Medical Tourism
Global Outlook & Indian Scenario

MEDICAL TOURISM
Global Outlook
&
Indian Scenario

PERCY K. SINGH

KANISHKA PUBLISHERS, DISTRIBUTORS
NEW DELHI-110 002

KANISHKA PUBLISHERS, DISTRIBUTORS
4697/5-21A, Ansari Road, Daryaganj
New Delhi -110 002
Phones : 2327 0497, 2328 8285
Fax : 011-2328 8285
E-mail : kanishka_publishing@yahoo.co.in
kanishkabooks@gmail.com

Medical Tourism: Global Outlook and Indian Scenario

First Published 2008

Edition 2026

ISBN : 978-81-8457-027-4

PRINTED IN INDIA

Published by Madan Sachdeva for Kanishka Publishers, Distributors, 4697/5-21A, Ansari Road, Daryaganj, New Delhi-110002, Typeset by Sunshine Graphics, Delhi, and Printed at G.S. Printers, Delhi.

Preface

This book entitled "Medical Tourism: Global Outlook & Indian Scenario" presents the readers with an Indepth comparative analysis of global and national medical tourism situation and future prospects. The book provides an introduction to tourism, the World Tourism Organisation, its global campaign, international standardization of tourism services, General Agreements for Trade in Services, Global Code of Ethics for tourism and WTO guidelines for the tourism industry. With such a background presentation, a global outlook of contemporary medical tourism process is given. Medical tourism has been defined and explained briefly in all its forms and functionalities. A service approach has been followed while discussing the industry of medical tourism and public health. The phenomenon involving rapid growth in medical tourism at a worldwide level has been explained briefly with famous and successful case studies from America, South-East Asia including Thailand, Malaysia, South Africa, Bardados, etc. The issues related to health tourism, health facilities and alternative healthcare and covered in detail while presenting the aforementioned case studies. Both a service industry perspective and an understanding of the darker side of medical tourism are presented. Besides, a policy perspective on impact of tourism and recreation is given, particularly with reference to local economic development and national development. The book also reflects briefly on tourism's potential as a sustainable development strategy with special reference to the Washington Declaration. One of the most important stakeholders in medical tourism is hospital. That is why its infrastructure, its services, precautionary measure and safety provisions become that very important. Besides giving general description about hospital, this book talks about the modern hospital information systems, national patient safety goals, with particular reference to the safety issues related to transport of critically ill patients. Case Studies are presented regarding the prevailing evaluation programmes for HIV / AIDs prevention and care in developing countries, in addition to a general comprehensive evaluation framework for country programmes. A global comparison of status of medical tourism in India has been made. India's suitability for aggressive marketing and facility development in medical tourism has been presented, including the cost-benefit analysis with other countries, such as UAE, etc. The healthcare system in India has been presented and critically evaluated. The case studies from some of India's federal states have been presented such as Karnataka and Rajasthan. For promoting medical tourism in India, the holiday and hospital package approach has been highlighted, with special focus on Ayurvedic therapies and regular health check-ups. This book is user friendly and provides readers with required glossary of terms, references/ bibliography and index select case-studies also make the book interesting enough for practical experience.

Percy K. Singh

Contents

Acronyms

A1	Mild Inflammation
A2	Moderate Inflammation
A3	Marked Inflammation
abnl	abnormal
AFP	Alpha Fetoprotein
AHP	Allied Health Professional
Alb	Albumin
ALT	Alanine Aminotransferase
AMA	Against Medical Advice
+ ANA	Antinuclear Antibody
APC	Ambulatory Payment Classification
ASC	Ambulatory Surgery Center
ASMA	Antismooth Muscle Antibody
AST	Aspartate Aminotransferase
AWP	Average Wholesale Price
beta-NAG	N-Acetyl-beta-Glucosaminidase
bid	twice a day
Bili	Bilirubin
bx	biopsy
CA	Carbohydrate Antigen
CABG	Coronary Artery Bypass Graft
CAH	Chronic Active Hepatitis
CC	Case Control
CD4	CD4 count (cell type)
CEA	Carcoembryonic Antigen
CHC	Chronic Hepatitis C
CI	Confidence Interval
CIF	Carriage, Insurance and Freight
CMPs	Care Management Protocols
CMS	Centers for Medicare and Medicaid Services.
COBRA	Consolidated Omnibus Budget Reconciliation Act of 1986.

CohP	Cohort Prospective
CohR	Cohort Retrospective
CON	Certificate of Need
CPH	Chronic Persistent Hepatitis
CPOE	Computerized Physician Order Entry
Cr	Creatinine
CS	Case Series
CSA	Cyclosporine
CT	Computerized Tomography
D	Day(s)
DDP	Delivered, Duty Paid
DDT	Dichlorodiphenyltrichlorethane
Des	Desmet
Disc/withdr	Discontinued Treatments or Withdrew from Study
DM	Diabetes Mellitus
DME	Durable Medical Equipment
Dose red	Dose Reduction
DRG	Diagnosis Related Group
dx	Diagnosis
EC	Emulsifiable Concentrate
EHC	Environmental Health Criteria
el	Elevated
ELISA	Enzyme-linked Immunosorbent Assay
EMTALA	Emergency Medical Treatment and Active Labour Act of 1986.
EPI	Expanded Programme on Immunization
ERISA	Employee Retirement Income Security Act
ESRD	End-Stage Renal Disease
ETR	End of Treatment Response
f/u	Follow-up
FFS	Fee-for-Service
FOB	Free on Board
G	Grade
g	Gram(s)
GGT	Gamma Glutamyl Transpeptidase
GNP	Gross National Product
GPO	Group Purchasing Organization
HA	Hyaluronic Acid
HAI	Histological Activity Index

HbsAg	Hepatitis B Surface Antigen
HBV	Hepatitis B Virus
HCC	Hepatocellular Carcinoma
HCV	Hepatitis C Virus
HEDIS	Health Plan Employer Data and Information Set
Hgb	Hemoglobin
HHI	Herfindahl-Hirschman Index
HIPAA	Health Insurance Portability and Accountability Act of 1996.
hr	Hour(s)
IDRC	International Development Research Centre
IDU	Intravenous Drug User
IFN	Interferon
Ig	Immunoglobulin
IL	Interleukin
IPA	Independent Practice Association
IPPS	Inpatient Prospective Payment System
ISH	Ishak
ITN	Insecticide-Treated Net
ITT	Intention To Treat
IV	Intravenous
IV-C7S	7S Type IV Collagen
Kno	Knodell
L	Liter(s)
LDH	Lactate Dehydrogenase
LL	Lower Limit
Ly IFN alpha	Lymphoid Interferon
M+C	Medicare + Choice
MA	Medicare Advantage
MAC	Maximum Allowable Cost
MCO	Managed Care Organization
MedPAC	Medicare Payment Advisory Commission
Met	Metavir
MFN	Most Favoured Nation
min	Minute(s)
mL	Milliliter(s)
MMP	Matrix Metalloproteinase
Mn-SOD	Manganese Superoxide Dismutase
mo(s)	Month(s)
MRI	Magnetic Resonance Imaging

MSA	Metropolitan Statistical Areas
MU	Million Units
n/s	not specified
NASH	Non-Alcoholic Steato Hepatitis
ng	nanograms
NGO	Non-Governmental Organization
NIBP	National Impregnated Bednet Programme
NIMR	Tanzanian National Institute of Medical Research
nl	normal
NP	n-terminal Polypeptide
NR	Not Reported
NS	Not Significant
OCPs	Oral Contraceptives
OLT	Orthotopic Liver Transplant
OPPS	Outpatient Prospective Payment System
ORS	Oral Rehydration Solution
PBM	Pharmacy Benefit Manager
P4P	Payment for Performance
PATH	Program for Appropriate Technology in Health
PCHE	Pseudocholinesterase
PCR	Polymerase Chain Reaction
peg-IFN	pegylated interferon
PHC	Primary Health Care
PHO	Physician-Hospital Organization
P-III-P	Procollagen Type III Peptides
plts	platelets
POS	Point of Service
PPO	Preferred Provider Organization
PT	Prothrombin Time
pts	patients
PTT	Partial Thromboplastin Time
qd	once a day
QIO	Quality Improvement Organization
r IFN	recombinant IFN
r/o	rule out
RBRVS	Resource-Based Relative Value Scale
RBV	Ribavirin
RCT	Randomized Controlled Trial
S	Staging
s.l.	sensu lato

s.s.	sensu stricto
S0	No Fibrosis
S1, S2	Mild (portal) Fibrosis
S3	Moderate (Bridging) Fibrosis
S4	Severe Fibrosis (Cirrhosis)
SBR	Sustained Biochemical Response
Sch	Scheuer
SCHIP	State Children's Health Insurance Programme
sec	second(s)
SP	Synthetic Pyrethroid
SR	Sustained Response
SSH	Single Specialty Hospital
SSS	Sugar-Salt Solution
SVR	Sustained Virological Response
TDR	UNDP/World Bank/WHO Special Programme for Research and Training in Tropical Diseases
tid	three times a day
TIMP	Tissue Inhibitor of Metalloproteinase
tiw	three times a week
TPA	Third-Party Administrator
tx	treatment
U/S	Ultrasound
ug	micrograms
UL	Upper Limit
UMCP	Urban Malaria Control Project (Dar es Salaam)
UNICEF	United Nations Children's Fund
w/	with
w/I	within
w/o	without
WBC	White Blood Cell
WHO	World Health Organization
wk	week(s)
WP	Wettable Powder
WSS	Water-Sugar-Salt (Solution)
XS	Cross-Sectional
yr(s)	year(s)

1

Tourism: A Brief Introductory Overview

TOURISM : AN INTRODUCTION

Tourism is the act of travel for predominantly recreational or leisure purposes, and also refers to the provision of services in support of this act. According to the World Tourism Organization, tourists are people who "travel to and stay in places outside their usual environment for not more than one consecutive year for leisure, business and other purposes not related to the exercise of an activity remunerated from within the place visited."

Tourism, however long its incident duration, has become an extremely popular, global activity. In 2004, there were over 763 million international tourist arrivals.

As a service industry, tourism has numerous tangible and intangible elements. Major tangible elements include transportation, accommodation, and other components of a hospitality industry. Major intangible elements relate to the purpose or motivation for becoming a tourist, such as rest, relaxation, the opportunity to meet new people and experience other cultures, or simply to do something different and have an adventure.

Tourism is vital for many countries, due to the income generated by the consumption of goods and services by tourists, the taxes levied on businesses in the tourism industry, and the opportunity for employment and economic advancement by working in the industry. For these reasons NGOs and government agencies may sometimes promote a specific region as a tourist destination, and support the development of a tourism industry in that area. The contemporary phenomenon of mass tourism may sometimes result in overdevelopment, however alternative forms of tourism such as ecotourism seek to avoid such outcomes by pursuing tourism in a sustainable way.

The terms *tourism* and *travel* are sometimes used interchangeably. In this context travel has a similar definition to tourism, but implies a more purposeful journey. The terms *tourism* and *tourist* are sometimes used pejoratively to imply a shallow interest in the cultures or locations visited by tourists.

Definition, Classification and Prerequisites

General Definition

One of the earliest definitions of tourism was provided by the Austrian economist Hermann Von Schullard in 1910, who defined it as, "sum total of operators, mainly of an economic nature, which directly relate to the entry, stay and movement of foreigners inside and outside a certain country, city or a region."

Hunziker and Krapf, in 1941, defined tourism as "the sum of the phenomena and relationships arising from the travel and stay of non-residents, insofar as they do not lead to permanent residence and are not connected with any earning activity."

In 1976 Tourism Society of England defined it as "Tourism is the temporary, short-term movement of people to destination outside the places where they normally live and work and their activities during the stay at each destination. It includes movements for all purposes."

In 1981 International Association of Scientific Experts in Tourism defined tourism in terms of particular activities selected by choice and undertaken outside the home environment.

United Nations Definition

United Nations classified three forms of tourism in 1994 in its Recommendations on Tourism Statistics as follows:

1. Domestic tourism, involving residents of the given country travelling only within this country;
2. Inbound tourism, involving non-residents travelling in the given country;

3. Outbound tourism, involving residents travelling in another country.

UN also derived different categories of tourism by combining the three basic forms of tourism:

1. Internal tourism, which comprises domestic tourism and inbound tourism;
2. National tourism, which comprises domestic tourism and outbound tourism;
3. International tourism, which consists of inbound tourism and outbound tourism.

New Definition

Intrabound tourism is a new academic terminology coined by the Korea Tourism Organization and widely accepted in Korea. Intrabound tourism differs from 'domestic tourism' in that the former is more dynamic and comprehensive, encompassing policy-making and implementation of national tourism policies in consideration of the tourism ecosystem consisting of inbound, outbound and intrabound tourism.

Entering into 21st century, the tourism industry has undergone a paradigm shift from the promotion of inbound tourism to the promotion of intrabound tourism since many countries are experiencing a tough competition for inbound tourists. Also realizing that it is impossible to advance the inbound tourism in the absence of active intrabound tourism, national policy-makers have shifted their policy priority onto the promotion of intrabound tourism such as the promotion of local tourism to contribute to the local economy.

Examples of such policies are "See America", "Getting Going Canada", and "See Korea Campaign". Taking a Korean case as an example, Korea Tourism Organization has recently launched a nation-wide campaign to promote intrabound tourism, named "Guseok Guseok", literally meaning corner to corner.

Prerequisites of Tourism

Before people are able to experience tourism they usually need at least:

1. Disposable income, i.e. money to spend on nonessentials
2. Leisure time
3. Tourism infrastructure, such as transport and accommodation.

Individually, sufficient health is also a condition, and of course the inclination to travel. Furthermore, in some countries there are legal restrictions on travelling, especially abroad. Certain states with strong governmental control over the lives of citizens (notably established Communist states) may restrict foreign travel only to trustworthy citizens. The United States prohibits its citizens from travelling to some countries, for example, Cuba.

History

Wealthy people have always travelled to distant parts of the world to see great buildings or other works of art, to learn new languages, to experience new cultures, or to taste new cuisine. As long ago as the time of the Roman Republic places such as Baiae were popular coastal resorts for the rich.

The terms *tourist* and *tourism* were first used as official terms in 1937 by the League of Nations. Tourism was defined as people travelling abroad for periods of over 24 hours.

Health Tourism and Leisure Travel

The history of European tourism can perhaps be said to originate with the medieval pilgrimage. Although undertaken primarily for religious reasons, the pilgrims in the Canterbury Tales quite clearly saw the experience as a kind of holiday (the term itself being derived from the 'holy day' and its associated leisure activities). Pilgrimages created a variety of tourist aspects that still exist—bringing back souvenirs, obtaining credit with foreign banks (in medieval times utilizing international networks established by Jews and Lombards), and making use of space available on existing forms of transport (such as the use of medieval English wine ships bound for Vigo by pilgrims to Santiago De Compostela). Pilgrimages are still important in modern tourism—such as to Lourdes or Knock in Ireland. But there are modern equivalents—Graceland and the grave of Jim Morrison in Père Lachaise Cemetery.

During the seventeenth century, it became fashionable in England to undertake a Grand Tour. The sons of the nobility and gentry were sent upon an extended tour of Europe as an educational experience. The eighteenth century was the golden age of the Grand Tour, and many of the fashionable visitors were painted at Rome by Pompeo Batoni. A modern equivalent of the Grand Tour is the phenomenon of the backpacker, although cultural holidays, such as those offered by Swann-Hellenic, are also important.

Health tourism has always existed, but it was not until the eighteenth century that it became important. In England, it was associated with Spas, places with supposedly health-giving mineral waters, treating diseases from gout to liver disorders and bronchitis. Bath was the most fashionable resort, but Buxton, Harrogate, and Tunbridge Wells, amongst others, also flourished. Of course, people visited these places for the balls and other entertainments, just as much as 'the waters'. Continental Spas such as Karlsbad attracted many fashionable travellers by the nineteenth century.

It could be argued that Britain was the home of the seaside holiday. In travelling to the coast, the population was following in the steps of Royalty. King George III made regular visits to Weymouth when in poor health. At the time, a number of doctors argued the benefits of bathing in sea water, and sea bathing as a widespread practice was popularized by the Prince Regent (later George IV), who frequented Brighton for this purpose.

Leisure travel was associated with the industrialization of United Kingdom—the first European country to promote leisure time to the increasing industrial population. Initially, this applied to the owners of the machinery of production, the economic oligarchy, the factory owners, and the traders. These comprised the new middle class. Cox & Kings were the first official travel company to be formed in 1758. Later, the working class could take advantage of leisure time.

The British origin of this new industry is reflected in many place names. At Nice, one of the first and best-established holiday resorts on the French Riviera, the long esplanade along the seafront is known to this day as the *Promenade des Anglais*; in many other historic resorts in continental Europe, old well-established palace hotels have names like the *Hotel Bristol*, the *Hotel Carlton* or the *Hotel Majestic*—reflecting the dominance of English customers.

THE WORLD TOURISM ORGANIZATION

Mission

The World Tourism Organization (UNWTO/OMT), a specialized agency of the United Nations, is the leading international organization in the field of tourism. It serves as a global forum for tourism policy issues and practical source of tourism know-how.

With its headquarters in Madrid, Spain, the UNWTO plays a central and decisive role in promoting the development of responsible, sustainable and universally accessible tourism, with the aim of contributing to economic development, international understanding, peace, prosperity and universal respect for, and observance of, human rights and fundamental freedoms. In pursuing this aim, the Organization pays particular attention to the interests of developing countries in the field of tourism.

The UNWTO plays a catalytic role in promoting technology transfers and international cooperation, in stimulating and developing public-private sector partnerships and in encouraging the implementation of the Global Code of Ethics for Tourism, with a view to ensuring that member countries, tourist destinations and businesses maximize the positive economic, social and cultural effects of tourism and fully reap its benefits, while minimizing its negative social and environmental impacts.

In 2006, the UNWTO's membership is comprised 150 countries, seven territories and more than 300 affiliate members representing the private sector, educational institutions, tourism associations and local tourism authorities.

Tourism for Prosperity and Peace

At the start of the new millennium, tourism is firmly established as the number one industry in many countries and the fastest-growing economic sector in terms of foreign exchange earnings and job creation.

International tourism is the world's largest export earner and an important factor in the balance of payments of most nations.

Tourism has become one of the world's most important sources of employment. It stimulates enormous investment in infrastructure, most of which also helps to improve the living conditions of local people. It provides governments with substantial tax revenues. Most new tourism jobs and business are created in developing countries, helping to equalize economic opportunities and keep rural residents from moving to overcrowded cities.

Intercultural awareness and personal friendships fostered through tourism are a powerful force for improving international understanding and contributing to peace among all the nations of the world.

The UNWTO recognizes that tourism can have a negative cultural, environmental and social impact if it is not responsibly planned, managed and monitored. The UNWTO thus encourages governments to play a vital role in tourism, in partnership with the private sector, local authorities and non-governmental organizations.

In its belief that tourism can be effectively used to address the problems of poverty, UNWTO made a commitment to contribute to the United Nations Millennium Development Goals through a new initiative to develop sustainable tourism as a force for poverty elimination. The programme, known as ST-EP (Sustainable Tourism-Eliminating Poverty), focuses the longstanding work of both organizations on encouraging sustainable tourism with a view to alleviating poverty and was implemented in 2003.

History

The World Tourism Organization had its beginnings as the International Congress of Official Tourist Traffic Associations set up in 1925 in The Hague. It was renamed the International Union of Official Travel Organizations (IUOTO) after World War II and moved to Geneva. IUOTO was a technical, non-governmental organization, whose membership at its peak included 109 National Tourist Organizations (NTOs) and 88 associate members, among them private and public groups.

As tourism grew and became an integral part of the fabric of modern life, its international dimension increased and national governments started to play an increasingly important role—their activities covering the whole spectrum from infrastructure to regulations. By the mid-1960s, it became clear that there was a need for more effective tools to keep developments under review and to provide tourism with intergovernmental machinery especially equipped to deal with the movement of persons, tourism policies and tourism's impacts.

In 1967, the members of IUOTO called for its transformation into an intergovernmental body empowered to deal on a worldwide basis with all matters concerning tourism and to cooperate with other competent organizations, particularly those of the United Nations' system, such as the World Health Organization (WHO), UNESCO, and the International Civil Aviation Organization (ICAO).

A resolution to the same effect was passed in December 1969 by the UN General Assembly, which recognized the decisive and central role the transformed IUOTO should play in the field of world tourism in cooperation with the existing machinery within the UN. Following this resolution, the UNWTO's Statutes were ratified in 1974 by the States whose official tourist organizations were members of IUOTO.

Thus IUOTO became the World Tourism Organization (UNWTO) and its first General Assembly was held in Madrid in May 1975. The Secretariat was installed in Madrid early the following year at the invitation of the Spanish Government, which provides a building for the headquarters.

In 1976, UNWTO became an executing agency of the United Nations Development Programme (UNDP) and in 1977, a formal cooperation agreement was signed with the United Nations itself. In 2003, the UNWTO was converted into a specialized agency of the United Nations and reaffirmed its leading role in international tourism.

Since its early years, UNWTO's membership and influence in world tourism have continued to grow. By 2005, its membership included 145 countries, seven territories and some 350 affiliate members, representing the private sector, educational institutions, tourism associations and local tourism authorities.

Key Events

1925: International Congress of Official Tourist Traffic Associations, The Hague, The Netherlands

1934: Creation of International Union of Official Tourist Propaganda Organizations (IUOTPO), The Hague, The Netherlands

1947: IUOTPO is converted to the International Union of Official Travel Organizations (IUOTO)

1969: Intergovernmental Conference in Sofia, Bulgaria and the UN General Assembly, call for creation of intergovernmental organization on tourism

1970: In Mexico, on 27 September (future date of World Tourism Day) IUOTO's Extraordinary General Assembly adopts the Statutes of World Tourism Organization

1975: First General Assembly of the World Tourism Organization is held in Madrid, Spain and UNWTO is officially launched with Robert Lonati (France) as Secretary-General

1976: UNWTO Secretariat moves from Geneva to Madrid

1977/1979: UNWTO General Assembly held in Torremolinos, Spain

1979: "World Tourism Day" created, to be celebrated every year on 27th September

1980: UNWTO convenes World Tourism Conference in Manila; the Manila Declaration on World Tourism is unanimously adopted

1981: UNWTO General Assembly held in Rome, Italy

1982: World Tourism Conference convened in Acapulco; Acapulco Document is adopted

1983: UNWTO General Assembly held in New Delhi, India

1985: Tourism Bill of Rights and Tourist Code adopted at UNWTO General Assembly, Sofia, Bulgaria

1986: Willibald Pahr (Austria) elected Secretary-General

1987: UNWTO General Assembly held in Madrid, Spain

1989: UNWTO General Assembly held in Paris, France

1989: Inter-Parliamentary Conference on Tourism, jointly organized with the Inter-Parliamentary Union, adopts The Hague Declaration on Tourism

1990: Antonio Enríquez Savignac (Mexico) elected Secretary-General

1991: UNWTO General Assembly held in Buenos Aires, Argentina

1993: UNWTO General Assembly held in Bali, Indonesia

1995: UNWTO General Assembly held in Cairo, Egypt

1996: Francesco Frangialli (France) appointed interim Secretary-General after Antonio Enríquez Savignac's early retirement

1996: Second UNWTO Forum on Parliaments and Local Authorities: Tourism Policy-Makers, adopts the Bali Declaration on Tourism, Indonesia

1997: UNWTO General Assembly held in Istanbul, Turkey
1997: Francesco Frangialli (France) elected Secretary-General
1999: UNWTO General Assembly held in Santiago, Chile
2001: Fourteenth General Assembly held jointly in Seoul, Republic of Korea and Osaka, Japan
2001: Francesco Frangialli (France) re-elected Secretary-General
2003: Fifteenth General Assembly held in Beijing, China
2003: Transformation of the UNWTO into a UN specialized agency
2005: Sixteenth General Assembly held in Dakar, Senegal
2005: Francesco Frangialli (France) re-elected Secretary-General

Structure

The bodies of the World Tourism Organization are the:

1. General Assembly

The General Assembly is the principal gathering of the World Tourism Organization. It meets every two years to approve the budget and programme of work and to debate topics of vital importance to the tourism sector. Every four years it elects a Secretary-General. The General Assembly is composed of Full Members and Associate Members. Affiliate Members and representatives of other international organizations participate as observers.

2. Executive Council

The Executive Council is UNWTO's governing board, responsible for ensuring that the organization carries out its work and adheres to its budget. It meets twice a year and is composed of 29 members elected by the General Assembly in a ratio of one for every five Full Members. As host country of UNWTO´s Headquarters, Spain has a permanent seat on the Executive Council. Representatives of the Associate Members and Affiliate Members participate in Executive Council meetings as observers.

3. Regional Commissions

UNWTO has six regional commissions—Africa, the Americas, East Asia and the Pacific, Europe, the Middle East and South Asia. The commissions meet at least once a year and are composed of all the

Full Members and Associate Members from that region. Affiliate Members from the region participate as observers.

4. Committees

Specialized committees of UNWTO Members advise on management and programme content. These include: the Programme Committee, the Committee on Budget and Finance, the Committee on Statistics and Macroeconomic Analysis of Tourism, the Committee on Market Intelligence and Promotion, the Sustainable Development of Tourism Committee, the Quality Support and Trade Committee, the UNWTO Education Council, the UNWTO Business Council and the World Committee on Tourism Ethics.

5. Secretariat

The Sécretariat is led by Secretary-General Francesco Frangialli of France, who supervises about 90 full-time staff at UNWTO's Madrid Headquarters. He is assisted by the Deputy Secretary-General Taleb Rifai of Jordan. These officials are responsible for implementing UNWTO's programme of work and serving the needs of members. The UNWTO Business Council is supported by a full-time Chief Executive Officer at the Madrid Headquarters, a position that is financed by the Spanish Government. The Secretariat also includes a regional support office for Asia-Pacific in Osaka, Japan, financed by the Japanese Government. The official languages of UNWTO are English, Spanish, French, Russian and Arabic.

Cooperation for Development

Shared Technical Skills

The transfer of tourism know-how to developing countries is one of the World Tourism Organization's fundamental tasks. As an executive agency of the United Nations Development Programme, UNWTO contributes decades of experience in tourism to the sustainable development goals of nations throughout the world.

Acting on requests from Member States, UNWTO secures financing, locates the world's leading experts, and carries out a gamut of development projects—large and small. Long-term projects have included:

- Tourism Master Plan for Pakistan (2001)
- Tourism Master Plans for eight Chinese provinces (2000-2002)
- Development of national parks in Rwanda (1999)
- Tourism development strategy for Moldova (1999-ongoing)
- Integrated development programme for Palestinian Authority (2000)
- Development activities in some 70 countries worth more than US$ 2.5 million (2001-2002)

Projects can also be short and targeted to address an immediate need, for example:

- Tourism legislation in Syria
- Ecotourism plan for Lithuania
- Statistics development in Botswana
- Social impact study for the Maldives
- Management of heritage sites in Ecuador
- Hotel classification for Bolivia
- Women's empowerment plan for Namibia
- Training for quality service in tourism in Peru

Tourism has proven to be a powerful tool in alleviating poverty. It has become the economic mainstay of many of the world's least developed countries (LDCs), providing them with one of the opportunities for development and job creation. A joint programme with UNCTAD called Sustainable Tourism—Eliminating Poverty (STEP) focuses on the twin subjects of sustainable tourism and alleviation of poverty, in order to increase their potential synergies and contribute more strongly to sustainable development in least developed and developing countries. STEP was launched at WSSD in Johannesburg in August 2002.

Regional Activities

Direct actions that strengthen and support the efforts of National Tourism Administrations are carried out by UNWTO's regional representatives.

Each region of the world—Africa, the Americas, East Asia and the Pacific, Europe, the Middle East and South Asia—receives special attention from its regional representative based at the Headquarters of the World Tourism Organization in Madrid.

Regional representatives are UNWTO's front line of contact with member countries. They are constantly on the go, but regional representatives are much more than travelling ambassadors.

- They meet with the top tourism officials from each of the countries in their region to analyze problems and offer solutions.
- To create specific development projects, they act as a liaison between tourism authorities and financing sources, especially the United Nations Development Programme.
- They represent UNWTO at national and regional tourism events.
- They organize national seminars on topics of particular relevance to an individual country.
- They hold regional conferences on problems that are shared by many countries so that Members can exchange experiences and work towards common goals. Recent conferences have been held on the Challenge of Globalization in the Middle East, Human Resource Development in East Asia and the Pacific, the Euro and Tourism in Europe and Quality Standards in the Americas region, Crisis Management in East Asia and the Pacific, etc.
- They help facilitate productive contacts between tourism authorities and other branches of government—often at the presidential level.

All of these activities are designed to help increase the stature of National Tourism Administrations within their own country, while at the same time building awareness of new developments in tourism and improving technical, operational skills.

In a special effort to help boost tourism to Sub-Saharan Africa, UNWTO has developed a specific programme of technical activities for the years 2003-2004.

UNWTO's six Regional Commissions meet at least once a year to discuss the Organization's activities and set priorities for the future. Affiliate Members from the region are encouraged to participate in the meetings and seminars.

Regional Promotion Projects

UNWTO is in a unique position to carry out special projects that promote tourism to a group of Member States. The Silk Road and the Slave Route are two of these projects, initiated in cooperation with the United Nations Scientific and Cultural Organization (UNESCO).

- *The Silk Road Project*, launched in 1994, aims at revitalizing the ancient highways used by Marco Polo through tourism. The Silk Road stretches 12,000 km from Asia to Europe and 22 countries have joined forces for this project: Armenia, Azerbaijan, China, DPR Korea, Egypt, Georgia, Greece, Islamic Republic of Iran, Italy, Israel, Japan, Kazakhstan, Kyrgyzstan, Mongolia, Pakistan, Republic of Korea, Russian Federation, Syrian Arab Republic, Tajikistan, Turkmenistan, Turkey and Uzbekistan. Joint promotional activities include seminars, a brochure and a video.
- *The Slave Route Project*, initiated in 1995 as part of the United Nations' International Year of Tolerance, aims to boost tourism to western African nations. Its immediate goals are to restore monuments, enhance history museums and launch joint information campaigns in selected tourism generating markets, which will motivate foreign visitors to learn about the history of these countries and to discover their roots.

World Tourism Day

Since 1980, Members of the World Tourism Organization have been celebrating World Tourism Day every year on September 27th. Events include parades, concerts, tourism fairs, seminars, dinners, dances, and free entrance to museums—anything and everything that draws attention to the important role that tourism plays in the local community.

Task Force for Destination Management

To reflect the growing decentralization of tourism administration, UNWTO formed a task force to focus on issues that are of special concern at the destination level. Some concerns of the task force include: management of congestion at coastal destinations; economic measurement of tourism at the local level; destination marketing for cities; information and communication technologies; human resource development; and risk and crisis management at individual tourism destinations. The Task Force for Destination Management meets periodically and acts as an informal advisory body of UNWTO, with the aim of encouraging new work in these areas and identifying ongoing UNWTO projects that are relevant to tourism officials working in destination management.

Business Council

UNWTO is unique among international inter-governmental organizations in that it is open to membership by the operating sector and promotes various methods of cooperation amongst its Members. Airlines, hotel chains, tour operators, trade associations, consultants, promotion boards and educational institutions make up approximately 350 Members of the UNWTO Business Council (UNWTOBC).

UNWTOBC utilizes a partnership approach to tourism as a method to promote public and private integration and as a model of understanding between the two sectors. To achieve their objectives, UNWTOBC aids Members in expanding their tourism businesses through industry networking, forming contacts with the necessary government officials strengthening industry-education relationship, and conducting specialized research projects of the private sector.

Currently, the UNWTOBC is undertaking numerous projects with the hope of creating more public-private partnerships and sustained cooperation amongst tourism industries. These projects include investigations into the factors that affect tourism, methods of managing congestion on sites, assisting small and medium size enterprises, and implementing new technology.

Under the guidance of its Board of Directors, UNWTOBC continues their research on the above-mentioned projects accompanied by annual studies, data compilation, research publication and organization of conferences. The Council continues to promote integration between public and private sectors with themes that are of special interest to the business community which include:

- Public-Private Sector Cooperation—Enhancing Tourism Competitiveness
- Marketing Tourism Destinations Online—Strategies for the Information Age
- E-Business for Tourism
- Tourism Taxation—Striking a Fair Deal
- Changes in Leisure Time

Tourism and Technology

The Internet and other computer technologies are revolutionizing the way tourism business is conducted and the way destinations are promoted. UNWTO's work in the area of new Information Technologies (IT) aims to provide leadership in the field of IT and tourism, as well as helping to bridge the digital divide between the have and have-nots among UNWTO's membership.

UNWTO carries out new research and studies of IT in connection with the promotion and development of tourism, such as the publications Marketing Tourism Destinations Online and E-Business for Tourism. It communicates the content of these studies throughout the world in a series of regional seminars. UNWTO also operates a Strategic Advisory Board on IT and Tourism that brings together a small number of high-level experts from destinations, private businesses and researchers.

Tourism technology is especially suited to cooperation projects between the public and private sectors. The objective is to keep all Members up-to-date on the constantly changing technologies that will affect the tourism industry in the years to come.

Education

UNWTO.HRD

The UNWTO Human Resource Development Department (UNWTO.HRD) works to add value to the tourism sector of

UNWTO Member States improving their capacity building and providing direct support in tourism education, training and knowledge. The UNWTO.HRD coordinates the activities of the UNWTO Education Council as well as those of the UNWTO. Themis Foundation with the common goal of achieving the tourism competitiveness and sustainability of UNWTO Members through excellence in tourism education.

Its mission is to build the knowledge capacity of UNWTO Members, providing leadership, initiative and coordination in quality tourism education, training and research through public-private partnerships among institutions and UNWTO Member States.

UNWTO.Themis Foundation

Based in Andorra and generously sponsored by its Government, the UNWTO.Themis Foundation provides the administrative back-up to UNWTO.HRD to develop and disseminate tourism education, training and knowledge products, thus optimizing service to UNWTO Members.

Its mission is to promote quality and efficiency in tourism education and training in close coordination with UNWTO and its Human Resource Development Department (UNWTO.HRD), facilitating administration and management in implementing its programme of work and enlarging the scope of services to UNWTO Members.

UNWTO Education Council

The UNWTO Education Council (UNWTO.EdC) is made up of leading tourism education, training and research institutions as well as business schools worldwide that have obtained the UNWTO.TedQual Certification for at least one of their tourism education programmes. With over 100 members, it forms a chapter of the UNWTO Affiliate Members, and is well represented in the Board of the Affiliates, their decision-making body. The UNWTO.EdC is an active agent within UNWTO and in the development and implementation of the UNWTO.HRD Programme of Work.

The main human resource development products are:

UNWTO.TedQual

A framework of programmes for quality in tourism education. The UNWTO.TedQual Certification is granted to training and education institutions by means of a quality audit. The TedQual institutions can request membership in the UNWTO Education Council (Affiliate Members). There are also TedQual Seminars (Educating the Educators) for Member States and TedQual Consulting on quality issues for education and training centres.

UNWTO.Practicum

This is a biannual programme for officials from UNWTO Member States. It is carried out at UNWTO Headquarters for a period of two weeks and includes GTAT.TPS seminars, workshops, technical visits and working meetings with the responsible staff of the Organization.

UNWTO.Themis TedQual Practicum

A practicum programme designed especially for officials from UNWTO Member States who are proposed by their governments as liaisons with UNWTO in matters of education and training.

UNWTO.GTAT

A set of programmes [General Tourism Achievement Test (GTAT)] designed to improve the performance of teaching and learning in tourism. These include software for examinations and course development and implementation, GTAT Courses to improve specific knowledge and/or prepare for exams, GTAT Diagnosis to ascertain strong and weak points in specific subjects, GTAT Exams and GTAT Certification of Proficiency for students and tourism professionals.

UNWTO.Sbest Initiative

A framework for a range of UNWTO Programmes aimed at contributing to excellence in destinations and tourism companies through quality training and education. Programmes include the UNWTO.Sbest Training, UNWTO.Sbest Audit and UNWTO Tourism Labour Market Observatory. Institutions, companies and destinations satisfactorily completing these programmes receive UNWTO.Sbest Awards. Many of these programmes are executed in coordination with the UNWTO Destination Management Task Force.

UNWTO.Tourism Labour Market Observatory

This programme was recently initiated by the UNWTO Education Council in conjunction with UNWTO.HRD and the UNWTO Destination Management Task Force. Its objective is to obtain quantitative and qualitative information on tourism labour markets in key destinations worldwide through panels of employers, workers, consumers and students. This is coordinated through UNWTO.Sbest tourism destinations and UNWTO TedQual Centres.

Other Products

- UNWTO.SIS Seminars
- Publications
- UNWTO.TedProm
- UNWTO Ulysses Awards for Innovation and the Application of Knowledge in Tourism
- Annual UNWTO.EdC Conference

Quality and Trade: In Search of Common Denominators, Fairness and Transparency

This activity follows the previous programme on Quality in Tourism Development. With an increased focus on the economics of tourism, trade and the enterprise it seeks to assist government and private sector Members in determining and pursuing quality-related objectives, standards and measures as a contribution to sustainable development and poverty alleviation.

The following specific areas are covered:

- Trade in tourism services, including access to tourism markets, competition and globalization
- Safety and security, including health issues
- Guidance, harmonization and recognition of quality-related standards.

Reference to standards is present in all these areas. On trade issues, UNWTO works closely with the United Nations Conference on Trade and Development (UNCTAD) and with the World Trade Organization (WTO-OMC). The aim is to relate tourism policies and strategies to multilateral negotiations according to the General Agreement on Trade in Services (GATS) designed to achieve progressively higher levels of liberalization with a view to promoting economic growth and the development of developing countries. Briefings and debate on trade in tourism are held periodically to help Members carry out comprehensive and informed trade policies.

The inclusion of the safety and security area is explained by it being considered as a fundamental quality factor. The current focus is on preparing a model work plan for tourism destinations based on objective safety and security criteria, a model code of conduct on travel advisories and a revised UNWTO document *Health Information and Formalities in International Travel*, was submitted to the 16th session of the General Assembly in 2005 and taking stock of the new *International Health Regulations of the World Health Organization (IHR 2005)*.

Under the chapter of quality standards, the specific aims include guidance to Members undertaking tourism quality programmes, the design of standards based on common denominators and cultural diversity, a hotel classification guidance document, and contributions to the work of the International Organization for Standardization (ISO) on tourism signs and symbols and other tourism related standards.

In relation to each area the Quality and Trade in Tourism department is also engaged in the preparation of "implementation parameters" for the Global Code of Ethics for Tourism. The operation of the Code and the secretariat of the World Committee on Tourism Ethics are now dealt with by Sustainable Development of Tourism department.

Key Publications and Instruments

- Tourism in the Least Developed Countries
- GATS and Tourism
- Tourist Safety and Security
- Tourism Signs and Symbols
- Recommended Measures for Tourism Safety

- Health Information and Formalities in International Travel
- Creating Tourism Opportunities for the Handicapped
- UNWTO Statement against organized sex tourism
- Quality, Hygiene and Safety of Food in the Tourism Sector

Global Code of Ethics for Tourism

Adopted by the UNWTO General Assembly in 1999 and acknowledged by the United Nations General Assembly in 2001 by a special resolution, the Code sets out a ten-point blueprint for safeguarding the resources upon which tourism depends and ensuring that its economic benefits are equitably shared.

The Code is based on the principles of sustainability that underpin all of UNWTO's programmes, with special emphasis on involving local communities in planning, managing and monitoring tourism development. It includes nine articles outlining the 'rules of the game' for destinations, governments, tour operators, travel agents, tourism workers and developers, and travellers themselves.

The tenth article involves implementation of the code through the activities of the World Committee on Tourism Ethics.

We, Members of the World Tourism Organization (WTO), representatives of the world tourism industry, delegates of States, territories, enterprises, institutions and bodies that are gathered for the General Assembly at Santiago, Chile on this first day of October 1999, Reasserting the aims set out in Article 3 of the Statutes of the World Tourism Organization, and aware of the "decisive and central" role of this Organization, as recognized by the General Assembly of the United Nations, in promoting and developing tourism with a view to contributing to economic development, international understanding, peace, prosperity and universal respect for, and observance of human rights and fundamental freedoms for all without distinction as to race, sex, language or religion.

Firmly believing that, through the direct, spontaneous and non-meditated contacts it engenders between men and women of different cultures and lifestyles, tourism represents a vital force for peace and a factor of friendship and understanding among the peoples of the world. In keeping with the rationale of reconciling environmental protection, economic development and the fight against poverty in a sustainable manner, as formulated by the United Nations in 1992 at the "Earth Summit" of Rio de Janeiro and expressed in Agenda 21 adopted on that occasion. Taking into account the swift and continued growth, both past and foreseeable, of the tourism activity, whether for leisure, business, culture, religious or health purposes, and its powerful effects, both positive and negative, on the environment, the economy and the society of both generating and receiving countries, on local communities and indigenous peoples, as well as on international relations and trade. Aiming to promote responsible, sustainable and universally accessible tourism in the framework of the right of all persons to use their free time for leisure pursuits or travel with respect for the choices of society of all peoples.

But convinced that the world tourism industry as a whole has much to gain by operating in an environment that favours the market economy, private enterprise and free trade and that serves to optimize its beneficial effects on the creation of wealth and employment, also firmly convinced that, provided a number of principles and a certain number of rules are observed, responsible and sustainable tourism is by no means incompatible with the growing liberalization of the conditions governing trade in services and under whose aegis the enterprises of this sector operate and that it is possible to reconcile in this sector economy and ecology, environment and development, openness to international trade and protection of social and cultural identities, considering that, with such an approach, all the stakeholders in tourism development—national, regional and local administrations, enterprises, business associations, workers in the sector, non-governmental organizations and bodies of all kinds belonging to the tourism industry, as well as host communities, the media and the tourists themselves, have different albeit interdependent responsibilities in the individual and societal development of tourism and that the formulation of their individual rights and duties will contribute to meeting this aim.

Committed, in keeping with the aims pursued by the World Tourism Organization itself since adopting resolution 364(XII) at its General Assembly of 1997 (Istanbul), to promote a genuine partnership between the public and private stakeholders in tourism development, and wishing to see a partnership and cooperation of the same kind extend, in an open and balanced way, to the relations between generating and receiving countries and their respective tourism industries.

Following up on the Manila Declarations of 1980 on World Tourism and of 1997 on the Social Impact of Tourism, as well as on the Tourism Bill of Rights and the Tourist Code adopted at Sofia in 1985 under the aegis of WTO.

But believing that these instruments should be complemented by a set of interdependent principles for their interpretation and application on which the stakeholders in tourism development should model their conduct at the dawn of the twenty-first century. Using, for the purposes of this instrument, the definitions and classifications applicable to travel, and especially the concepts of "visitor", "tourist" and "tourism", as adopted by the Ottawa International Conference, held from 24 to 28 June 1991 and approved, in 1993, by the United Nations Statistical Commission at its twenty-seventh session.

Referring in particular to the following instruments:

- Universal Declaration of Human Rights of 10 December 1948;
- International Covenant on Economic, Social and Cultural Rights of 16 December 1966;
- International Covenant on Civil and Political Rights of 16 December 1966;
- Warsaw Convention on Air Transport of 12 October 1929;
- Chicago Convention on International Civil Aviation of 7 December 1944, and the Tokyo, The Hague and Montreal Conventions in relation thereto;
- Convention on Customs Facilities for Tourism of 4 July 1954 and related Protocol;
- Convention concerning the Protection of the World Cultural and Natural Heritage of 23 November 1972;
- Manila Declaration on World Tourism of 10 October 1980;
- Resolution of the Sixth General Assembly of WTO (Sofia) adopting the Tourism Bill of Rights and Tourist Code of 26 September 1985;
- Convention on the Rights of the Child of 20 November 1989;
- Resolution of the Ninth General Assembly of WTO (Buenos Aires) concerning in particular travel facilitation and the safety and security of tourists of 4 October 1991;

- Rio Declaration on the Environment and Development of 13 June 1992;
- General Agreement on Trade in Services of 15 April 1994;
- Convention on Biodiversity of 6 January 1995;
- Resolution of the Eleventh General Assembly of WTO (Cairo) on the prevention of organized sex tourism of 22 October 1995;
- Stockholm Declaration of 28 August 1996 against the Commercial Sexual Exploitation of Children;
- Manila Declaration on the Social Impact of Tourism of 22 May 1997;
- Conventions and recommendations adopted by the International Labour Organization in the area of collective conventions, prohibition of forced labour and child labour, defence of the rights of indigenous peoples, and equal treatment and non-discrimination in the work place.

Affirm the right to tourism and the freedom of tourist movements, state our wish to promote an equitable, responsible and sustainable world tourism order, whose benefits will be shared by all sectors of society in the context of an open and liberalized international economy, and solemnly adopt to these ends the Principles of the Global Code of Ethics for Tourism.

Article 1: Tourism's contribution to mutual understanding and respect between peoples and societies

1. The understanding and promotion of the ethical values common to humanity, with an attitude of tolerance and respect for the diversity of religious, philosophical and moral beliefs, are both the foundation and the consequence of responsible tourism; stakeholders in tourism development and tourists themselves should observe the social and cultural traditions and practices of all peoples, including those of minorities and indigenous peoples and to recognize their worth;
2. Tourism activities should be conducted in harmony with the attributes and traditions of the host regions and countries and in respect for their laws, practices and customs;

3. The host communities, on the one hand, and local professionals, on the other, should acquaint themselves with and respect the tourists who visit them and find out about their lifestyles, tastes and expectations; the education and training imparted to professionals contribute to a hospitable welcome;
4. It is the task of the public authorities to provide protection for tourists and visitors and their belongings; they must pay particular attention to the safety of foreign tourists owing to the particular vulnerability they may have; they should facilitate the introduction of specific means of information, prevention, security, insurance and assistance consistent with their needs; any attacks, assaults, kidnappings or threats against tourists or workers in the tourism industry, as well as the willful destruction of tourism facilities or of elements of cultural or natural heritage should be severely condemned and punished in accordance with their respective national laws;
5. When travelling, tourists and visitors should not commit any criminal act or any act considered criminal by the laws of the country visited and abstain from any conduct felt to be offensive or injurious by the local populations, or likely to damage the local environment; they should refrain from all trafficking in illicit drugs, arms, antiques, protected species and products and substances that are dangerous or prohibited by national regulations;
6. Tourists and visitors have the responsibility to acquaint themselves, even before their departure, with the characteristics of the countries they are preparing to visit; they must be aware of the health and security risks inherent in any travel outside their usual environment and behave in such a way as to minimize those risks.

Article 2: Tourism as a vehicle for individual and collective fulfillment

1. Tourism, the activity most frequently associated with rest and relaxation, sport and access to culture and nature, should be planned and practised as a privileged means of individual and collective fulfillment; when practised with

a sufficiently open mind, it is an irreplaceable factor of self-education, mutual tolerance and for learning about the legitimate differences between peoples and cultures and their diversity;

2. Tourism activities should respect the equality of men and women; they should promote human rights and, more particularly, the individual rights of the most vulnerable groups, notably children, the elderly, the handicapped, ethnic minorities and indigenous peoples;
3. The exploitation of human beings in any form, particularly sexual, especially when applied to children, conflicts with the fundamental aims of tourism and is the negation of tourism; as such, in accordance with international law, it should be energetically combated with the cooperation of all the States concerned and penalized without concession by the national legislation of both the countries visited and the countries of the perpetrators of these acts, even when they are carried out abroad;
4. Travel for purposes of religion, health, education and cultural or linguistic exchanges are particularly beneficial forms of tourism, which deserve encouragement;
5. The introduction into curricula of education about the value of tourist exchanges, their economic, social and cultural benefits, and also their risks, should be encouraged.

Article 4: Tourism, a user of the cultural heritage of mankind and a contributor to its enhancement

1. Tourism resources belong to the common heritage of mankind; the communities in whose territories they are situated have particular rights and obligations to them;
2. Tourism policies and activities should be conducted with respect for the artistic, archaeological and cultural heritage, which they should protect and pass on to future generations; particular care should be devoted to preserving and upgrading monuments, shrines and museums as well as archaeological and historic sites which must be widely open to tourist visits;
Encouragement should be given to public access to privately-owned cultural property and monuments,

with respect for the rights of their owners, as well as to religious buildings, without prejudice to normal needs of worship;

3. Financial resources derived from visits to cultural sites and monuments should, at least in part, be used for the upkeep, safeguard, development and embellishment of this heritage;
4. Tourism activity should be planned in such a way as to allow traditional cultural products, crafts and folklore to survive and flourish, rather than causing them to degenerate and become standardized.

Article 5: Tourism, a beneficial activity for host countries and communities

1. Local populations should be associated with tourism activities and share equitably in the economic, social and cultural benefits they generate, and particularly in the creation of direct and indirect jobs resulting from them;
2. Tourism policies should be applied in such a way as to help to raise the standard of living of the populations of the regions visited and meet their needs; the planning and architectural approach to and operation of tourism resorts and accommodation should aim to integrate them, to the extent possible, in the local economic and social fabric; where skills are equal, priority should be given to local manpower;
3. Special attention should be paid to the specific problems of coastal areas and island territories and to vulnerable rural or mountain regions, for which tourism often represents a rare opportunity for development in the face of the decline of traditional economic activities;
4. Tourism professionals, particularly investors, governed by the regulations laid down by the public authorities, should carry out studies of the impact of their development projects on the environment and natural surroundings; they should also deliver, with the greatest transparency and objectivity, information on their future programmes and their foreseeable repercussions and foster dialogue on their contents with the populations concerned.

Article 6: Obligations of stakeholders in tourism development

1. Tourism professionals have an obligation to provide tourists with objective and honest information on their places of destination and on the conditions of travel, hospitality and stays; they should ensure that the contractual clauses proposed to their customers are readily understandable as to the nature, price and quality of the services they commit themselves to providing and the financial compensation payable by them in the event of a unilateral breach of contract on their part;
2. Tourism professionals, insofar as it depends on them, should show concern, in cooperation with the public authorities, for the security and safety, accident prevention, health protection and food safety of those who seek;
3. Family, youth, student and senior tourism and tourism for people with disabilities, should be encouraged and facilitated; their services; likewise, they should ensure the existence of suitable systems of insurance and assistance; they should accept the reporting obligations prescribed by national regulations and pay fair compensation in the event of failure to observe their contractual obligations;
4. Tourism professionals, so far as this depends on them, should contribute to the cultural and spiritual fulfillment of tourists and allow them, during their travels, to practice their religions;
5. The public authorities of the generating States and the host countries, in cooperation with the professionals concerned and their associations, should ensure that the necessary mechanisms are in place for the repatriation of tourists in the event of the bankruptcy of the enterprise that organized their travel;
6. Governments have the right and the duty - especially in a crisis, to inform their nationals of the difficult circumstances, or even the dangers they may encounter during their travels abroad; it is their responsibility however to issue such information without prejudicing in an unjustified or exaggerated manner the tourism industry of the host countries and the interests of their

own operators; the contents of travel advisories should therefore be discussed before hand with the authorities of the host countries and the professionals concerned; recommendations formulated should be strictly proportionate to the gravity of the situations encountered and confined to the geographical areas where the insecurity has arisen; such advisories should be qualified or cancelled as soon as a return to normality permits;

7. The press, and particularly the specialized travel press and the other media, including modern means of electronic communication, should issue honest and balanced information on events and situations that could influence the flow of tourists; they should also provide accurate and reliable information to the consumers of tourism services; the new communication and electronic commerce technologies should also be developed and used for this purpose; as is the case for the media, they should not in any way promote sex tourism.

Article 7: Right to tourism

1. The prospect of direct and personal access to the discovery and enjoyment of the planet's resources constitutes a right equally open to all the world's inhabitants; the increasingly extensive participation in national and international tourism should be regarded as one of the best possible expressions of the sustained growth of free time, and obstacles should not be placed in its way;
2. The universal right to tourism must be regarded as the corollary of the right to rest and leisure, including reasonable limitation of working hours and periodic holidays with pay, guaranteed by Article 24 of the Universal Declaration of Human Rights and Article 7.d of the International Covenant on Economic, Social and Cultural Rights;
3. Social tourism, and in particular associative tourism, which facilitates widespread access to leisure, travel and holidays, should be developed with the support of the public authorities;

Article 8: Liberty of tourist movements

1. Tourists and visitors should benefit, in compliance with international law and national legislation, from the liberty to move within their countries and from one State to another, in accordance with Article 13 of the Universal Declaration of Human Rights; they should have access to places of transit and stay and to tourism and cultural sites without being subject to excessive formalities or discrimination;
2. Tourists and visitors should have access to all available forms of communication, internal or external; they should benefit from prompt and easy access to local administrative, legal and health services; they should be free to contact the consular representatives of their countries of origin in compliance with the diplomatic conventions in force;
3. Tourists and visitors should benefit from the same rights as the citizens of the country visited concerning the confidentiality of the personal data and information concerning them, especially when these are stored electronically;
4. Administrative procedures relating to border crossings whether they fall within the competence of States or result from international agreements, such as visas or health and customs formalities, should be adapted, so far as possible, so as to facilitate to the maximum freedom of travel, and widespread access to international tourism; agreements between groups of countries to harmonize and simplify these procedures should be encouraged; specific taxes and levies penalizing the tourism industry and undermining its competitiveness should be gradually phased out or corrected;
5. So far as the economic situation of the countries from which they come permits, travellers should have access to allowances of convertible currencies needed for their travels.

Article 9: Rights of the workers and entrepreneurs in the tourism industry

1. The fundamental rights of salaried and self-employed workers in the tourism industry and related activities,

should be guaranteed under the supervision of the national and local administrations, both of their States of origin and of the host countries with particular care, given the specific constraints linked in particular to the seasonality of their activity, the global dimension of their industry and the flexibility often required of them by the nature of their work;

2. Salaried and self-employed workers in the tourism industry and related activities have the right and the duty to acquire appropriate initial and continuous training; they should be given adequate social protection; job insecurity should be limited so far as possible; and a specific status, with particular regard to their social welfare, should be offered to seasonal workers in the sector;
3. Any natural or legal person, provided he, she or it has the necessary abilities and skills, should be entitled to develop a professional activity in the field of tourism under existing national laws; entrepreneurs and investors - especially in the area of small and medium-sized enterprises should be entitled to free access to the tourism sector with a minimum of legal or administrative restrictions;
4. Exchanges of experience offered to executives and workers, whether salaried or not, from different countries, contributes to foster the development of the world tourism industry; these movements should be facilitated so far as possible in compliance with the applicable national laws and international conventions;
5. As an irreplaceable factor of solidarity in the development and dynamic growth of international exchanges, multinational enterprises of the tourism industry should not exploit the dominant positions they sometimes occupy; they should avoid becoming the vehicles of cultural and social models artificially imposed on the host communities; in exchange for their freedom to invest and trade which should be fully recognized, they should involve themselves in local development, avoiding, by the excessive repatriation of their profits or their induced imports, a reduction of their contribution to the economies in which they are established;

6. Partnership and the establishment of balanced relations between enterprises of generating and receiving countries contribute to the sustainable development of tourism and an equitable distribution of the benefits of its growth.

Article 10: Implementation of the principles of the Global Code of Ethics for Tourism

1. The public and private stakeholders in tourism development should cooperate in the implementation of these principles and monitor their effective application;
2. The stakeholders in tourism development should recognize the role of international institutions, among which the told Tourism Organization ranks first, and non-governmental organizations with competence in the field of tourism promotion and development, the protection of human rights, the environment or health, with due respect for the general principles of international law;
3. The same stakeholders should demonstrate their intention to refer any disputes concerning the application or interpretation of the Global Code of Ethics for Tourism for conciliation to an impartial third body known as the World Committee on Tourism Ethics.

Sustainable Development

Ensuring the sustainable development and management of tourism so that its benefits can be enjoyed for generations to come is the philosophy behind the activities carried out by the Sustainable Tourism Development Section. UNWTO creates practical instruments that allow tourism managers, in both the public and private sectors, to apply the principles of sustainability to concrete situations. The Section has issued several publications, manuals, inventories and analyzes of best practices, which have been widely circulated and organized seminars have been held throughout the world.

Some major projects include:

(a) *International Year of Ecotourism 2002*: Recognizing the global importance of ecotourism, the United Nations designated the year 2002 as the International Year of Ecotourism. A

World Ecotourism Summit in Quebec, Canada (May 2002), jointly organized with the United Nations Environment Programme, gathered around 1,200 participants and resulted in the Quebec Declaration on Ecotourism, containing 49 specific guidelines for sustainable ecotourism development and management.

(*b*) *World Summit on Sustainable Development*: The World Tourism Organization was actively involved in the preparations for the World Summit on Sustainable Development that took place in Johannesburg on 26 August, 4 September 2002.

(*c*) *Planning for Sustainable Development of Tourism*: UNWTO has published several manuals for tourism planning at the national, regional and local levels. It organizes national seminars on tourism planning for local authorities in developing countries.

(*d*) *Indicators of Sustainable Tourism*: Sustainable tourism indicators are fundamental tools for the planning and monitoring of tourism development. UNWTO has been involved in this area since 1992, conducting pilot studies, producing a manual and teaching how to use indicators through a series of regional technical workshops in different regions and types of destinations.

(*e*) *Good Practices in Sustainable Development of Tourism*: Providing successful examples of tourism development and management is an important way of disseminating experiences that can be adapted at other destinations. UNWTO has published three compilations of good practice cases in sustainable tourism, each of them containing around 50 case studies from more than 30 countries in a structured format.

Key Publications

- Sustainable Development of Tourism: Guide for Local Authorities, with three regional supplements (Africa, Americas, Asia and the Pacific)
- A Practical Guide to the Use of Sustainable Tourism Indicators Agenda 21 for the Travel and Tourism Industry
- Guidelines for the Development of National Parks and protected areas

- Sustainable Development of Tourism—A Compilation of Good Practices
- Sustainable Development of Ecotourism—A Compilation of Good Practices
- Voluntary Initiatives for Sustainable Tourism
- Series of ecotourism market studies

Statistics

Proving the economic impact of tourism with solid facts and figures is the goal of UNWTO's Section on Statistics and Economic Measurement of Tourism. It helped create the Tourism Satellite Account (TSA) and is now assisting governments implement this accurate system of measuring the demand and supply sides of tourism.

UNWTO sets international standards for tourism measurement and reporting. Its recommendations on tourism statistics were adopted by the United Nations in 1993, creating a common language of tourism statistics that allows destinations to compare their success with that of their competitors. In 2000, the United Nations approved the Tourism Satellite Account methodology, making tourism the world's first sector to have international standards for measuring its economic impacts in a credible way.

UNWTO also provides the world's most comprehensive tourism statistics. Member States, private tourism companies, consulting firms, universities and the media all recognize UNWTO as the world's most comprehensive and reliable source of global tourism statistics and forecasts. Tourism data collected from 190 countries around the world include: arrivals, receipts, overnight stays, mode of transport, length of stay, tourist spending, and origin of visitors.

Tourism Satellite Account

Endorsed by the United Nations Statistical Commission, the Tourism Satellite Account is a joint project of several intergovernmental bodies and industry representatives. It sets a series of global standards and definitions that measure the tourism industry's true contribution in terms of: percentage of GDP, direct tourism jobs and capital investment. In compliance with United Nations recommendations, it runs alongside the national accounts framework. It will provide internationally comparable data developed by a country's own statistical institutions. TSA also puts tourism for the first time on an equal footing with other, less diversified economic sectors. Developing TSA is an opportunity for defining cooperative work between National Tourism Administrations, National Statistical Offices and Central Banks.

Key Publications

- Compendium of Tourism Statistics
- Yearbook of Tourism Statistics
- Tourism Satellite Account as an ongoing process: past, present and future developments
- Enzo Paci Papers on Measuring the Economic Significance of Tourism, Vol. 1 and 2
- Measuring Visitor Expenditure for Inbound Tourism

Market Intelligence

Assisting governments and tourism professionals in understanding the constantly changing tourism marketplace is the aim of UNWTO's Section on Market Intelligence and Promotion. Identifying market trends as they are happening; short-term and long-term forecasting; analyzing the world's generating markets; conducting research into niche markets; and providing evaluation tools for promotional campaigns are just some of the activities carried out each year.

The annual series of Tourism Market Trends reports provides a timely and comprehensive analysis of tourism results around the world. It enables tourism authorities to compare their performance to other countries of the same region, examining arrivals, receipts and the main factors affecting growth in the previous season.

Special attention is paid to studying tourism products, such as sports, cruises, MICE tourism (meetings, incentives, congresses and exhibitions) and market segments, such as ecotourism, youth or senior tourism. Another important task is the analysis of outbound tourism of both consolidated and emerging markets. Research can be initiated in any specific topics relevant for tourism development. For instance, to increase insight in the evolution of the tourism sector, it was studied how consolidation by means of alliances, mergers and acquisitions in the sub-sectors of accommodation, air transport and distribution is impacting destinations, travel agents, small businesses and the consumer.

To assist Member States with tourism promotion, the Section conducts periodic surveys on tourism budgets and sources of financing. It also provides practical guidance whenever pertinent. For instance, after the September 11th attacks it monitored the subsequent situation of uncertainty, studied lessons learned from past crises and helped Members with strategies to adapt to sudden change in market conditions.

UNWTO's seven-volume forecast Tourism 2020 Vision on worldwide forecasts is a landmark study based on data gathered from Member States and interviews with over 75 tourism visionaries about the future of the industry. It predicts that international tourist arrivals will grow by an average of 4.1 per cent annually for the 25-year-period 1995-2020. Tourism 2020 Vision includes forecasts of inbound and outbound tourism growth for countries in every region of the world and examines the outlook for several market segments.

Results are disseminated in various ways, such as through presentations and seminars, the UNWTO website and in a broad range of publications, including:

- Tourism Market Trends—five regional volumes and a world volume
- Tourism Highlights
- Tourism 2020 Vision—six regional volumes and a world volume
- Budgets of National Tourism Administrations
- Tourism Generating Markets
- World Tourism Barometer

Communications

A Focal Point for Tourism Information

Increasing awareness of the importance of tourism, promoting the UNWTO's work and objectives through effective communication in order to provide transparency of its activities, helping achieve the goals of all sections and keeping you informed about new projects, studies, seminar results and upcoming

UNWTO activities are the primary goals of UNWTO's Press and Communications Section.

Members receive the UNWTO News, published quarterly, and the electronic Members' Update, published fortnightly. Non-members are reached through the media. The Press and Communications Section maintains a database of 2,000 key journalists around the world and contacts them regularly through news releases and press conferences.

The entire tourism industry is reached by UNWTO's website on the Internet and through major international tourism trade fairs where UNWTO operates an information booth, including:

- FITUR, Madrid
- ITB, Berlin
- MITT, Moscow
- WTM, London

Improving the promotional efforts of Member States through effective media relations, organizing press trips and seminars on media relations and crisis management, are even more goals of UNWTO's Press and Communications Section. It publishes Shining in the Media Spotlight, a communications manual that includes a directory of major media in the world's top tourism generating markets. The World Conference on Tourism Communications (TOURCOM), was held in early 2004, and became a regular meeting place of tourism professionals from both, public and private sectors, with the international media.

www.world-tourism.org

Completely renovated in 2001, UNWTO's popular website on the Internet is available in English, French and Spanish, with a growing section in Russian and—to follow—in Arabic. The attractive homepage offers the latest news from UNWTO and easy-to-use links to all activities and products. Users have access to basic statistics on world tourism, seminars' programmes, a complete calendar of worldwide tourism events, details on special programmes such as the meetings of the Tourism Recovery Committee, the Silk Road Project, Protection of Children from Sexual Exploitation in Tourism and Sustainable Tourism—Eliminating Poverty (ST-EP).

Publications

One of UNWTO's most important functions is to serve as a permanent source of information for its Members and the world community. UNWTO fulfills this task in part through its extensive programme of publications and the new programme of electronic products. The broad span of these products corresponds to the vast sweep both of the Organization's concerns and of the needs of its Members.

Today, UNWTO has already more than 250 titles available. Every year this list is extended by some 30 to 40 new titles in up-to four official languages which are produced by the UNWTO publications department together with the originating sections. The Publications Department runs at UNWTO headquarters in Madrid a bookshop from which all publications and electronic products can be ordered. Besides, all books and electronic products are displayed in a very detailed form and with excerpts in the UNWTO Info shop at www.world-tourism.org/infoshop. Easy purchase and credit card payment options are just some of the comfortable features the shop offers. All products can also be ordered directly from a world-wide network of local distributors.

With the aim of improving the dissemination of our information as much as possible, translation and reproduction rights are also available to editorials that wish to publish UNWTO publications into other official and non-official languages. Untill today UNWTO publications have been translated into more than 30 different languages.

With its recently launched Depository Library Programme, the UNWTO publications section encourages libraries to collect all UNWTO publications and make them available to a wider audience. All libraries which are complying with the requirements for Depository Libraries are invited to share this initiative and are offered interesting financial conditions.

Documentation Resources

With the goal of acting as a true clearing-house, the UNWTO Documentation Centre's endeavour to provide up-to-date qualitative information on tourism activities and related components on a theme-oriented basis.

The Documentation Centre concentrates its efforts to improve the information linkage networking between itself, UNWTO Members and other institutional partners, so as to facilitate tourism information access, transfer and exchange worldwide.

With these objectives in mind, the Centre offers online access to a tourism legislation database (LEXTOUR) providing bibliographic and textual data on laws and regulations existing both at the UNWTO Secretariat and in similar external legislative information systems.

As visible output products, the Centre delivers regular research reports on strategic issues, such as the role, spheres of competence and activities of tourism administrations and tourism investment policies. It also collaborates with other departments within the Secretariat in establishing a permanent tourism taxation monitoring information system.

To consolidate its function as a referral service, a specific database administrated by the Centre disseminates factual data on national and international tourism information holders and brokers (INFODOCTOUR) via the UNWTO Website. In addition, the Documentation Centre provides an authoritative tool for indexing and retrieving information on tourism and allied fields with the Multilingual Thesaurus on Tourism and Leisure Activities.

Who can join the World Tourism Organization?

UNWTO has three categories of membership: Full Members, Associate Members and Affiliate Members.

- Full membership is open to all sovereign States.
- Associate membership is open to territories not responsible for their external relations. Membership requires the prior approval of the government which assumes responsibility for their external relations.
- Affiliate membership comprises a wide range of organizations and companies working directly in travel, tourism and related sectors. These may include: airlines and other transport, hotels and restaurants, tour operators and travel agents, banking institutions, insurance companies, travel assistance, publishing groups, etc.

Affiliate membership is made up of three groups, the UNWTO Business Council, the UNWTO Education Council, and the UNWTO Task Force on Destination Management. Affiliate membership requires endorsement by the government of the state in which the headquarters of the applicant is located.

UNWTO is the only intergovernmental organization that offers membership to the operational sector and in this way offers a unique contact point for discussion between government officials and industry leaders. UNWTO's broad-based Affiliate membership also has its own programme of activities which includes regular meetings and technical seminars on specific study topics.

WTO GLOBAL CAMPAIGN

"Tourism enriches individuals, families, communities and all the world." This is a central, simple but straight-forward message of the new awareness campaign with which the World Tourism Organization (WTO) wants to raise awareness of the positive impacts tourism can have on life, culture and economy, in short on society at all levels.

In Madrid, on 16 February 2004, the "Tourism Enriches" campaign was launched at the First World Conference on Tourism Communications (TOURCOM) end of January in Madrid. "This is the first time WTO has aimed a campaign at the general public", said WTO Secretary-General Francesco Frangialli. "It is a simple, upbeat idea and a simple beginning, but ultimately the campaign is intended to be developed and used by the tourism industry, especially ministries in our member countries, as they see fit."

The initiative came from the WTO Members and was discussed at the 15th Session of the General Assembly in Beijing, China.

"Governments have been putting a higher priority on tourism in the time of recent crises," stressed Mr. Frangialli, explaining that this resulted in recognition of tourism as the most prospective activity, important for environmental, cultural and social awareness, pursuit of peace and international cooperation recognition and in particular of its ability to alleviate poverty through the creation of small and medium sized tourism businesses and the creation of new jobs. "That same recognition has taken place at the highest level in the General Assembly of the United Nations, which unanimously agreed on December 23rd to make the UNWTO its newest specialized agency."

"We are calling upon governments to implement this importance of tourism in practice and invest more funds in tourism development and communications", said the Secretary-General. "The success of "Tourism Enriches" also depends in part on its diffusion in the media, so we are inviting them to become the third member in the already established public-private partnership in international tourism."

The aims of "Tourism Enriches" campaign are to promote tourism as a basic human right and way of life, to stimulate communication about the benefits of tourism as the most prospective economic activity for the local communities and countries, to enhance cooperation between destinations and the tourism industry with the local, regional and international media and to link individual tourism entities to the larger community of international tourism.

Cooperating in the campaign is offered to all destinations, tourist companies and the media, unconditionally with the membership status in the WTO. "While we believe that the principles of this campaign are acceptable for all, we in particular invite the developing world to adopt them and link them to the United Nations Millennium Development Goals," added Mr. Frangialli.

The campaign features five basic components that can be adapted and expanded for use by Member States, Affiliate Members of the WTO and the rest of the tourism industry in their own tourism promotion and awareness building activities: the slogan "Tourism Enriches", the graphic image or logo of the campaign, a six-page A4 size flyer outlining positive impacts of tourism, such as economic benefits, increased international understanding, rural jobs, environmental protection, etc., an attractive poster using the same art work and a thirty-second video public service announcement for free use on national television channels, airlines, and satellite TV (in progress).

The TOURCOM Network of Communications Experts, a new consultative body to the WTO Press and Communications Section, will be responsible for implementing the campaign within the scope of their own activities around the world.

COLLABORATION IN THE INTERNATIONAL STANDARDIZATION OF TOURISM SERVICES

This section provides a description of the organization, role, and added value of the International Organization for Standardization (hereinafter "ISO"), and outlines some of its current and potential activities for standardization of tourism services of potential interest to the World Tourism Organization. It is intended to inform, and to foster dialogue, and provide a basis to explore possible areas of cooperation between the two organizations. The document is divided into a general description of ISO, its added value, activities undertaken in standardization of tourism services upto the present, and potential future developments. In addition, three annexes provide, respectively, a summary of how standards are developed, ISO's added value, and examples of national standards on tourism services currently implemented by various ISO members.

ISO (International Organization for Standardization - www.iso.org) is the world's largest developer of voluntary technical standards. ISO is a nongovernmental organization established in 1947 with members consisting of the national standards organizations of 146 countries, on the basis of one member per country. These national standards organizations are in some cases national associations made up of industry and consumer interests; in other cases they are specific government ministries or departments that have a national mandate for the development of standards. All, however, have some form of official recognition of their national role and international involvement in this area.

ISO has a Central Secretariat, based in Geneva, Switzerland, that employs approximately 150 staff. The work in developing and maintaining the portfolio of some 14,000 technical International Standards is shared amongst the membership, with individual national members providing and financing the Chairmanships and Secretariats for one or more of the 188 technical committees and 550 subcommittees managing 2,200 working groups and the Central Secretariat providing the general coordination of procedures, electronic tools and final production and dissemination. Further information on the ISO standards development process is attached at Annex 1.

ISO develops standards to meet market requirements. The work is carried out by experts on loan from the industrial, technical and business sectors which have asked for the standards, and which subsequently put them to use. These experts may be joined by others with relevant knowledge, such as representatives of government agencies, consumer organizations, educational establishments and testing laboratories. Collaboration with relevant international organizations is provided through liaison arrangements

While one of the best-known standards in the ISO portfolio is ISO 9001:2000, *Quality management systems—Requirements*, the great majority of ISO standards do not relate to management system requirements. Rather they include terminology, sampling, test and analytical methods, as well as specifications and performance requirements for industrial and agricultural products, equipment, processes and, to a growing extent, services.

ISO is able to act as a bridging organization in which a consensus can be reached on solutions that meet both the requirements of business and the broader needs of society, such as the needs of stakeholder groups like consumers and users. ISO's work programme includes something to offer for the entire range of business and technology, from standards for traditional activities, such as agriculture and construction, through mechanical engineering, to medical devices, banking cards and toys, to the latest information technology developments. Its extensive national memberships enables taking into account the implications and concerns of developing countries.

The ISO system provides added benefit for all stakeholders participating in, and affected by the development of International Standards and other normative documents. Suppliers benefit through easier access to markets and facilitation of trade. Consumers benefit through enhanced choice and improved safety, fitness for purpose, and other criteria. International Standards also provide a valid basis for legislation and for trade agreements by governments. The international consensus on the state-of-the-art provides Developing Countries with an important source of technical knowledge and therefore access to the world's markets. This knowledge includes both product and manufacturing standards and also the good management practices provided by the ISO 9000 and ISO 14000 series of quality and environmental management standards. More relevant information appears at Annex 2.

ISO—together with IEC (International Electrotechnical Commission) and ITU (International Telecommunication Union)—has built a strategic partnership with the World Trade Organization (WTO) with the common aim of promoting a free and fair global trading system. The political agreements reached within the framework of the WTO require underpinning by technical agreements.

ISO cooperates with three committees of the World Trade Organization: the Committee on Technical Barriers to Trade (TBT), the Committee on Sanitary and Phytosanitary Measures (SPS) and the Committee on Trade and the Environment (CTE). Several provisions within the text of the General Agreement on Trade in Services (GATS), particularly Article VI:5 and VII:5, recognize the value of International Standards to facilitate trade in services.

Standardization of Tourism Services and Related Issues—ISO's Activities to Date

Commercial services occupy an increasingly important share of the world's trade. The contribution of the service sector to the world gross domestic product was 64 per cent in the year 2000, compared to 57 per cent in 1990, with tourism the largest single category in the area. In 2001, tourism accounted for 37.8 per cent of all services traded in developing countries, and 29.3 per cent of all services traded in developed countries. Services are a particularly crucial area for developing countries. According to the World Trade Organization, 25 developing countries depend on the export of commercial services for more than half of their total export revenues.

Realizing this trend, the ISO Committee on consumer policy (ISO/COPOLCO), which is a policy development structure reporting directly to the ISO Council and which includes delegated representatives from most of the participating members of ISO, held an international workshop on standardization of services in 1995. This event, as well as a decision by the ISO Technical Management Board, led ISO to organize a series of regional workshops jointly with the GATS Committee of the World Trade Organization in 1998. These were held in Argentina, France, Singapore and the USA.

While the conclusions of these workshops suggested that there was good support for developing International Standards on tourism services, few ISO International Standards have since been developed on this subject. At this point in time, the only existing ISO International Standard is the recently-published ISO 18513, *Tourism services—Hotel and other types of tourism accommodation—Terminology*, directly adopted from a European (CEN) standard.

As a result of a subsequent ISO/COPOLCO workshop on services standardization in 2001, ISO/COPOLCO resolved to develop generic guidelines for standardization of services, and to identify consumer priorities in the standardization of two specific areas: financial services, and tourism. Particularly in the area of tourism, preliminary investigations revealed a strong interest in standardization of tourism services and an abundance of existing national standards. The summarized results of this survey to the members of COPOLCO showing existing national standards, appears at Annex 3.

COPOLCO agreed that input from industry operators was necessary in developing feasible proposals for standardization of tourism services. Further research by COPOLCO specialists led them to contact representatives from other tourism-related organizations (e.g. Rainforest Alliance, Swiss Tourism Association, World Tourism Organization, International Hotel and Restaurant Association).

Exchange of information between ISO/COPOLCO consumer representatives and representatives from the hospitality industry has been fruitful. Input from representatives of the hospitality industry, notably by a representative of the International Hotel and Restaurant Association (IH&RA), has helped COPOLCO focus on priority areas of tourism standardization. In September 2003, COPOLCO identified the following subjects as both important for consumers and conducive to standardization: hygiene, sustainable tourism, safety (particularly concerning child and fire safety) and accessibility (including "design for all" concepts).

On the basis of continued work to refine these subjects, ISO/COPOLCO will consider a more in-depth proposal at its forthcoming plenary meeting on 18-19 May. This proposal will form the basis for a formal request to ISO to initiate standards initiatives in tourism security and safety, accessibility and hygiene.

The ISO 9000 and ISO 14000 series of standards have been successfully used in a variety of different service areas, including financial and tourism services, to improve the overall quality of service delivery. Notably, ISO has also published International Workshop Agreements (a precursor to an International Standard, with a shorter development process) on implementation of ISO 9001 in the areas of health-care and education. Actual case examples of hospitality industry providers benefiting from ISO 9000 and ISO 14000 certification include German tour operators and fair organizers, hotel and catering associations and hotels in France, hotels in Singapore and Malaysia, and an airline catering service in Singapore. The Italian ISO member has published handbooks providing guidance on implementation of ISO 9000, and later ISO 14000, in the hotel and tourism sector. Other examples include parks in Italy and Ecuador, and the administration of island tourist destinations in Italy and South Korea. Of the 561,747 organizations certified to ISO 9000 worldwide at the end of 2002, 123,128 were providers of services. Hotels and restaurants accounted for 1840 of these certifications.

Standardization of Tourism Services—Potential New Initiatives, Related Issues

The European Commission (DG Enterprise) has mandated the Comité Européen de Normalisation (CEN) to develop a framework for standardization of services (Mandate 340). CEN is to research and write a list of possible areas of standardization of services by December 2004. CEN is currently conducting an enquiry to list areas of service standardization at the national level and has created a working group, led by the ISO member for Spain, AENOR. Criteria for inclusion in the listing are (1) Sartorial interest in the project, and (2) Feasibility of standardization within a reasonable length of time. As was demonstrated by ISO 18513 on terminology, standards emanating from this mandate have the potential to be adopted as International Standards.

In related initiatives, the DG-Internal Markets is developing a European Directive on cross-border trade in services and the DG-SANCO is performing research on possible directives concerning safety of services in the area of sports and leisure, including adventure tours.

The ISO Committee on conformity assessment (CASCO) has produced a "tool box" or set of International Standards which set out requirements for how conformity to International Standards should be assessed. Areas covered include certification of products, services, persons, management and systems. The tool box also includes International Standards on how to self-declare conformity, be peer-assessed or accredited.

Since the beginning of 2004, three separate ISO members from different points of the globe have contacted the ISO Secretary-General expressing interest in developing International Standards for tourism services. The areas for work that each has proposed under a new Technical Committee structure are Ecotourism, Exhibition terminology and audit procedures, and Tourism as a whole.

The ISO Central Secretariat is currently considering the most optimal Technical Committee and Subcommittee structure for these different proposals on tourism standardization, for deliberation by the Technical Management Board at its next meeting. Other issues being considered include the feasibility of a cooperative, or "twinning" arrangement with another ISO member, and fast-tracking an already existing national standard on Exhibition terminology as the basis of an International Standard. Depending on the outcome of discussion, a full enquiry on launching a new area of technical work on standardization of tourism services will likely go out to the entire membership of ISO.

It is worth noting that the World Tourism Organization already acts in a formal liaison organization to ISO/TC 145/SC 1—*Public information symbols* and TC 154 *Processes, data elements and documents in commerce, industry and administration.* In addition, other related standards may be of interest to the World Tourism Organization; one example is ISO/IEC 7501 *Identification cards — Machine readable travel documents.* ISO has a number of Technical Committees with work programmes impacting on tourism (ISO/TC 42 *Photography,* TC 68 *Financial services,* ISO/TC 204 *Intelligent transport systems,* TC 177 *Caravans,* TC 83 *Sports and recreational equipment,* TC 188 *Small craft*).

Conclusion: ISO has a great deal of experience in consensus-based development of standards in many fields, especially in relevant areas such as management system and conformity assessment standards. A number of formal proposals for international standardization of tourism services are underway among the ISO membership and within COPOLCO.

ISO would therefore like to present its skills and experience to the World Tourism Organization, to discuss shared priorities, opportunities for synergy and expanded modes of cooperation, both at the strategic and technical levels.

Annex 1: Simplified Explanation of Stages in the Development of ISO International Standards

An International Standard is the result of an agreement between the member bodies of ISO. It may be used as such, or may be implemented through incorporation in national standards of different countries.

International Standards are developed by ISO technical committees (TC) and subcommittees (SC) by a six-step process:

Stage 1 : Proposal stage
Stage 2 : Preparatory stage
Stage 3 : Committee stage
Stage 4 : Enquiry stage
Stage 5 : Approval stage
Stage 6 : Publication stage

If a document with a certain degree of maturity is available at the start of a standardization project, for example a standard developed by another organization, it is possible to omit certain stages. In the so-called "Fast-track procedure", a document is submitted directly for approval as a Draft International Standard (DIS) to the ISO member bodies (stage 4) or, if the document has been developed by an international standardizing body recognized by the ISO Council, as a Final Draft International Standard (FDIS, stage 5), without passing through the previous stages.

For greater detail on how an International Standard is developed, refer to the publication ISO/IEC Directives, Part 1: *Procedures for the technical work* (available on ISO's Standards Developers' Information Site SDIS at www.iso.org/sdis).

The following is a summary of each of the six stages:

Stage 1: Proposal Stage

The first step in the development of an International Standard is to confirm that a particular International Standard is needed. A new work item proposal (NP) is submitted for vote by the members of the relevant TC/SC to determine the inclusion of the work item in the programme of work. The proposal is accepted if a majority of the P-members of the TC/SC votes in favour and at least five P-members declare their commitment to participate actively in the project. At this stage a project leader responsible for the work item is normally appointed.

Stage 2: Preparatory Stage

Usually, a working group of experts, the chairman (convener) of which is the project leader, is set up by the TC/SC for the preparation of a working draft. Successive working drafts may be considered until the working group is satisfied that it has developed the best technical solution to the problem being addressed. At this stage, the draft is forwarded to the working group's parent committee for the consensus-building phase.

Stage 3: Committee Stage

As soon as a first committee draft is available, it is registered by the ISO Central Secretariat. It is distributed for comments and, if required, voting, by the P-members of the TC/SC. Successive committee drafts may be considered until consensus is reached on the technical content. Once consensus has been attained, the text is finalized for submission as a Draft International Standard (DIS).

Stage 4: Enquiry Stage

The Draft International Standard (DIS) is circulated to all ISO member bodies by the ISO Central Secretariat for voting and comment within a period of five months. It is approved for submission as a Final Draft International Standard (FDIS) if a two-thirds majority of the P-members of the TC/SC are in favour and not more than one-quarter of the total number of votes cast are negative. If the approval criteria are not met, the text is returned to the originating TC/SC for further study and a revised document will again be circulated for voting and comment as a Draft International Standard.

Stage 5: Approval Stage

The Final Draft International Standard (FDIS) is circulated to all ISO member bodies by the ISO Central Secretariat for a final Yes/No vote within a period of two months. If technical comments are received during this period, they are no longer considered at this stage, but registered for consideration during a future revision of the International Standard. The text is approved as an International Standard if a two-thirds majority of the P-members of the TC/SC are in favour and not more than one-quarter of the total number of votes cast are negative. If these approval criteria are not met, the standard is referred back to the originating TC/SC for reconsideration in the light of the technical reasons submitted in support of the negative votes received.

Stage 6: Publication Stage

Once a Final Draft International Standard has been approved, only minor editorial changes, if and where necessary, are introduced into the final text. The final text is sent to the ISO Central Secretariat which publishes the International Standard.

Review of International Standards (Confirmation, Revision, Withdrawal)

All International Standards are reviewed at least once every five years by the responsible TCs/SCs. A majority of the P-members of the TC/SC decides whether an International Standard should be confirmed, revised or withdrawn.

Annex 2: "ISO's Added Value"—What ISO Contributes

1. Recognized experience in international consensus building
2. Brand name and wide recognition
3. Diversified scope, broad range of deliverables and cross-sector consistency
4. Strong national membership base, ensuring adequate consensus, dissemination of deliverables and market feedback for their maintenance and development
5. Extensive networking, at both the international and regional levels
6. Ability to provide International Standards to assist in the implementation and harmonization of regulations
7. Leadership for the production of standards and guides for conformity assess men
8. Leadership in the use of IT tools for the production and dissemination of standards

Annex 3: Examples of national standards for tourism services

Country	*Tourism sector standards as a whole*	*Specific standards*
Botswana	Standards address physical facility requirements for grading of hotels, lodges, bed and breakfast, and guesthouses	(a) BOS 50-1:2001 Hotels and related establishments—Grading requirements—Part 1: Fully serviced hotels. (b) BOS 50-2:2001 Hotels and related establishments—Grading requirements—Part 2: Selected service hotels. (c) BOS 50-3:2001 Hotels and related establishments—Grading requirements—Part 3: Game lodges and camps. (d) BOS 50-4:2001 Hotels and related establishments—Grading requirements—Part 4: Domestic guesthouses. (e) BOS 50-5:2001 Hotels and related establishments—Grading requirements—Part 5: Commercial guesthouses. (f) BOS 50-6:2001 Hotels and related establishments—Grading requirements—Part 6: Self-catering establishments.
Canada	Standards on hotels, campgrounds, vacation centers, bed and breakfasts, youth hostels, residences in teaching establishments	Published standards—in French only NQ 1014-010/2001 *Bus Transportation Services.* NQ 9700-010/2001 **Tourism** — *Customer Service* — *Guidelines for Standards.* NQ 9700-050/2001 **Tourism** — *Customer Service* — *Travel Agencies.* P 9700-065 **Tourism** — *Customer Service* — *Adventure and Ecotourism.* NQ 9700-075/2002 **Tourism** — *Customer Service* — *Cruise Ships and Ferries.* NQ 9700-085/2002 **Tourism** — *Customer Service* — *Attractions and Events.* P 9700-100 **Tourism** — *Customer Service* — *Vacation Centers.* NQ 9700-110/2002 **Tourism** — *Customer Service* — *Hotels.* NQ 9700-120/2002 **Tourism** — *Customer Service* — *Campgrounds.* Standards in Development (in French only) P 9700-060 **Tourism** — Ecotourism Products. P 9700-130 **Tourism** — *Customer Service* — Outfitters.
France		NF237—Service d'accueil et d'information des offices de tourisme et syndicates d'initiative PR NF EN 14804—Séjours linguistiques—Organisateurs de séjours linguistiques NF X 50-055—Service organisateurs de séjours linguistiques NF EN ISO 18513—Services touristiques—Hôtels et autres types d'hébergements touristiques—Terminologie NF S52-104—Pistes de ski—Information sur les risques d'avalanche—Drapeaux d'avalanche

(*Contd.*)

Country	*Tourism sector standards as a whole*	*Specific standards*
Germany	Hotel Classification System by German Hotel Assn (DEHOGA)	DIN 77001, Publication date:1999-09 **Tourism** services—Symbols used in travel brochures DIN EN 13809, Publication date:2003-06 **Tourism** services— Travel agencies and tour operators—Terminology DIN EN ISO 18513, Publication date:2003-12 **Tourism** services—Hotels and other types of tourism accommodation—Terminology SN EN 13809, Publication date:2003-03 **Tourism** services—Travel agencies and tour operators—Terminology
Ireland	Compulsory registration system for Hotels and Guesthouses (but not Bed and Breakfasts and Self-catering businesses) Voluntary, widely-use classification system for Hotels and Guesthouses	
Korea, Rep.	Standards on outbound travel services	
Lebanon	Standards on Hotels and Furnished Apartments Rating system for Hotels only	
Lithuania	Law on **tourism** requires all hotels, motels and camps to be classified	
Netherlands		NEN-EN-ISO 18513:2003—**Tourism** services—Hotels and other types of **tourism** accommodation—Terminology NEN-EN 13809:2003—**Tourism** services—Travel agencies and tour operators—Terminology

(Contd.)

Country	Tourism sector standards as a whole	Specific standards
Singapore	Standards, Productivity and Innovation Board (Spring Singapore) is working on NSRS skills standards in the hotel, travel agent and **tourism** retail sectors. Eventually, NSRS will be extended to all **tourism** sectors	
Spain		UNE 150101:2001 EX Sistemas de gestión medioambiental. Guía para la implantación de un sistema de gestión medioambiental conforme a UNE-EN ISO 14001 en hoteles y otros alojamientos turísticos UNE-EN 13809:2003 Servicios turísticos. Agencias de viajes y turoperadores. Terminologia UNE 41512:2001 Accesibilidad en las playas y su entorno PNE 150104 Sistemas de gestión ambiental. Guía para la implantación de sistemas de gestión ambiental conforme a la Norma UNE-EN ISO 14001 en playas Registrada
South Africa	Standards for Hotels, Guest Houses, Self-catering, Game and Nature Reserves, Caravan Parks, Restaurants, Info. Offices, etc.	
Turkey	Standard on general **rules** on **tourism** services	
UK		BS EN ISO 18513:2003—**Tourism** services. Hotels and other types of **tourism** accommodation. Terminology BS EN 13809:2003—**Tourism** services. Travel agencies and tour operators. Terminology
USA		ISO 18513:2003—**Tourism** services—Hotels and other types of **tourism** accommodation—Terminology BSR/NSF 166-200x—Hotels: Public Health Protection PREN 13809—**Tourism** services—Travel Agencies and Tour Operators Terminology NFPA 1194: Standard for Recreational Vehicle Parks and Campgrounds, 2002 Edition

GATS AND TOURISM

The General Agreement on Trade in Services (GATS) tries to put into action the principle that free market forces are the best means of providing consumers with the best possible products at the best possible prices.

GATS sets in place a system that will lead to the gradual elimination of some barriers to tourism growth, such as restrictions on hiring of foreign personnel, establishment of management operations and opening of franchise companies. This report explains how that will happen.

The guiding philosophy of GATS is that the easier it is for companies to compete and do business, the more trading ensues and the more economies grow.

In order to do business as effectively as possible, companies need level playing fields so that they can have equal access to natural resources, expertise, technologies and investment, both within countries and across borders.

GATS objective is to liberalize trade in services by setting the same rules for both foreign and domestic trading partners, providing "most favoured nation" treatment for all GATS members, and by avoiding disruptive changes in policies affecting trade.

GATS lays the foundations of a new multilateral trading system that will be implemented gradually over the upcoming years. Contrary to widespread belief, nothing will happen overnight.

GATS is a new international trade agreement signed by 125 nations in Marrakesh, Morocco, on 15 April, 1994. It sets global trading rules for service industries, such as telecommunications, financial services, transportation/business services and tourism. It provides procedures for governments to liberalize trade in services through negotiations.

GATS is administered by the Geneva-based World Trade Organization. Formerly called GATT, the World Trade Organization is also charged with supervising 14 other treaties on international commerce that resulted from the Uruguay Round of trade negotiations between 1986 and 1993. Some of the other agreements include the "new" GATT (General Agreement on Trade Related Aspects of Intellectual Property Rights).

GATS signatory countries have submitted schedules of commitments that specifically spell out their national trading rules for each service sector. One hundred countries have submitted schedules of commitments on tourism services, more than any other services sector.

The World Trade Organization will bring countries together to negotiate and balance their commitments on liberalization in successive rounds of negotiations across all services sectors.

GATS recognizes that countries are at different stages in their development and services regulations. It provides special treatment for developing countries, particularly the least developed ones, with a view to increasing their participation in world trade.

GATS applies to measures affecting trade in services in three ways:

- *Juridical*: GATS is legally binding on the signatory countries.
- *Contractual*: GATS signatory countries agree to specific rights and obligations which may be disputed, settled or enforced through established procedures.
- *Strategic*: In their commercial policies, member countries are expected to be guided by GATS rules towards progressive liberalization. This means gradually according market access, national treatment and most-favoured-nation treatment to all members.

GATS is not a free trade agreement, but a tool leading to trade in services without discrimination or other non-tariff barriers. GATS does not mean immediate and full liberalization, but a beginning of the liberalization process.

GATS does not intervene in the economic policies and regulations of its member countries, such as taxes, incentives, interest rates, etc., unless such policies are applied unequally to domestic and foreign services suppliers.

GATS does not deal with frontier formalities which affect travellers, such as visas, passports, customs duties, exit taxes, or taxes on tourism services. Nor does it apply to foreign exchange allowances or restrictions affecting international travellers.

Presently, much of international trade in services is clouded by discriminatory practices, protectionism and a lack of transparency.

In tourism, restrictions affect companies in many ways, such as:

- Their ability to move staff to a foreign country (intra-company transfers),
- To create and operate branch offices abroad,
- To effect currency payments and transfers,
- To use trademarks, etc.

Even when meeting all of a country's requirements for doing business in that country, a foreign tourism enterprise—hotel, travel agency, restaurant, transport company may still be prevented from conducting business it the national government claims there is not an "economic need" for that business.

GATS intends to do away with this cloudy trading environment by first:

- Clearly defining the general obligations or rules for trading, such as: market access, national treatment and most-favoured-nation (MFN) status.
- Determining the modes of supply of services or types of service transactions to which such rules should apply.
- Asking countries to define their measures by making specific commitments that all in line with the general obligations or rules.
- While stating that the Agreement is for total coverage and applies to all services sectors, hence the tourism sector.

The Two Pillars of GATS

- **National treatment**: Each government shall treat foreign services suppliers no less favourbaly than its own services and service suppliers.
- **Market access**: Each government shall accord services and services suppliers of other governments treatment no less favourable than that agreed and recorded in its "schedule".

Most Favoured Nation (MFN)

A government must not discriminate between services or services suppliers of other members.

Modes of Supply of Services Under GATS

- Cross-border (e.g. tour operation travel assistance)
- Consumption abroad (e.g. by international visitors)

- Commercial presence (e.g. establishing a branch office)
- By natural persons (e.g. hotel manage, consultant tour guide).

In the future, countries that agree to GATS are supposed to allow foreign service suppliers full access to their domestic markets and thus be treated equally as domestic suppliers.

For tourism and travel-related businesses this will mean:

- Tour operators, hotel enterprises and other tourism and travel-related companies from one country will be able to set up operations in other countries.
- In the hotel sector, GATS will facilitate franchising, management contracts, technical service agreements, licensing and patents.
- If national treatment is fully granted, foreign companies will be able to sell their services under the same terms and conditions as domestic companies and suppliers.
- Such treatment will also make foreign companies eligible for a government's domestic incentives and benefits.
- They will be able to move staff to a foreign country and base thorn there without restrictions.
- They will be allowed to effect international transfers and payments for current transactions without restrictions.

Commitments relating to market access and national treatment obligations and, in a different way, to most favoured nation treatment. Measures mean laws, regulations, rules, procedures, decisions, administrative action and guidelines, and practices. Commitments introduce such measures to the Agreement. It produces several effects:

- It allows the country to actually form part of the Agreement.
- It determines, the degree of openness of the country's market to foreign suppliers of the services in question.
- It makes commitment points of reference for post and future negotiations.

Theoretically, a country can enter GATS solely on the basis of just one service sector.

Depending on the possible commercial value and rationale of commitment, it can be regarded as a concession, compensation, benefit or restriction on behalf of that government.

Four "levels" of commitments are foreseen in the schedules:

- Full (no limitation—*"none"*)
- With limitations (citing an actual measure that binds or improves the existing restrictive regulatory situation)
- No commitment (*"unbound"* for measures inconsistent with market access or national treatment); or
- Simply explaining that *"no commitment is technically possible"*.

Normally, commitments are related to specific services sectors, although there may also be horizontal commitments, i.e. relating to all sectors at once.

Countries may also enter additional commitments in the form of undertakings which apply to domestic regulations such as qualifications, technical standards, licensing requirements and procedures.

Once fixed in GATS/commitments may be withdrawn or modified. After 1 January 1998, governments can withdraw or modify their commitments. If such amendments affect the benefits of members, compensation must be offered on a MFN basis (e.g. available to all members).

GATS promotes multilateralism in international trade: a measure expressed by a commitment affects all GATS member countries, even if the commitment is a result of a bilateral negotiation.

Measures inconsistent with MFN treatment (which originate because of members' bilateral and regional agreements concluded outside the GATS negotiations) must be published in Lists of Article II (MFN) Exemptions forming an integral part of the Agreement. It provides for machinery and negotiations by which measures corresponding to exemptions must be terminated. Normally, they should disappear as of 1 January 2005. GATS records some MFN exemptions concerning GRS.

GATS provides for rules regarding recognition of the education or experience obtained, requirements met, or licenses or certifications granted in a particular country, for the purpose of authorization, licensing or certification of services suppliers in another country.

Such recognition is not deemed as a commitment in the GATS sense, i.e. it does not spread to all members. It may be based on an agreement with the country concerned or may be accorded autonomously. The GATS principles for such recognition apply in the way that the country offering recognition to another country must afford adequate opportunity for other interested members to negotiate their accession to such agreements or to demonstrate their eligibility to recognition.

The transparency discipline of GATS requires each Member to publish promptly (at the latest by the time of their entry into force) all laws, regulations or administrative guidelines as well as international agreements which significantly affect trade in services covered by the member's specific commitments. Members must also respond promptly to all requests for specific information, particularly through enquiry points which should be established by the end of 1996.

This can be looked at from the following angles:

- Economic importance of tourism services
- The definition and coverage of tourism services
- Actual commitments on tourism
- Controversy over the meaning of consumption abroad
- The degree of actual liberalization in the tourism sector
- Relationship between the main tourist generating countries and developing tourist receiving countries.

Economic Importance of Tourism

The value of internationally-traded tourism services can be related to the receipts from international tourism. According to WTO/OMT estimates, at the world level such receipts (excluding international fare receipts) in 1993 accounted for nearly thirty-two per cent of the total exports of commercial services, of which over thirty-five per cent were in developing countries.

Tourism is seen as the largest services sector and the largest item of international trade.

Coverage of Tourism Services

GATS deals with services supplied by natural persons (individual services suppliers) and juridical persons (formally established companies), also to natural or juridical persons, in other words, in the tourism context, to travellers and tourism-related enterprises whenever such transactions are carried out between national and foreign persons.

Supply of a Service

Supply of a Service includes the Production, Distribution, Marketing Sales and Delivery of a Service. For the purpose of identifying commitments, GATS conventionally singles out so-called tourism and travel related services (TTRS), along with other sectors corresponding to business; communication; construction; distribution; education; environment; finance; health; recreation, culture and sports; and transport. Within this classification TTRS sub-sectors are not further developed unlike in the majority of other sectors.

Sector 9. *Tourism and Travel Related Services Under GATS Classification*

- Hotel and restaurant (including catering)
- Travel agencies and tour operator services
- Tourist guide services
- Other (unspecified)

For tourism this classification can be considered "open-ended" or even incomplete since a number of important, distinct tourism-oriented services such as computer reservation systems (CRS), travel assistance, car rental, tourist health services, convention centres, and many others are scattered under various sectors or are not specified at all.

This situation was responsible for the non-uniform presentation of commitments, thus giving rise to a certain confusion: while some countries registered rent-a-car commitments under the item "other" of TTRS, others did it under road transport services; while some included "hotel management" under TTRS, others would rather identify it under business services; for some, "marina operations" was part of TTRS ("other"), for others of recreational, cultural and sporting services, etc.

Although an important and inseparable part of the tourism sector, tourist transport services, including passenger transportation by air, are all included under transport services. However, as regards air transport services, GATS applies temporarily only to measures affecting:

- The selling and marketing of air transport services,
- Computer reservation system (CRS) services, and not:
- Traffic rights, however granted, or
- Services directly related to the exercise of traffic rights.

Tourism Commitments

Commitments on tourism and travel-related services ranked higher than for any other services sector. As many as 100 countries (including the European Union's twelve members in 1994) and dependent territories submitted commitments under this item out of the 107 countries and territories which entered their schedules in the Marrakesh Agreement. This figure is well above those for financial and business services which came next. There were four countries which submitted only TTRS commitments.

Thirty-seven countries presented commitments on computer reservation systems. They were entered under air transport services and TTRS ("other"). Two countries mentioned GRS in their lists of MFN exemptions. A careful reading of the Services Agreement suggests that when entering specific commitments regarding tourism, countries were rather cautious by actually fixing the existing regulatory situation governing at the time of the negotiations, or by fixing measures below the already existing market access opportunities.

Understanding Consumption Abroad

Consumption abroad, i.e. by international visitors, is the most important mode of delivery of tourism services. International tourism is a sector where consumers need to travel to a foreign destination in order to buy a service or product. Yet, the measures affecting such travel are not yet dealt with by GATS.

Consumption abroad should be understood as the freedom for one member's residents to purchase services in the territory of another member, once they are already there. In other words, the movement of consumers across international borders is not regarded as pertaining to consumption abroad under the present GATS text.

Limitations of consumption abroad occur when this freedom is curtailed in whatever way (thus, e.g. diminishing the sales of tourism companies) or when the supply of a service by foreign-based companies to internal consumers is obstructed in the national territory. Limitations to this mode of supply of tourism services can be identified by analyzing what is meant by "supply of a service", being the production, distribution, marketing, sales and delivery of a service.

Actual Liberalization in Tourism

The tourism sector was considered relatively "easy" to negotiate in the core, frontline activities such as hotel and tour operations, although actual commitments revealed a number of limitations particularly in the area of national treatment and the presence of individual service suppliers. Nevertheless, it was not found necessary to open a separate track of negotiations on tourism, as was the case for financial services, telecommunications or maritime transport services, on which special annexes had to be drafted.

Underdeveloped or developing tourist destinations attract rather than discourage the main suppliers of tourism services for commercial presence combined with investment. If there had been market access restrictions, these could have been overcome without great problems by large companies.

Tourism and Developing Countries

GATS Article IV advocates increasing participation of developing countries. This objective is of special relevance to tourism in which there exist considerable imbalances between developed and developing countries with regard to tourism receipts and tourism-accrued economic benefits.

Vertical integration and the concentration of distribution channels which are managed from within the developed tourist generating countries can be held responsible for such effects as:

- Retention of economic receipts from tourism within the distribution channels
- Low remuneration of destination services (domestic accommodation, attractions, local guides, etc.)

- Imports (leakages) from destination countries which are needed to maintain tourism facilities in service order.

The developing countries must strengthen their domestic services capacity/efficiency and competitiveness, improve their access to and share in distribution channels and information networks, as well as receive market access in modes of supply of export interest to them (such as, e.g., the presence of individual services suppliers). Under GATS all such improvements can be negotiated by means of commitments. Members, especially developed countries, must establish, by 31 December 1996, contact points to facilitate the attainment by developing countries of these goals.

GATS intends to bring order to the conditions of trade in services. From the perspective of a single country the price to pay will be less flexibility but the advantages seem important. Abiding by GATS creates a predictable trading environment and thus contributes to increased confidence of potential investors in the recipient market. The exercise of all freedom in trade policy measures is not feasible either. It undermines the sustainability of trade in general, including for those who now exercise their dominant position in this area.

On the other hand, GATS does not clash with traditional incentives: grants, tax holidays, work permits, etc. which are so important to attract tourism investments, but which are designed for brief periods. Some countries, particularly the developing ones, due to their weak negotiating capacity, may also have found it difficult to extract durable, equitable benefits from investor countries by simply using incentives. In the case of GATS measures, equitable compensation is sought and should be offered.

Fixing incentives as GATS commitments is risky. The result could be the distortion of the competitive conditions between different sectors or too high a price to pay by offering new concessions should the incentive-type commitment be withdrawn. It is therefore advisable not to bind incentives as commitments, but to retain flexibility in this area. On the other hand, when incentives are offered and not fixed as commitments, they should still be available to all eligible companies, national and foreign, in order to go by the national treatment obligation.

Not always. The right to personnel mobility, for example, will not apply to measures affecting persons seeking access to the local employment market, nor to measures regarding citizenship, residence or employment on a permanent basis.

The right to effect international payments may be subject to foreign exchange controls and restrictions to safeguard the balance of payments; however such measures, should they occur, will require notification and consultations.

If governmental agencies purchase services for governmental purposes (e.g. contracting a state reception), the GATS principles of most favoured nation treatment, market access and national treatment, will not apply.

Members of the Agreement will also be free to adopt restrictive measures in order to protect public morals, privacy of individuals, and the environment, to maintain public order, prevent deceptive and fraudulent practices, and for safety and security in general. This requirement may apply differently to domestic and foreign companies.

GATS will benefit tourism and travel in several ways. Since the overall objective of GATS and other accords of the Marrakesh Agreement is to spur trade and economic growth, there will be more demand for exhibitions, incentive and business travel, meetings and conventions. More trade in both goods and services will mean more movements of people and more business opportunities for the travel trade.

With disappearing trade restrictions for tourism companies, tourism will grow and increasingly focus on quality. The tourism sector will benefit not only by allowing major tour operators and hotel chains to expand their reach worldwide, but also by opening up competition to small-medium scale companies. So far, they have been overshadowed by big companies and monopolies, and not strong enough to overcome the existing trade barriers. Under GATS, a monopoly situation will be dealt with by the GATS rules on monopolies and exclusive service suppliers.

Liberalization in all other than TTRS sectors (business services, communication, construction, finance) will help tourism companies to do their job better: quicker and at lower cost. Other Marrakesh accords will also help. GATT 1994 reduced barriers to the importation of tourism activity related merchandise, and TRIPS will sort out problems with trademarks and service marks of which tourism services abound. For example, requirements that foreign marks be used in conjunction with local marks would, as a general rule, be prohibited.

The following example shows how GATS will benefit the tourism industry, national economy and employment.

Global Distribution System Through CRS

A developing country may restrict the establishment of CRS, because it is perceived as putting its national airline at a disadvantage.

Under GATS, Country A where a CRS is based will be able to approach Country B where it is restricted and ask that the restrictions (e.g. to commercial presence) be lifted. Country B will then decide what market liberalizing measure it wants in return from Country A or from other countries in which CRSs are based and which may equally be interested in accessing its market. In addition to fair access terms, the compensating measures sought by Country B could be in the tourism sector or in another sector. Countries involved will then negotiate.

If the talks succeed in lifting the limitations and allowing the CRS into the new market, this market opening will be available to CRSs from all countries and the following advantages could result:

- *Investment*: The CRS that is seeking to establish itself in Country B will have to invest in Country B. This will have a positive result on the latter's balance of payments and economy.
- *Access*: Country B will receive fair access terms in the CRS for its tourism services suppliers.
- *Training and employment*: Local staff will have to be trained and employed because bringing in a full expatriate staff may be prohibitively expensive. This will attract know-how and technology and create new jobs.
- *Payments*: Local telecommunications costs have to be paid, thus increasing country's revenues.
- *Taxes*: Payment of local taxes boosts revenues for national treasuries.
- *Prices*: Declining prices for consumers and increasing commissions for travel agents can result because of the new competition.
- *Benefits in other services sectors*: The negotiated compensations vary and could include, for example,

increased business services opportunities for professionals of Country B in all other GATS countries.

The potential recipients of CRSs are regarded as late coiners. National regulations are outdated or do not exist, and uncertainty still governs as regards the multilaterally agreed rules on CRS. Thus regulations can neither be cited as commitments nor used as a reference for hypothetical negotiations.

There is a high concentration of CRSs and the possibilities of building alternative networks are low. Barriers to new entrants are high. These include:

- Difficulties in making effective use of the network.
- In using networks, small air carriers and tour operators face prohibitive booking fees.

Once foreign-based networks are established, they may develop anti-competitive attitudes: CRSs, e.g., may present problems of bias in the priority accorded to different service suppliers.

The CRS commitments were received from a few groups of countries: the European Union's members (12), EFTA countries (6), a few other developed and European countries, as well as ten developing countries outside Europe. Only one country committed itself to grant market access and national treatment without limitations. The remaining countries included a number of limitations, e.g., EU and EFTA countries in respect of national treatment for cross-border supply and commercial presence, the developing countries in respect of both national treatment and market access, and almost all countries restricted the presence of natural persons. On the other hand, consumption abroad was not bound (not fixed as a commitment) by two countries only.

The absence of CRS-related lull or restricted commitments in GATS does not prevent CRS from being effectively established in the new recipient markets. The difference is that the actual arrangements with CRS may not yet be reflected in GATS.

Taking into account the specificity of tourism services under GATS as already discussed, that depends on how much the developing countries will actually open their markets and how rapidly they will strengthen their industries and make them competitive internationally.

Though people in some developing countries reacted negatively to GATS at the early stages of negotiations, fearing a "foreign invasion", it must again be emphasized that liberalization measures will not be implemented overnight. Liberalization by GATS is a long-term process of consultations and negotiations to be carried out at five-year intervals, usually between groups of countries which have been identified as principal suppliers and recipients of a specific service.

As pointed out in the example concerning GRS, GATS will help strengthen the ability of developing countries to compete by attaching conditions to their market opening commitments and requesting the transfer of technology and expertise.

Also, the least-developed countries were given an additional year to negotiate and present their first package of commitments.

Moreover, developing countries will be the main ones to use the safeguard provisions of GATS, such as protecting the balance of payments. Compared with the present situation, the advantage of GATS will be that all the relevant measures are adopted in a transparent way, in a multilateral framework and as a result of consultations.

Developing countries can seek the freedom to deploy not only their key personnel, but also regular personnel in the main tourist generating countries. They can also request the presence in these countries of their individual services suppliers: GRS experts, chefs, hotel managers and developers, and many others, without the requirement of commercial presence. Such permission must be fixed in the schedules of commitments.

There is plenty of work to do. GATS opens the tourism market to business opportunities and pressure from all countries which will eventually form the World Trade Organization (already today the bulk of transactions related to international tourism is effected among World Trade Organization countries). GATS challenges the traditional tourism policies carried out at national, bilateral or regional levels. So far, they have been usually targeted at tourism infrastructure and plant, and the facilitation of travel flows, but not to trade issues.

National Tourism Policies

Without neglecting these objectives national tourism policies should now shift to address commercial aspects, better capitalize on comparative advantages (tourism resources) and move towards creating a competitive trading environment for national companies by fostering their efficiency and the ability to supply quality products and exploit all the modes specified in the Agreement and the elements of supply of a service (distribution, marketing, etc.).

GATS calls for more tourism staff training (inclusive of tourism policy-makers and negotiators in the GATS context) to respond to international demand, the enhancement of investment incentives, a new generation of international tourism agreements (e.g. regarding tourism promotion abroad), efficient help to small-medium scale tourism companies to identify and consolidate their market position vis-à-vis large tourism projects, the adequacy of tourism products which can be traded internationally, harmonization between national tourism policies and those regarding international transport, a new regulatory framework for tourism (e.g., for GRS, consumer protection, taxes).

Tourism Industry Organizations

Since GATS, after all, is all about helping to improve market conditions for the private sector to do business, tourism industry organizations must take an interest in, and be admitted to, decision-making regarding the implementation of this agreement. This can be done on both national and international levels. Tourism companies must be aware of what is negotiated on their behalf by governments, and how to defend their interests, particularly using GATS dispute settlement procedures. The tourism industry should also be able to view their individual interests in a broader context of all services sectors.

National Tourism Administrations

National Tourism Administrations and Tourist Boards may wish to re-define their field of competence and action to take stock of the commercial aspects of tourism and work with national trade representatives, chambers of commerce, transport organizations and bodies representing other services sectors.

Given the results of the Uruguay Round, governments should increase their awareness of the importance and specificity of tourism services and provide for measures allowing tourism industry representatives, legislators and tourism-related public bodies and officials to share responsibility for decisions concerning the operation and development of GATS, particularly in future rounds of negotiations.

In order to take a better stock of the content and volume of the tourism sector, for the purpose of future negotiations, it would be advisable to develop a new, all-inclusive and dynamic classification of tourism and travel related services, whenever work on services classification is resumed. This possibility happily coincides with the current activities of the World Tourism Organization geared to implement satellite accounts for tourism and the Standard International Classification of Tourism Activities (SICTA), recently adopted by the United Nations Statistical Commission. SICTA identifies tourism and travel related activities by the percentage of sales going to tourist consumption and the share of each activity in tourist expenditure.

World Tourism Organization

The World Tourism Organization plans to cooperate with the World Trade Organization and other international bodies concerned with economic development and integration such as UNCTAD and OECD, as well as regional and tourism industry organizations with a view to:

- Monitoring the GATS implementation process in respect of tourism policies of its member States.
- Organizing tourism policy forums and expert groups.
- Assisting countries in negotiating their tourism and travel related commitments in conformity with their tourism development plans and policies.
- Fostering the creation of statistical tools to measure the economic importance of tourism.
- Developing the concepts of liberalization of trade in tourism services for regional or sub-regional economic integration projects.

Partly no and partly yes. Countries are free to engage in such projects. If a country however, is a party to GATS, it must assume the corresponding consequences derived from GATS principles. A country may simultaneously engage in regional integration projects if:

- They provide for substantial sectoral coverage (most services sectors must be included, no mode of supply of services is a priori excluded); and
- The regional agreement in question aims at the absence or elimination of substantially all discrimination.

The countries which are already parties to the agreements of this kind should provide to WTO/OMC's Council for Trade in Services all relevant information on the implementation of the agreements, and receive from the Council its recommendations concerning such agreements.

An example of a regional agreement using GATS principles is the North American Free Trade Agreement (NAFTA). Its principles apply automatically to tourism along with other services sectors, except for those sectors (not tourism) which are singled out in the annexes to the general NAFTA agreement.

GATS should not be considered a panacea for solving all the problems of tourism development, but forming part of the Agreement can help countries give a more adequate response to the needs of the tourism mega market of the future. It will discipline their tourism policies and encourage them to seek equitable advantages from tourism development.

GLOBAL CODE OF ETHICS FOR TOURISM

We, the representatives of the States, bodies, enterprises and institutions, Members of the World Tourism Organization (WTO), gathered for the General Assembly in Santiago, Chile on this 1st day of October 1999, Recalling the Principles of the Universal Declaration of Human Rights.

Reasserting the aims set out in Article 3 of the Statutes of the World Tourism Organization, and aware of the central and decisive role of this Organization, as recognized by the General Assembly of the United Nations, in promoting and developing tourism with a view to contributing to economic development, international understanding, peace, prosperity and universal respect for, and observation of, human rights and fundamental freedoms for all without distinction as to race, sex, language or religion.

Firmly believing that, through the direct and non-intrusive contacts it engenders between men and women of different cultures and lifestyles, tourism represents a vital force for peace and sustainable development and a factor of friendship and of understanding among the peoples of the world.

In keeping with the (drop: tendency) [replace with: REQUIREMENT] to reconcile environment, economic development and the fight against poverty in a sustainable manner, as formulated by the United Nations in 1992 at the 'Earth Summit' of Rio de Janeiro, and expressed in Agenda 21, adopted on this occasion.

Taking into account the swift and continued growth, both past and foreseeable, of tourism activity, whether for reasons of leisure, business, religion or health, and its powerful effects, both positive and negative, on the economic, social, cultural and educational sectors of countries and on international relations and exchanges.

Aiming to promote responsible, sustainable and universally accessible tourism in the framework of the right to leisure and travel, and in respect of the choice of society of all peoples.

Convinced that, provided a certain number of principles are observed, responsible and sustainable tourism is not at all incompatible with the growing liberalization of the national and international conditions and rules which guide the conduct of enterprises in the sector, as undertaken in the framework of the General Agreement on Trade in Services of 15 April 1994.

Equally convinced that the world tourism industry as a whole has a lot to gain by moving in an environment which favours freedom of enterprise, investment and trade, and which serves to maximize its beneficial effects in terms of creating activity and employment.

Considering that all the actors in tourism development national and local administrations, tourism enterprises and bodies but also the host communities, the workers engaged in tourism and tourists themselves, have different albeit interdependent roles in the individual and social development of tourism and that the definition of their individual rights and duties will contribute to meeting this aim.

Concerned with promoting a real partnership between all the public and private actors in tourism development, in keeping with the aim pursued by the World Tourism Organization since adopting resolution 364(XII) at its General Assembly of 1997 (Istanbul).

With the aim of following up on the Manila Declarations of 1980 on World Tourism and of 1997 on the Social Impact of Tourism, and the Tourism Bill of Rights and the Tourist Code adopted in Sofia in 1985 under the aegis of WTO, but believing that these instruments should be (completed) [COMPLEMENTED] by a set of interdependent principles on the basis of which the main actors in tourism development should regulate their conduct at the dawn of the 21st century.

(State our wish to promote responsible and sustainable tourism in the context of an open and competitive international market economy, and) [STATE OUR WISH TO PROMOTE RESPONSIBLE TOURISM SO THAT IT CONTRIBUTES TO JUST AND SUSTAINABLE DEVELOPMENT BY INVOLVING ALL SECTIONS OF SOCIETY IN THE PROCESS OF ASSESSING DEVELOPMENT STRATEGIES AND OF SHARING THE BENEFITS FROM TOURISM ACTIVITIES].

Solemnly adopt to this end the Global Code of Ethics for Tourism.

I. Principles

Article 1

1. The understanding and respect of the diversity of cultural values, and of religious, philosophical and moral beliefs are both the condition for and the consequence of tourism; the actors in tourism development and [THE] tourists themselves are duty-bound to observe the social and cultural (traditions) [RIGHTS] and practices of all peoples, including (national) [ETHNIC] minorities and indigenous peoples.
2. Tourism activities shall be conducted in harmony with the attributes and traditions of the host regions and countries, and in respect for their laws, habits and (customs) [VALUES].
3. (The host communities and local professional actors shall acquaint themselves with and respect the tourists who visit them and find out about their lifestyles, tastes and expectations)—OMIT.
4. When visiting other places, tourists shall [BE BOUND TO] refrain from any criminal or wrongful act [SUCH AS THE EXPLOITATION OF PEOPLES IN THE HOST

COMMUNITIES, IN PARTICULAR CHILDREN AND WOMEN, DRUG TRAFFICKING, SMUGGLING OF RARE AND COMMERCIALLY PROFITABLE SPECIES, ARTEFACTS, ANTIQUES, AND FROM] (or) any conduct which is considered to be shocking or injurious to the local populations.

***Article* 2**

1. Tourism, the activity most frequently associated with rest and relaxation, sport and access to culture, should be planned and practised as a factor of individual and collective fulfilment; when practised with (a sufficiently open mind) [ALL DUE RESPECT], it is an irreplaceable factor of self-education, mutual tolerance and for learning about the (legitimate differences between) [DIVERSITY OF] peoples and cultures.
2. Tourism activities shall aim to promote human rights and, more particularly, the individual rights of the more vulnerable groups, notably women, children, the elderly or handicapped [ETHNIC MINORITIES AND INDIGENOUS PEOPLES].
3. The exploitation of other people in any form, notably sexual, breaches the fundamental rights of (tourism; it is not a deviation of tourism, but the negation of tourism and, as such) [INDIVIDUALS AND] shall be strictly prohibited and penalized.

***Article* 3**

1. Following the guidelines set out in Agenda 21, all the actors in tourism development are duty-bound to safeguard the natural environment [AND RESOURCES OF LIVELIHOOD] in the perspective of continued and sustainable development geared to satisfying equitably the needs and aspirations of present and future generations.
2. Forms of tourism development which are conducive to saving [SCARCE AND PRECIOUS RESOURCES] energy and reducing waste production shall be given priority and financially encouraged.
3. The staggering in time and space of tourist flows,

particularly those generated by paid holidays and school holidays, shall be promoted in such a way as to reduce the pressure of tourism activity on the environment.

4. Tourism infrastructures and activities shall be designed in such a way as to protect and ensure the protection of the ecosystem and biodiversity, and to preserve endangered species of wild fauna and flora.
5. Nature tourism and ecotourism (are recognized as being particularly conducive to enriching and enhancing the standing of tourism) [CAN CONTRIBUTE TO SUSTAINABLE DEVELOPMENT], provided they (respect natural environments and) [ARE REALIZED WITH THE INFORMED PARTICIPATION OF HOST COMMUNITIES AND UNDER THE GUIDANCE OF LOCAL INHABITANTS WHO ARE THE EXPERTS OF THEIR OFTEN FRAGILE ENVIRONMENTS, AND ACCORDING TO STRINGENT GUIDELINES RESPECTING NATURAL RESOURCES], the carrying capacity [AND THE CULTURAL ASSETS] of the sites visited.

Article 4

1. Tourism resources [BELONG TO THE COMMUNITIES IN WHICH THEY ARE LOCATED, AND] are part of the common heritage of mankind.
2. Tourism policies and activities shall be conducted with respect for the artistic, archaeological, cultural and monumental heritage of countries, which they should contribute to identifying, protecting, enhancing and passing on to future generations; particular care shall be devoted to preserving and enhancing monuments and museums which (are a magnet for) [ATTRACT] tourists; public access to privately-owned cultural goods and monuments shall be encouraged.
3. The resources derived from visits to cultural sites and monuments shall, at least partially, be used for (the) [THEIR] upkeep (and embellishment) [AND THE DEVELOPMENT OF LOCAL TECHNIQUES, MATERIALS AND ARTISANS FOR CONSERVATION] of this heritage.
4. Tourism activity shall be planned in such a way as to allow

traditional cultural products, crafts and folklore to survive and flourish, rather than causing them to degenerate and become standardized.

Article 5

1. Local communities and populations are associated with tourism activities and shall participate [EQUITABLY] in the economic, social and cultural benefits they generate, and particularly in the creation of direct and indirect jobs resulting from these activities.
2. Tourism policies shall be (planned in such a way as) [ORIENTED AND TAILORED TO THE NEEDS OF THE LOCAL HOST POPULATIONS IN ORDER] to contribute to improving (the) [THEIR] standard of living (of the populations of the regions visited); [TOURISM PLANNING SHALL TAKE ACCOUNT OF ALL THE ECONOMIC, SOCIAL, CULTURAL AND ENVIRONMENTAL ASPECTS AND THE POTENTIAL DRAWBACKS OF THE DEVELOPMENT OF TOURISM]; tourism resorts and accommodation shall be planned and (run) [MANAGED] in such a way as to integrate them (to the extent possible) in the local economic and social fabric; (where skills are equal), [TRAINING SHALL BE PROVIDED TO ALLOW FOR] priority (shall) [TO] be placed on using local labour.
3. Special attention shall be paid to the specific problems of island countries or territories and to fragile rural zones, for which tourism often represents a (rare) [IMPORTANT COMPLEMENTARY] opportunity for development (in the face of the decline of traditional economic activities).

Article 6

1. [TOURISM PROFESSIONALS, INCLUDING INVESTORS, AND TOURISM AUTHORITIES HAVE AN OBLIGATION TO ESTABLISH FULL TRANSPARENCY ON DEVELOPMENT SCHEMES AND MASTERPLANS, AND TO GUARANTEE THE INFORMED PARTICIPATION OF ALL SEGMENTS OF LOCAL POPULATION AT ALL

LEVELS OF DECISION MAKING, PLANNING AND IMPLEMENTATION OF TOURISM DEVELOPMENT].

2. [Tourism professionals (have an obligation to) [SHALL] provide tourists with reliable information on their place of destination and on the conditions of travel, hospitality and sojourns; they shall ensure that the contractual clauses proposed to their clients are readily understandable with regard to the nature, price and quality of the services they commit themselves to providing and their financial compensation in the event of any claims against the contract.
3. Tourism professionals (insofar as it depends on them) [IN COOPERATION WITH THE CONCERNED AUTHORITIES], shall guarantee security and safety, accident prevention, health protection and the food safety of those who seek their services [AND OF THOSE WHO PROVIDE THE SERVICES]; they shall develop specific systems of insurance and assistance; they shall accept the obligation to be held liable.
4. The public authorities of the generating countries and the host countries shall ensure that these rules are established and respected by tourism professionals, and shall (repatriate) [ASSIST] tourists in the event of a serious default on their part.
5. The press, particularly the specialized tourism press, shall contribute to supplying the consumers of tourism services with accurate and reliable information (new information technologies shall also be developed and used to this end).

Article 7

1. Special attention shall be paid to guaranteeing the fundamental rights of salaried and free lance workers, [ESPECIALLY WOMEN] engaged in tourism and connected activities (including their social welfare, bearing in mind the specific constraints they are subject to and the flexibility required of them by virtue of their jobs) [AS A MINIMUM AS SET OUT IN THE CORE STANDARDS OF THE INTERNATIONAL LABOUR ORGANIZATION (ILO), INCLUDING THE NEW CONVENTION AGAINST

THE MOST INTOLERABLE FORMS OF CHILD LABOUR].

2. Workers engaged in tourism are entitled and bound to acquire appropriate initial and continuous training.
3. Workers engaged in tourism shall be protected against financial or social exploitation under the control of the national and local administrations both in their countries of origin and in the host countries (so far as possible); job insecurity should be kept to a minimum; a specific status should be offered to seasonal workers in the tourism sector.
4. All individuals and legal entities shall be entitled to develop a professional activity in the field of tourism within the framework of existing national laws.

Article 8

1. The universal right to tourism is the consequence of the right to rest and leisure, including reasonable limitation of working hours and periodic holidays with pay, guaranteed by Article 24 of the Universal Declaration of Human Rights and Article 7.d of the International Covenant on Economic, Social and Cultural Rights.
2. Social tourism, and notably associative tourism, which facilitates widespread access to leisure and holidays, should be encouraged and developed.
3. Family, youth and student tourism, and tourism for the elderly and the handicapped should be facilitated.

Article 9

1. Tourists and workers engaged in tourism, salaried or otherwise, shall benefit, in compliance with international and national legislation, from the liberty to move freely within their country and from one state to another, in compliance with Article 13 of the Universal Declaration of Human Rights; they shall have access to places of transit and sojourn and to tourism and cultural sites without being subject to meaningless formalities or discrimination.
2. Tourists and workers engaged in tourism are entitled to

have access to all available forms of communication, internal or external; the safety of their persons and the security of their belongings should be guaranteed; they shall benefit from prompt and easy access to local administrative, legal and health services; they may freely contact the consular representatives of their countries of origin in compliance with the diplomatic agreements in force.

3. Administrative procedures related to border crossings, such as visas, and health and customs formalities shall be designed in such a way as to facilitate to the maximum freedom of travel and widespread access to international tourism [EQUALLY FOR ALL INHABITANTS OF THIS PLANET].

Article 10

1. The public and private actors in tourism development shall commit themselves to cooperating in the implementation of these principles and to monitoring their proper application [BY DEVELOPING PUBLICLY AVAILABLE CODES OF CONDUCT AND PRECISE GUIDELINES FOR THEIR SPECIFIC ACTIVITIES].
2. The actors in tourism development shall recognize the role played by international institutions and non-governmental organizations [,] whose activities are related to tourism, human rights and environmental protection [ESPECIALLY BY SEEKING THEIR ADVICE AND ASSISTANCE FOR THE APPLICATION AND THE MONITORING OF THESE PRINCIPLES].
3. The same actors shall agree to refer any disputes concerning the interpretation or application of this Global Code of Ethics for Tourism to an impartial third party in the conditions defined hereinafter.

II. Implementation of the Principles

Article 11

The actors in tourism development—national and local tourism administrations, tourism enterprises and bodies—the host communities, [AND THE] workers engaged in tourism (and tourists themselves) shall respect the principles embodied in this Code and implement them in accordance with the provisions set out in this section and in Section III hereafter.

Article 12

The principles embodied in this Code are interdependent in their interpretation and in their application and each one should be understood on the basis of the others.

Article 13

On interpreting and applying the principles embodied in this Code, the following instruments shall be taken into account:

- Warsaw Convention of 12 October 1929;
- Chicago Convention on international civil aviation of 7 December 1944, and the Tokyo, Hague and Montreal Conventions in relation thereto;
- Universal Declaration of Human Rights of 10 December 1948;
- International Covenant on Economic, Social and Cultural Rights of 16 December 1966;
- International Covenant on Civil and Political Rights of 16 December 1966;
- Convention for the protection of the world cultural and natural heritage of 23 November 1972;
- Manila Declaration on World Tourism of 10 October 1980;
- Tourism Bill of Rights and Tourist Code of 26 September 1985;
- Convention on the Rights of the Child of 26 January 1990;
- Rio Declaration on the Environment and Development of 13 June 1992;
- General Agreement on Trade in Services of 15 April 1994;
- Resolution of the Eleventh General Assembly of WTO (Cairo) on the prevention of organized sex tourism of 22 October 1995;
- Stockholm Declaration of 28 August 1996 against the Commercial Sexual Exploitation of Children;

— Manila Declaration on the Social Impact of Tourism of 22 May 1997;

[Add: The ILO "core" conventions:

Nos. 87 (1948) and 98 (1949) on freedom of association and collective bargaining,

Nos. 29 (1930) and 105 (1957) on forced labour,

Nos. 100 (1951) and 111 (1958) on equality of treatment and non-discrimination,

No. 138 (1973) on minimum age for admission to work and the new convention (1999) against the worst forms of child labour,

The ILO conventions Nos. 107 (1957) and 169 (1991) on indigenous and tribal peoples,

The UN Convention on the Elimination of All Forms of Discrimination Against Women (1979),

The Beijing Declaration and the platform for action (1995)].

Article 14

The procedures for applying the principles set out in Articles 6, 7, 9 and, where necessary, Article 10 of this Code shall be subject to guidelines which will clarify their contents. Prepared by the World Committee on Tourism Ethics [?], these guidelines shall be submitted to the Executive Council of WTO and proclaimed by the General Assembly. They shall be periodically reviewed and adjusted in the same conditions.

Article 15

All persons, whether individuals or corporate bodies, public or private, involved in any form of tourism activity shall [BE URGED TO] regulate their conduct in accordance with this Global Code of Ethics for Tourism. Although they are not legally bound to do so, member or non-member States of WTO are nonetheless urged to accept expressly the principles of this Code and to integrate them in their national laws. Likewise, tourism enterprises and bodies, whether WTO Affiliate Members or not, and their associations, are urged to include the provisions of this Code in their contractual instruments or make specific reference to them in their internal codes of conduct or professional rules [WHICH SHALL BE PUBLICLY AVAILABLE].

Article 16

WTO Member States shall publish and make known as widely as possible the Global Code of Ethics for Tourism, mainly by disseminating it among all the actors in tourism development and inviting them to give it broad publicity.

III. Evaluation and Regulation of Disputes

A. World Committee on Tourism Ethics [?]

[The internal control, by members and bodies of the WTO, of the application of the global code of ethics is very important. This could be the task of the WTO regional commissions.

For the sake of credibility and reliabilty of the code there needs to be a form of external impartial monitoring of the code. This cannot be assured by government officials, who could belong to WTO-members, or to legal advisers alone. This crucial impartial third party as referred to in Article 10 (3) could be constituted on the model of the multi-stakeholder dialogues for the application of agenda 21.

This impartial third party might be called "world committee on tourism ethics". Its constituency and tasks as well as its relationship with other implementing and monitoring bodies of the global code of ethics for tourism shall be exactly defined hereafter.

Any reference made hereafter to the role and the competencies of the world committee on tourism ethics, its sub-committee and the WTO regional commissions shall be revised in accordance to the role and competencies of the impartial third party.

Article 17

A World Committee on Tourism Ethics [?] shall be created consisting of eleven independent government officials and eleven alternates, selected on the basis of their jurisdiction in the field of tourism and connected fields.

Article 18

The members of the World Committee on Tourism Ethics shall be appointed as follows:

- Six members and six alternate members designated by the WTO Regional Commissions; four members and four alternate members elected by the General Assembly of WTO from the representatives of the (tourism industry) [DIFFERENT STAKEHOLDERS] after conferring with the Committee of Affiliate Members.
- A chairman and an alternate chairman elected by the other members of the Committee, on the proposal of the Secretary-General of WTO.

On appointing these members, account shall be taken of the need for a balanced geographical composition of the Committee and for a diversification of the specific qualifications of its members, mainly from an economic, social and legal standpoint. The members shall be appointed for four years; their term may only be renewed once. In the event of a vacancy, the member who fails to appear shall be replaced by his alternate; if a member and his alternate fail to appear, the Committee itself shall fill the vacancy.

Article 19

The WTO Regional Commissions shall act, in the cases provided for in Articles 24 and 26 of this Code, as regional committees on tourism ethics.

Article 20

The World Committee on Tourism Ethics shall establish its own Rules of Procedure. The presence of two-thirds of the members of the Committee shall be necessary to constitute a quorum at its meetings; in the event that a member is absent, he may be replaced by his alternate; in the case of a tie, the chairman shall have the casting vote.

Article 21

The operating expenses of the Committee and the travel expenses and daily subsistence allowances of its members, who shall not receive any remuneration, shall be covered by a trust fund financed by the voluntary contributions of member States and by donations from private bodies, or, failing that, by the WTO budget.

Article 22

The World Committee on Tourism Ethics shall meet at least once a year and as often as necessary each time an urgent problem arises, notably for the purpose of settling disputes arising out of the application of the provisions of Section IIIB; in the event of any such petition, the chairman shall consult the other members as to the need to convene an extraordinary meeting.

Article 23

The functions of the World Committee on Tourism Ethics and the WTO Regional Commissions shall be the evaluation of the implementation of this Code and arbitration of disputes.

Article 24

On the basis of periodical reports submitted by Full Members, Associate Members and Affiliate Members of WTO, the WTO Regional Commissions shall, every two years, examine the application of the Code in their respective regions. They shall record their findings in a report addressed to the World Committee on Tourism Ethics. The reports of the Regional Commissions may contain suggestions to amend or increase the scope of the Global Code of Ethics for Tourism. The World Committee on Tourism Ethics shall summarize the reports drafted by the Regional Commissions and complete them with the information it has collected with the assistance of the Secretary-General and the participation of the Committee of Affiliate Members. This summary shall include, should the need arise, proposals to amend or increase the scope of the Global Code of Ethics for Tourism.

Article 25

The Secretary-General shall pass on the report of the World Committee on Tourism Ethics to the Executive Council together with his own observations. The Executive Council shall examine the report and submit it to the General Assembly with its own recommendations. The General Assembly shall decide what action to take with regard to the report and the recommendations thus submitted to it.

B. Methods of Arbitration for the Settlement of Disputes

Article 26

1. In the event of a dispute concerning the interpretation or application of the Global Code of Ethics for Tourism, (two) actors in tourism development
[WHY ONLY TWO—THERE COULD BE MORE ACTORS? WHO ARE THESE ACTORS? THERE MUST BE A PROVISION TO MAKE SURE THAT THIRD PARTIES WHO ARE NOT MEMBERS OF WTO AND THEREFORE AUTOMATICALLY BOUND TO THIS CODE CAN PUT A COMPLAINT TO THE BODIES OR USE THE DISPUTE SETTLEMENT AS SET OUT HERE?]
may jointly refer it to the World Committee on Tourism Ethics. If the dispute is between two actors belonging to the same region, the two parties may jointly refer to the competent WTO Regional Commission acting in its capacity as a Regional Committee on Tourism Ethics.
2. The States and tourism enterprises and bodies (may) [MEMBERS OF WTO SHALL] declare that they accept (in advance) the competence of the World Committee on Tourism Ethics or of a WTO Regional Commission for any dispute concerning the interpretation or application of this Code, or for certain categories of dispute. In this case, the Committee or the competent Regional Commission shall validly be referred to unilaterally by the other Party to the dispute.

Article 27

When a dispute is first submitted to the consideration of the World Committee on Tourism Ethics, its Chairman shall appoint a sub-committee made up of three members who shall be responsible for examining the dispute.

Article 28

The World Committee on Tourism Ethics to which a dispute has been referred shall reach a decision on the basis of the report drafted by the Parties to the dispute. The Committee may ask these Parties to submit additional information and, if deemed useful, may listen to them at their request. The expenses incurred by this hearing shall be borne by the Parties unless circumstances arise that are assessed (as exceptional) by the Committee [SUCH AS INDIVIDUAL LOCAL EMPLOYEES OR COMMUNITY MEMBERS DIRECTLY AFFECTED]. The failure of one of the Parties to appear shall not prevent the Committee from making a ruling.

Article 29

Unless otherwise agreed by the Parties, the World Committee on Tourism Ethics shall announce its decision in the six months following the date on which it was referred to. It shall present its conclusions to the Parties by way of recommendations which shall form the basis of a settlement. The Parties shall immediately inform the chairman of the Committee that has examined the dispute of the action they have taken on these conclusions.

Article 30

In the event of a dispute being referred to a WTO Regional Commission, it shall announce its decision by following the same procedure, mutatis mutandis, as the one applied to the World Committee on Tourism Ethics when it announces a decision in the first instance.

Article 31

If, two months after notification of the conclusions of the Committee or of a Regional Commission, the Parties are unable to agree on the terms of a final settlement, the Parties or one of them may refer the dispute to a plenary session of the World Committee on Tourism Ethics. When it is the World Committee on Tourism Ethics that has made a ruling in the first instance, the members of the sub-committee which examined the dispute may not take part in this plenary session, but shall be replaced by their alternates; if these were initially on the sub-committee, the members whom they replaced shall not be prevented from participating in the plenary session.

Article 32

The plenary session of the World Committee on Tourism Ethics shall make its ruling, mutatis mutandis, by following the procedures set out in Articles 28 and 29 above and shall formulate the final conclusions for the settlement of the dispute.

Article 33

Full Members, Associate Members and Affiliate Members of WTO as well as States [WHICH] are not Members of WTO, (may) [SHALL BE URGED TO] declare that they accept in advance as fully binding and, where applicable, subject to the sole condition of reciprocity, the final conclusions of the World Committee on Tourism Ethics in the disputes, or in a private dispute, to which they are party. Likewise, the States (may) [SHALL BE URGED TO] accept as fully binding or subject to exequatur the final conclusions of the World Committee on Tourism Ethics regarding the disputes to which their nationals are party or which should be applied in their territory.

Article 34

Tourism enterprises and bodies (may) [SHALL] include in their contractual documents a provision making the final conclusions of the World Committee on Tourism Ethics fully binding in their relations with their co-contractors.

WTO GUIDELINES FOR THE TOURISM INDUSTRY

Horrific terrorist attacks and acts of war have cast dark clouds over the tourism sector in many parts of the world, underscoring the urgent need for good crisis management in this industry—which usually prefers to be thought of as happy and carefree.

While news of large-scale crises has filled the newspapers and airwaves over the past few months, a tourism crisis can take an infinite variety of forms and have been occurring regularly for many years. Natural disasters, such as floods, hurricanes, fires or volcanic eruptions sometimes do more harm to the image of a destination than to the infrastructure itself. Civil unrest, accidents, crime and disease will damage the attractiveness of the strongest destinations. While even economic factors, such as a sharp fluctuation in exchange rates can contribute to a tourism crisis.

Simply put: "A crisis is any unexpected event that affects traveller confidence in a destination and interferes with the ability to continue operating normally."

Crisis management strategies are needed to help retain the confidence of travellers and the travel industry, and to minimize the impact of a crisis on the destination.

No matter what kind of crisis occurs, the techniques for dealing with it effectively are quite similar. Good communications based on the principles of honesty and transparency is the key to successful crisis management, but other tourism specialities also need to be involved, especially:

(*a*) Communications
(*b*) Promotion
(*c*) Safety and security
(*d*) Market research

To assist WTO members with this process, the following guidelines suggest specific actions to take:

I. Before a crisis
II. During the actual problems
III. Immediately after a crisis

The goal is to get tourists returning to the destination as quickly as possible and good crisis management techniques can speed up that process.

I. Before the Crisis: Preparing for the Worst

Never underestimate the possible harm a crisis can do to your tourism. Crises are like viruses—sudden, insidious and virulent. They are extremely dangerous. The best way to minimize the impact of a crisis is to be well-prepared.

A. Putting a Communications Strategy in Place

- *Prepare a crisis management plan*: A crisis can take a myriad of forms so begin to plan by imagining the worst-case scenario. Audit current resources for dealing with a crisis. Designate responsibilities and a chain of command for decision-making. Collect a list of key contacts in an emergency. Involve public services and private tourism companies in the planning process—one key to effective crisis management is good cooperation. Rehearse for a crisis and update the plan annually.

- *Designate spokespersons*: It is essential that information to the media in a crisis be authoritative and coordinated. For this, the designated spokesperson should be a high-ranking official, but not necessarily the top person in your organization. Additional spokespersons also need to be designated to take turns during a crisis. Train spokespersons by practising in mock news conferences and crisis rehearsals.
- *Establish a press and communications department*: To be prepared for a crisis, every tourism organization needs to set up a communications department. The department should include staff trained in working with the media, a good contact list of local and international media, several telephone lines, fax broadcast machines or a mass email computer programme capable of reaching the media on short notice, and background information on your organization—including maps, stock photos, arrivals statistics and fact sheets on previous crises. If possible, make this background information available in a special media section of your destination's website.
- *Communicate regularly with media*: Reputations can take years to develop, so it is important to communicate frequently in good times as well as bad. The policy should be one of honesty and transparency. You can face a crisis with a certain degree of credibility, if you have made an effort to establish good contacts with the media by supplying them with information about what is new in your destination, if you have promptly responded to any questions they have and if you have made good friends with reporters during fam trips organized for foreign journalists.
- *Pay attention to local media*: Local newspapers, television reports and radio are a primary source of information for international media. In a crisis, local news reports can go global within minutes. So even though your principal target is media in the main generating markets, you cannot afford to ignore local journalists. Local newsmen and newswomen will also stay interested in your crisis recovery story long

after the international media has moved elsewhere to a new crisis.

- *Train spokespersons in safety and security issues*: Communications on security should be responsive rather than pro-active. When a crisis erupts, the spokesperson should be able to communicate in an authoritative manner on security issues, striking a good balance between providing enough information without putting too much emphasis on security issues. According to one tourism minister experienced in such matters: "You do security, you don't talk about it."

B. Promotion Planning

- *Develop a data base of partners in the travel trade*: All tour operators sending tourists to your destination, as well as major travel agencies and transport companies in your key generating markets should form the foundation of the data base, but also include incoming operators and tour organizers, as well as local hotels, transport companies, local promotion boards and tourism associations.
- *Build an e-mail or fax broadcast system*: Communications systems capable of reaching the partners in your database should be in place for use in a crisis. But begin communicating news directly to your partners on a regular basis before a crisis strikes. If you only communicate during problematic periods, the image transmitted will be one of nothing but trouble.
- *Be honest and ethical in promotion*: Just as in communications, building and maintaining credibility is fundamental in tourism promotion. Avoid overselling or misrepresenting your product and be ethical in the choice of promotional content or you could create your own crisis. The Bahamas, for example, was recently slammed in the international media for using photos in its advertising that were taken in Hawaii, the Seychelles and Florida.
- *Set aside budget reserves for emergencies*: Recuperating from a crisis requires money for additional promotion and communication activities. A prudent manager will set aside budget reserves in a special emergency fund for use if a

crisis occurs. Try to get advance permission to spend crisis funds without going through lengthy bureaucratic procedures to permit a quick and flexible response in an emergency.

- *Stay out of the travel advisory war*: Travel advisories should be issued in accordance with Article 6 of WTO's Global Code of Ethics for Tourism, which states: "...governments should issue such information without prejudicing in an unjustified or exaggerated manner the tourism industry of host countries and the interests of their own operators." Travel advisories should be discussed with authorities in the host country and travel professionals before they are issued. Warnings should be limited to specific geographical areas rather than blanket an entire country and be lifted as soon as the situation returns to normal. Avoid retaliatory travel advisories.
- *Improve communication of security issues with tourists*: Make tourist safety and emergency information available on your website. Some of the most useful information to include is: emergency telephone numbers; exchange rates; design of banknotes; common rules of behaviour; places to avoid travelling; safe places to leave luggage; average prices of common purchases; the need to report crimes before a tourist returns home; and the importance of keeping photocopies of travel documents. The Tourism Authority of Thailand (TAT) website, for example, includes information on tough laws aimed at ending child prostitution and urges visitors to report incidents.
- *Encourage tourists to learn food safety practices*: The World Health Organization has prepared an excellent booklet of advice called "Safe Food for Travellers". Adapt this information on how to avoid illness while travelling for use in promotional material, especially on the destination website or provide link to the booklet on the WHO website: www.who.int/fsf/Documents/brochure/travellers.PDF.

C. Reviewing Security Systems

- *Maintain a working relationship with other government departments responsible for safety and security*: Decisions made by police agencies, emergency services, as well as the departments of interior, health, consumer affairs, judiciary, foreign affairs, and civil defence have a great influence on how a crisis involving tourists is managed. Start a Safety and Security working group to bring these partners together on a regular basis to discuss tourism. In South Africa, for example, the Tourism Safety Task Group is made up of the Department of Environmental Affairs and Tourism, the national police, the tourism board (SATOUR), the Tourism Business Council, the Department of Foreign Affairs and nine provincial tourism departments.

- *Get involved in defining security procedures*: Tourism authorities need to make sure they are aware of all security measures being taken that affect the industry. Review the entire tourism chain—airport arrivals, ground transport, hotels, restaurants, shopping zones and all tourist sites. Consider the need for enhanced security at all sites, including places like beaches or entertainment districts. The goal is to provide a safe environment with procedures that are as invisible as possible and do not restrict the arrival of tourists.
- *Designate a national tourist safety and security focal point*: Every National Tourism Administration should designate a person to act as a liaison with other government bodies, specialized services, the tourism sector and the WTO services on safety and security issues. The NTSS Focal Point will also keep records on basic facts of tourist security, such as rules and regulations, identification of risks, safety statistics and incidents. In addition, this person should join the WTO Safety and Security Network, sharing information with their counterparts around the world and posting safety information on the WTO website.
- *Train local personnel in security issues*: NTAs can take an active role in improving safety and security by sponsoring workshops on safety issues for local tourism workers and especially by encouraging partnerships between public security and private security companies in the tourism sector, such as local police and hotel security guards. In addition, undertake community awareness programmes that help local residents recognize the value of tourism to their communities. They can help make it safer for visitors by reporting suspicious activities.

- *Establish tourism police and emergency call centres*: Special tourism police forces, such as the ones in Argentina, the Dominican Republic, Egypt, Greece and Malaysia, are trained to offer assistance in several languages. Mexico's Green Angels patrol the highways with bilingual crews. Other countries offer call centres with multi-lingual operators to handle emergencies involving visitors. Information on how to contact these emergency services needs to be communicated clearly to tourists on arrival.

D. Research Readiness

- *Establish strong contacts with key partners in the private sector*: Set up reciprocal agreements with major hotels, airlines and tour operators to exchange up-to-the-minute data on overnight stays, occupancy rates, pricing, etc. Build an e-mail or fax system capable of exchanging your data with these key partners.
- *Monitor hospital admissions involving tourists*: Information on non-crisis situation hospital admissions of tourists can be used as a point of comparison to put any possible problems in the future in a proper perspective.
- *Monitor crime against tourist*: Statistics on crimes against tourists can help experts find gaps in security services, improve the quality of the destination and possibly help avoid crisis-scale problems in the future. Crime statistics can also be used as background information, providing a context for crisis communication and a reference point for demonstrating a return to normalcy.

II. During a Crisis: Minimizing Damage in a Crisis

The first 24 hours of a crisis are crucial. An unprofessional response could wreck further havoc on the destination, while responsible management of the crisis can actually enhance relations with the travel trade and help the destination recuperate faster.

A. Communications from the Front Line

- *Be honest and transparent*: To protect your credibility, adopt policy of full disclosure about what is known and what is not known. Deliver facts in a non-patronizing manner. Do not try to cover-up an incident and do not lie. Be assured that the true facts about a crisis will eventually come out and news of lies or a cover-up could do greater harm than the crisis itself.

- *Do not impose a news blackout*: Failure to provide information to the media will not only deprive you of the chance to express your point of view, it will also force the media to seek alternative news sources—often less careful with their words than you would be.
- *Establish a media çentre*: The media will come to your offices immediately in a crisis, so set aside a room they can use that is equipped with desks, phones and data lines. Use it for media briefings. If the crisis occurs in a different location, set up a second media centre there with a second spokesperson who is in constant communication with the headquarters. Work with security services to help television reporters gain access to positions with good backgrounds for on-camera reports.
- *Act fast*: News travels around the world in a matter of seconds. In order to work effectively with the media, you need to respond as quickly as they do. Begin to release information once you are ready to answer the five key questions: who, what, where, when and why? If some of the information is still missing, simply say that it is not yet available and promise to get back to the journalists as soon as possible. Set up a timetable for regular bulletins. Provide background information on your destination.
- *Remember the victims*: The first communication about the crisis should include information about what is being done to help the victims. News about economic losses to the tourism industry comes across as insensitive where loss of life or injury is concerned. Tourism is a humane industry and needs to show its compassionate face in a crisis. When two French sunbathers were run over during a police chase recently on Miami Beach, the tourism director immediately arranged to fly in the grieving parents, he met them personally at the airport and spent the evening with the family in hospital. His personal involvement, rather than police negligence, was the focus of the story that ran in the morning newspaper.

- *Avoid speculation and categorical reassurances*: Speculation about what caused a disaster or who is to blame damages your credibility. Information has to be perceived as accurate and reliable and not contaminated by efforts to encourage people. While the safest time to visit a troubled destination is possibly immediately following an incident, categorical reassurances such as "it is completely safe here" can have the opposite effect by making travellers suspicious. It is better to stick to information about what is being done to make the destination safer.
- *Put the crisis into context*: Use good maps and plenty of statistics to demonstrate that the crisis is limited to a specific area or that it has only affected a portion of your country's tourism industry. When highly-publicised health problems among British tourists to the Dominican Republic created a crisis in 1997, part of the recovery strategy was to show through statistics that less than one per cent of the two million British tourists in the past year had fallen ill. This fact emphasized the hundreds of thousands of people who had travelled safely to the Dominican Republic.
- *Challenge untrue statements*: Take time to contact media outlets that are making mistakes in their reporting immediately—before the inaccuracies can be repeated by other journalists. Be prepared with facts and offer interviews or other assistance. Don't automatically assume the media is against you, credibility sustains their businesses and, while journalists don't enjoy being corrected, they value the truth.
- *Use the media spotlight to highlight positive aspects*: During the crisis period, you have an unprecedented opportunity to speak with reporters in depth about your destination. Make sure to work positive details into news releases, for example: new tourism developments, growth statistics or how important tourism is to the community. Look for human interest stories, such as local residents helping victims.
- *Place information about the crisis on website*: Internet allows each tourism destination to become its own news channel. Communicate directly to potential tourists over your destination website, emphasizing which areas are affected

by the crisis and which are unaffected, as well as what is being done to end the crisis. Be honest and factual. Update the information on a daily basis.

- *Network with other news sources*: Other organizations that are providing information on the crisis to the media, such as police, disaster relief, airlines, hotel associations, tour operator groups and WTO should be kept informed about your response so that they can refer to it in their communication. Let these partners know how to reach your spokesperson in order to correct any possible errors or request more information.

B. Hard Decisions about Promotion

- *Communicate directly with travel trade*: Don't make your key partners rely on the media for information about the crisis. Provide details about the extent of the disaster, what is being done to assist victims, how security services are working to end the crisis and what is being done to make sure it doesn't happen again. UK tour operators have successfully used conference calls in crisis situations to link up the various people responsible for safety, promotion and tourism policy so that everyone is getting the same information at the same time. Fam trips organized for tour operators during or immediately following the crisis are the best way to allow them to assess the true situation for themselves.
- *Change promotional message to address safety concerns*: Rather than suspending promotion when a crisis hits, immediately change the message to reflect the current situation and address safety concerns about the destination. Advertising should express sympathy for victims or provide information about what is being done to end the crisis. Use ads to direct potential tourists to a hotline or website for more detailed information. After the Prestige oil tanker sank off the Spanish coast, for example, huge billboards sponsored by the regional tourism board went up thanking Madrid residents for their concern over the crisis.
- *Press ahead with promotional events and travel shows*: The travel trade needs to understand that your destination is

stable and not going to disappear because of the crisis. The best way to demonstrate that is to press ahead with scheduled promotional events. A crisis will undoubtedly create more attention for a destination at a trade show and allow more opportunities to communicate positive developments, as well as up-to-date information about the end of the crisis.

- *Seek increases in promotional budgets*: A crisis usually results in more government attention for the tourism industry than it would receive under normal circumstances with everything operating smoothly. Use the opportunity to seek increases in promotional budgets—which will be needed to help the industry recover and stimulate visitors to return.
- *Initiate financial assistance and/or fiscal measures to support tourism companies*: Governments need to work closely with the industry in difficult times to ensure that there is not a damaging loss of product that could limit the recovery when better times come. Temporary tax incentives, subsidies, reduced airport charges and free visas are some of the measures taken to encourage tour operators, airlines, and cruise companies to continue operating immediately following a crisis.

C. Ensuring Security

- *Set up a hotline*: If there is an emergency call centre in operation, it can become the hotline/or inquiries from tourists and their families during a crisis. If there is no call centre, one needs to be set up immediately/allowing a crisis with multi-lingual operators who have a good understanding of security issues. A sample hotline questionnaire is included in WTO's Handbook on Natural Disaster Reduction. Promote the existence of the hotline in news briefings and on the destination website.
- *Monitor what is being done to improve safety and security*: Use inter-agency contacts and relationships to help keep your organization informed about what security services are doing to end the crisis and improve safety.
- *Coordinate with security services for media access*: Where possible, try to help organize with security services/or reasonable media access to the stricken area. A few years

ago, a Caribbean country tried to restrict access to an area hit by a hurricane. CNN simply hired a helicopter to fly over and take 'exclusive' pictures of the devastation. The images were all the more powerful because they were 'banned' by authorities.

- *Communicate internally*: In the heat of a crisis, internal communication often gets overlooked. But it is important to keep all tourism staff up-to-date on the seriousness of the crisis and what is being done to end it. Not only does it strengthen the tourism team, it can also prevent erroneous information from being spread.

D. Quick Research Tactics

- *Get to know your visitors*: Send out survey teams to find out who is travelling during the crisis, where they come from and why, then feed information back immediately to the promotion department.
- *Monitor media reports*: Keep track of what is being published and broadcast about your destination during the crisis and feed that information back to the communications and promotion departments. Even if media monitoring is normally the responsibility of the communications department, they will be stretched too thin during a crisis and will appreciate the assistance.

III. Following a Crisis: Recovering Tourist Confidence

While media attention moves quickly to fresh stories, the damage wrought by a crisis can stay in the minds of potential tourists for a long time. Recovery demands a redoubling of efforts, especially in the areas of communications and promotion.

A. Image Building Communications

- *Be pro-active in communications*: Promote what you are doing to restore tourism to normalcy. Tell journalists about your recuperation plans and how long it will take for them to have effect. Provide plentiful information, including copies of speeches, editorial pieces, maps and photos. Recuperating from a crisis requires extra budgetary and human resources in communications.

- *Look for positive news*: Gear news items to reflect the normalcy of tourism activity, for example, the arrival of specialized tour groups or the opening of new attractions. The goal is to demonstrate "business as usual" in your destination. Egypt has effectively promoted the discovery or reopening of archaeological sites as part of its recovery strategy. Promote news not directly related to tourism, such as cultural events, scientific discoveries, sporting triumphs, film shoots and shopping trends.
- *Increase fam trips for journalists*: Invite the press back to show them what has been achieved. Target the theme of the fam trip to address your particular image problem and make sure it includes plenty of contact between journalists and local residents. Concentrate on positive television coverage to counteract the harmful effect of TV images of the crisis in the minds of potential tourists. The great thing about fam trips is that they allow plenty of time to make friends with individual journalists—who are often motivated to take a special interest in your country for years to come.
- *Remember anniversaries*: A major crisis will be revisited by the media during year-end reviews and on key anniversaries—100 days, six months, one year, two years. These dates offer a good opportunity to communicate. Anticipate this attention and be prepared with materials and stories that reflect the recovery of the destination.
- *Anticipate legal actions*: People affected by international incidents will lobby/or investigations, make complaints and pursue lawsuits. If the media reports something about you that is not accurate, write a letter to the editor to correct the matter. If someone takes you to court, the inaccurate media report could be produced as evidence and it does no good to claim is was not true. You will need some evidence to show that you disagreed with the report at the time.
- *Create your own news outlet on the destination website*: Provide an alternative to mass media news sources on your own website. Make the website as newsy as possible, taking advantage of its unlimited space to provide more in-depth information. To demonstrate that your website is providing up-to-date information it needs to include today's date in

a prominent place. And it needs to be updated daily with positive stories that demonstrate a return to normalcy following a crisis.

- *Join the global communications campaign for tourism*: A global campaign promoting the positive impacts of tourism is being prepared by WTO for presentation as part of the 'First International Conference on Tourism Communications' (Tourcom) was held on 2-3 July, 2003 in Madrid. The campaign featured five basic components that can be adapted for use by WTO members in their own promotion and awareness building activities—a slogan, logo, poster, flyer and 30-second public service announcement. It aimed to stimulate communication about the benefits of tourism on the local level and at the same time link individual tourism entities to the larger community of international tourism.

B. Flexibility in Promotion

- *Create new niche market products*: Packages should be targeted at the most resistant market segments, such as: golf, skiing, sporting events, culture, honeymoons.
- *Target experienced and special interest travellers*: More experienced travellers and repeat visitors are less likely to be scared away by the crisis. Individual travellers with a particular passion, be it diving, mountain climbing, or archaeology, will go where they need to go to enjoy their hobby.
- *Create special price offers*: Rather than engaging in price wars in a crisis stricken region or slashing prices across the board, create special offers. Malaysia and Sri Lanka build their special offers around holiday weekends and festivals. The key is not necessarily to offer the cheapest prices, but rather to offer value-for-money.
- *Quickly shift promotion to most promising markets*: Be prepared to shift promotional campaigns to markets that promise the most resilience. Usually these are the source markets closest to home because travellers there are more familiar with your destination. But pay attention to research and beware of wasting money on markets that are not yet ready

to travel. A joint Caribbean ad campaign recently launched to win back US tourists had little effect because Americans are still wary of going abroad.

- *Step up promotion to domestic market*: In larger countries, domestic tourism can make up for lack of foreign demand during the recovery period. The Ball Tourism Board began promoting to the domestic market following the terrorist bombing there in order to keep hotels functioning. Persian Gulf tourists vacationed closer to home and kept hotels in Dubai, Bahrain and other Arab countries operating following the September 11, 2001 attacks. Tourism officials were surprised to discover they spent more than long-haul visitors.
- *Increase fam trips for tour operators and special events*: As soon as the situation permits, bring in tour operators and travel agents to see what has been done to restore the destination. Organize special events and meetings to create an opportunity to communicate with your partners in the travel trade and with the international community.
- *Take travel advisories seriously*: Establish contact with governments that have issued travel advisories against the destination. Provide a regular flow of information on the crisis, including details of the exact location of the incident, what is being done to make the area more secure and where it is safe for visitors to travel. Begin lobbying the government and invite representatives to see the situation for themselves.
- *Intensify cooperation*: A crisis brings people together in a spirit of solidarity and cooperation is essential to a quick recovery. Improve coordination among tourism promotion boards throughout the country and redouble collaboration between public and private sectors in marketing campaigns. Also explore the possibility of multi-country regional promotions and products.

C. Security for the Future

- *Evaluate security procedures*: Following a crisis, a second look is needed at security systems to make sure they are in place, but not in an obvious way and not contributing to a negative image of the destination. Do not let the 'hassle' of dealing with security frighten visitors or prevent tourism from resuming.

- *Push to improve quality of services and facilities*: Encourage quality through feedback of survey results on tourist perceptions, by rewarding excellence and by setting up tourist complaint services. Tourists should have somewhere to complain if services do not meet expectations. Peru's Tourist Protection Service (SPT), which operates under the auspices of the country's consumer protection commission, provides this service by mediating complaints, providing general tourist information and analyzing data on the nature of complaints to help point out where improvement is needed.

D. Using Research Effectively

- *Survey generating markets on perceptions of your destination*: Research potential tourists and survey your travel partners in primary source markets for readiness to travel and for information about their perceptions or apprehensions about your destination. Feeding this information back to promotion officials will allow them to tailor campaigns to correct damaging impressions. In order to begin in perceptions, it is essential to know where you stand.

IV. Crisis Action Team

Responding quickly to a tourism crisis demands solidarity, flexibility and expertise. That is why the World Tourism Organization has put together a Crisis Action Team made up of 11 of the world's top experts in the area of communications, marketing and promotion and safety and security—all of them with solid experience collaborating with WTO. These professionals have agreed to make themselves available to help member countries that are hit by a crisis and request urgent assistance from the Secretary-General. The kind of assistance would be at the discretion of the Secretary-General depending on the nature of the crisis, but could include such services as: audits of crisis preparedness, developing crisis management plans, communications training seminars, providing advice by phone or e-mail, or giving emergency on-site assistance during a crisis.

2

Medical Tourism: A Global Outlook

Medical tourism, or *medical travel*, is the act of travelling abroad to obtain medical, surgical and dental healthcare. The term was initially coined by travel agencies and the media as a catchall phrase to describe a rapidly growing industry where people travel internationally to obtain healthcare services. The leisure aspect of travelling may be also included on a medical tourism trip. Medical tourism healthcare procedures can include elective surgeries (e.g., cosmetic surgery, dental implants) as well as complex specialized surgeries (e.g., knee/hip replacement, heart surgery. Some medical tourism companies, such as Healthbase Online, Inc. and Medical Excursions, Inc., inspect overseas healthcare facilities to help their patients find qualified and affordable medical service providers.

Description

A combination of many factors has led to the recent increase in popularity of medical tourism: the high cost of healthcare in industrialized nations, the ease and affordability of international travel, and the improvement of technology and standards of care in many countries of the world.

A large draw to medical travel is the convenience in comparison to that of other countries. Some countries that operate from a public health care system are so taxed that it can take a considerable amount of time, to get needed medical care. The time spent waiting for a procedure, such as a hip replacement, can be a year or more in Britain and Canada; however, in Singapore, Bangkok or Bangalore, a patient could feasibly have an operation the day after their arrival.

Reasons pushing medical travel include lower healthcare costs as well as the search for medical expertise and safety. According to research found in an article by the University of Delaware publication, UDaily:

> "The cost of surgery in Bolivia, Argentina, India, Thailand or South Africa can be one-tenth of what it is in the United States or Western Europe, and sometimes even less. A heart-valve replacement that would cost US $ 200,000 or more in the U.S., for example, goes for $10,000 in India—and that includes round-trip airfare and a brief vacation package. Similarly, a metal-free dental bridge worth $5,500 in the U.S. costs $500 in India or Bolivia, a knee replacement in Thailand with six days of physical therapy costs about one-fifth of what it would in the States, and Lasik eye surgery worth $ 3,700 in the U.S. is available in many other countries for only $ 730. Cosmetic surgery savings are even greater: A full facelift that would cost $ 20,000 in the U.S. runs about $2,500 in South Africa or $ 2,300 in Bolivia."

To understand the phenomenon of medical travel, we can compare the average costs of cosmetic surgeries between the industrialized nations and the most popular countries in Latin America which are specialized in medical tourism and cosmetic surgery tourism (Argentina, Bolivia, Brazil, Costa Rica, India, Mexico). All the prices have been provided us by the offices affiliated with the ministries of health in USA, Europe (France, Spain, Switzerland), Argentina, Bolivia, Brazil, Costa Rica, India and Mexico.

Table 2.1

	USA	*Europe*	*Argentina*	*Bolivia*	*Brazil*	*Costa Rica*	*India*	*Mexico*
Rhinoplasty	$ 6,000	$ 5,500	$ 2,300	$ 1,200	$ 2,100	$ 2,000	$ 1,500	$ 1,700
Face Lift	$ 15,000	$ 12,500	$ 4,300	$ 2,600	$ 4,500	$ 4,200	$ 2,900	$ 4,500
Breast Augmentation	$ 8,000	$ 7,500	$ 3,700	$ 2,500	$ 3,800	$ 3,400	$ 2,900	$ 3,900
Breast Reduction	$ 9,000	$ 8,000	$ 3,900	$ 2,400	$ 3,600	$ 3,200	$ 3,000	$ 3,700
Complete Liposuction	$ 13,500	$ 11,000	$ 4,500	$ 2,700	$ 4,700	$ 3,800	$ 3,200	$ 4,800
Gluteal Augmentation	$ 9,000	$ 9,000	$ 4,000	$ 3,000	$ 4,200	$ 3,800	$ 3,200	$ 4,500

Medical tourists can come from anywhere in the world and may seek essential healthcare services such as cancer treatment and brain and transplant surgery as well as complementary or 'elective' services such as aesthetic treatments (cosmetic surgery).

Popular *Medical travel* worldwide destinations are:

- Colombia
- Singapore
- India
- Thailand
- Brunei
- Cuba
- Hong Kong
- Hungary
- Israel
- Jordan
- Lithuania
- Malaysia
- The Philippines
- Singapore, and recently
- UAE

Popular *Cosmetic Surgery travel* destination are:

- Colombia
- Argentina
- Bolivia
- Brazil
- Costa Rica
- Mexico, and
- Turkey

In Europe Belgium and Poland are also breaking into the business. South Africa is taking the term "medical tourism" very literally by promoting their "medical safaris": Come to see African wildlife and get a facelift in the same trip. However, feelings towards medical tourism are not always positive. In places like the US, where most have insurance and access to quality healthcare, medical tourism is viewed as risky. In some parts of the world, wider political issues can influence where medical tourists will choose to seek out healthcare; for example, in late 2006 some patients from the Middle East were choosing to travel to Singapore or Hong Kong for healthcare rather than to the USA.

While the tourism component might be a big draw for some South-East Asian countries that focus on simple procedures, India is positioning itself the primary medical destination for the most complex medical procedures in the world. India's commitment to this is demonstrated with an ever growing number of hospitals that are attaining the US Joint Commission International accreditation.

Singapore positions itself as a medical hub where healthcare services, medicine, biomedical research and pharmaceutical manufacturing converge. Singapore has made international news for many complex surgeries in specialities such as neurology, oncology and organ transplants procedures. Currently Singapore boasts the largest number of US Joint Commission accredited hospitals in the region.

On the other hand, in South America, countries such as Argentina, Bolivia, Brazil lead on plastic surgery medical skills relying on the vast experience their surgeons have in treating the style-obsessed. It is estimated that 1 in 30 Argentinians had taken plastic surgery procedures, making this population the most operated in the world after the US and Mexico.

In Bolivia the situation is impressive. According to the "Sociedad Boliviana de Cirugia Plasticay Reconstructiva", more that 70 per cent women who belong to the middle and upper class had taken plastic surgery procedure.

There are companies emerging to offer global healthcare options that will allow North American patients to take full advantage of dramatic reductions in air travel and access world class healthcare at a fraction of the cost. Companies that focus on 'Medical Value Travel' typically will have experienced nurse case managers to assist patients with pre- and post-travel medical issues. They will also help provide resources for follow-up care upon the patient's return. While these services will initially be of interest to the self-insured patient, several studies indicate that the rapid growth of Health Savings Accounts will also drive interest to healthcare in other countries.

Because standards are everything when it comes to healthcare, there is a parallel issue around hospital accreditation. Potential medical tourists may be assisted in making their choices by whether or not hospitals have been assessed and accredited by reputable external accreditation bodies. In the USA, JCI (Joint Commission International) fulfills such a role, while in the United Kingdom and Hong Kong, the Trent Accreditation Scheme is a key player.

India

India is one of the most touted destinations in the world for medical tourists. It is known in particular for heart surgery and hip resurfacing, areas of advanced medicine in which India is generally considered a global leader. Probably no country has been in the news for medical tourism than India in 2005-06, and the government and private hospital groups both seem committed to a goal of making the subcontinent a world leader in the industry. Indian medical industry's main appeal is low-cost treatment. Most estimates claim treatment costs in India start at around a tenth of the price of comparable treatment in America or Britain. Morever Indian hospitals also provides more personalized care than available in west.

For example, in April, Madras Medical Mission, a Chennai-based hospital, successfully conducted a complex heart operation on an 87-year-old American patient at a reported cost of $8,000 (€ 7,000, £4,850) including the cost of his airfare and a month's stay in hospital. The patient claimed that a less complex operation in America had earlier cost him $40,000. Take the rising popularity of "preventive health screening". At one private clinic in London a thorough men's health check-up that includes blood tests, electrocardiogram tests, chest X-rays, lung tests and abdominal ultrasound costs £ 345 ($574, € 500). By comparison, a comparable check-up at a clinic operated by Delhi-based healthcare company Max Healthcare costs $84.

A lady from Vero beach, FL, who was featured in CBS 60 min in April 2005, went to India for hip surgery. In USA only hip replacements are possible, but India allows hip resurfacing that does not need the full hip replacement rather saves part of the hip to achieve the same result as the hip replacement.

Escorts Heart Institute and Research Centre in Delhi and Faridabad, India performs nearly 15,000 heart operations every year, and the post-surgery mortality rate is only 0.8 per cent, which is less than half of most major hospitals in the United States.

Medical Tourism in India is one of the best options available to people across the globe. Millions come to India every year to get treated and then enjoy their recuperative holidays across India. People from different walks of life cut across America, United Kingdom, Pakistan, Sri Lanka, Europe, Maldives, Germany and numerous other countries come to India to have their treatments done with peace of mind. India provides world class medical facilities with hospitals and specialized multi-speciality health centres providing their expertize in the areas of Cosmetic Surgery, Dental Care, Heart Surgeries, Coronary Bypass, Heart Checkup, Valve replacements, Knee replacements, Eye surgeries, Indian traditional treatments like Ayurvedic Therapies and much more, practically covering every aspect of medicine combining modern treatments with traditional experience.

Estimates of the value of medical tourism to India go as high as $ 2 billion a year by 2012. In 2003, Indian Finance Minister Jaswant Singh called for India to become a "global health destination". However, the biggest stumbling block preventing the rapid growth of India as a healthcare destination is its poor infrastructure and lack of quality hotels.

Singapore

Singapore's healthcare services built on a heritage of excellent quality, safety and trustworthiness, coupled with advanced research and international accreditation, and is Asia's leading medical hub. Nine hospitals and two medical centres in Singapore have obtained Joint Commission International (JCI) accreditation. JCI is the main hospital accreditation agency in the United States.

According to statistics at the official website, www.singaporemedicine.com, 374,000 visitors came to Singapore purely to seek healthcare in 2005.

Many of these patients come from neighbouring countries such as Indonesia and Malaysia. However, patient numbers from Indo-China, South-Asia, the Middle East and Greater China to Singapore are seeing fast growth. On top of that, patients from developed countries such as United States also choose Singapore as their medical travel destination for relatively affordable quality healthcare services in a clean cosmopolitan city for a peace of mind.

Singapore made news for many complex and innovative procedures such as the separation of conjoined twins and tooth-in-eye surgery. The successful separation of the 10-month-old Nepalese conjoined twins in 2001 puts Singapore's medical expertise onto the World's headlines. Singapore has since accomplished many more milestones both in Asia and in the world arena.

Recently, Singapore also hosted the first International Medical Travel Conference (IMTC) from 12 to 15th December 2006. The four-day event attracted participants and media from 21 countries, setting pace and platform for the development of the budding medical travel industry. The conference aims to bring together thought leaders to examine some of the fundamentals, issues and challenges involved in the burgeoning international medical travel industry. Curiously however major media did not pay attention to this awkwardly managed event.

However, upto late 2006 Singapore Hospitals have only chosen to accredit themselves through Joint Commission International (JCI), a US-based group, and this approach may have little appeal to potential health tourists based in other parts of the world. In time, Singapore Hospitals may look towards other European or Asian-based systems of hospital accreditation in an attempt to broaden their credibility and appeal.

Thailand

Medical tourism is a growing segment of Thailand's tourism and health care sectors. Lower labour costs translate into significant cost savings on procedures, compared to hospitals in the United States, and a higher, more personalized level of nursing care than Westerners are accustomed to receiving in hospitals back home. In 2005, one Bangkok hospital took in 150,000 treatment seekers from abroad. In 2006, medical tourism was projected to earn the country 36.4 billion baht.

One patient who received a coronary artery bypass surgery at Bumrungrad International Hospital in Bangkok said the operation cost him US$12,000, as opposed to the $100,000 he estimated the operation would have cost him at home in the US.

Hospitals in Thailand are a popular destination for other Asians. Another hospital that caters to medical tourists, Bangkok General Hospital, has a Japanese wing and Phyathai Hospitals Group has interpreters for over 22 languages, besides the English speaking medical staff. When Prime Minister of Nepal Girija Prasad Koirala needed medical care in 2006, he went to Bangkok.

While it is not commonly known outside Thailand, the modern Thai medical system had its origins in the United States when Prince Mahidol of Songla, the King's father, earned his MD degree from Harvard Medical School in the early 20th century. Prince Mahidol and another member of the Thai Royal Family paid for an American medical education for a group of Thai men and women. Prince Mahidol also convinced the Rockefeller Foundation to provide scholarships for Thai citizens to study medicine and nursing. Funds from the Rockefeller Foundation were also used to help build modern medical training facilities in Thailand. The men and women who studied medicine and nursing as a result of Prince Mahidol's efforts became the first educators for the modern Thai medical system.

Today many Thai physicians hold US professional certification. A number of Thai hospitals have relationships with facilities in the US. The US Consular information sheet gives the Thai healthcare system high marks for quality, particularly facilities in Bangkok. In Thailand, there is modern infrastructure, with clean, safe streets. According to the US Consular information sheets, the crime rate in Bangkok is lower than that of many US cities. Personal safety is another factor to consider when travelling abroad both for vacation as well as healthcare. Thailand offers everything from cardiac surgery to organ transplants at a price much lower than the US or Europe, in a safe, clean environment.

Thailand has long been a destination for medical tourists, and has a growing number of hospitals with JCAHO accreditation. Over one million people per year travel there for everything from cosmetic surgery to cutting edge cardiac treatment. Don Ho, the famous Hawaiian entertainer, recently received cutting-edge adult stem cell cardiac treatment at a Bangkok hospital. Six weeks later he had recovered sufficiently from his nonischemic cardiomyopathy and was able to return to the stage.

Medical Travel Risks and Rewards

Medical tourism does carry risks that local medical procedures do not. Should complications arise, patients might not be covered by insurance or be able to seek adequate compensation via malpractice lawsuits, though it should be noted that the malpractice insurance is a considerable portion of the cost in the West.

For some living in remote rural areas, travel to another country is almost as expensive as travel to a large city in their own country.

Nations such as India or Thailand have different infectious diseases, and different prevalence of the same diseases, than home nations such as the US, Canada, UK. Exposure to foreign diseases without having built up natural immunity can be a hazard for weakened individuals, specifically for gastrointestinal diseases (e.g. Hepatitis A, amoebic dysentery, bacteria) which could weaken progress, mosquito transmitted diseases, and influenza, TB, etc. (75 per cent of South Africans have latent TB).

Also, travel soon after surgery can increase the risk of complications, as can vacation activities. For example, scars will be darker and more noticeable if they sunburn while healing. Long flights can be bad for those with heart (thrombosis) or breathing related problems (low oxygen environment), not to mention uncomfortable.

However, because in poor tropical nations diseases run the gamut, doctors seem to be more open to the possibility of any disease, including HIV, TB, and typhoid, there are cases in the West where patients were consistently misdiagnosed for years because it is perceived to be "rare" in the West, a famous case of the misdiagnosis and death of a CDC researcher from TB, something that few would rule out in India or Thailand.

The term *Medical Tourism* has emerged from the practice of citizens of highly industrialized nations such as the United States, Canada, Great Britain, Western Europe etc. travelling to other countries around the globe to receive a variety of medical and healthcare services, mainly due to cóntinually rising costs of the same services and procedures in their own countries. In addition, these people also take on the role of tourists, vacationing and taking advantage of all the major sites and attractions that these nations have to offer, in conjunction with receiving medical treatment. In addition to the rising costs of healthcare in places like the United States and Great Britain, the increasing ease and affordability of international travel via air and sea, as well as the rapid advancement of medical technologies in lesser-developed nations all around the world have all contributed to the growing global interest in Medical Tourism. Places like India, the East Indies, Mexico and South America are becoming very popular when it comes to Medical Tourism. Not only do these nations provide a high level of quality medical care at significantly lower rates, but they also offer an abundant number of touring, site-seeing, shopping, dining, and relaxation options as well. Other Medical Tourism hot spots are the West Indies, the Philippines. Africa, the Middle East, and Mexico. Ample data by virtue of surveys is available on the Medical Tourism concept and increasing number of people are joining this bandwagon every year.

MEDICAL TOURISM: MEANING AND DIMENSIONS

Medical tourism can be broadly defined as provision of 'cost effective' private medical care in collaboration with the tourism industry for patients needing surgical and other forms of specialized treatment. This process is being facilitated by the corporate sector involved in medical care as well as the tourism industry—both private and public. Medical tourism refers to travelling to other countries to obtain medical, dental, and surgical treatment. At the same time they could also tour, and fully experience the attractions of the countries they visit. Exorbitant costs of healthcare in industrialized nations, ease and affordability of international travel, favourable currency exchange rates in the global economy, rapidly improving technology and standards of care in many countries of the world, and most importantly proven safety of healthcare in select foreign nations have all led to the rise of medical tourism.

More and more people are travelling abroad as an affordable, enjoyable, and safe alternative to having treatment in their home countries. Medical tourists are generally residents of the industrialized nations of the world and primarily come from The United States, Canada, Great Britain, Western Europe, Australia, and The Middle East. But more and more, people from many other countries of the world are seeking out places where they can combine vacationing and obtaining their medical care at an affordable cost. Non-resident Indians form a big group of medical tourists to India.

Currently medical tourists are travelling in large numbers abroad where the quality of healthcare is equal to anywhere else in the world and yet the cost is significantly lower. These regions also offer numerous options for touring, sight-seeing, shopping, exploring, and yes, even lounging on sun drenched beaches. Although India, the East Indies, and South America are currently the most popular choices for medical tourists, the industry is growing so rapidly that more and more countries and medical centres around the world are beginning to tailor services aimed specifically at medical tourists, and the expectation is that the options for where medical tourists can choose to travel will continue to increase at a rapid pace.

In general the reasons to choose medical tourism include:

- Avoid waiting list in native countries
- Less cost
- Quality accommodation and nursing care
- Touring the place
- Medical Treatment in West = A tour to India + Medical Treatment + Savings

The ranges of treatment the medical tourists obtain vary widely. They start from simple comprehensive medical check up to elective procedures such as rhinoplasty, liposuction, breast augmentation, orthodontics and LASIK surgery. Often they do visit for larger and life-saving procedures such as joint replacements, bone marrow transplants, and cardiac bypass surgery etc. Medical tourists can now obtain essentially any type of medical or surgical procedure abroad in a safe and effective manner for a fraction of the cost that they would face in their home countries.

The average cost of private heart surgery in the United States is $50,000. That same operation with comparable rates of success and complications costs only $10,000 in the finest and most state-of-the-art hospital in Mumbai. A bone marrow transplant that costs $250,000 in the U.S. costs only $25,000 in India. For the same price as a week-long vacation for two in Hawaii, a couple can travel to India's south coast to include airfare, boarding and lodging, personal tour guide/concierge, and have LASIK corrective surgery for two. Large price disparities such as these exist across the board for numerous medical and surgical procedures. And because of favourable currency exchange rates for medical tourists, the costs associated with accommodations, food, shopping, and sight-seeing are similarly very favourable.

The countries where medical tourism is being actively promoted include Greece, South Africa, Jordan, India, Malaysia, Philippines and Singapore. India is a recent entrant into medical tourism. According to a study by McKinsey and the Confederation of Indian Industry, medical tourism in India could become a $1 billion business by 2012. The report predicts that: "By 2012, if medical tourism were to reach 25 per cent of revenues of private up-market players, upto Rs. 10,000 crore will be added to the revenues of these players." The Indian government predicts that India's $17-billion-a-year health care industry could grow 13 per cent in each of the next six years, boosted by medical tourism, which industry watchers say is growing at 30 per cent annually.

Analysts say that as many as 150,000 medical tourists came to India last year. However, the current market for medical tourism in India is mainly limited to patients from the Middle East and South Asian economies. Afro-Asian people spend as much as $20 billion a year on healthcare outside their countries—Nigerians alone spend an estimated $1 billion a year. Most of this money would be spent in Europe and America, but it is hoped that this would now be increasingly directed to developing countries with advanced facilities.

How to Identify a Hospital Abroad? What is the Check List?

India has one of the best qualified professionals in each and every field, and this fact has now been realized the world over. Regarding medical facilities India has the most competent doctors and world class medical facilities. With most competitive charges for treatment, India is a very lucrative destination for people wanting to undergo treatment.

Before entering the hospital and package, one has to identify with prior mail communication regarding:

- Whether the specialist in that area is available.
- Whether the hospital has all investigations required within campus.
- The credentials of the hospital.
- The credentials of the specialist.

In summary India offers world class medical facilities, comparable with any of the western countries. India has state-of-the-art hospitals and the best qualified doctors. With the best infrastructure, the best possible medical facilities, accompanied with the most competitive prices, the treatment can be done in India at the lowest charges.

Medical Tourism has become a serious enterprise in India over the last two years. However some hospitals have been practising it for quite a few years. Regular patient inflow from neighbouring Indian countries like Sri Lanka, Nepal, Bangladesh and sometimes Malaysia has been happening for over a decade. These are some real case histories. The names and circumstances of the patients have been changed to protect their confidentiality.

There are quite a few examples of Indian patients who have had a liver transplant abroad and are living with an English or American liver. There are few examples of kidney failure patient living with an Englishman's kidney. In fact the longest living kidney transplant patient in India had his transplant in London way back in 1970's. Here is an example of a Canadian lady living with an Indian kidney.

Case Study

1. Canadian Lady with Indian Kidney

Betty was an Anglo-Saxon Canadian lady who was on 42 and on hemo-dialysis for twelve years. She first had treatment at Toronto and then moved on to Montreal after she got employment in a local school. She was young and getting very frustrated being on dialysis three times a week. She had been on the transplant waiting list for many years and should have got a couple of kidneys in that period of waiting. However every time she was called it was found that her cross-match was positive. She also had a rare blood group (AB positive). As she had had multiple blood transfusions, this had resulted in a very high level of antibodies developing in her system. This meant that the chances of a transplanted kidney getting immediately rejected were very high. She then spoke to a few doctors and her well-wishers and someone suggested that maybe the solution was to try and get a kidney from a patient from another race. Immediately she thought of countries like Hong Kong, China and India. She contacted Sri Ramachandra Hospital and was told that they did not do any unrelated transplants, however if she was interested she could go on a cadaver transplant list provided there were no Indian patients waiting for AB kidney.

Betty was not keen to indulge in purchasing a kidney from a stranger and having waited for a kidney for many years in Canada she did not mind waiting for some time in India to get a cadaver kidney. She travelled to India and got admitted to the hospital and was started her hemo-dialysis.

As luck would have it for her, three weeks after her arrival and waiting, AB cadaver donor was available in the hospital and there was only one Indian patient on the waiting list hence there was a possibility that the second kidney could be given to her provided her cross-match was not positive. However as a precaution multiple special hemo-dialysis was done to extract some of her antibodies and the cross-match results were awaited with donor's blood.

The cross-match was weakly positive. She was told this however Betty said she would take her chance and go for the transplant. Her transplant was successful and within a couple of weeks she made remarkable progress and within a month after her transplant she flew back to Canada with her brother who had accompanied her for the surgery.

2. *The Wet Little Pretty Girl from Seychelles*

Maggy, a very pretty seven-year-old was the only child of Dorothy—a single parent from Seychelles. She refused to go to school because she was constantly wetting her underwear and felt embarrassed. She had changed three schools, as her friends teased her for smelling of urine. Vince was born with some kind of congenital anomaly of her kidneys and had double kidneys on both sides with four tubes from the kidney to the bladder (normally there are two kidneys with two tubes).

It was suspected that one of her tubes was opening somewhere in her vagina and this was causing the leakage of urine. Repeated examination did not reveal any such opening and it was a perplexing problem for the pediatricians at Seychelles. The mother decided to take her out of the country and seek help. Singapore was an option as many of the Seychelles patients were travelling there for treatment for the past many years.

However the cost of treatment was very high and she could not afford it. The pediatrician had known that a few of the adult patients had travelled to Chennai and had been successfully treated at the urology department of Sri Ramachandra Hospital. Knowing the mother personally the doctor got in touch with the department on the phone and made enquiries. She spoke to the head of the department Dr. Shroff and was assured that the problem could be solved as the department was fully staffed with various sub-specialists and they also had a full time pediatric urologist

Dr. Ramesh Babu who had trained in the UK. The young lady and her mother travelled by the first available flight and landed in the hospital. The girl was thoroughly investigated and taken up for investigations. Following this she was checked under anesthesia. At first everything appeared normal, however a closer and thorough examination revealed one of the tubes from her left kidney opening next to her vagina close to her skin. An operation was undertaken and the problem was immediately fixed. She went home after two weeks with a big smile on her face, for the first time she did not have to constantly wear nappies.

3. The Headmaster from Nigeria

James, a headmaster at a local school, near the city was exploring the possibility of undergoing his transplant in India, as he was not sure which centre he should visit. He made enquiries with his friends and a few of them had travelled to Sri Ramachandra Hospital in Chennai and liked their facilities and reasonable costs. In fact one of the patients who was undergoing dialysis in his place had a transplant at Sri Ramachandra Hospital and he decided to travel to Chennai to have the transplant.

He had a large family and his youngest brother who was in a garment business agreed to donate his kidney. A few initial investigations were done and they took a flight to Chennai via Mumbai. A month after his arrival he had a kidney transplant and he did well post-operatively. The total cost of the treatment was within five lakhs and this included the 1.5 lakhs for the special three injections that would prevent early rejection of his kidney.

Atsu was a frail 72-year-old Japanese who had travelled the world as a Merchant Navy officer. He had always enjoyed good health however a test during his annual health check-up showed that his creatinine was starting to go up. His doctor said he might require a transplant. This came as a shock to the old man. His only son worked in the USA running many beautiful Golf courses. They spoke on the phone and the next day he flew to the states. They decided to visit Cleveland and seek an opinion from one of the most renowned clinics in the world. Here he underwent tests and he was told to return after six months as they felt that his creatinine and other parameters were not high enough for a transplant.

4. The Best Hospital in the World is Not the Best

In Singapore one his lawyers heard this and suggested that they next time should travel to India to Chennai as they knew of this hospital that had good facilities and doctors doing a number of transplants. After six months his son decided to travel his father to Chennai and visited Sri Ramachandra Hospital. He was found to have a borderline raised creatinine. Looking at the frail structure of the body they reassured him that a transplant though an option in future was not the only option. He was told about 'Continuous Ambulatory Peritoneal Dialysis'. He was also shown how this could be done and he met a couple of patients at the hospital undergoing similar procedures. He was also explained and shown a machine was that could do the process overnight. He was delighted that he had an option besides transplant in the future. He and his son were a bit annoyed that the busy doctors at the world famous hospital in Cleveland never discussed these options with his father. The son summed it up in one line 'the so-called best hospital in the world is not the best'. He returned back to his country only to promise to come back for the procedure when required.

These are some of the interesting anecdotal stories from the department of Urology, Nephrology and Transplantation at Sri Ramachandra Hospital. The department is no stranger to medical tourism and has always attracted patients since 1996. At first it used to get patients from Nepal and Sri Lanka with various problems and now gets patients from all over the world.

Dr. Sunil Shroff the Head when asked about the departments experience with medical tourism said: As the department has grown over the years our volumes of both local and foreign patients have gone up. Initially when we started a lot of patient came for treatment from Eastern part of the country, but now we get them from everywhere in the world especially Nigeria, Yemen and Oman. On being asked why do they choose their hospital in comparison to others he said: 'I think we have all the facilities under one roof with world-class doctors. The rooms are spacious and overall the value for money I think is good for these patients.' He also added: 'We do not believe in marketing our services though we are an ISO 9000 certified department. I firmly believe the traffic grows because happy and satisfied patients refer other patients to us.'

He is aware of the CII-McKinsey report on Medical tourism and its potential for India. He thinks that we need to get better-standardized practice in the hospital and the need to improve our infrastructure facilities. The recent JCIA accreditation for which his own hospital is working towards would help tremendously, he felt.

The Department of Urology and Renal Transplants is an ISO 9000:2000 certified departments and is an integral part of Sri Ramchandra Medical College and Research Institute. They have so far treated about 300 patients from various countries. Another interesting phenomenon that he mentioned was the desire of foreign students from all over the world to undertake medical electives in India. In his own department he has had students from Sweden, Germany, France and England.

Dr. Shroff's dream on Medical Tourism, he said: "I went abroad to get my training in Surgery and Urology, but in my lifetime I would like to see foreigners come to India for training. He feels that tide is slowly changing, first it is the patients and medical students, and next it will be doctors. There are already some laparoscopic centres that are attracting foreigners who are getting trained.

One does not know the potential and magnitude of the market and Dr. Sunil Shroff feels that the market is much larger than projected by the CII-McKinsey report, if total picture is taken into consideration. He feels that once we train the foreign health manpower the doctors would feel comfortable to send their patients to India for treatment. His department is already recognized by WHO for training of doctors. The department has trained doctors and nurses from North Korea, Burma and Nepal over the years.

Dr. Shroff further said: 'Many South-East Asian countries would want their doctors to get trained in India and once our infrastructure improves, India will become an important hub in providing treatment healthcare services.'

INDUSTRY OF MEDICAL TOURISM AND PUBLIC HEALTH: A SERVICE APPROACH

The most recent trend in privatization of health services is medical tourism, which is gaining prominence in developing countries. Globalization has promoted a consumerist culture, thereby promoting goods and services that can feed the aspirations arising from this culture. This has had its effect in the health sector too, with the emergence of a private sector that thrives by servicing a small percentage of the population that has the ability to "buy" medical care at the rates at which the "high end" of the private medical sector provides such care. This has changed the character of the medical care sector, with the entry of the corporate sector. Corporate run institutions are seized with the necessity to maximize profits and expand their coverage. These objectives face a constraint in the form of the relatively small size of the population in developing countries that can afford services offered by such institutions. In this background, corporate interests in the medical care sector are looking for opportunities that go beyond the limited domestic "market" for high cost medical care. This is the genesis of the "medical tourism" industry.

Medical tourism can be broadly defined as provision of 'cost effective' private medical care in collaboration with the tourism industry for patients needing surgical and other forms of specialized treatment. This process is being facilitated by the corporate sector involved in medical care as well as the tourism industry—both private and public. In many developing countries it is being actively promoted by the government's official policy. India's National Health Policy 2002, for example, says: "To capitalize on the comparative cost advantage enjoyed by domestic health facilities in the secondary and tertiary sector, the policy will encourage the supply of services to patients of foreign origin on payment. The rendering of such services on payment in foreign exchange will be treated as 'deemed exports' and will be made eligible for all fiscal incentives extended to export earnings." The formulation draws from recommendations that the corporate sector has been making in India and specifically from the "Policy Framework for Reforms in Health Care", drafted by the Prime Minister's Advisory Council on Trade and Industry, headed by Mukesh Ambani and Kumaramangalam Birla.

The countries where medical tourism is being actively promoted include Greece, South Africa, Jordan, India, Malaysia, Philippines and Singapore. India is a recent entrant into medical tourism. According to a study by McKinsey and the Confederation of Indian Industry, medical tourism in India could become a $1 billion business by 2012. The report predicts that: "By 2012, if medical tourism were to reach 25 per cent of revenues of private up-market players, upto Rs. 10,000 crore will be added to the revenues of these players." The Indian government predicts that India's $17-billion-a-year health care industry could grow 13 per cent in each of the next six years, boosted by medical tourism, which industry watchers say is growing at 30 per cent annually.

In India, the Apollo group alone has so far treated 95,000 international patients, many of whom are of Indian origin. Apollo has been a forerunner in medical tourism in India and attracts patients from Southeast Asia, Africa and the Middle East. The group has tied up with hospitals in Mauritius, Tanzania, Bangladesh and Yemen besides running a hospital in Sri Lanka, and managing a hospital in Dubai. Another corporate group running a chain of hospitals, Escorts, claims it has doubled its number of overseas patients—from 675 in 2000 to nearly 1,200 this year. Recently, the Ruby Hospital in Kolkata signed a contract with the British insurance company, BUPA. The management hopes to get British patients from the queue in the National Health Services soon. Some estimates say that foreigners account for 10 to 12 per cent of all patients in top Mumbai hospitals despite roadblocks like poor aviation connectivity, poor road infrastructure and absence of uniform quality standards. Analysts say that as many as 150,000 medical tourists came to India last year. However, the current market for medical tourism in India is mainly limited to patients from the Middle East and South Asian economies. Some claim that the industry would flourish even without Western medical tourists. Afro-Asian people spend as much as $20 billion a year on health care outside their countries—Nigerians alone spend an estimated $1 billion a year. Most of this money would be spent in Europe and America, but it is hoped that this would now be increasingly directed to developing countries with advanced facilities.

The key "selling points" of the medical tourism industry are its "cost effectiveness" and its combination with the attractions of tourism. The latter also uses the ploy of selling the "exotica" of the countries involved as well as the packaging of healthcare with traditional therapies and treatment methods. Price advantage is, of course, a major selling point. The slogan, thus is, "First World treatment at Third World prices". The cost differential across the board is huge: only a tenth and sometimes even a sixteenth of the cost in the West. Open-heart surgery could cost up to $70,000 in Britain and upto $150,000 in the US; in India's best hospitals it could cost between $3,000 and $10,000. Knee surgery (on both knees) costs 350,000 rupees ($7,700) in India; in Britain this costs £10,000 ($16,950), more than twice as much. Dental, eye and cosmetic surgeries in Western countries cost three to four times as much as in India. The price advantage is however offset today for patients from the developed countries by concerns regarding standards, insurance coverage and other infrastructure. This is where the tourism and medical industries are trying to pool resources, and also putting pressure on the government. We shall turn to their implications later. In India the strong tradition of traditional systems of healthcare in Kerala, for example, is utilized. Kerala Ayurveda centres have been established at multiple locations in various metro cities, thus highlighting the advantages of Ayurveda in health management. The health tourism focus has seen Kerala participate in various trade shows and expos wherein the advantages of this traditional form of medicine are showcased. A generic problem with medical tourism is that it reinforces the medicalized view of healthcare. By promoting the notion that medical services can be bought off the shelf from the lowest priced provider anywhere in the globe, it also takes away the pressure from the government to provide comprehensive healthcare to all its citizens. It is a deepening of the whole notion of healthcare that is being pushed today which emphasizes on technology and private enterprise. The important question here is for whom is 'cost effective' services to be provided. Clearly the services are "cost effective" for those who can pay and in addition come from countries where medical care costs are exorbitant—because of the failure of the government to provide affordable medical care. It thus attracts only a small fraction that can pay for medical care and leaves out large sections that are denied medical care but cannot afford to pay. The demand for cost effective specialized care is coming from the developed countries where there has been a decline in public spending and rise in life expectancy and non-communicable diseases that requires specialist services.

Medical tourism is going to only deal with large specialist hospitals run by corporate entities. It is a myth that the revenues earned by these corporates will partly revert back to finance the public sector. There is ample evidence to show that these hospitals have not honoured the conditionalities for receiving government subsidies—in terms of treatment of a certain proportion of in patients and out-patients free of cost. If anything, increased demand on private hospitals due to medical tourism may result in their expansion. If they expand then they will need more professionals, which means that they will try to woo doctors from the public sector. Even today the top specialists in corporate hospitals are senior doctors drawn the public sector. Medical tourism is likely to further devalue and divert personnel from the public sector rather than strengthen them. Urban concentration of healthcare providers is a well-known fact—59 per cent of India's practitioners (73 per cent allopathic) are located in cities, and especially metropolitan ones. Medical tourism promotes an "internal brain drain" with more health professionals being drawn to large urban centres, and within them, to large corporate run speciality institutions. Medical tourism is going to result in a number of demands and changes in the areas of financing and regulations. There will be a greater push for encouraging private insurance tied to systems of accreditation of private hospitals. There is a huge concern in the developed countries about the quality of care and clinical expertise in developing countries and this will push for both insurance and regulatory regimes. The potential for earning revenues through medical tourism will become an important argument for private hospitals demanding more subsidies from the government in the long run. In countries like India, the corporate private sector has already received considerable subsidies in the form of land, reduced import duties for medical equipment etc. Medical tourism will only further legitimize their demands and put pressure on the government to subsidize them even more. This is worrying because the scarce resources available for health will go into subsidizing the corporate sector. It thus has serious consequences for equity and cost of services and raises a very fundamental question: why should developing countries be subsidizing the healthcare of developed countries?

WORLDWIDE GROWTH OF MEDICAL TOURISM

Falling ill while aboard seems like the worst sort of travelling nightmare. Yet, for growing numbers of travellers, the lure of combining affordable medical care with attentive room service is a chief draw for packing a suitcase and boarding a plane.

Medical tourists have good cause to seek out care beyond the United States for many reasons. In some regions of the world, state-of-the-art medical facilities are hard to come by, if they exist at all; in other countries, the public health care system is so overburdened that it can take years to get needed care. In Britain and Canada, for instance, the waiting period for a hip replacement can be a year or more, while in Bangkok or Bangalore, a patient can be in the operating room the morning after getting off a plane.

For many medical tourists, though, the real attraction is price. The cost of surgery in India, Thailand or South Africa can be one-tenth of what it is in the United States or Western Europe, and sometimes even less. A heart-valve replacement that would cost $200,000 or more in the U.S., for example, goes for $10,000 in India—and that includes round-trip airfare and a brief vacation package. Similarly, a metal-free dental bridge worth $5,500 in the U.S. costs $500 in India, a knee replacement in Thailand with six days of physical therapy costs about one-fifth of what it would in the States, and Lasik eye surgery worth $3,700 in the U.S. is available in many other countries for only $730. Cosmetic surgery savings are even greater: A full facelift that would cost $20,000 in the U.S. runs about $1,250 in South Africa.

Inferior medical care would not be worth having at any price, and some skeptics warn that Third World surgery cannot possibly be as good as that available in the United States. In fact, there have been cases of botched plastic surgery, particularly from Mexican clinics in the days before anyone figured out what a gold mine cheap, high-quality care could be for the developing countries.

Yet, the hospitals and clinics that cater to the tourist market often are among the best in the world, and many are staffed by physicians trained at major medical centres in the United States and Europe.

Bangkok's Bumrungrad hospital has more than 200 surgeons who are board-certified in the United States, and one of Singapore's major hospitals is a branch of the prestigious Johns Hopkins University in Baltimore. In a field where experience is as important as technology, Escorts Heart Institute and Research Centre in Delhi and Faridabad, India, performs nearly 15,000 heart operations every year, and the death rate among patients during surgery is only 0.8 per cent—less than half that of most major hospitals in the United States.

In some countries, clinics are backed by sophisticated research infrastructures as well. India is among the world's leading countries for biotechnology research, while both India and South Korea are pushing ahead with stem cell research at a level approached only in Britain. In many foreign clinics, too, the doctors are supported by more registered nurses per patient than in any Western facility, and some clinics provide single-patient rooms that resemble guestrooms in four-star hotels, with a nurse dedicated to each patient 24 hours a day.

Add to this the fact that some clinics assign patients a personal assistant for the post hospital recovery period and throw in a vacation incentive as well, and the deal gets even more attractive. Additionally, many Asian airlines offer frequent-flyer miles to ease the cost of returning for follow-up visits.

Ten years ago, medical tourism was hardly large enough to be noticed. Today, more than 250,000 patients per year visit Singapore alone—nearly half of them from the Middle East. This year, approximately half a million foreign patients will travel to India for medical care, whereas in 2002, the number was only 150,000.

In monetary terms, experts estimate that medical tourism could bring India as much as $2.2 billion per year by 2012. Argentina, Costa Rica, Cuba, Jamaica, South Africa, Jordan, Malaysia, Hungary, Latvia and Estonia all have broken into this lucrative market as well, or are trying to do so, and more countries join the list every year.

Some important trends guarantee that the market for medical tourism will continue to expand in the years ahead. By 2015, the health of the vast Baby Boom generation will have begun its slow, final decline, and, with more than 220 million Boomers in the United States, Canada, Europe, Australia and New Zealand, this represents a significant market for inexpensive, high-quality medical care.

Medical tourism will be particularly attractive in the United States, where an estimated 43 million people are without health insurance and 120 million without dental coverage—numbers that are both likely to grow. Patients in Britain, Canada and other countries with long waiting lists for major surgery will be just as eager to take advantage of foreign health care options.

Major centres for medical tourism are Bangkok and Phuket, with six medical facilities in Bangkok boasting hospital accreditation from the United States.

As in most tourist-oriented medical communities, the major attractions are cosmetic surgery and dental treatments. However, eye surgery, kidney dialysis and organ transplantation also are among the most common procedures sought by medical vacationers in Thailand.

For a few patients, Phuket has another attraction as well: Bangkok Phuket Hospital is the premier place to go for sex-change surgery. In fact, that is one of the top 10 procedures for which patients visit Thailand.

India is a relative newcomer to medical tourism, but is quickly catching up with Thailand, and recent estimates indicate that the number of foreign patients is growing there by 30 per cent each year.

India has top-notch centres for open-heart surgery, pediatric heart surgery, hip and knee replacement, cosmetic surgery, dentistry, bone marrow transplants and cancer therapy, and virtually all of India's clinics are equipped with the latest electronic and medical diagnostic equipment.

Unlike many of its competitors in medical tourism, India also has the technological sophistication and infrastructure to maintain its market niche, and Indian pharmaceuticals meet the stringent requirements of the U.S. Food and Drug Administration. Additionally, India's quality of care is up to American standards, and some Indian medical centres even provide services that are uncommon elsewhere. For example, hip surgery patients in India can opt for a hip-resurfacing procedure, in which damaged bone is scrapped away and replaced with chrome alloy—an operation that costs less and causes less post-operative trauma than the traditional replacement procedure performed in the U.S.

For North American patients, Costa Rica is the chosen destination for inexpensive, high-quality medical care without a trans-Pacific flight, and it is the particular mecca for westerners seeking plastic surgery.

South Africa also draws many cosmetic surgery patients, especially from Europe, and many South African clinics offer packages that include personal assistants, visits with trained therapists, trips to top beauty saloons, post-operative care in luxury hotels and safaris or other vacation incentives. Because the South African rand has such a long-standing low rate on the foreign-exchange market, medical tourism packages there tend to be perpetual bargains as well.

Additionally, Argentina ranks high for plastic surgery, and Hungary draws large numbers of patients from Western Europe and the U.S. for high-quality cosmetic and dental procedures that cost half of what they would in Germany and America.

Lastly, Dubai—a destination already known as a luxury vacation paradise—is scheduled to open the Dubai Healthcare City by 2010. Situated on the Red Sea, this clinic will be the largest international medical centre between Europe and Southeast Asia. Slated to include a new branch of the Harvard Medical School, it also may be the most prestigious foreign clinic on the horizon.

One of the shared priorities among the provincial/territorial and federal governments is the "wait time guarantee". The proposed guarantee is a way to assure patients waiting for treatment that they will receive it within clinically acceptable wait times. The guarantee will inform patients how soon they can expect to receive care and what to do if the wait becomes excessive. The Hon. Tony Clement, Federal Minister of Health, says that Ministers of Health have already agreed on an initial set often common benchmarks for medical treatment and screening services in key care areas such as cancer, cardiac care, orthopedic areas and vision treatment—namely cataracts. Funding to ensure that action is taken is included in the 41 billion dollars over ten years agreed to in the 2004 health accord. Clement sums up the guarantee by saying that there will be a guarantee in place "in each and every province and territory [and that it] will mean that a patient in Prince Edward Island will get the same health service as a patient anywhere else in Canada in a timely manner even if it means sending that patient to another province" (Clement, August 16, 2006 and August 17, 2006).

Proposed wait time guarantees do not take into account sending patients to other countries for services that they cannot get at home in a timely fashion. As well, the proposed guarantees speak to only "medically necessary" services that are publicly funded. However, there are some patients who have taken matters into their own hands and travel abroad (usually offshore) to receive treatment. Some go abroad for elective procedures while some choose to do so for treatment that they have to wait too long for at home. Ease of international travel, costs of healthcare, wait times, globalization and rapidly expanding technology and improving standards of care in many countries around the world have led to an increasingly lucrative industry called medical tourism.

According to the Wikipedia online encyclopedia, medical tourism is "the act of travelling to other countries to obtain medical, dental and surgical care". Medical tourists are generally residents of industrialized countries (like Canada, Britain and the US) who travel to less developed ones where the currency exchange ratios are favourable. In the past, the most typical medical tourist was one who was looking for an elective procedure such as cosmetic surgery at a cost that was lower than they would have to pay at home. While the reasons patients had for travelling for treatment varied, many from the United States sought treatment abroad for the significantly lower costs. Today, medical tourists from Canada are often people who are frustrated with long waiting times. Patients from Britain are often those who cannot wait for treatment from the public health system but also cannot afford to see a physician in private practice (CBC News Indepth, 2004).

There are a number of developing countries that actively promote medical tourism and among them, India is considered a leader. Its National Health Policy states that the treatment of foreign patients is legally an export and is deemed to be eligible for all fiscal incentives extended to export earnings. India is moving into a system of "medical outsourcing" where hospitals and clinics subcontract to western countries to provide services dedicated to relieving their overburdened health systems. An example is the largest of about half a dozen medical corporations serving medical tourists in India is the Apollo Hospital. Its aggressive move into medical outsourcing has provided overnight computer services for US insurance companies and hospitals as well as working with pharmaceutical companies with drug trials. In 2004, it began working with Britain to work as a subcontractor to do surgery and tests for patients at a fraction of the cost for both the public and private systems. In the case of Apollo, the first patients were Indian expatriates who returned home for treatment. Patients from Europe, the Middle East and Canada followed. Apollo now has 37 hospitals in India and is in partnership in hospitals in Kuwait, Sri Lanka and Nigeria. Western patients frequently get a package deal that includes flights, transfers, hotels, treatment and a post-operative vacation (CBC Indepth News, 2004).

In the past, horror stories of botched surgeries in other countries coloured the idea that high quality care could be received offshore and patients still need to weigh the risks against saving money and reducing wait time for treatment. However, according to an American futurist Marvin Cetron, many of the hospitals and clinics catering to western patients are the best in the world and are staffed by physicians trained at major medical centres in the US and Europe. Physicians are supported by more registered nurses per patient than in any western facility and some of these hospitals or clinics provide single patient rooms that resemble accommodations in four-star hotels with a nurse dedicated to treat patient 24 hours a day (Cetron, 2006).

Medical tourism may never become a component of wait time guarantees in Canada. However, there are already patients who have chosen to go abroad for care that they could not get in a timely fashion at home. In 2004, CBC reported that there were about 45 patients in Alberta who had used this means of getting "medically necessary" treatment abroad with reimbursement for the treatment costs from the provincial medicare system. However as medical tourism gains momentum, patients need to do a considerable amount of research as well as discussion with their personal physician before a decision is made to take this route to care. Quality of care can be variable abroad and while there is value in the accreditation from source country regulators accreditation from international bodies should be checked. Lists of accredited international providers are maintained by both the Joint Commission International www.jointcommissioninternational.com and the British Standards Institute www.bsi-global.com (Carrera, 2006).

Future Prospects of Global Medical Tourism

Tourism Minister of India, Ambika Soni said that medical tourism, has a potential of growing by a whopping 25 per cent annually to fetch India Rs.100 billion ($2.15 billion) a year by 2012.

"The sector has a huge potential and looking at the response from foreign patients, we estimate that the country may fetch Rs.100 billion annually by 2012," said Soni while releasing the "Incredible India: The Global Healthcare Destination" brochure.

"We have just drawn up a year-long campaign to promote a holistic picture of India. In the medical tourism front all the wings including the Indian form of medicine and naturopathy will be promoted in a strategic way."

"In order to promote Brand India, we are partnering in the International Tourism in Berlin 2007, the leading tourism trade fair", the minister said at a meet organized by the Confederation of Indian Industry (CII).

Health Minister Anbumani Ramadoss said the government was considering a bill that to provide for accreditation of all hospitals down to the district level.

"Besides, we are working on a quality control body, like the Joint Commission International of the US, to provide quality hospitals to every one," the minister said.

He said only two to three per cent Indians have any form of health insurance. "We hope there will be a massive surge in medical insurance in the next five years," he said.

Ramadoss said "the government had launched a Rs.1.25 billion project for scientific validation of traditional healthcare systems of ayurveda, homoeopathy, unani and siddha.

The aim is to integrate these systems with the allopathic systems of medicine and thereby increase their acceptance."

The chairman of CII's National Committee on Healthcare, Naresh Trehan, said India was being recognized as a quality destination for medical value travel.

"There are 50 million people in the US without medical insurance and for them domestic treatment costs are prohibitive. Their treatment in India is now facilitated by tie-ups between the insurance companies in the US and private Indian hospital chains", said the leading cardiologist.

US MEDICAL TOURISM

While medical tourism is certainly not a new phenomenon, the L.A. Times reports that some companies outside the U.S. have begun marketing it more aggressively. It certainly is an attractive option for Americans facing healthcare costs which are spiralling out of control. One patient featured in the article needed surgery to correct a painful herniated disc in her lower back—a procedure which would cost $30,000 in the U.S., but only $3500 in Thailand. She was able to bring her sister with her to enjoy a little vacation for $6,400, about 1/5 of the cost of having the surgery here in the U.S.

Of course, there are risks involved in getting medical and dental procedures performed overseas. There are excellent and highly qualified doctors, surgeons, and dentists all over the world, but other countries may not regulate professional licensing and continuing education as heavily as we do here in the U.S., so finding the right provider can be hit or miss. This article includes some helpful advice on things to avoid (e.g. do not hit the beach right after you get a face lift), and also directs you to the Joint Commission on the Accreditation of Healthcare Organizations International Accreditations website. The Joint Commission accredits U.S. hospitals, and in 1997 began to also accredit international hospitals that meet their quality standards.

SOUTH-EAST ASIAN SCENARIO MEDICAL TOURISM

Propelled by health conscious people and escalating medical costs the West is looking towards East for medical support. South-east countries with their indigenous advantages of supreme medical treatment with low cost production and skilled workforce have emerged as the hot seats for medical tourism of the world, according to a study analysis on "The Healthcare Scenario of the South-east Asia", released by Imprimis Life, a leading life sciences specialist.

While a heart surgery costs $30,000 in the US, it costs $6,000 in Southeast Asia. Similarly, a bone marrow transplant costs $26,000 here compared to $250,000 in the US, this disparity in cost difference has leveraged South-east Asia as a competitive strength to promote medical tourism.

India as a healthcare hub is growing 30 per cent annually and has a potential to attract over a million tourists per annum, augmenting its economic growth. India is also fast moving towards adopting international standards like accreditation of hospitals, providing the state-of-art healthcare facilities at far lesser prices compared to its western counterparts, the report says.

Aman Gupta, CEO, Imprimis Life Pvt. Ltd said, "With global revenues of an estimated $2.8 trillion, the healthcare industry is the world's largest industry. The Indian healthcare industry has the potential to show the same exponential growth that the software and pharmaceutical industries have shown in the past decade."

The research is a comparative analysis of the five South-east Asian countries namely India, Malaysia, Singapore, Indonesia and Thailand. The study gives a comprehensive break up of the market scenario of the five potential nations, individually highlighting their strengths and weakness.

CASE STUDY OF PHUKET—THAILAND

Fly to Phuket, Thailand and have the very best private medical care in:

- Annual check-ups at our health centre
- Dental treatment by dentists
- MRI scanning and other imaging diagnostic
- Dialysis treatment at our dialysis centre
- Rejuvenation treatments without surgery
- Surgery. at our aesthetic centre

  - *Plastic Surgery Procedures*

    Abdominoplasty, Blepharoplasty—Eyelid Surgery, Brachioplasty, Breast Enlargement (Augmentation Mammoplasty), Breast Lift, Breast Reduction, Dermabrasion, Face-Lift, Forehead Lift, Liposuction, Mid-Face Lift, Neck Lift, Otoplasty—Surgery of the Ear, Plastic Surgery for Men, Rhinoplasty—Nose Surgery

  - *Sex reassignment*
  - *Hip or knee replacements*

Combine health and holiday aspects of travel and enjoy great savings in time and money. The health and holiday package from one of our partners could include pre-arrangement for your entire trip, all transfers, personal airport pick-up, hotel accommodation, pre-doctor appointment, quotation for healthcare treatment, optional sightseeing city/island tours and night entertainment attraction bookings.

Phuket, in Southern Thailand, is world famous as the tourist destination. Its natural beauty and variety of holiday facilities attract millions of visitors each year. Its glorious beaches, tropical climate, delicious cuisine and friendly people are an unforgettable experience for all who visit her welcoming shores. But Phuket is much more than just a holiday island. It is a centre of international commerce, a hub for the development of the entire Andaman region as well as a centre of higher education and fast becoming a medical holiday destination.

The Bangkok Hospital, Phuket has been meeting the medical

needs of international clients for more than ten years, with English-speaking, UK and America-trained health professionals on staff. Bangkok Hospital Phuket is a member of the first and largest integrated hospital group in South-East Asia—the Bangkok Hospital Group—where medical care and patient comfort are second to none. Today, with world-class facilities, patients from all around the world come to Bangkok Hospital in Phuket for treatments.

Post Operative Care in Phuket

Directly after an operation you will in stay in a private hospital room for one or several nights depending on your operation. After that you will move to a hotel or resort.

Our Agents in Other Countries

If you want to book a package including airfare and accommodation please contact our agents.

Australia: All about beauty, Gorgeous Getaways, Noosa Travel
Holland : Be-Nice
Thailand : Health Vision Asia
Sweden : RelaxU
Norway : Phuket Ferie

MEDICAL TOURISM FOR HIV/AIDS CARE: A CASE STUDY OF NORTHERN THAI COMMUNITIES

Obstacles to effective healthcare access have opened therapeutic markets to itinerant healthcare seekers, or medical tourists, who may travel long distances for effective and anonymous HIV/AIDS care. This ethnographic research examined social and economic contexts of healthcare-seeking behaviour and reported reasons for care-seeking travel by low-income medical tourists in two Northern Thai communities. Methods: Case studies were conducted comparing two districts in Chiang Kai province, one highly touristed, using 10 months of participant observation and multiple in-depth interviews with 12 itinerant HIV treatment seekers, who were contacted through district hospital-based HIV support groups. Results: Medical tourists reported seeking access to efficacious HIV treatment in combination with other needs, including spiritual support, anonymous services, supportive advice, respite from stigma, and hope for longevity. Within the touristed district, over 50 private sector venues for HIV/AIDS treatment attracted incoming medical tourists while competing with community-based HIV/AIDS treatment and support programmes. Medical tourists residing in the touristed district reported greater dissatisfaction with their governmental AIDS care programmes. They described more detailed fantasies of AIDS cures, with less skepticism, than those in the community with more support services. Conclusions: Even in low-income communities, medical tourism can emerge from areas with poor access to effective community-based HIV/AIDS care.

MALAYSIAN APPROACH TOWARDS HEALTH TOURISM

The idea of Health Tourism was first mooted in 1997 when the government realized how important health is to a budding nation. Therefore, it has embarked on a programme that combines activities relating to healthcare and tourism.

Such activities involved trekking, cycling, jogging and swimming complemented with medical services treatment, which also includes massages, spa and sauna.

Three organizations undertook this task and formed a committee; the Ministry of Health, the Malaysia External Trade Development Corporation (Matrade), and Tourism Malaysia. The efforts combined, escalate the programme to the international level.

For the last few years, the committee had gone for successful trade missions to countries such as the Middle East, Bahrain, United Arab Emirates, Saudi Arabia, Myanmar and Vietnam.

Matrade has also organized Specialized Healthcare Missions to various countries, which include Cambodia and Brunei.

MEDICAL TOURISM IN CAPE TOWN, SOUTH AFRICA

The medical tourism business in Cape Town is booming—fuelled by the rand exchange rates clients get unrivalled value for your money: instead of cut-rate procedures that compromise on quality and standards, they are sure of state-of-the-art facilities and world-renowned medical practitioners.

This has led to the city's first one-stop gateway for potential international patients. Mediscapes (http://www.mediscapes.com) has brought under one roof the full spectrum of top medical specialists, post-operative treatments, luxury accommodation and tours to other parts of South Africa.

Mediscapes's managing director Peter Ordway says, "Each client's needs are different, so we adopt a completely personalized approach. We work extremely closely with each individual client, providing tailor-made packages to address their unique needs, and at the same time, we guarantee their personal safety and privacy.

A simple facelift in South Africa costs about R20,000 whereas in England or the US the same procedure will set a client back upwards of R80,000. As a result when patients are in town for one medical procedure they often just go ahead and get plastic surgery done, while no one back home is the wiser.

What Mediscapes is successfully doing is offering a combined package of carefully selected top medical professionals for any medical request and combining it with visits to world-class tourists attractions. Mediscapes handles the entire package for a client or patient—from finding the best medical care available, to making doctor's, hospital ward and theatre bookings, as well as handling transport, hotel and travel itineraries.

HEALTH FACILITIES AND ALTERNATIVE HEALTHCARE IN BARBADOS

The very first tourists that came to Barbados were enticed here because of the clean air, sunshine, and a spirit of vitality. The East coast with its rugged landscape, strong winds and pounding seas became the retreat of choice for the wealthy European and American visitors and a number of health services and retreats grew up to cater to this clientele.

Over the years the tourism industry has widened and diversified, but Barbados has continued to attract the health conscious because of its well-known healing qualities. It remains a haven for those needing to get away and relax, those who seek a more spiritual experience and those looking for alternatives to traditional medicine.

Barbados is known as one of the healthiest places in the world. Indeed, George Washington chronicled a trip here in 1751 to aid his half-brother in his fight against a severe lung infection.

Barbados has a high standard of healthcare which is easily accessible to all. The main Government hospital—the Queen Elizabeth Hospital—has 600 beds and offers specialized care in areas such as pediatrics, obstetrics, plastic surgery, radiology, etc.

There are also 8 government Polyclinics providing free medical treatment for minor ailments, 5 Geriatric hospitals for care of the elderly, and a network of Child Care facilities.

Visitors prescriptions may be filled at local pharmacies. However visitors should consult with a local physician first. A list of pharmacies and medical practitioners may be found in the Barbados Yellow Pages (a copy of which is in most hotel rooms).

Vaccinations are not required for entry into Barbados.

Exception: Yellow Fever vaccination certificate is required from travellers over one year of age, coming from infected areas.

Alternative Health and Medicine Areas:

- Chiropractic
- Osteopath
- Acupuncture
- Massage
- Spiritual Retreats
- Self Improvement
- Reiki
- Reflexology

MEDICAL TOURISM: HIDDEN DIMENSIONS

Wayne Steinard, on the wrong side of the 50s, was leading a normal citizen's life in Florida as a building contractor specializing in poor peoples' homes, when discovery of a heart ailment brought dark clouds over his future. Medical tests alone, he found to his horror, would cost as much as US $10,000 which is all he could have raised from his own resources. Where would the funds for the expensive surgery come from? Steinard is among the large number of citizens of the world's only super power (some estimates put the figure at 45 million) who have either no medical insurance cover or are under-insured. Along with prayers he took refuge in the internet which is where he found relief.

India, he was told was one country where he could get the right treatment at the right cost even without an insurance cover.

But, then all he knew of India was what he learnt at school half a century ago, that although it was a great country with a glorious past, it was ridden with poverty. Two things helped him get over his misgivings—the presence of a very large number of Indian doctors in America (and even in his own Florida), and, a chance encounter on the internet with a Tom Borta, who had a rewarding experience of treatment in India. What made him take a final decision in favour of India was in contact with Planet Hospital, an America-based agency that connects patients with low cost medical facilities around the world including India.

To cut Steinard's long story short, Planet Hospital organized a teleconference between him, his local doctor, and Max Devki Devi Heart and Vascular Institute in South Delhi. Accompanied by his daughter, Beth Keigans (who works for Walmart), he flew into the Indian capital and underwent a triple bypass under the care of Dr Anil Bhan, chief cardio thorasic surgeon at Max. A beaming Steinard told this writer as he was being discharged from Max Hospital on May 25, that in India he had found an answer to his prayer to God (and internet he added with a smile). "I still cannot believe", he said, "that expenses on the surgery, other hospital charges, airfares and hotel stay do not add up to US $10,000." He was very touched by the personalized attention he received from doctors and nurses, something unknown in his own country. Steinard had a special word for Planet Hospital whose executives stayed 'connected' throughout with the cell phones provided to both father and daughter and said they were impressed with the meeting arrangements at the airport, transfers to hotel and hospital. Asked if he would visit the Taj Mahal, Steinard shot back, "You bet we will. Right tomorrow. Vipul Jain (head of Planet Hospital in India) has already organized that."

Surprisingly the Wayne Steinard story has yet to find space in the Indian media, TIME magazine has covered it in its latest Asia Pacific issue.

The genesis of Planet Hospital is an interesting development in itself. Three young entrepreneurs in America — an Indian (Vipul Jain), a Canadian (Rudy Rupak) and an American (Valarie Capleito) had been planning to set up a business together. On a visit to Bangkok, Valarie Capleito had to be hospitalized. Sensing the quality of treatment in the so-called "developing nations", the low cost and no wait-list, the trio saw immense potential for an outfit that could "help patients find the best and least expensive medicare." Planet Hospital was thus incorporated at Los Angeles just three years ago. According to Jain, it has already emerged as the largest agency in the field with marketing offices apart from India, in the United States, UK, France, Australia and New Zealand with access to treatment in India, Thailand, Belgium, Costa Rica, Brazil, Mexico and Argentina. The Indian tie-ups include Apollo, Wockhardt, Hiranandani and Max. Starting with small numbers, Jain said, the Indian arm is handling a patient a day from abroad. The Indian chief of Planet Hospital pointed out that it is not only the cost factor or the on-demand availability that will attract patients to India. It is also the fact that India offers certain surgeries and orthopedic procedures which are not available in advanced countries like America, and that makes India a preferred destination. He gave the example of hip-resurfacing which is not on offer in the USA but available in India.

Jain estimated that last year as many as 200,000 patients came to India. But this figure should be viewed in comparison with Bangkok where one hospital alone took care of 150,000 treatment seekers from abroad. Airfares to India are higher than, say, Thailand, hotels more expensive and visas not hassle-free.

A SERVICE INDUSTRY PERSPECTIVE ON MEDICAL TOURISM

History shows that tourism is one sector in which the wealthy really are early adopters and innovators. In the middle of the nineteenth century, the growth of national railroad and telegraph systems, rise of steamship travel, the invention of the funicular (which made it possible to develop mountain resorts), and the growth of travel services, combined to make recreational travel— and destinations that previously had been reserved for those wealthy enough to be able to spend several months a year on leisurely trips— accessible to the middle classes and labourers. When this happened, rich travellers moved on, to the Alps or the south of France, the Rockies (the town of Aspen was developed by rich Chicago advertising executives), Hawaii, etc.

Now, the latest high-end tourist innovation is going mass-market. As Firedoglake reports:

> Carl Garrett, a paper mill technician in Canton, N.C., needed gall bladder and shoulder surgery. So his employer, Blue Ridge Paper Products, came up with an increasingly less- than-novel solution: Send him overseas for surgery.

India, in this case.

In this case, the choice was employer-driven, thought Garrett was offered a cut of the savings. It is not clear how many examples like this there are, but it is a good bet that they'll become more common. The medical tourism industry is growing rapidly, and is configuring itself to project a high-tech, professional image reassuring to Western patients and employers (even if its Web page design sometimes remains wonderfully exuberant). Some marketers have already started appealing to small business owners and self-employed professionals, who are not just in the market for plastic surgery or other elective work, but are in the market for more basic services:

> In the past several years, trip organizers say, more patients have been pursuing not just elective and cosmetic surgeries, but also medically necessary procedures, including hip and knee replacements, angioplasty and hysterectomies.

UNDERSTANDING THE DARKER SIDE OF MEDICAL TOURISM

The phenomenon of medical tourism—of patients travelling abroad for surgery or other medical procedures—has received a certain amount of attention recently. Most of the stories chronicle how both patients and practitioners are taking advantage of global differences in labour costs: one Thai plastic surgeon returned his home country after decades of practising in northern California, opened a clinic near a resort—and sees some of the same patients he had in Marin County.

But there's a dark side to medical tourism, captured in the title of this recent *Guardian* article:

> *UK Transplant Patients go to China for Organs from Executed Prisoners.*

The British Transplantation Society said that "an accumulating body of evidence suggests that the organs of executed prisoners are being removed for transplantation without the prior consent of either the prisoner or their family."

Thousands of organs are thought to be involved in the lucrative trade, it said. Transplant centres, patients, and the Chinese authorities and judiciary could all be implicated in a breach of human rights...

Evidence from doctors who have left China suggests that many patients are travelling for kidney or liver transplants, perhaps in desperation because of the shortages of donor organs in their own country. Most patients came from Japan and Korea and there were quite a few reports of Chinese Americans returning to China for their operation, he said.

Websites of Chinese transplant centres openly tout in English for business from foreigners. Although they do not suggest the organs come from executed prisoners, they offer a fast supply—between a week and a maximum of a month for a kidney transplant. One website declares: "Viscera providers can be found immediately!"

There's something lost in any translation that comes out "viscera providers".

3

Impacts of Tourism and Recreation: A Policy Perspective

INTRODUCTION TO TOURISM AND RECREATION

At both global and national scales, tourism is the fastest-growing economic sector today. Here are some basic facts about the tourism industry to highlight its importance and impacts:

- In 1998, it accounted for over 10 per cent of the world GNP and directly or indirectly for 200 million jobs worldwide.
- In 2000, 700 million people visited a foreign country—62 per cent of them for leisure? Accounting for US$ 478 billion of international receipts/revenues.
- Tourism is one of the five top export categories for 83 per cent of countries, and the main one for 38 per cent of them.
- Tourism employs 3 per cent of the total global workforce (8% if indirect/informal jobs are included, or one in every 12 workers).
- In France, the world's number one tourism destination, tourism accounts for over 7 per cent of GDP.

For many coastal, tropical, developing countries, tourism plays an important role in the economy often representing the major source of employment, foreign exchange earnings, and national government revenue. The World Tourism Organization has estimated that tourism receipts account for some 25 per cent of total export earnings in the Pacific and over 35 per cent for Caribbean islands. However, much of the income generated by tourism does leak back to developed countries (30-50 per cent in the Caribbean), mostly to foreign air carriers, hotel owners and suppliers of imported food and beverages. Tourism is mainly a natural resource based industry and, as such, affects air, land and water and can damage natural systems if its planning, development and operation are not properly managed. On the other hand, if developed sustainably, tourism can be a positive force for conservation and environmental protection.

IMPACTS OF TOURISM

As one of the world's largest industries and one of its fastest growing economic sectors, tourism has a multitude of impacts, both positive and negative, on people's lives and on the environment. The quality of the environment, both natural and man-made, is essential to tourism. However, tourism's relationship with the environment is complex. It involves many activities that can have adverse environmental effects. Negative impacts from tourism will arise when the level of visitor use is superior to the environment's ability to cope with this use.

Uncontrolled coastal tourism development poses potential threats to many natural areas around the world as it can put enormous pressure on a very narrow area. Many of these impacts are linked with the construction of general infrastructure such as roads and airports, and of tourism facilities, including resorts, hotels, restaurants, shops, golf courses and marinas. Such developments often lead to impacts such as soil erosion, increased pollution, waste discharges into the sea, natural habitat loss and associated loss in biodiversity and increased pressure on endangered species. This is particularly true for some of the world's most ecologically fragile areas such as wetlands, mangroves, coral reefs and sea grass beds. Furthermore, it often puts a strain on water resources, and it can force local populations to compete for the use of critical resources such as fish. By involving many activities that can have adverse environmental effects tourism has the potential to gradually destroy the environmental resources on which it depends. Usually these effects are dynamic and often interactive.

On the other hand, tourism has the potential to create beneficial effects on the environment by contributing to environmental protection and conservation. It is a way to raise awareness of environmental values and it can serve as a tool to finance protection of natural areas and increase their economic importance.

1. Impacts of Nature-Related Tourism

How can tourism develop in a sustainable fashion, while respecting local conditions and local communities? Produced through the co-operation of IUCN's World Commission on Protected Areas (WCPA), the United Nations Environment Programme (UNEP) and the World Tourism Organization (WTO) the new publication Sustainable Tourism in Protected Areas: Guidelines for Planning and Management aims to advise and guide protected area planners and managers, governments at all levels, local communities, tourism enterprises and organizations and tourists themselves.

Tourism has become a major sector of economic activity worldwide. A substantial portion of Gross Domestic Product (GDP) and employment, especially in developing countries, is related to tourism. International arrivals globally amounted to more than 700 million in 2001. Domestic tourism—the movement of nationals in their own country—is also displaying significant growth in countries experiencing increases in disposable incomes. All indications are that tourism will continue growing in the years to come: the WTO predicts that international travel will grow at 4.1 per cent annually until 2020, with the major source countries being in North America, Europe and East Asia.

With this growth, a diversification of tourism products and destinations is taking place, with increased demand for nature-related tourism. Tourists themselves are becoming increasingly sophisticated in their demands, seeking more than pure leisure and relaxation.

The expected growth and the new trends observed put tourism in a strategic position to make a positive contribution to the sustainability of protected areas management and the development of surrounding areas and their communities.

The Kakum Conservation Area Project in Ghana, supported technically and financially by Conservation International, an IUCN member, and by U.S. Agency for International Development was planned and implemented in the belief that ecotourism can be both an effective conservation tool and a successful community development model. Local people were helped to assist and manage their own ecotourism businesses, which created jobs that directly depend on a healthy environment, and motivated people to protect their surroundings. Tangible benefits to local people included purchase of agricultural products for the restaurant, purchase of furnishings, crafts and services from local artisans, provision of guide training to local teachers and creation of full-time, direct and indirect employment. Visitation to the site increased from 700 in 1990 to 80,000 in 1999 with little direct impact on the environment.

The protection of reef sharks in the Maldives is another illustration of how tourism can be a major tool for the conservation of protected areas. It also shows that tourism can raise the environmental awareness of residents and visitors. After a survey in 1992 estimated that dive operations focusing on reef sharks generated about 100 times more revenue than the shark fishery, objectives were set to protect important dive sites, conserve biodiversity and achieve the sustainable development of tourism by prohibiting certain damaging activities. Tourist divers were used as a resource to monitor and report on law breakers, deliberate or otherwise. This created awareness among locals of the importance of protecting the shark and its environment, and illegal mining and garbage dumping stopped in these areas.

The increasing pressure of tourism however poses a real threat to the deterioration of biodiversity found in protected areas. This was experienced by local communities in the Nepalese Himalaya. Tourism started to become a significant activity in Nepal in the 1950s, resulting in the construction of hotels and lodges for the growing numbers of visitors. One notable negative effect was the depletion of forests to meet the tourism industry's demand for firewood and timber, which left local people with a firewood crisis and resulted in increased erosion and landslides.

Nature-based tourism is not, by definition, sustainable. Hence, tourism operations within protected areas need to be carefully planned, managed and monitored in order to ensure their long-term sustainability.

2. Economic Impacts of Tourism

The tourism industry generates substantial economic benefits to both host countries and tourists' home countries. Especially in developing countries, one of the primary motivations for a region to promote itself as a tourism destination is the expected economic improvement.

As with other impacts, this massive economic development brings along both positive and negative consequences.

According to the World Tourism Organization, 698 million people travelled to a foreign country in 2000, spending more US$ 478 billion. International tourism receipts combined with passenger transport currently total more than US$ 575 billion—making tourism the world's number one export earner, ahead of automotive products, chemicals, petroleum and food.

3. Negative Economic Impacts of Tourism

There are many hidden costs to tourism, which can have unfavourable economic effects on the host community. Often rich countries are better able to profit from tourism than poor ones. Whereas the least developed countries have the most urgent need for income, employment and general rise of the standard of living by means of tourism, they are least able to realize these benefits. Among the reasons for this are large-scale transfer of tourism revenues out of the host country and exclusion of local businesses and products.

Leakage

The direct income for an area is the amount of tourist expenditure that remains locally after taxes, profits, and wages are paid outside the area and after imports are purchased; these subtracted amounts are called leakage. In most all-inclusive package tours, about 80 per cent of travellers' expenditures go to the airlines, hotels and other international companies (who often have their headquarters in the travellers' home countries), and not to local businesses or workers. In addition, significant amounts of income actually retained at destination level can leave again through leakage.

A study of tourism 'leakage' in Thailand estimated that 70 per cent of all money spent by tourists ended up leaving Thailand (via foreign-owned tour operators, airlines, hotels, imported drinks and food, etc.). Estimates for other Third World countries range from 80 per cent in the Caribbean to 40 per cent in India.

Of each US$ 100 spent on a vacation tour by a tourist from a developed country, only around US$ 5 actually stays in a developing-country destination's economy. The figure below shows how the leakage happens.

There are two main ways that leakage occurs:

(*a*) *Import Leakage*. This commonly occurs when tourists demand standards of equipment, food, and other products that the host country cannot supply. Especially in less-developed countries, food and drinks must often be imported, since local products are not up to the hotel's (i.e. tourist's) standards or the country simply does not have a supplying industry. Much of the income from tourism expenditures leaves the country again to pay for these imports.

The average import-related leakage for most developing countries today is between 40 per cent and 50 per cent of gross tourism earnings for small economies and between 10 per cent and 20 per cent for most advanced and diversified economies, according to UNCTAD.

Even in developed regions, local producers are often unable to supply the tourism industry appropriately even if goodwill is present: the 64-room hotel "Kaiser im Tirol" in Austria, an award-winning leader in sustainable practices, cannot find organic food suppliers in the local farming networks in the appropriate quantity, quality and reliability, as production cycles and processes are not compatible with its needs. (Source: Austian Preparatory Conference for the International Year of Ecotourism, September, 2001.)

(*b*) *Export Leakage*. Multinational corporations and large foreign businesses have a substantial share in the import leakage. Often, especially in poor developing destinations, they are the only ones that possess the necessary capital to invest in the construction of tourism infrastructure and facilities. As a consequence of this, an export leakage arises when overseas investors who finance the resorts and hotels take their profits back to their country of origin.

A 1996 UN report evaluating the contribution of tourism to national income, gross levels of incomes or gross foreign exchange, found that net earnings of tourism, after deductions were made for all necessary foreign exchange expenditures, were much more significant for the industry. This report found significant leakage associated with: (a) imports of materials and equipment for construction; (b) imports of consumer goods, particularly food and drinks; (c) repatriation of profits earned by foreign investors; (d) overseas promotional expenditures, and (e) amortization of external debt incurred in the development of hotels and resorts. The impact of the leakage varied greatly across countries, depending on the structure of the economy and the tourism industry. From the data presented in this study on the Caribbean, St. Lucia had a foreign exchange leakage rate of 56 per cent from its gross tourism receipts; Aruba had 41 per cent, Antigua and Barbuda 25 per cent and Jamaica 40 per cent. (*Source*: Caribbean Voice.)

4. Enclave Tourism

Local businesses often see their chances to earn income from tourists severely reduced by the creation of "all-inclusive" vacation packages. When tourists remain for their entire stay at the same cruise ship or resort, which provides everything they need and where they will make all their expenditures, not much opportunity is left for local people to profit from tourism.

The Organization of American States (OAS) carried out a survey of Jamaica's tourist industry that looked at the role of the all-inclusives compared to other types of accommodation. It found that 'All-inclusive hotels generate the largest amount of revenue but their impact on the economy is smaller per dollar of revenue than other accommodation subsectors.'

It also concluded that all-inclusives imported more, and employed fewer people per dollar of revenue than other hotels. This information confirms the concern of those who have argued that all-inclusives have a smaller trickle-down effect on local economies.

The cruise ship industry provides another example of economic enclave tourism. Non-river cruises carried some 8.7 million international passengers in 1999. On many ships, especially in the Caribbean (the world's most popular cruise destination with 44.5 per cent of cruise passengers), guests are encouraged to spend most of their time and money on board, and opportunities to spend in some ports are closely managed and restricted.

5. Other Negative Impacts

Infrastructure Cost

Tourism development can cost the local government and local taxpayers a great deal of money. Developers may want the government to improve the airport, roads and other infrastructure, and possibly to provide tax breaks and other financial advantages, which are costly activities for the government. Public resources spent on subsidized infrastructure or tax breaks may reduce government investment in other critical areas such as education and health.

Increase in Prices

Increasing demand for basic services and goods from tourists will often cause price hikes that negatively affect local residents whose income does not increase proportionately. A San Francisco State University study of Belize found that, as a consequence of tourism development, the prices for locals increased by 8 per cent.

Tourism development and the related rise in real estate demand may dramatically increase building costs and land values. Not only does this make it more difficult for local people, especially in developing countries, to meet their basic daily needs, it can also result in a dominance by outsiders in land markets and in-migration that erodes economic opportunities for the locals, eventually disempowering residents. In Costa Rica, close to 65 per cent of the hotels belong to foreigners. Long-term tourists living in second homes, and the so-called amenity migrants (wealthy or retired people and liberal professionals moving to attractive destinations in order to enjoy the atmosphere and peaceful rhythms of life) cause price hikes in their new homes if their numbers attain a certain critical mass.

Economic Dependence of the Local Community on Tourism

Diversification in an economy is a sign of health, however, if a country or region becomes dependent for its economic survival upon one industry, it can put major stress upon this industry as well as the people involved to perform well. Many countries, especially developing countries with little ability to explore other resources, have embraced tourism as a way to boost the economy.

In The Gambia, for instance, 30 per cent of the workforce depends directly or indirectly on tourism. In small island developing states, percentages can range from 83 per cent in the Maldives to 21 per cent in the Seychelles and 34 per cent in Jamaica, according to the WTO. Over-reliance on tourism, especially mass tourism, carries significant risks to tourism-dependent economies. Economic recession and the impacts of natural disasters such as tropical storms and cyclones as well as changing tourism patterns can have a devastating effect on the local tourism sector.

Malta has only 380,000 residents, but received 1.2 million tourists in 1999. As 25 per cent of GDP (and indirectly 40%), tourism generated more than $650 million in foreign exchange earnings. Malta's high *dependence on tourism and a limited number of export products makes its trade performance vulnerable to shifts in international demand.*

Seasonal Character of Jobs

The seasonal character of the tourism industry creates economic problems for destinations that are heavily dependent on it. Problems that seasonal workers face include job (and therefore income) insecurity, usually with no guarantee of employment from one season to the next, difficulties in getting training, employment-related medical benefits, and recognition of their experience, and unsatisfactory housing and working conditions.

6. Other Industry Impacts Affecting Tourism

Economic crises, like the Asian crisis that hit Thailand, Malaysia and Indonesia a few years ago, can be devastating to inbound tourism flows. The financial turmoil triggered a sharp fall in tourism flows to affected countries during 1997 and 1998. In the Philippines, the crisis and the temporary closure of Philippine Airlines affected inbound arrivals significantly as there was a decline of almost 3.3 per cent in 1998

How Tourism can Contribute to Economic Conservation

The main positive economic impacts of tourism relate to foreign exchange earnings, contributions to government revenues, and generation of employment and business opportunities. These are discussed briefly here; further information on economic contributions from tourism can be found at the World Travel and Tourism Council's home page.

Foreign Exchange Earnings

Tourism expenditures and the export and import of related goods and services generate income to the host economy and can stimulate the investment necessary to finance growth in other economic sectors. Some countries seek to accelerate this growth by requiring visitors to bring in a certain amount of foreign currency for each day of their stay and do not allow them to take it out of the country again at the end of the trip.

An important indicator of the role of international tourism is its generation of foreign exchange earnings. Tourism is one of the top five export categories for as many as 83 per cent of countries and is a main source of foreign exchange earnings for at least 38 per cent of countries.

Contribution to Government Revenues

Government revenues from the tourism sector can be categorized as direct and indirect contributions. *Direct* contributions are generated by taxes on incomes from tourism employment and tourism businesses, and by direct levies on tourists such as departure taxes. *Indirect* contributions are those originated from taxes and duties levied on goods and services supplied to tourists.

The United States National Park Service estimates that the 273 million visits to American national parks in 1993 generated direct and indirect expenditures of US$ 10 billion and 200,000 jobs. When visits to land managed by other agencies, and to state, local, and privately-managed parks, are added, parks were estimated to bring around US$ 22 billion annually to the US economy. These expenditures also generate significant tax revenues for the government.

The World Travel and Tourism Council estimates that travel and tourism's direct, indirect, and personal tax contribution worldwide was over US$ 800 billion in 1998—a figure it expects to double by 2010.

Employment Generation

The rapid expansion of international tourism has led to significant employment creation. For example, the hotel accommodation sector alone provided around 11.3 million jobs worldwide in 1995. Tourism can generate jobs directly through hotels, restaurants, nightclubs, taxis, and souvenir sales, and indirectly through the supply of goods and services needed by tourism-related businesses. According to the WTO, tourism supports some 7 per cent of the world's workers.

Stimulation of Infrastructure Investment

Tourism can induce the local government to make infrastructure improvements such as better water and sewage systems, roads, electricity, telephone and public transport networks, all of which can improve the quality of life for residents as well as facilitate tourism.

Contribution to Local Economies

Tourism can be a significant, even essential, part of the local economy. As the environment is a basic component of the tourism industry's assets, tourism revenues are often used to measure the economic value of protected areas. For example, Dorrigo National Park in New South Wales, Australia, has been estimated to contribute 7 per cent of gross regional output and 8.4 per cent of regional employment. The importance of tourism to local economies can also be illustrated by the impacts when it is disrupted: the catastrophic 1997 floods that closed Yosemite National Park in California cause locally severe economic losses to the areas around the park. In the most heavily impacted county, Mariposa County, 1997 personal income was reduced by an estimated US$1,159 per capita (US$18 million for the entire county)—a 6.6 per cent decline. The county was also estimated to have lost US$1.67 million in county occupancy and sales tax revenues, and 956 jobs, a significant number in a county of fewer than 16,000 residents.

There are other local revenues that are not easily quantified, as not all tourist expenditures are formally registered in the macro-economic statistics. Money is earned from tourism through informal employment such as street vendors, informal guides, rickshaw drivers, etc. The positive side of informal or unreported employment is that the money is returned to the local economy, and has a great multiplier effect as it is spent over and over again. The World Travel and Tourism Council estimates that tourism generates an indirect contribution equal to 100 per cent of direct tourism expenditures.

Visualizing Tourism as a Tool for Economic Development

Tourism is an attractive tool for economic development, specifically in the developing world. Viewed as an export industry of three Gs—"get them in, get their money, and get them out—tourism has assisted many developing countries to move away from a dependency on agriculture and manufacturing (Tooman, 1997).

Chosen for its ability to bring in needed foreign exchange earnings, income and employment, tourism has become a popular addition to economic development policies in many African, Asian, South and Central American countries. Although tourism seems to be adding substantially to the economic growth of many of these regions, many developing countries are not reaping full benefits from tourism. Pleumarom (1999) writes that more than two-thirds of the revenue from international tourism never reaches the local economy because of high foreign exchange leakage. Understanding the many ways that tourism profits can leak out of an economy, and devising strategies to minimize leakage could make tourism a more effective economic development agent. The purpose of this topic is two-fold: to describe the nature and sources of leakage of foreign exchange earnings from tourism, and to suggest strategies to maximize the economic benefits of tourism in developing countries.

Tourism has become an important source of income for most of the countries of the world. Worldwide, international tourist arrivals in 1999 are estimated at approximately 700 million, resulting in over $500 billion in tourist receipts (Edgell, 1999), and tourism generates nearly 250 million jobs worldwide (WTO, 1999). The increasing fascination with tourism has been motivated in large part due to its potential economic benefits for destination areas. Early literature in tourism development emphasized the role of tourism in economic development, particularly for developing countries (Erbes, 1973).

However, in the past two decades increased attention to the negative social, cultural and environmental impacts of tourism has also emerged, calling for more careful planning and management of tourism development (WTO, 1996; Mathieson and Wall, 1982, Wahab, 1997). As discussion of responsible tourism growth is still in its infancy, the dilemma for many countries is devising a way to develop a sustainable tourism industry—one that maintains economic benefits and limits associated negative impacts. In other words, how can countries develop a tourism industry which provides the much needed economic benefits such as foreign exchange, employment and income while protecting the human and natural resources it is built upon?

Again, emphasis in tourism literature suggests that avenues to achieve this goal lie in minimizing negative impacts by strategies such as environmental and social impact analysis, community control, and segmenting markets (Harrison and Husbands, 1996, Cater, 1993). While a shift has occurred among researchers to try and devise ways to minimize the "ills" associated to tourism, little attention has been paid to retaining the positive contributions it can make to developing countries. If the ultimate goal of sustainable tourism development is to balance the scales, or maximize positive impacts and mitigate the negative, increased attention must be devoted to preventing positive economic benefits from leaking out of developing countries.

The potential economic benefits of tourism are a major attraction for developing countries due to three pro-tourism arguments (Mill and Morrison, 1999). First, the trend in demand for international travel is projected to continue at astonishing rates due to the economic stability and travel preferences of people in the developed regions such as Europe, Asia and North America. Second, the income elasticity of demand for tourism means that as the household incomes of people in the developed world increase, more disposable income will be directed towards travel. And thirdly, developing countries are in need of foreign exchange earnings to support their economic development initiatives and to satisfy the demands of their own residents.

Due to these pro-tourism arguments, many developing countries are choosing, or being encouraged to develop tourism over some of the more traditional industry alternatives such as agriculture and manufacturing. Although between 50 -70 per cent of people in developing countries are directly dependent on agriculture, reliance on the industry can result in numerous problems (World Bank, 1979). One of the primary problems with agriculture is that countries can be overly dependent upon a few specific crops or products (Mill and Morrison, 1999). In the competitive global market, where externalities are uncontrollable and price unpredictable, countries dependent on agriculture have an unreliable and inconsistent source of revenue. In these cases, tourism may play a role in diversifying the economy and complementing the income brought in through agriculture. For example, after introducing tourism into the Caribbean island economies, the $9 billion tourism sector brought in six times the revenue of all traditional agricultural exports (Simon, 1995).

Other developing countries have sought manufacturing as an economic development policy option. As with agriculture, there are inherent problems when relying upon manufacturing. In order to manufacture something, a country must have easy access to a source of raw materials for production. "Thus, manufacturing is more successful in nations that are richly endowed with natural resources. Many developing countries are also plagued with chronic shortages of skilled labour, one of the necessary inputs for a strong manufacturing base. And, even when these problems are nonexistent, export oriented industries still face full international competition in selling their products (Mill and Morrison, 1999).

Tourism, like manufacturing, requires similar access to land, labour and capital resources. Yet, tourism, in the way that the product is produced and delivered, may be a more viable alternative for developing countries. Most countries have the basic raw materials required to establish a tourism industry. Whether using its heritage, architecture, landscape, water or people, the mix of natural and cultural resources is what makes a destination unique and marketable to visitors. As international policy agreements on trade of services advances, there are fewer restrictions on international travel than trade (Edgell, 1999). Demand for tourism is expected to remain strong into the new millennium and with advances in technology reducing the time required to travel, the distance between the consumer and the tourism product is becoming negligible. Finally, unlike other industries, tourism prices are more under the control of the seller than the buyer. These traits combined, tourism is seen as an attractive economic development option for many countries in the developing world. But, as the OECD cautions, "there are few if any developing countries which could, or perhaps even should, rely principally on tourism for their economic salvation" (Erbes, 1973).

Assessing whether tourism is a good choice for economic development requires more than simply understanding its projected growth. A number of other reasons make tourism a suitable fit for developing countries. Tourism differs substantially from agriculture and manufacturing industries in that it produces an invisible export. As a service industry, the product is consumed in the destination that it is produced in. The transportation costs for the experience are borne by the consumer who must travel to the exporting country to obtain the product. This eliminates any freight costs associated to delivering tangible products overseas.

Tourism also allows countries more leverage in manipulating exchange rates to influence visitor expenditures on site. For example, destination areas can lower exchange rates to attract a greater number of visitors. More than other industry, tourism is multifaceted and either directly or indirectly affects other sectors of the economy. For example, the tourism product relies directly on, and produces economic benefits for, transportation, accommodations, food and beverage and entertainment sectors. Indirectly, other businesses that are involved in servicing the aforementioned sectors receive increased economic benefits as well.

It is not the intent of the author to advocate tourism as an economic development tool for all developing countries. The decision whether or not to enter into the tourism system in not one to be made lightly. The industry differs from agriculture and manufacturing in many ways including the organization, nature of the activity, required human, social, technical and natural capital, and resulting economic, social and environmental impacts. And, although scant evidence exists in the literature, the development of tourism differs from the developing and developed worlds (Liu, 1998). To put it most succinctly, Jenkins (1980:27) suggests that "tourism in developed countries can be regarded as mainly a social activity with economic consequences; in developing countries it is largely an economic activity with social consequences". Many of the suggestions in this study reflect the difference that tourism has from other industries, and from the developed world. Partly, the intent of this topic is to bring attention to these differences in order to suggest strategies which will work given the context and unique position of developing countries on the path to sustainable tourism development. The following section will turn attention to some of the not so attractive features of tourism, which need to be considered by those organizing tourism in developing countries.

International tourism is usually price-elastic and income elastic, meaning that it is sensitive to changes in price or income. Shifts in either can result in significant changes in travel patterns. This can be positive when the household incomes of visiting markets are stable, but can result in problems for destinations dependent on visitors who are experiencing an economic crisis. This effect was recently experienced in the Pacific Asian region where many countries who depended on Asian visitors experienced lower visitation levels due to the 1997 Asian economic crisis (WTO, 1999).

Perhaps more importantly, tourism is different from other industries in that it brings a number of other non-monetary benefits and costs (such as social, environmental and cultural) to destination areas. It is this feature of the tourism industry, which has forced destinations to consider a new, more balanced approach to tourism planning and policy in the 1990's. Sustainable tourism development, as promoted by the United Nations, should seek to reduce or control the negative environmental and social impacts resulting from tourism, while continuing to benefit local economies. A complex goal, sustainable tourism development is beyond the scope of this article. However, achieving sustainable tourism development requires additional costs for destination areas. Therefore every dollar that can be retained in the local economy will help to balance the impacts resulting from tourism.

Issues in Retaining Foreign Exchange Earnings

The positive economic impacts of tourism are commonly listed as increased foreign exchange earnings, increased income, and increased employment in destination areas (WTO, 1996; Mill and Morrison, 1999; Edged, 1999: Lundberg *al et.*, 1995). All three forms of economic impact are central to economic development. There has been a lot of attention on economic impacts of tourism in the literature (Loomis and Walsh, 1996; WTO, 1999), mostly focused however on methods to estimate income from tourism via economic impact assessments, or claims of direct and indirect employment generated by tourism. This has not been without good reason, as both of these methods produce convincing figures that are used to show the significance of tourism. In fact, public relations literature for tourism destinations are often laced with claims of the economic expenditures and jobs created by tourism. For example:

> "Tourism is one of the most promising aspects of Zimbabwe's economy, attracting thousands of visitors and earning millions of dollars. Over the past 10 years Zimbabwe's tourist sector has scored impressive annual growth rates of nearly 20 per cent. According to the Zimbabwe Tourism Authority (ZTA) total tourism receipts account for 4.6 per cent of the country's GDP. It is estimated that tourism employs close to 100,000 Zimbabweans, up from 40,500 in 1990. This growth in employment is impressive considering Zimbabwe's unemployment rate is more than 50 per cent of the potential workforce and that employment figures have remained static since 1990." *African Business, 1999*

These figures also convince local residents that tourism is benefiting the society economically. Yet, income and employment aside, one of the primary motives for choosing tourism to assist in economic development is to bring in much needed foreign currency to produce the investment necessary to finance growth in other economic sectors (Archer, 1995, Liu, 1998). Tourism, for example, has been one of the few growth industries in the Caribbean, and for many has become the main source of hard currency earnings, accounting for 50 to 70 per cent of the area's foreign exchange earnings (Shurland, 1998). Perhaps then, increased attempts need to be made to understand the significance of foreign exchange earnings in developing countries, specially how much is being generated, retained and used for the economic goals of the region.

Economic impacts from tourism typically report the amount of new income being received in a destination area, and then use a multiplier to account for the additional re-spending that result afterwards. There is a danger however, of overstating the foreign exchange earnings of tourism when leakage is not taken into consideration. Leakage refers to the amount of money that leaves an economy to import goods and services needed for tourism development. For example, materials imported from another country to build tourism infrastructure, people brought in to fill tourism positions, and supplies purchased elsewhere to cater to specific needs of tourists are all examples of leakage. This leakage must be subtracted from foreign exchange earnings to obtain a true estimate of the economic impacts associated to tourism.

Leakage results from at least six factors (Mill and Morrison, 1999). First, the costs of goods and services purchased to satisfy the needs of visitors. If, for example, visitors to a destination want to eat food that is not grown domestically, the destination must make arrangements and pay to bring in the food from places it can be obtained. If the destination is marketing itself on being able to deliver this aspect of the tourism experience, it must then satisfy the desires of the visitors it has attracted. A second form of leakage occurs when destinations must purchase materials and equipment from other countries to supply the needed infrastructure for tourism. Many developing countries do not produce for example, the materials or expertise required to build hotels, transportation and sewage facilities that are essential to support tourism. A third form of leakage is for payments to foreign factors of production. Here, any commissions, interest payments, rent or profits that are paid outside the country for tourism related products should be considered as leakage. Many foreign owned hotel chains and entertainment corporations for example, import everything from building materials, furnishings and labour to construct and operate in developing countries (Pleumarom, 1999). A fourth form of leakage to consider is the expenditure for promoting a destination abroad. For example, most countries operate a National Tourism Organization either inside or outside the destination. Costs involved in promoting the destination and attracting tourists must be deducted as leakage, which is not a common practice among countries economic impact assessments (Mill and Morrison, 1999). Transfer pricing is a fifth form of leakage. Here, profits and taxes accruing to a destination area are reduced when payments are made in the country of visitor origin rather than the destination. For example, many visitors purchase packages from tour operators who use foreign owned hotels, attractions and services in the destination area. These visitors, particularly when purchasing all-inclusive packages, leave very little new money in the destination area. Local banks can also miss out on the opportunity to generate income when visitors rely on the use of credit cards and traveller's cheques for purchases. Finally, a sixth form of leakage occurs when destination areas exempt foreign owned companies from paying duties or taxes as an incentive to attract investment. This is particularly common among developing countries in the early stages of tourism development when tourism infrastructure needs are high (Mill and Morrison, 1999).

Getting an estimate on the amount of and forms of leakage from tourism is a critical issue for developing countries. Unfortunately, many countries are under pressure to bring in foreign exchange earnings quickly to offset the initial costs involved in developing tourism infrastructure. As well, many do not have access to the materials or human resources needed to establish tourism, and therefore depend heavily on imported content. Some small island nations such as in the Caribbean have import content levels of over 50 per cent for tourism (Mill and Morrison, 1999; Archer *et al.*, 1995). Hastily, many of these developing countries see no other way to establish tourism than to import capital and labour, and attract foreign investment. The critical issue for developing countries then, is to devise strategies to minimize leakage.

Maximizing Economic Benefits from Tourism in Developing Countries

In short, the way that developing countries can maximize the economic benefits from tourism is to bring in more money from visitors and organize tourism to minimize leakage of both money and jobs. Although this sounds rather simple, the number and agenda's of various stakeholders involved in tourism development make it complex. This section will discuss some strategies to enhance the economic benefits to host countries.

Tourism in the developing world differs in the role that government and the private sector play in establishing policy and encouraging development. National policies on tourism in developing countries are usually the domain of the state, whereas in more developed countries, private entrepreneurs often dominate policy formation and enactment (Liu, 1998). In most developing countries, owing to the small size of the private sector and the shortage of funds, the government necessarily takes on the role of entrepreneur (Shurland, 1998). This is usually in response to proposed private foreign investment. The aims of the private sector often oppose those of the public sector, with the former hinging upon profitability. The state, on the other hand, must take into account non-economic ramifications as well — for without governmental involvement, short-term developments can foster long-term problems. Governments in the developing world generally have the responsibility of formulating and enforcing tourism policy, and for many, sustainable tourism goals are central to their tourism plan. This should include, as already stated, increasing the economic impact of tourism to the local economy by reducing the leakage of foreign exchange earnings.

As previously mentioned, one of the ways to increase economic impacts of tourism is to bring in tourists who spend money in the developing country. As mass tourism markets have been criticized for the negative environmental and social impacts they cause, there is growing attention on targeting fewer visitors, and those with higher household incomes expecting that they will spend more during their visit. Although this sounds logical, the strategy has its critics (Mill and Morrison, 1999). There is little known about the net foreign exchange earnings that result from different types of visitors and types of tourism purchases. Although it has not been clearly shown, visitors with high household incomes may spend more, but they may also require substantial investment in infrastructure and facilities with high import content. The question for many destinations to consider carefully is: "is it better for the destination to mass market visitors who arrive in greater numbers and spend less but require fewer imported goods and services?" Clearly, as this strategy is being chosen by many destination areas, further research into the nature of tourism expenditures by different visitors is needed, especially in comparison to the amount and types of infrastructure needed to attract high spending tourists.

Another strategy to maximize economic benefits is to encourage import substitution within developing countries. If quality products and services are available within the host country at a reasonable price, then the amount of imports [and therefore leakage] does not have to be so high. Unfortunately, many developing countries do not have these products and services readily available, but governments who are keen to establish tourism as a form of economic development could become involved by offering subsidies, grants or loans to local businesses. As well, to encourage use of local goods and services, quotas or tariffs on the use of imported goods could be implemented. The last strategy may be viewed as aggressive by other countries, however, it may be necessary in developing countries where loyalties to brand images on foreign products has already been established.

Governments of developing countries may want to consider implementing incentive programmes to local and foreign investors to encourage the use of local architecture, design and materials. Through a range of fiscal and other incentives (see Table 3.1), governments can stimulate and influence the amount of local content used in tourism development. Many of the incentives listed in table one are to attract capital investment, however for many developing countries the issue is a shortage of local labour. In this case, efforts to train and educate the local workforce may be necessary to ensure that leakage from employing outside labour is kept to a minimum.

Table 3.1: Categories and types of government incentives

Categories of incentives	*Types of incentives*	*Description*
Fiscal incentives	Tax holidays or deferrals	Government agency defers the payment of income taxes or other taxes for predetermined time period.
	Remission of tariffs	Government agency relaxes or removes import duties on goods and services required by the project.
	Tax reductions	Government agency lowers the normal tax rates that would be paid by the project.
Direct and Indirect Incentives	Non-refundable grants	Reduces a project's capital budget.
	Low interest loans	Reduced the amount of interest that the project must pay during its operating life.
	Interest rebates	Government agency rebates a portion of the project's interest costs during its operating life.
	Forgivable loans	Government agency loans funding to the project and then "forgives" all or part of these over an agreed-upon time period.
	Loan guarantees	Government agency guarantees loan given to a project by a private financial institution.
	Working capital bans	Government agency loans funds to meet the working capital of a project.
	Equity participation	Government agency purchases some of the available shares in the project, and becomes an equity investor.
	Training grants	Government agency provides a non-refundable grant to the project for staff training purposes.
	Infrastructure assistance	Government agency assumes the costs of some or all of the infrastructure required for the project.
	Leasebacks	Government agency purchases land, buildings, or equipment and then leases them to the project.
	Land donations	Government agency donates land free of charge to the project.

Source: Mill and Morrison, 1999, p. 290.

Perhaps one of the more complicated but necessary strategies for developing countries to consider is finding a way to work with transnational tourism corporations (TNC's). The demand for travel in the past few decades, coupled with the globalization of trade and services sectors has resulted in the rise of numerous TNC's in the tourism sector. Hotels, airlines, restaurants, travel agencies and tour operators have become more sophisticated in marketing and serving millions of travellers. With their success, has come a wave of criticism from smaller companies who view TNC's as operating for their own profitability at the expense of destination areas. For example, Pleumarom (1999) writes that many overseas chain hotel and resort properties are operated without any foreign equity involvement with headquarters in the developed world. Others, with their own agenda, can engage in policies that run counter to the national tourism plans. TNC's generate lower foreign exchange receipts than do smaller local owned operations, an important realization for many developing countries.

Many international hotel chains employ a core of expatriate managerial staff. Thus, another criticism of multinationals is that they do little to provide meaningful employment opportunities for local populations. To maximize the employment benefits for local populations, the governments of developing countries should ensure that when attracting TNC's, that there is direct financial involvement in developing the human capital in the destination's tourism mix. The World Tourism Organization has been working with many countries such as China, Russia, North Korea and Mongolia to identify ways to address manpower scarcity in tourism (WTO, 1999). An alliance with major TNC's may prove to be valuable in financing the development of human capital in these tourism projects.

A significant portion of international tourism expenditures are made on transportation to and from the destination. Although most developing countries own and operate a centrally owned airline, people from developing countries tend to use airlines from their country or origin. This may be due to the aggressive marketing of airlines to develop customer loyalty through rewards programmes, or the fact that safety standards on airlines in the developing world are substandard. Regardless of the cause, the economic benefits involved in transportation are not reaching many developing countries. Again, to survive in the competitive airline industry and to reap more of the profits, airlines in developing countries may want to partner with the larger airlines and focus on providing safe, reliable domestic air transportation.

Once destination areas have made substantial investments into the infrastructure necessary to cater to their chosen tourism markets, they can often become dependent upon large foreign tour operators to supply them with visitors. This important intermediary role can make it difficult for small local tour operators to survive. The large tour operators can bring in more people and often deal directly with local hotel chains and transportation services. Without the smaller local operator, these sectors can become dependent upon foreign tour operators to supply them with visitors. Due to the differing interests of foreign vs. local tour operators, developing countries can find themselves in a precarious position when foreign tour operators follow trends and pull out of the destination and provide packages in other locations. It is therefore in the long-term interest of developing countries to invest in, and encourage support of local tour operators who establish and secure their role in providing packages with local flavour.

Another obvious way to maximize foreign exchange earnings is for developing countries to ensure that foreign currency is spent as much as possible. Some countries such as Cuba, have limited the amount of foreign currency that visitors can bring into and take out to ensure that foreign currency is used. Other countries like Belize, require that visitors show that they have $ 50.00 U.S. for every day of their visit. Developing countries may want to ensure that all possible foreign exchange earnings are staying within the country by tightening up on these loopholes which will inevitably be found and used if unchecked.

Research Needs

There is great need for further research into the role of tourism as an economic tool for developing countries. Through advanced economic impact techniques, measurements of tourism's overall economic impacts are becoming more sophisticated, particularly in the developed world. These impact statements are being used to encourage further entry into the tourism industry by rural communities, and by countries in the developing world. But further attention to the economic benefits that accrue to these areas needs to be better understood, considering the differences in the ability of these areas to organize tourism, and supply the products desired by those whose have the propensity to travel. Although we can measure the amount of money entering an economy from tourism, more attention needs to be paid to measure the amount leaving an economy. Without subtracting the amount of these "leaks", rural areas and developing countries may be entering into tourism without a complete understanding of its consequences. While waiting for the promised economic benefits to arrive, these areas may be incurring more of the social and environmental costs of tourism development.

Research in this area should explore the types of, and extent of leakage incurred in tourism in the developing world. A thorough description of foreign exchange leakage may help to identify where experimental research could be done to "plug the holes" and measure the resulting benefits to destination areas. With increasing attention being paid to alternative forms of tourism such as ecotourism, researchers should attempt to measure the economic impacts and compare them to those brought about by mass tourism. Indeed, these forms of tourism are being considered due to their ability to limit the negative social and environmental impacts of tourism, but if they are found to contribute to the positive economic benefits as well, they may be an even more attractive alternative for areas to consider.

Differing from the traditional industries of agriculture and manufacturing, the service industry of tourism is a viable alternative for developing the economies of many third world countries. In need of foreign exchange earnings, income and employment opportunities, developing countries often make the decision to become involved in tourism hastily. Due to the initial costs required to establish tourism infrastructure and attract visitors, developing countries can enter into tourism by importing a significant amount of materials and labour, and by attracting heavy foreign investment. With these systems left unchecked however, the potential for leakage of money from the destination is high. This section outlined some of the ways that developing countries may be losing out on significant revenues from tourism and suggested strategies that could be considered to reduce leakage of much needed tourism profits. Indeed the critical issues of retaining tourism revenues in developing countries is essential in order to achieve the broader goal of sustainable tourism development. For developing countries will need to utilize financial resources to mitigate the negative environmental and social impacts resulting from tourism in the long term.

LINKING TOURISM AND LOCAL ECONOMIC DEVELOPMENT

Tourists are often enjoined to "leave only footprints" in order to minimize adverse environmental effects—the greater challenge is to find ways of leaving a larger economic impact in the local economy by increasing local tourist spend and the value of tourism to the local economy. Tourists, international and domestic, constitute a significant additional market in the local economy during their holiday; they consume a very wide variety of goods and services, many of which are not readily identified as tourism. The diversity of goods and services consumed directly by tourists and by the tourism industry as inputs to hotels, restaurants and tourism facilities often goes unrecognized and uncounted, it is for this reason that WTO has advocated the creation of tourism satellite accounts, which allow the desegregation of tourism as a sector in the national economy. Using the methodologies developed by WTO it is possible to identify the value of tourism to the national economy and its impacts through different industries.

The contribution of tourism to the local economy is also often undervalued. It has five kinds of positive economic impacts on livelihoods, any or all of which can form part of a poverty reduction strategy:

- Wages from formal employment
- Earnings from selling goods, service or casual labour
- Dividends and profits arising from locally owned enterprises
- Collective income which may include profits from a community run enterprise, land rental, dividends from a joint venture or levies—these incomes can provide significant development capital and provide finance for corn-grinding mills, a clinic, teachers housing and school books
- Infrastructure gains, for example roads, piped water, electricity and communications.

Understanding the Leakages and Linkages

The term 'leakage' is used to refer to the amount spent on importing goods and services to meet the needs of tourists, leakages can occur across national boundaries and will then impact on the Balance of Payments or between economic areas with national boundaries. Leakages occur when the local economy is unable to provide a reliable, continuous, competitively priced supply of the required product or service and of a consistent quality to meet the market demand. From a tourism and poverty perspective it is generally more productive to focus on the other side of the coin: linkages. It is when the local economic linkages are weak that revenue from tourism receipts in a local economic area leaks out. Engaging with local suppliers, using local capital and resources and developing the skills necessary to deliver consistently at an appropriate quality and at a competitive price can reduce leakage. This can have a demonstrable benefit for the poor as is clear from the Nepal case study which provides an example of what can be achieved for one small economic area.

From the perspectives of local economic development and poverty reduction, what matters is not how much of a tourist's total expenditure on a trip is spent outside the country, but rather how much is not spent in the local economy, thereby limiting the benefit to local communities and the poor among them. Leakages which reduce the development impact of tourism are:

- Imported skills, expatriate labour,
- Imported commodities, goods and services,
- Imported technology and capital goods,
- Increased oil imports,
- Repatriation of profits,
- Advertising and marketing efforts abroad,
- Transporting tourists to the destination country.

However developing local sources of supply, encouraging local ownership and enhancing linkages to the local economy can ameliorate all but the last two of these, creating at the same time more jobs and opportunities for SMME development.

One of the best ways to enhance economic benefits to the local community and to increase the contribution to poverty reduction is to increase the extent of linkages between the formal tourism sector (hotels, lodges, restaurants, tour operators and transport providers) and the local economy. If the linkages to the local economy can be increased, the extent of leakages will be reduced.

Increased integration can develop strong linkages between tourism and other economic sectors including agriculture, fisheries, manufacturing, construction and crafts production. If the tourism industry purchases from domestic industries, it strengthens them and provides additional revenue and jobs, at the same time reducing the import content and foreign exchange leakage from the tourism industry.

The creation of local linkages needs to be part of the overall tourism development strategy of governments and development agencies in the planning, construction and operational phases. Three key sets of factors are important in enhancing the extent of local linkages:

- The creation of employment at all skill levels and particularly where there is existing capacity.
- New "attractions" created through anti-poverty tourism development strategies need to be integrated into the tour programmes of the ground handlers and inbound operators. Creating mutually beneficial business linkages between the formal and informal sector is critical. Local government needs to ensure that micro enterprises and emerging entrepreneurs are promoted in local tourism marking initiatives, where they are often neglected. Visitor attractions, parks, cultural sites and hotels should be encouraged to provide information about local products and services provided by the poor.
- The requirements of new micro enterprises for credit, marketing skills and a thorough understanding of tourist expectations need to be met. Micro enterprises may have particular difficulties in meeting health and safety, licensing and other regulatory requirements. Such regulations themselves need to be crafted to encourage inclusion through assisted education and training to ensure engagement by the poor in the industry.

For the development of successful linkages it is necessary to develop the quality, reliability and competitiveness of local products so that they can be successful in the local market. The local formal sector business community needs to be actively engaged through partnership approaches in the process. The making of effective partnership-based linkages often requires a catalyst and a sustained effort. If new planning permission, leases or concessions are being granted, private sector companies can be asked to make the development of such linkages part of their bid.

Tourism can provide an important diversification for other sectors of the local economy and create new ones, offering additional community livelihood opportunities. If local communities and businesses participate in the development of tourism, local economic benefits and ownership are likely to be greater. Increasingly governments are adopting policies, to encourage and facilitate participation by the local communities and the poor in the development of tourism projects, resulting in increasing employment and growth of complementary products.

Benefits can be maximized through partnerships at the destination level. Hotels and tour operators working with local communities, local government and NGOs, can develop forms of tourism that bring sustainable development which contribute to poverty reduction and provide a richer experience for domestic and international tourists. Such partnerships will benefit both the host communities and the tourism industry, ensuring that more tourism dollars, euros or pounds stay in the local community where they can make significant contributions to the reduction of poverty.

Enterprises, in both their constructional and operational phases, can do a great deal to increase beneficial local economic impact through affirmative policies for employment, training, food furnishings and craft. In the South African Responsible Tourism Guidelines a whole range of practical strategies for developing local economic linkages are identified.

Increasing Market Access and Enclave Tourism

All too often, particularly in rural areas, local people are denied any significant opportunity to participate in the tourism market. Tourists are not accessible to the local community when they are within their hotels, coaches, and safari vehicles or inside sites and attractions such as museums. These are all enclave forms of tourism, where those wishing to sell goods or services to tourists are often reduced to hawking or touting at the enclave entry and exit points. Cruise ship passengers and tourists on "all inclusive" hotel or resort packages are particularly difficult for local entrepreneurs to access (and these sectors are growing rapidly).

Local involvement in the tourism industry depends to a large extent on access to the market. In many cases local benefits are greatest in the informal sector; the return on local skills and services is often maximized where the scale of capital investment is low. This aspect is sometimes neglected in tourism planning, and access to tourists for the informal sector is often restricted.

All-inclusive packages can offer tourists who do not always feel safe in a new destination a protected environment, isolated from the poverty and hassle from beggars, touts and hawkers in some destinations. Tourism can however be organized in ways that enable local people to have better access to tourists, this will require partnership approaches based on agreements where hotels facilitate access for informal sector traders and the traders reciprocate by not hassling tourists. These partnerships can create an environment in which tourists feel secure in moving beyond the enclave to local "hassle-free" craft markets and to approach local guides committed to rotation systems and abiding to codes of conduct, which they have developed and agreed amongst themselves.

Poorer members of communities can be helped to access the tourism market by measures designed to assist the informal sector and by developing their links with the formal sector. In The Gambia, the Association of Small Scale Enterprises in Tourism (ASSET) is working to improve the linkages between community-based tourism attractions, SMMEs and the formal tourism sector, represented by hotels, ground agents and the tour operating companies based in the tourist originating countries. The Gambia case study shows what can be achieved by partnership approaches to improving the relationships between the formal and informal sectors through 'badging', licensing and codes for the informal sector, increased promotion for these trades, improved access to the hotels and resorts, 'free market days' or similar arrangements, where craft workers are given access on a rotation basis to sell inside hotels; they can make a dramatic difference to their sales and earnings.

Enhancing Economic Benefits

There are a number of strategies that can be used to enhance overall economic benefits and can have a poverty reduction focus.

Growth and Selection

The tourism sector in the poorest countries is generally highly dependent on international markets, as they do not have significant domestic markets. However, it has been noted before that a significant number of developing countries have strong domestic tourism sectors as well as significant outbound tourists. Whilst the domestic market should always be considered, for the poorest countries, and in order to maximize foreign exchange revenues, the primary focus continues to be on international arrivals. The challenge is to attract larger numbers of those international and domestic tourists most likely to benefit the poor—those predisposed to visit local markets and to seek tourism experiences of nature, culture and daily life which are most likely to be provided by poor people.

The importance of intra-regional tourism in this regard should also be noted; WTO reported intra-regional tourism as growing in most regions of the world. It is significant that 40 per cent of Africa's tourism comes from neighbouring African countries. Opening up the roads and improving the modes of transport between countries in Africa would greatly enhance the movement of people and contribute to poverty reduction. Intra-regional tourism is especially valuable for pro-poor tourism and local economic development because of the greater likelihood of shared cultural values and familiarity with social systems between peoples of neighbouring countries.

Whilst there is a case for attracting more visitors in order to increase the economic impact, this strategy will only assist in poverty reduction if the additional visitors can be encouraged to spend in ways that benefit the poor and if they meet overall sustainability criteria. The World Bank's World Development Report, recognized that economic growth does not necessarily result in swift poverty reduction; this requires an explicitly pro-poor strategy. Such growth requires that the benefits flow in a disproportionate way to the poor. Some of the key components of broad-based growth which assist in benefiting the poor include:

- Government commitment and responsiveness to the needs of the poor,

- The expansion of employment opportunities for the poor,
- Improved productivity for the poor,
- Improved access for the poor to credit, knowledge and Infrastructure, and
- Investment in the human capital of the poor (particularly education and health).

Increasing Tourists' Length of Stay

Strategies which extend the average length of stay through the development of the product increase the numbers of bed nights and the expenditure of tourists on board and accommodation, and increase the economic returns which can be earned from the same number of visitor arrivals. If the additional bed nights create extra employment or create greater opportunities for the poor to sell goods and services to the tourists or to the tourism industry, then there will be a poverty reduction impact.

Increasing Visitor Expenditure

There is a market trend towards more experiential holidays; holidaymakers want to learn more about the countries they are visiting: the people their cultures, traditions, cuisine, etc. The trend is towards more active holidays, greater personal involvement and active participation instead of passive relaxation. This encourages the diversification and enrichment of the tourism product. Developing more activities and attractions, with interpretation, and providing the services of guides and transport necessary to their enjoyment increases both, expenditure and length of stay. Making more extensive use of natural and cultural heritage, whilst carefully managing the tourism impacts so as to ensure the conservation of resources, can make an important contribution both to economic development and conservation. Special interest tourists tend to spend more money on and during their holidays and to stay longer, whether those interests are based on natural, archaeological, historical or cultural heritage, or based on adventure and physical challenge.

Developing Complementary Products

A greater variety and richness of attractions and activities in a destination will increase the propensity of travellers to visit the destination and may extend the length of stay and increase visitor expenditure. Market trends towards more experiential holidays suggest that there are promising opportunities for the development of complementary products that enable the poor to engage in the industry and to profit from it. The established industry has an interest in the development of complementary products: tourism services (like guided walks and the performing arts) and goods (particularly crafts and other local specialities), which complement the core tourism facilities of transport, excursions and accommodation. These complementary tourism products, often provide experiences that are not provided by the tour operators but which enrich their product. Hoteliers and tour operators can encourage local people to develop tourism products and services and to support them in doing so with training and marketing. The development of appropriate complementary products will increase the attractiveness of the destination and increase tourist expenditure in the local economy.

Some examples of complementary products drawn from Africa:

- Drumming and dance classes
- Story telling
- Hair braiding
- Bush craft
- Bird watching
- Guided walks to look at plants and their medicinal uses
- Craft and cookery classes
- Village and agricultural tours
- Language classes
- School visits
- Visits to craft workers
- Sharing a meal with a family in a village
- History tours

Local communities can often engage in the provision of complementary products because it requires less capital investment and is therefore less risky. Tourism is often best considered as an additional diversification option for the poor, rather than a substitute for their core means of livelihood. As an additional source of income (or other benefits) it can play an important part in improving living standards and raising people above the poverty threshold. The poor can maximize their returns by choosing forms of participation which complement their existing livelihood strategies and which realize their cultural and social assets. Tourists are interested in the "everyday lives" of local communities and there are a host of small enterprise opportunities for local people. Local guides and cycle-rickshaw driver/ guides in India's Keoladeo National Park, and guides and charter-boat operators in Indonesia's Komodo National Park are examples of local people diversifying their livelihood strategies. The boat operators also fish, and many of the cycle-rickshaw drivers work in town in the low season.

Spreading the Benefits of Tourism Geographically

Tourism experiences are shaped by the geographical diversity of beach, mountain and urban attractions, and holiday-makers can be encouraged to travel further, beyond established destinations, in order to experience particular environmental, cultural or natural heritage attractions. Heritage trails and other similar products have been developed to extend length of stay and to spread the advantages of tourism development to new areas and communities, they can be used for initiatives which specifically benefit the poor.

National Parks, cultural sites and World Heritage sites are often the major attractions, the primary "tourism magnets" in significant parts of the developing world and they often attract people to marginal rural areas. As the major attractions in areas which would not otherwise be of interest to tourists, it can be argued that natural and cultural heritage sites should be taking a wider view of their potential to contribute to tourism development and the well-being of local communities. Changing the way in which tourism is organized in and around attractions can increase the economic development impact. For example, at Komodo National Park in Indonesia, 85 per cent of tourism trip expenditure bypasses the local economy due to the dominance of non-local carriers and package tour operators. Estimates for average local expenditure at Komodo per visitor demonstrate the importance of minimizing enclave tourism. Cruise ship tourists spent on average US$0.03 in the local economy, package tourists spent US$52.5 and independent travellers US $97.4. There is scope for Parks and other major tourism attractions in rural areas to assist the development of small scale, locally owned attractions and tourism services.

Nature-based tourism and cultural heritage tourism in rural areas can provide significant local markets and economic development opportunities, which contribute to integrated rural development and offer local employment and supplementary or alternative income-generating opportunities for poor people. The development of tourism in such areas can significantly improve incomes for local communities and the poor, if these flagship attractions can be planned and managed so as to maximize the opportunities for local economic development and poverty reduction.

Infrastructure and Planning Gain

Tourism can contribute to overall socio-economic development through the provision of roads, telephones, electricity, piped and treated water supplies, waste disposal and recycling and sewage treatment. Roads developed for tourism provide opportunities for trade and conversely new roads opened to improve trade also bring tourism opportunities if they open access to tourism resources. New economic corridor development projects often create tourism development opportunities for local communities in addition to improving trade linkages. These facilities enhance opportunities for other forms of local economic development, but more could be done at local and national level to maximize those benefits, particularly when new projects are licensed. Through appropriate interventions by government and tourism planners, it is possible to maximize these planning gains and to tilt them so that they encourage local economic development and benefit the poor.

Local Management of Tourism and Partnerships

Local communities and the poor amongst them are more likely to benefit from planning gain where they are involved in discussions and decisions about tourism developments and where the complementarities between different forms of tourism development and their livelihood strategies are considered. The Manila Declaration called for "greater involvement of communities, in the planning, implementation, monitoring and evaluation processes of tourism policies, programmes and projects" and for "community awareness campaigns to inform people of the benefits to be gained from tourism development". Only in this way could the negative effects of tourism be managed and the positive economic benefits maximized to benefit communities, through great employment of the local labour force in tourism and to provide for more positive participation by women and youth.

Appropriate planning structures can facilitate effective community participation in the tourism development process and provide a mechanism for capturing planning gain through infrastructural, employment and economic linkages. A planning process that addresses carrying capacity and sets limits of acceptable change is most likely to achieve local communities' active influence in tourism development as well as anti-poverty goals. It is through participatory forms of these technical processes, informed by traditional and local knowledge, that local communities can most effectively be empowered, and the environmental, social and cultural integrity of destinations maintained.

SMME Development

As local experience of tourism deepens, there are often increased opportunities for the development of new locally owned enterprises providing competitive and complementary goods and services; this follows trends in developed country destinations and can be supported by government policy and SMME development strategies. The tourism industry offers viable opportunities for the development of a wide range of SMMEs; even in the developed countries they constitute the largest part of local tourism supply. In Europe 70 per cent of total tourist accommodation capacity is provided by small and medium-sized firms. Some estimates for the developing world put the comparable figure as high as 85 per cent.

In well-established developing country destinations, like The Gambia and Goa, increasing numbers of international tourists are staying in locally owned accommodation. SMMEs are very important in the provision of restaurants and bars, handicrafts, the supply of furnishings and other consumables to hotels, the provision of transport, local tour operating, guiding and attractions. The development of SMMEs in developing countries often requires access to capital and training in business management and critically in marketing. Providing information, advisory and mentoring to small and micro enterprises and emerging entrepreneurs can make a powerful contribution to their success.

Reducing Seasonality

Seasonality in tourist arrivals is the major cause of seasonal and casual employment. There are a number of strategies that can be employed to extend the tourism season, including festivals, the development of special interest products, attracting seminars and conventions, and pricing policies, specially addressing senior citizens who have more flexibility to travel in the low season. Strategies that reduce seasonality and successfully attract tourists in significant numbers for a larger part of the year, benefit the hotels and tour operators, their employees and those in the destination who earn all or part of their livelihood by direct or indirect sales to tourist or the tourism industry. These beneficiaries will often include the poor.

Employment and Training

The employment impact of tourism includes both direct employment in tourism enterprises and indirect employment in those enterprises and micro-enterprises that supply the tourism industry. The amount of direct employment in tourism is dependent upon the scale and form of tourism development and the extent of tourists' engagement in the local economy and with SMMEs. Maximizing the employment of locals and nationals in tourism including managerial grades, keeps income within the local and national economies and reduces wage and salary leakages (wages and salaries remitted or spent out of the local economy). However, the success of the tourism enterprise will depend upon the delivery of the appropriate level of service, and in this global industry maintaining high levels of training is an important consideration in the economic sustainability of businesses.

One of the ways in which the industry can contribute to poverty reduction is by committing to employ more local poor people and demonstrating that with training and staff development programmes those commitments can be met. The South African Responsible Tourism Guidelines include a number of specific ways in which enterprises can adopt employment practices and targets, which will benefit the poor. Elsewhere in Southern Africa, ZimSun committed themselves in their lease agreement to employ as many local people as possible from the Mahenye community, and to train these staff to take on middle management roles. In the construction phase of the lodges, local labour was recruited and a number of local workers completed apprenticeships. Electricians, plumbers, carpenters, bricklayers, plasterers and steel fixers were trained, creating a cadre of skilled labour in the local community available to work on other projects and able to undertake the maintenance on the lodges. In March 1997 the Mahenye and Chilo Lodges were employing 63 per cent of their labour from the local community, and whilst only seven women were employed in the lodge, six of them came from the local community.

Tourism can contribute to poverty alleviation through the creation of employment and changes in existing employment practices where pro-poor employment strategies are pursued, for example prioritizing the employment of women and youth. Tourism is a relatively labour intensive industry providing direct employment in hotels and tour companies, and indirect employment in taxis, bars, restaurants and suppliers, where a proportion of employee time serves the tourism industry and tourists. Tourism can create jobs, which benefit the poor where specific measures are taken to recruit and train workers from amongst the poor. Where tourism enterprises make these efforts, there is a strong case for careful monitoring of employment effects to determine to what extent local people, and particularly the poor, benefit and to ensure that they gain kudos for it.

Beyond the hotels, particular efforts should be made to train and employ local guides, artists, performers and craft workers who are able to interpret their heritage and in so doing maintain some control over it. Entrepreneurship development programmes for tourism SMMEs are usually necessary. These programmes typically include developing business opportunity awareness, business planning including project feasibility analysis and training in management skills. Provision of continuing business advisor and mentoring services may be needed for emerging entrepreneurs over several years. Many countries already have small business development and credit programmes and tourism

SMME development can sometimes be attached to these existing programmes.

Moving Beyond "Trickledown" Effect

It has long been assumed that tourism development projects, if successful, would attract international investment, contribute foreign exchange earnings to the national accounts and generate economic development. By a process of trickledown, local communities would benefit through employment and local economic development generated by the additional spending and the new entrepreneurial opportunities which this would create.

Accepting that tourism operations need to be profitable in a competitive world market if they are to be sustainable, there are a number of things, which can be done to increase the benefits to the local economy in tourist destination areas to:

- Facilitate local community access to the tourism market.
- Maximize the linkages into the local economy and minimize leakages.
- Build on and complement existing livelihood strategies through employment and small enterprise development.
- Evaluate tourism projects for their contribution to local economic development not just for their national revenue generation and the increase in international arrivals.
- Ensure the maintenance of natural and cultural assets.
- Control negative social impacts.

The South African case study, which follows, demonstrates how a national government can use policy to lead tourism to address the economic development of local communities and to engage with the poor and disadvantaged. The data reported for the three enterprises on which the monitoring methodologies were tested, demonstrate that it is possible to move beyond the assertion of 'trickledown' and to measure and report local economic benefits.

PROMOTING TOURISM FOR NATIONAL DEVELOPMENT

Tourism emerged as a global phenomenon in the 1960's and the potential for tourism to generate economic development was widely endorsed by national governments, which looked at tourism to generate foreign exchange earnings, to create employment and to bring economic benefits to regions with limited options for alternative economic development. National tourism authorities were created to promote tourism and to maximize international arrivals. The success of these authorities and of Tourism Ministries was judged by the growth in international arrival figures. As tourism expanded and its significant economic contributions were lauded, an awareness of its negative environmental and social impacts also increased. A more skeptical attitude to the economic benefits of tourism also emerged. The importance of environmental and social sustainability was more widely accepted, and emphasis has increasingly been placed on the generation of economic benefits at the local level.

The tourism industry can be viewed as "a great school for the modernization of a people's values". The regional and international connections of the industry, and its international competitive nature, mean that tourism can be an important conduit for the introduction of modern management techniques and technologies. This can be a problem if the industry is reliant on imported technologies and labour brought in from abroad or from the metropolitan centres. On the other hand, it presents excellent opportunities for developing entrepreneurship, for staff training and progression and for the development of transferable skills.

Tourism development has generally been focused at the macro level: on international promotion, attracting inward investment and major hotel and resort developments, and on national and regional master planning. The primary concern has been with maximizing foreign exchange earnings, in part to finance investment in technology and other imports for economic development and to finance debt.

Performance of Developing Countries and LDCs

International Tourist Arrivals

Since the 1950's developing countries have received increasing numbers of international tourists, largely from developed countries. International tourist arrivals have been growing significantly faster in developing countries than they have in the European Union (EU) or Organization for Economic Cooperation and Development

(OECD) countries. Developing countries had 292.6 million international arrivals in 2000, an increase since 1990 of nearly 95 per cent. The sub-group of 49 LDCs had 5.1 million international arrivals in 2000, they achieved an increase of nearly 75 per cent in the decade. This performance by developing countries compares very favourably with the growth of tourism to countries of the OECD and the EU, which achieved around 40 per cent growth.

International Tourism Receipts

Over the last ten years there has been a higher rate of growth in the absolute value of tourism expenditure as recorded in the national accounts in the developing countries than in the developed countries. The absolute earnings of developing countries grew by 133 per cent between 1990 and 2000 and in the LDCs by 154 per cent, this compares with 64 per cent for OECD countries and 49 per cent for EU countries.

Table 3.2: International tourist arrivals in thousands

Country Groups	*1990*	*2000*	*Increase*	*% increase*
OECD	338,200	471,164	132,964	39.3
EU	204,961	283,604	78,643	38.4
Other Countries	3,465	6,652	3,187	92.0
Developing Countries	150,563	292,660	142,097	94.4
Least Developed Countries (LDCs)	2,921	5,106	2,185	74.8
Other Developing Countries	13,755	25,562	11,807	85.8

Source: WTO

For list of countries by country groups see Annex 3.

Table 3.3: Absolute value (US$ Million) of tourism expenditure by country group

Country Groups	*1990*	2000	*Increase*	*% increase*
OECD	201,082	330,464	129,382	64.3
EU	119,998	179,041	59,043	49.2
Other Countries	1,366	2,388	1,022	74.0
Developing Countries	59,645	138,937	79,292	132.9
Least Developed Countries (LDCs)	1,021	2,594	1,573	154.1
Other Developing Countries	11,045	17,041	5,996	54.3

Source: WTO

Figures relate to the credit component of the Travel item of the Balance of Payments of the corresponding countries of reference. *This item is traditionally referred to as Tourism.*

The developing countries and particularly the LDCs secured a larger increase in the income per international arrival between 1990 and 2000 than did the OECD or the EU. The LDCs secured an increase of 45 per cent between 1990 and 2000 and the developing countries nearly 20 per cent, this compares with 18 per cent for OECD countries and 7.8 pèr cent for the EU.

Table 3.4: Average value per international arrival of tourism expenditure by country group

Country Groups	*1990*	*2000*	*Increase*	*% Increase*
OECD	595	701	107	18.0
EU	585	631	46	7.8
Other Countries	394	359	-35	-8.9
Developing Countries	396	475	79	19.8
Least Developed Countries (LDCs)	350	508	158	45.3
Other Developing Countries	803	667	-136	-17.0

Source: WTO

Figures relate to the credit component of the Travel item of the Balance of Payments of the corresponding countries of reference. This item is traditionally referred to as Tourism.

The average value has been calculated by dividing absolute value taken for the travel item in the Balance of Payments by the international arrival figure.

Data from the Balance of Payments can be used to calculate the importance of tourism (the Travel item in the Balance of Payments) as a proportion of international trade in services. For the OECD and EU country groups tourism constitutes around 28 per cent of trade in services in 2000, this significantly less than the 43 per cent recorded for developing countries and 70 per cent for LDCs. For the OECD and EU country groups the credit travel item of the Balance of Payments, taken to equate to tourism receipts, amounts to around 6 per cent of total Goods and Services in 2000 In the developing countries group it averages 6.5 per cent and in the LDCs 15.3 per cent.

In 2000 tourism ranked third among the major merchandize export sectors for both developing countries and LDCs.

Table 3.5: Travel as share of total trade in services and as share of total goods and services in 2000

Country Groups	*Travel as share of total Services (%)*	*Travel as share of total Goods and Services (%)*
OECD	28.1	5.9
EU	28.6	6.3
Developing Countries	43.3	6.5
Least Developed Countries (LDCs)	70.6	15.3
Other Developing Countries	29.0	4.9

Source: WTO

Figures relate to the credit component of the Travel item of the Balance of Payments as percentage of items on "Services" and "Goods and Services" in the countries of reference. In such cases (6 in 1990 and 5 in 2000) wherein the percentage exceeds a 100, obviously is a question of a lack of consistence in the information provided by those countries.

Table 3.6: Value in US$ million of major merchandize exports by country group

	Developing Country	*R*	*LDCs*	*R*
Manufactures	900,649	1	720	2
Food	120,262	2	334	4
Tourism	113,902	3	335	3
Fuels	73,624	4	2316	1
Ores and metals	41,585	5	111	5
Agriculture	25,167	6	68	6

Source: WTO

Figures relate to the credit component of the Travel item of the Balance of Payments of the corresponding countries of reference. This item is traditionally referred as Tourism.

Merchandize exports show the f.o.b. value of goods provided to the rest of the world valued in 'J S. dollars. These items have been obtained from 2001 World Development Indicators, published by the World-Bank. Data for 2000 have been estimated Agricultural raw materials comprise SITC section 2 (crude materials except fuels) excluding divisions 22, 27 (crude fertilizers and mineral excluding coal, petroleum and precious stones), and 28 (metalliferous ores and scrap).

Fuels comprise SITC section 3 (mineral fuels).

Ores and metals comprise the commodities in SITC divisions 27, 28 and 68 (nonferrous metals). Manufactures comprise the commodities in SITC sections 5 (chemicals), 6 (basic manufactures), 7 (machinery and transport equipment) and 8 (miscellaneous manufactured goods), excluding division 68.

In the developing countries the export value of tourism grew by 154 per cent in developing countries second only to the growth in the manufacturing sector. In the LDCs tourism grew 47 per cent, behind manufactures and fuel but ahead of food, which declined.

Table 3.7: Growth between 1990 and 2000 in top 4 export sectors for developing countries and LDCs

	Developing Country	*R*	LDCs	*R*
Manufactures	208%	1	217%	2
Food	58%	2	-71%	4
Tourism	154%	3	47%	3
Fuels	16%	4	1444%	1

International Tourism in the LDCs

The category of Least Developed Country was first used by the United Nations in 1971 to encourage the international community to recognize these countries as structurally disadvantaged and facing the risk of being overcome by those disadvantages. Since 1971 only Botswana has graduated from LDC status, and tourism played a very significant role in that process with the annual number of international tourism arrivals increasing by more than half a million visitors between 1985 and 1998. Cape Verde, Maldives, Samoa and Vanuatu have all been considered for graduation since 1994 and in all four of them tourism has been the single most important factor explaining the socio-economic progress which would form the basis of their graduation. As Pierre Encontre of UNCTAD concludes, "international tourism has been one of the very few economic sectors able to place some poor countries on a better development path" and to enable them to reduce their marginalization from the global economy.

In the Maldives, annual visitor arrivals tripled between 1985 and 1998, in the same period the proportion of tourism exports to GNP increased from 75 per cent to 89 per cent, making the Maldives the LDC most dependent on international tourism, followed by Samoa and Vanuatu, both with over 20 per cent. International arrivals to other LDCs grew fast between 1995 and 1998 Angola and Chad experienced more than 75 per cent growth (albeit from low base lines), Cape Verde, The Gambia, Lao, Mali and Zambia all enjoyed growth above 20 per cent. Sudan, Sierra Leone, Sao Tome, Kiribati, Ethiopia, Eritrea, the Central African Republic and Burundi, however, all saw reductions in international visitor arrivals.

If petroleum industry exports are discounted (and they are significant only in Angola, Yemen and Equatorial Guinea) tourism is the primary source of foreign exchange earnings in the 49 LDCs. The combined tourism export receipts of all LDCs in 1998 accounted for 16.2 per cent of their non-oil export receipts. This is 39 per cent more than cotton and 82 per cent more than textiles, their second and third most significant non-oil exports. In more than one third of LDCs tourism ranks among the top three sources of foreign exchange earnings, and it is the most important source of foreign exchange earnings in seven of them.

Table 3.8: International tourism receipts as per cent of GDP, 2000

LDC	*% of GDP*
MALDIVES	57.7
VANUATU	27.4
SAMOA	17.0
TANZANIA	8.2
COMOROS	7.4
CAMBODIA	7.2
LAO P. DEM.R.	6.7
ERITREA	5.9
KIRIBATI	4.6
SENEGAL	3.2
ZAMBIA	3.1
MALI	3.1
MADAGASCAR	3.1
NEPAL	3.0
LESOTHO	2.7
BHUTAN	2.1
SIERRA LEONE	1.9
MALAWI	1.6
RWANDA	1.3
HAITI	1.3

(Contd.)

ETHIOPIA	1.1
YEMEN	0.9
TOGO	0.4
GUINEA	0.4
SUDAN	0.3
ANGOLA	0.2
BURUNDI	0.1
BANGLADESH	0.1

Tourism as per cent of GDP data from the World Development Indicator database, World Bank.

Table 3.9: Change in revenue from international arrivals in current US$ values

LDC	*% of GDP*
LAO P.DEM. R	3700
TANZANIA	1037
COMOROS	650
BHUTAN	400
MYANMAR	367
BANGLADESH	355
YEMEN	280
MALDIVES	261
MADAGASCAR	198
ETHIOPIA	172
NEPAL	161
RWANDA	140
ZAMBIA	122
KIRIBATI	100
SAMOA	100
MALAWI	69
MALI	51
VANUATU	49
SUDAN	43
LESOTHO	41
ANGOLA	39
HAITI	17
SENEGAL	-16
SIERRA LEONE	-37
GUINEA	-60
BURUNDI	-75
TOGO	-91
EQ.GUINEA	-100

Tourism as per cent of GDP data from the World Development Indicator database, World Bank.

There are 28 LDCs for which there is adequate data to calculate tourism as a proportion of GDP. As can be seen from Table 3.9, in 8 of the 28 LDCs for which there is data, international tourist receipts is greater than 5 per cent of the domestic economy, in a further 8 countries it is more than 2 per cent. Table 3.9 reports the change in the dollar value (at current prices) of international arrivals. Sixteen countries saw the revenues in current dollar values increase by more than 100 per cent in the ten years from 1990-2000. 22 of the 28 had significant increases in tourism revenues at current values—mostly from low base figures. Amongst those countries that had significant reductions in tourism earnings were Sierra Leone, Guinea, Burundi, and Equatorial Guinea all of which have suffered from political instability.

Tourism and Development

Tourism can contribute to development and the reduction of poverty in a number of ways. Economic benefits are generally the most important element, but there can be social, environmental and cultural benefits and costs. Tourism contributes to poverty reduction by providing employment and diversified livelihood opportunities. This in turn provides additional income or contributes to a reduction in vulnerability of the poor by increasing the range of economic opportunities available to individuals and households. Tourism also contributes to poverty alleviation through direct taxation and the generation of taxable economic growth; taxes can then be used to alleviate poverty through education, health and infrastructure development. It should not be forgotten that some tourism facilities also improve the recreational and leisure opportunities available for the poor themselves at the local level.

Tourism, Taxation and Poverty Alleviation

Tax revenue from tourism is an important economic benefit at national and local level. Taxes can provide the financial resources for development of infrastructure, some types of attractions and other public facilities and services, and tourism marketing and training required for developing tourism, as well as to help finance poverty alleviation programmes by governments. In addition, tourism-related tax revenues can, and do, help to finance general community improvements and services used by all residents.

WTO's 1998 report on tourism taxation emphasizes that taxation policies in a country must be carefully evaluated in an integrated manner to ensure that tourism-related taxes are giving the necessary substantial revenues; but taxes should not be so high for the country's international competitive position to be adversely affected and produce a loss of tourist markets. A balance must be achieved between, on the one hand, a level of taxation that maintains, a competitive position for the country and reasonable profits for the industry and, on the other hand, receiving adequate revenues to support investment in and maintenance of the tourism sector, and to contribute towards general community welfare.

Tourism and Poverty Reduction

Tourism is not very different from other productive sectors, but it has four potential advantages for pro-poor growth:

- It has higher potential for linkage with other local enterprises because customers come to the destination.
- It is relatively labour intensive and employs a high proportion of women.
- It has potential in poor countries and areas with few other competitive exports.
- Tourism products can be built on natural resources and culture, which are assets, that some of the poor have.

Many disadvantages of tourism such as leakage and volatility of revenue are common to other economic sectors. But tourism may involve greater trade-offs with local livelihoods through more competition for natural resources, particularly in coastal areas.

The Comparative Advantages

The WTO is convinced that tourism has considerable potential for growth in many developing countries and LDCs where it is a significant economic sector and growing; and that it has advantages when compared with other economic sectors. This case can be summarized:

Comparative Advantages of Tourism as a Development Strategy for Developing Countries

1. Tourism is consumed at the point of production. Because of this the opportunities for individuals and micro-enterprises, in urban centres or marginal rural areas, to sell additional products (e.g. handicrafts and souvenirs) or services (e.g. guiding or music) to these potential consumers is therefore considerable.
2. Access to international markets is a serious problem for developing countries particularly in traditional sectors like food, agriculture and textiles where they confront tariff and non-tariff barriers. This is not the case for the tourism sector. The developed countries have not erected significant tariff barriers against tourism exports from the developing countries. In fact, principal trade barriers to international tourism are visa restrictions and similar taxes imposed by the exporting country as a source of revenue (or sometimes in retaliation for visa restrictions imposed by the tourist originating countries). The position of Cuba is instructive in this regard. Whilst Cuba has struggled to find export markets for its sugar and tobacco it has been much more successful in maintaining a dynamic tourism industry.
3. Most export industries depend on financial, productive and human capital. Tourism not only depends on these, but also on natural capital (e.g. wildlife, scenery and beaches) and culture, which are assets possessed by the poor.
4. Tourism has particular potential in many countries with few other competitive exports.
5. Tourism is a much more diverse industry than many others and can build upon a wide resource base. Diversity increases the scope for wide participation, and for the informal sector through livelihood diversification—for example where a farming household produces crafts or sells produce to a local lodge.
6. Tourism is often reported to be more labour intensive than other productive sectors. Data from six countries with satellite tourism accounts does indicate that it is more labour intensive than non-agricultural activities, particularly manufacturing, although less labour intensive than agriculture.

7. There is a greater uptake of jobs by women than in other sectors although it is not known if more jobs are taken by the poor and unskilled. (The percentage of female employment varies enormously by country, ranging from over 60 per cent in Bolivia to fewer than 10 per cent in some Muslim countries).
8. In many developing countries, for example South Africa, China, the Philippines and India, domestic tourism is growing rapidly and like international tourism brings relatively wealthy consumers to areas where they constitute an important local market, one which the poor can access at low cost and again where tourists bear the transport costs. It is not always appropriate to focus on international tourists. Recent work in Palawan (Philippines) demonstrated that domestic tourists are more "valuable" than international tourists in that the Filipino tourists were spending about 6 per cent more per day in Puerto Princesa than were the international tourists.

Perceived Disadvantages of Tourism as a Development Strategy

- Foreign private interests drive tourism and it is difficult to maximize local economic benefits due to the high level of foreign ownership, which means that there are high levels of leakage and few local linkages.
  There is no body of evidence to confirm that the leakages associated with tourism are typically greater than for other comparable export sectors, nor of any evidence that the supposed levels of foreign ownership are any higher than for comparable sectors. It is clear that the many small enterprises and individual traders sustain themselves around hotels and other tourism facilities and that these SMMEs are not foreign owned. There is often confusion about levels of foreign ownership, local ownership is often masked by franchize agreements and management contracts. WTO is studying this issue in collaboration with UNCTAD as part of its poverty elimination research.
- Tourism can impose substantial non-economic costs on the poor through loss of access to resources (particularly beaches), displacement from agricultural land and social and cultural disruption and exploitation.

Many forms of development bring with them disadvantages of this kind, negative impacts that need to be managed. The economic and non-economic negative impacts need to be determined and the issues addressed. It is for this reason that the WTO supports a holistic livelihoods approach to assessing the impacts of tourism—positive and negative on the poor. The issues of environmental management and planning at local level are real, and not unique to tourism; they need to be addressed through the good governance agenda.

- Tourism is vulnerable to changes in economic conditions in the originating markets, which cause major swings in levels of economic activity in tourism in the destinations, and international visitor arrivals are also vulnerable to civil unrest, crime, political instability and natural disasters in destinations.

  It is not clear that the volatility of export markets for tourism is significantly greater than for other commodities. Tourism has the advantage noted above that it is not subject to tariff or other non-tariff barriers and that the destination has some control over civil unrest, crime and political instability.
- Tourism requires highly sophisticated marketing.

  International tourism marketing is expensive, although there are more efficient and less costly forms of marketing, which are not always deployed. Attendance at international trade fairs is expensive but these marketing costs are carried at national level. The individual traders and SMMEs should not be marketing there—their market is the international and domestic tourists in the destination where they live and the hotels, resorts and inbound operators who are in contact with the tourists. Individual handicraft producers rarely export directly, they sell through wholesalers into international markets.

Tourism to many developing countries and many LDCs has been growing strongly in recent years and there are strong reasons to think that these trends will continue. There is a market opportunity in tourism for many, but not all, developing countries. Many developing countries have comparative advantage in tourism—or at least tourism constitutes one of their better opportunities for development. The disadvantages, which are often identified in relation to international tourism in developing countries, are more apparent than real when tourism is compared with other sectors. WTO has long advocated that tourism is considered alongside other industries as a development option and that where tourism presents the best opportunity for local economic development and anti-poverty strategies, development banks and bilateral and multilateral development agencies should back it with determination.

TOURISM'S POTENTIAL AS A SUSTAINABLE DEVELOPMENT STRATEGY

The WTO Tourism Policy Forum marked the first time that donor agencies, developing countries, and civil society have met together at a high-level international conference to focus specifically on ways to cooperate and harness the economic power of tourism for sustainable development.

Organized by WTO and The George Washington University—chair of the WTO Education Council—the forum attracted 200 participants and more than 200 observers from 52 countries, including 20 tourism ministers or top-level government officials. Participating donor agencies included multilateral banks such as the World Bank and Inter-American Development Bank, as well as bilateral development agencies such as USAID, DGSC/MAE Italy, AECI Spain, DGCID/MAE France, SNV Netherlands, GZT Germany, CIDA Canada, and JICA Japan.

The forum opened on October 19, 2004 with keynote speeches by WTO Secretary-General Francesco Frangialli, Inter-American Development Bank President Enrique Iglesias, and World Bank Vice-President James Adams. All three speakers stressed that properly managed tourism can be a powerful tool for sustainable development. But they also agreed that the complex, multifaceted nature of the tourism industry presents special management challenges for donor agencies as well as governments. Some challenges identified were ensuring cooperation and communication among the diverse tourism development stakeholders and developing analytical measurement tools to evaluate the success or failure of sustainable tourism development projects.

Mr. Iglesias also described the importance of tourism in the Latin American region, where 54 million international visits per year translate into 2.5 million jobs, or roughly 15 per cent of the region's workforce. Mr. Iglesias also mentioned that although IDB has been involved in tourism projects for 30 years, the focus has changed from big infrastructure projects to more community-based projects. Mr. Adams reported that in the past five years, the World Bank Group has undertaken approximately 100 projects involving tourism in 56 countries, representing 3 per cent of the bank's total investment. He also stressed how tourism development is not only about economic growth but also about conservation and social sustainability. Finally, Mr. Frangialli reviewed WTO activities in the area of sustainable tourism development, asserting WTO's intention to lead a global partnership for sustainable tourism development to help the developing world harness its tremendous tourism potential.

An additional keynote speech was later delivered by USAID Administrator Andrew Natsios, who stressed the need for community involvement to ensure tourism is sustainable. He also underscored the importance of capacity building, which he said represented the essence of development.

This was followed by a tourism minister panel discussion, moderated by Mr. Frangialli. Participants included the tourism ministers from Lesotho, Nicaragua, South Africa, Honduras, Andorra, and Jordan. Some messages that were echoed by all participants were that tourism is the most efficient sector for generating jobs and economic growth, master plans need to stress long-term sustainability and poverty reduction, and that legal and regulatory frameworks for investors are needed.

The afternoon session on October 19, 2004 included several important announcements. First, a Memorandum of Understanding was announced and signed between WTO and The George Washington University for a new project called DANTEI (Development Assistance Network for Tourism Economic Initiatives). DANTEI is a website designed to increase communication and the exchange of information about sustainable tourism projects.

In the afternoon session, Eduardo Fayos-Solá, Head of WTO Human Resource Development, discussed the value of knowledge management as a key instrument for tourism policy and outlined the framework of a WTO approach to Tourism Policy for Development consisting of (i) building public/private partnerships for action; (ii) using knowledge management as the main instrument in tourism for development policies, and (iii) creating strategic tourism policy plans with development as the main objective. Some specific initiatives such as a sustainability indicators study, an e-learning programme, and a WTO Education Council volunteer programme were then discussed during the WTO Knowledge Management panel that concluded the activities on October 19, 2004.

Following this, Geoffrey Lipman, WTO Special Advisor, announced the creation of the new ST-EP (Sustainable Tourism—Eliminating Poverty) Foundation, which is set to begin operations next year. ST-EP will finance new research and development projects that link sustainable tourism to the UN Millennium Development Goals (MDGs), especially poverty alleviation. The foundation, to be based in Seoul, aims to attract US$100 million in financing and sponsor 5,000 projects by 2015.

Young-Shim Dho of the Korean Culture and Tourism Policy Institute, which is providing US$5 million in seed money for the ST-EP Foundation, was one six panelists in a donor session held later in the afternoon of October 19, 2004. She was joined on the panel by Richard Scobey of the World Bank, Paul McGinnis of Canadian International Development Agency, Martin Tampe of German Technical Cooperation GZT, and Don Martin of the Critical Ecosystem Partnership Fund. The session was moderated by Antonio Vives of the Inter-American Development Bank.

The focus of October 20, 2004 was on working group sessions organized according to eight tourism development themes. The themes of the four morning concurrent sessions were Strategic Assessment Planning and Implementation; Decentralized Governance and Community Capacity Building; SME Business Development and Competitiveness; Natural Resource and Protected Area Management. The themes of the four afternoon sessions were Cultural Heritage Preservation; Marketing Sustainable Tourism Product; Rural Development; and Financial Instruments and Enabling Environments.

In each session, five or six tourism experts presented case studies. Next, session attendees divided into three groups, each discussing an issue that was identified through a pre-conference survey. More specifically, each group identified three important recommendations related to their issue and then determined how and by which organizations these recommendations should be carried out.

After the afternoon working group sessions, a panel of tourism experts from USAID, DGSC/MAE Italy, AECI Spain, DGCID/MAE France, SNV Netherlands, and GZT Germany discussed their organizations' tourism activities and avenues for future collaboration.

The forum concluded with a reading of the *Washington Declaration on Tourism as a Sustainable Development Strategy* by University of Hawaii, Professor Pauline Sheldon and concluding statements by WTO Special Advisor Geoffrey Lipman. Lipman pointed out the emergence of a new mindset among top officials of the international financing institutions, who had asserted that tourism can be the "entry point" to development in areas like infrastructure and rural renewal. He also called upon all participants to collaborate in order to leverage their strengths, offering the WTO as reference point for the sector and focal point for linkages with the Millennium Development Goals.

WASHINGTON DECLARATION

The first international forum focusing on tourism development and assistance met for the Tourism Policy Forum held in Washington DC from October 18-20, 2004, convened by the World Tourism Organization and The George Washington University, Chair of the WTO Education Council.

The Assembly Proposes the Following Declaration

- Whereas, the World Tourism Organization (WTO) has recently become the United Nations Specialized Agency for Tourism, vested with a central role in promoting the development of responsible, sustainable and universally accessible tourism;
- Whereas, the purpose of the WTO Tourism Policy Forum (WTO.TPF) is to convene educators and knowledge management experts of the WTO Education Council and

other informed professionals, together with representative government policy-makers and business leaders, to focus on critical policy issues facing global tourism and to offer recommendations for future directions;

- Whereas, 200 delegates and 200 observers from 52 countries participated in global consensus building activities focused on development assistance issues and strategic recommendations;
- Taking into consideration that tourism is the largest industry in the world today with significant economic, environmental and socio-cultural impacts, requiring sustainable, knowledge-based policies;
- Taking into consideration that tourism is an increasingly important development strategy to positively address poverty reduction, economic growth, biodiversity conservation, and socio-cultural integrity generally, as well as the UN Millennium Development Goals (MDGs) specifically;
- Recognizing that tourism can contribute to equitable redistribution of income and liberalization with a human face;
- Recognizing also the active role of other United Nations agencies and their assistance to developing countries;
- Acknowledging that sustainable tourism development necessitates private and public sector, donor agency and stakeholder cooperation and input;
- Acknowledging that the measurement and monitoring of tourism's impact with rigorous analytical tools and relevant indicators is crucial;
- Acknowledging the importance of the WTO ST-EP programme to bring sustainable tourism development into the service of poverty alleviation.

We agree to the following:

- To build partnerships of equal opportunity and fair representation within destinations, and to strengthen their leadership;
- To engender local community awareness of the tourism planning process and its benefits;

- To foster buy-in for the concept of sustainability by all sectors including the sharing of guidelines and good practices;
- To delegate the authority for decision-making to the appropriate community level and build capacity there, and empower local development authorities;
- To encourage and facilitate brand awareness and a collective image for a destination community;
- To recognize the uniqueness of the business perspective as different from that of the public sector and to communicate effectively in business language;
- To develop cross-sectoral demonstration projects that illustrate linkages, inter-relationships and working partnerships;
- To call upon governments, biateral and multilateral institutions to facilitate access to capital of all kinds, and to provide guidance, training and support on how to access such funding;
- To develop land-use policies through a participatory process, and to provide policy incentives for private land owners;
- To enhance communication and coordination between agencies including the use of advanced information communication technologies;
- To develop educational programmes directed to tourism policy stakeholders including local communities to promote the understanding of cultural/heritage resources, and the need for preservation and social responsibilities;
- To encourage the development of a regional network of researchers, practitioners and donor agencies for sustainable tourism development.

Therefore, be it resolved that:

- These Forum findings and recommendations will be reported to the relevant bodies and WTO organs for consideration of further action.
- The Forum delegates call upon aid donors and recipients, to join together with government, private sector, universities and civil society stakeholders to form a global network to enhance tourism's potential to contribute positively to the fulfillment of Millennium Development Goals.

4

Hospitals, Patient Safety and Healthcare Programmes

HOSPITALS : AN INTRODUCTION

A *hospital* is an institution for healthcare provided by physicians, surgeons, nurses and other professionals.

During the Middle Ages the hospital could serve other functions, such as almshouse for the poor, or hostel for pilgrims. The name comes from Latin *hospes* (host), which is also the root for the English words *hotel, hostel* and *hospitality*. The modern word *hotel* derives from the French word *hostel*, which featured a silent s, which was eventually removed from the word; French for *hospital* is *hôpital*.

Some patients just come for diagnosis and/or therapy and then leave (outpatients); while others are admitted and stay overnight or for several weeks or months (inpatients). Hospitals are usually distinguished from other types of medical facilities by their ability to admit and care for inpatients.

The best-known type of hospital is the general hospital (in the UK known as a District General Hospital), which is set up to deal with many kinds of disease and injury, and typically has an emergency ward/A&E department to deal with immediate threats to health and the capacity to dispatch emergency medical services. A general hospital is typically the major healthcare facility in its region, with large number of beds for intensive care and long-term care; and specialized facilities for surgery, plastic surgery, childbirth, bioassay laboratories, and so forth. Larger cities may have many different hospitals of varying sizes and facilities.

Very large hospitals are often called Medical Centres in the United States (US) and usually conduct operations in virtually every field of modern medicine.

Most hospitals in the United Kingdom (UK) are run by the National Health Service.

Specialized Hospitals

Types of specialized hospitals include trauma centres, children's hospitals, seniors' (geriatric) hospitals, and hospitals for dealing with specific medical needs such as psychiatric problems (see psychiatric hospital), pulmonary diseases, and so forth.

A hospital may be a single building or a campus. Some hospitals are affiliated with universities for medical research and the training of medical personnel. Within the United States, many hospitals are for profit, while elsewhere in the world most are non-profit.

Clinics

A medical facility smaller than a hospital is called a *clinic,* and is often run by a government agency for health services or a private partnership of physicians (in nations where private practice is allowed). Clinics generally provide only outpatient services.

Other Facilities

Many hospitals have hospital volunteer programmes where people (usually students and senior citizens) can volunteer and provide various ancillary services.

Most cities (especially in the U.S.) have laws that require hospitals to have alternative backup power generators, in case of a blackout. Additionally they may be placed on special high priority segments of the public works (utilities) infrastructure to insure continuity of care during a state of emergency.

Early History of Hospitals

In ancient cultures religion and medicine were linked. The earliest known institutions aiming to provide cure were Egyptian temples. Greek temples dedicated to the healer-god Asclepius might admit the sick, who would wait for guidance from the god in a dream. The Romans adopted his worship. Under his Roman name

Æsculapius, he was provided with a temple (291 BC) on an island in the Tiber in Rome, where similar rites were performed. State-supported hospitals also appeared in China later during the first millennium A.D.

Early Hospitals in Southern and Western Asia

The Sinhalese (Sri Lankans) are perhaps responsible for introducing the concept of dedicated hospitals to the world. According to the Mahavamsa, the ancient chronicle of Sinhalese royalty written in the sixth century AC, King Pandukabhaya (fourth century BC) had lying-in-homes and hospitals (Sivikasotthi-Sala) built in various parts of the country after having fortified his capital at Anuradhapura. This is the earliest literary evidence we have of institutions specifically dedicated to the care of the sick anywhere in the world. Mihintale Hospital is perhaps the oldest in the world.

Institutions created specifically to care for the ill also appeared early in India. King Ashoka founded 18 hospitals c. 230 BC. There were physicians and nursing staff, and the expense was borne by the royal treasury.

The first teaching hospital, however, where students were authorized to methodically practice on patients under the supervision of physicians as part of their education, was the Academy of Gundishapur in the Persian Empire. One expert has argued that "to a very large extent, the credit for the whole hospital *system* must be given to Persia".

Hospitals in the Roman Empire

The Romans created *valetudinaria* for the care of sick slaves, gladiators and soldiers around 100 BC. The adoption of Christianity as the state religion of the empire drove an expansion of the provision of care, but not just for the sick. The First Council of Nicaea in 325 A.D. urged the Church to provide for the poor, sick, widows and strangers. It ordered the construction of a hospital in every cathedral town. Among the earliest were those built by the physician Saint Sampson in Constantinople and by Basil, bishop of Caesarea. The latter was attached to a monastery and provided lodgings for poor and travellers, as well as treating the sick and infirm. There was a separate section for lepers.

Hospitals in Medieval Europe

Medieval hospitals in Europe followed a similar pattern. They were religious communities, with care provided by monks and nuns. (An old French term for hospital is *hôtel-Dieu,* "hostel of God".) Some were attached to monasteries; others were independent and had their own endowments, usually of property, which provided income for their support. Some hospitals were multi-function while others were founded for specific purposes such as leper hospitals, or as refuges for the poor or for pilgrims: not all cared for the sick.

Hospitals in the Medieval Islamic World

Meanwhile Muslim hospitals developed a high standard of care between the eighth and twelfth centuries A.D. Hospitals built in Baghdad in the ninth and tenth centuries employed up to twenty-five staff physicians and had separate wards for different conditions and lead to the modern hospital.

Hospitals in the Modern Era

In Europe the medieval concept of Christian care evolved during the sixteenth and seventeenth centuries into a secular one, but it was in the eighteenth century that the modern hospital began to appear, serving only medical needs and staffed with physicians and surgeons. The Charité (founded in Berlin in 1710) is an early example.

Guy's Hospital was founded in London in 1724 from a bequest by wealthy merchant Thomas Guy. Other hospitals sprang up in London and other British cities over the century, many paid for by private subscriptions. In the British American colonies the Pennsylvania General Hospital was chartered in Philadelphia in 1751, after £2,000 from private subscription was matched by funds from the Assembly.

When the Viennese General Hospital (Allgemeines Krankenhaus) opened in 1784 (instantly becoming the world's largest hospital), physicians acquired a new facility that gradually developed into the most important research centre. During the 19th century, the Second Viennese Medical School emerged with the contributions of physicians such as Karl Rokitansky, Josef Skoda, Ferdinand von Hebra and Ignaz Philipp Semmelweis. Basic medical science expanded and specialization advanced. Furthermore, the first dermatology, eye, as well as ear, nose and throat clinics in the world were founded in Vienna—it was the birth of specialized medicine.

By the mid-nineteenth century most of Europe and the United States had established a variety of public and private hospital systems. In Continental Europe the new hospitals were generally built and run from public funds. In the UK the giant State-run National Health Service, founded in 1948 and one of the world's five largest employers, dominates the hospital sector.

In the United States the traditional hospital is a non-profit hospital, usually sponsored by a religious denomination. One of the earliest of these "almshouses" in what would become the United States was started by William Penn in Philadelphia in 1713. These hospitals are tax-exempt due to their charitable purpose, but provide only a minimum of charitable medical care. They are supplemented by large public hospitals in major cities and research hospitals often affiliated with a medical school. In the late twentieth century chains of for profit hospitals arose.

Mechanical, Electrical, Plumbing and Other Systems

The surgical, special procedures, radiological, intensive care unit, and patient rooms typically have medical gases, emergency and normal electrical power, and heating, air conditioning and ventilation systems.

Electrical

The reliability of the electrical power systems that serve a hospital is important. In order to provide higher electrical reliability, the National Institutes of Health (NIH), requires that all secondary substations > 500 kVA at their Bethesda, MD campus be the spot network type. The spot network substations cost more than other arrangements.

Pneumatic Tube Conveying Systems

Pneumatic tube conveying systems are often used to move the actual paper prescriptions for medicines to the pharmacies, and to move medicines, especially intra venous (IV), bags to the patient care rooms. Tissue samples can be sent to the laboratory. Medical notes can be transcribed, printed, and then transported via a pneumatic tube conveying system.

As measured by the weight of the item be transferred, the 6″ diameter tube systems have about 225 per cent of the lifting and moving capacity of a 4″ system. When the seals are new, the 4″ tube carriers will move a 2+ pound IV bag. But when the seals on the tube carriers are worn, the tubes can stop moving in the piping, and require a trained technician to recover the tube carrier.

MODERN HOSPITAL INFORMATION SYSTEMS

The purpose of a hospital information system (HIS) is to manage the information that health professionals need to perform their jobs effectively and efficiently. Information requirements:

- Operational requirements
  - Up-to-date factual information
  - Necessary for day-to-day tasks
- Planning requirements
  - Short- and long-term decisions about patient care
  - Decisions about hospital management
- Documentation requirements
  - The maintenance of records
  - Accreditation
  - Legal record

It costs a lot of money to deal with the information in a hospital. The Friedman and Martin functional model for an HIS:

- Core systems
  - Patient scheduling
  - Admission
  - Discharge
  - Admission-discharge-transfer (ADT)
- Business and financial systems
  - Payroll
  - Accounts receivable
- Communications and networking systems
  - Integration of all parts of the HIS

  - Order entry and results reporting
- Departmental-management systems
  - The needs of individual departments can be met
  - Those subsystems can be useful in a macro-system
- Medical-documentation systems
  - Collecting, organizing, storing and presenting
  - Quality assurance (QA)
- Medical support systems
  - Assistance in interpreting data
  - Issue alerts, provide advice

It can be useful to integrate the clinical and the administrative information into the same information system. This can create a "rich database for decision making".

Alternative architectures for hospital information systems:

- Central systems
  - Total or holistic system
  - One main computer handling all the information
  - Many terminals and printers for information exchange
  - TMIS
  - Problems:
    - Very difficult to backup
    - Hard to keep up-to-date technology
    - All or nothing effect
- Modular systems
  - Distinct software modules carry out specific tasks
  - "Plugging in" new task performance
  - HELP
  - Problems:
    - "Plugging in" never works very well
- Distributed systems
  - LAN structure
  - Independent computers tailored for specific uses
  - Autonomous
  - Computers with shared data
  - Can connect multiple LANs
  - PROMIS (Problem-Oriented Medical Information System)

Comparison

- Technicon medical information system (TMIS)
    - Among the oldest (started in 1965)
    - Developed between Lockheed and El Camino Hospital
    - Only accomplished information management
- HELP system
    - Developed at the LDS hospital
    - Provided information management, physician guidance, and clinical-research support
    - Physician guidance was accomplished through "knowledge frames"
        - Set alarms
        - Warning if "this is true" then "do this"
- PROMIS (Problem-Oriented Medical Information System)
    - Developed at the medical centre hospital of Vermont and the University of Vermont
    - Designed to completely replace paper
    - Used by the physician during a session to guide his/her analysis
    - Severely constrictive and not well received
    - Made an impact upon later HISs

Trends in HIS Development

- Local area communication networks
    - LANs are cheaper and more effective
- Workstations and personal computers
    - On a LAN you need some computers
- Bedside terminals
    - Have not caught on yet due to cost
- Linkages between hospitals and physicians
    - As automation occurs natural links occur

2007 NATIONAL PATIENT SAFETY GOALS

The Joint Commission on Accreditation of Healthcare Organizations on June 12, 2006 at OAK BROOK TERRACE announced the 2007 national patient safety goals and related requirements for each of its accreditation programmes and its Disease-Specific Care certification programme. The goals and requirements, recently approved by the Joint Commission's Board of Commissioners, apply to the nearly 15,000 Joint Commission-accredited and certified healthcare organizations and programmes.

Major changes in this fifth annual issuance of National Patient Safety Goals include extension of a Requirement that accredited organizations define and communicate the means for patients and their families to report concerns about safety, across all Joint Commission accreditation and certification programmes. The Requirement—first applied to the Home Care, Laboratory, Assisted Living, and Disease-Specific Care programmes in 2006—is the central expectation of the Goal: "Encourage patients' active involvement in their own care as a patient safety strategy."

In addition, a new requirement specifies that behavioural healthcare organizations, as well as psychiatric hospitals and patients being treated for emotional or behavioural disorders in general acute-care hospitals, identify patients at risk for suicide. This requirement is part of the goal: "The organization identifies safety risks inherent in its patient populations." For home care organizations, a corresponding requirement under this goal stipulates that these organizations are to identify risks associated with long-term oxygen therapy such as home fires. Finally, new language in one of the two requirements under the existing medication reconciliation goal stipulates that a complete list of current medications be provided to the patient on discharge from care. This expectation is applicable to the Ambulatory Care, Assisted Living, Behavioural Healthcare, Critical Access Hospital, Disease-Specific Care, Home Care, Hospital, Long Term Care, and Office-Based Surgery programmes.

"The 2007 National Patient Safety Goals target critical areas where patient safety can be improved through specific actions in healthcare organizations," says Dennis S. O'Leary, M.D., president, Joint Commission. "Organizations that truly integrate these requirements into their daily operations will realize major opportunities to improve patient safety."

The development and annual updating of the National Patient Safety Goals and Requirements continue to be overseen by an expert panel that includes widely recognized patient safety experts, as well as nurses, physicians, pharmacists, risk managers and other professionals who have hands-on experience in addressing patient safety issues in a wide variety of healthcare settings. Each year, the Sentinel Event Advisory Group works with the Joint Commission to undertake a systematic review of the literature and available databases to identify candidate new goals and requirements. Following a solicitation of input from practitioners, provider organizations, purchasers, consumer groups, and other parties of interest, the Advisory Group determines the highest priority goals and requirements and makes its recommendations to the Joint Commission.

JCI has been testing tracer methodology as an enhanced patient-focused survey process during accreditation surveys in 2006. During accreditation surveys, the JCI surveyors will follow the experience of individual patients through the healthcare system, visiting multiple care units, departments, and/or areas to "trace" the care, treatment, and services rendered to an individual. The JCI survey process will focus on validating compliance with the standards, evaluating that structures and processes are in place to sustain quality improvement and safety, and result in continuous quality improvement and better outcomes for the patients, organization and staff.

Organizations seeking further information on either the IPSGs or tracer methodology are encouraged to attend JCI's 2006 Joint Commission International Executive Briefings, 31 October-1 November in Dublin, Ireland. Registration has been extended through 9 October 2006.

JCI is also planning a variety of educational programmes regarding accreditation, standards, and survey process over the coming months.

SAFETY DURING TRANSPORT OF CRITICALLY ILL PATIENTS

The care of acutely ill patients routinely includes transportation, both within a given hospital to undergo tests and procedures, and between hospitals, as patients may require transfer to other facilities for specialized services. Critically ill patients in particular commonly require such transfers and are at high risk for complications en route. Developing practices to reduce or minimize this necessary risk represents a potentially important area of patient safety research. This section focuses on transportation of critically ill patients by health professionals (paramedics, nurses, physicians and/or respiratory therapists) between hospitals (to receive higher levels of care) and within the hospital (for diagnostic or therapeutic procedures).

Stabilization before transport, in the field or in the transferring hospital, and the mode of transferring patients from the field to specialized centres also present important research and policy questions. However, we regarded these issues as clinical research topics and quality improvement issues for the fields of pre-hospital and emergency medicine, rather than patient safety in general, and so do not review this literature here.

Intrahospital transport refers to transportation of patients within a hospital for the purpose of undergoing diagnostic or therapeutic procedures or transfer to a specialized unit. In the context of this section, this generally involves movement of critically ill patients from intensive care areas of the hospital (including intensive care units, emergency departments, operating theaters and recovery rooms) to areas typically not involved in the delivery of such care (e.g., a hospital radiology department). Equipment and staffing used for intrahospital transport varies by hospital, clinical service and patient acuity. Studies of intrahospital transport have mainly focused on the adequacy of patient monitoring and ventilator support. The specific practices evaluated in this section include:

- *The continued use of mechanical ventilation instead of switching to manual ventilation.* Manual ventilation involves a self-inflating bag with or without a volumeter, while mechanical ventilation consists of a portable, time-cycled, volume-constant transport ventilator.
- *The use of specialized transfer units during intrahospital transport.* The unit is attached to the patient's bed and contains all equipment necessary to meet the patient's needs (ventilation, monitoring and infusion of drugs) in the ICU (Intensive Care Unit) and during transport. The unit works as a stand-alone unit.

Interhospital transport refers to transportation of patients between hospitals by ground or air ambulance. Interhospital transport teams vary widely in composition, training and experience. The transport team does not always include a physician; even when a physician is present, his or her training may not include skills necessary for this task. Nurses and respiratory therapists frequently accompany critically ill patients during interhospital transport. Some paramedics receive special training in skills necessary for the interhospital transport of critically ill patients. As with physicians, the training of nurses and respiratory therapists assigned responsibility for interhospital transport varies widely. Equipment used during interhospital transport also varies widely, but the practices evaluated in the literature mainly relate to the use of *specialized transport teams.*

Specialized transport teams characteristically receive consistent and high levels of training and experience in the transportation of critically ill patients, compared with teams assembled ad hoc.

Prevalence and Severity of the Target Safety Problem

Adverse events during transport of critically ill patients fall into two general categories: mishaps related to intensive care (e.g., lead disconnections, loss of battery power, loss of intravenous access, accidental extubation, occlusion of the endotracheal tube, or exhaustion of oxygen supply), and physiologic deteriorations related to critical illness (e.g., worsening hypotension or hypoxemia). Unfortunately many studies do not distinguish clearly between these two categories. Further complicating assessments of patient transport as a safety problem is the confounding effect of patient selection, as patents requiring intra- or interhospital transport likely represent a sicker patient population than unselected critically ill patients. In fact, one case control study reported no differences in adverse events (equipment-related or physiologic) in critically ill adults during the period of intrahospital transportation as compared to matched subjects in the ICU.

Death during transport is a rare event. The majority of studies reported no mortality during intrahospital transport or interhospital transport, and some do not mention deaths.

For intrahospital transport of critically ill patients, reported rates of adverse events range from 5.9 per cent to 66 per cent. (We could find no comparable reports of event rates for critically ill children). Much of this variation undoubtedly reflects definitional differences, but differences in patient populations also contribute to this wide range. For instance, a prospective study of 50 high-risk adult cardiac patients reported arrhythmias in 84 per cent of patients, with 52 per cent of these arrhythmias providing an indication for emergency treatment.These event rates are clearly much higher than would be observed in an unselected population of critically patients. Similarly, Insel *et al.* showed a significantly higher incidence of hemodynamic changes requiring therapeutic intervention when intrahospital transport involved transfers from the operating room to the ICU compared with patients transported from the ICU to diagnostic procedures.

In contrast to the above, the literature on adverse events during interhospital transport has generally involved critically ill children, not adults. Reported rates of adverse events during pediatric interhospital transport range from 0 to 75 per cent. In one of these studies, a prospective cohort design reported a morbidity ratio of 1.85 (95 per cent CI: 1.12-3.06) for pediatric patients transported from another hospital to the pediatric ICU (PICU) as compared with those admitted directly (emergency room and wards). Importantly, this increased morbidity reflected an increased rate of "intensive care events" such as plugged endotracheal tubes and loss of intravenous access, not an increase in physiologic events. Patients experiencing such adverse events tended to have higher morbidity scores (on the PRISM scale) and lower therapy level (TISS) scores prior to transport. Thus, as noted above, confounding of differences in patient sickness and intensity of therapy could account for much of the observed variation in transport-associated morbidity.

A survey conducted in 1990 to review voluntary compliance with the American Academy of Pediatrics (AAP) recommendations to include physicians with higher level of training (at least 3rd year residency) reported that only 28 per cent of hospitals with a pediatric critical care transport team met this recommendation. All teams included a nurse with pediatric experience and a varying degree of training, and 50 per cent of teams included a respiratory therapist.

Interhospital Transport

Study Designs and Outcomes

We identified three studies with at least a Level 3 study design and Level 2 outcomes. Two of these studies involved pediatric patients.

The prospective comparison of outcomes for high-risk pediatric patients admitted to two different ICU's, one of which employed a specialized transport team, while the other followed the standard practice of using non-specialized teams. The specialized team consisted of a second-year pediatric resident and a pediatric ICU nurse, both trained in pediatric advanced life support, and a respiratory therapist with pediatric experience. Non-specialized teams varied in composition—a physician was not always present and level of training in pediatric care for other personnel was not standardized. The other pediatric study, from England, retrospectively compared outcomes using a specialized team for the transport of intubated newborns from hospitals within 80 miles to a NICU at a referral centre to outcomes during a control period in which transport was performed by *ad hoc* doctor/nurse teams. The specialized teams included physicians with more years of experience and dedicated transport nurses with specialized training, as well as slight equipment improvements (humidifier for ventilator and invasive/non-invasive blood pressure monitoring).

The third study (the one involving adults) describes the experience of a London teaching hospital that receives critically ill patients from other facilities by two methods: either accompanied by the receiving hospital's special retrieval team consisting of an ICU physician, nurse, and medical physics technician (a technician to fix and maintain equipment) or standard ambulance transport, with an escorting physician supplied by the referring hospital.

The two pediatric studies reported adverse events during transportation. We counted adverse events related to intensive care (e.g., accidental extubation) as Level 2 and physiologic events (e.g., ph < 7.2) as Level 3. (A case could be made for classifying both types of adverse events as Level 3, as neither has a clearly established relationship to adverse events of interest). All studies provided information on case mix in the study and control groups.

Evidence for Effectiveness of the Practice

Although of theoretical and practical concern, the literature to support the scope, frequency and outcome of adverse events during transportation is sparse and methodologically weak. Most studies are small descriptive studies of local practices. Factors that limit comparability between studies include a variety of definitions for transport-related adverse events, unclear descriptions of transport team training and experience, diverse equipment availability and different scoring systems for severity of illness (APACHE II, APACHE III, Glasgow Coma Scale, PRISM, etc). Many confounders affect the evaluation of transportation of a critically ill patient, among them selection bias, the intervention received at primary hospital, time spent at primary hospital, adequate stabilization before transport and duration of transport.

In one of the studies, patients transported by the standard (non-specialized) team were older and more likely to have trauma as a diagnosis. This difference in patient populations clearly limits the ability to interpret the results, although the direction of bias this might introduce is not clear. The other pediatric study reported no significant differences in basic clinical and demographic factors between the 2 patient populations, but did not report PRISM scores.

The single study in adults did not report intensive care-related adverse events, but did observe significant reductions in surrogate physiologic markers and a non-significant reduction in mortality within 12 hours of arrival at the receiving facility. Although an observational study, there were no differences in the patient populations in terms of demographic factors, basic physiology measurements (FiO_2, PaO_2, $PaCO_2$, PaO_2/FiO_2, MAP, heart rate and temperature) or sophisticated measures of severity of illness (APACHE II, simplified Acute Physiological Score-SAPS II).

Potential for Harm

A delay in the transfer of critically ill patients to referral hospitals because the specialized team is not available in timely fashion could create a potential for harm although one study showed no delay or cancellation due to unavailability of specialist team.

Costs and Implementation

Although no firm recommendation can be made, the costs and implementation requirements may only be feasible for tertiary centres that have enough volume to justify the investment in human and physical resources. Time out of hospital will vary depending on the time required to stabilize the patient—not the focus of our study. (One study reported an increase in stabilization time from 80-105 minutes ($p<0.0001$) after the implementation of a specialized team and another reported no difference in duration of transport between non-specialized and specialized team). The third study did not mention duration of transport.

EVALUATING PROGRAMMES FOR HIV/AIDS PREVENTION AND CARE IN DEVELOPING COUNTRIES

Role of Evaluation in HIV/AIDS Programmes

Conceptual Approach and Framework for Monitoring and Evaluation

Evaluating HIV/AIDS prevention and care programmes is a never-ending challenge, but recognizing its importance in improving current interventions may help to enhance the success of future initiatives.

There are probably as many definitions of "programme evaluation" or "evaluation research" as there are programme evaluators. Our approach to evaluating HIV/AIDS prevention and care programmes is best captured by a description of evaluation provided by Michael Quinn Patton:

> "I use the term evaluation quite broadly to include any effort to increase human effectiveness through systematic data-based inquiry. When one examines and judges accomplishments and effectiveness, one is engaged in evaluation. When this examination of effectiveness is conducted systematically and empirically through careful data collection and thoughtful analysis, one is engaged in evaluation research.... Evaluation is applied research, or a type of "action science". This distinguishes evaluation research from basic academic research....The purpose of applied research and evaluation is to inform action, enhance decision-making, and apply knowledge to solve human and societal problems....Applied evaluative research is judged by its usefulness in making human actions and interventions more effective and by its

practical utility to decision-makers, policymakers and others who have a stake in efforts to improve the world."

Such an evaluation approach is utilization-focused. This approach emphasizes the interests of key stakeholders and primary users of the information at all levels, for example the donor, the host country, and the implementing agencies. It applies socio-epidemiological research to identify ways to improve the design and implementation of HIV/AIDS prevention and care programmes.

This chapter first describes several considerations that are fundamental to planning an evaluation effort. It then presents a comprehensive framework for country programmes by explaining the major types of evaluation and discussing several important issues related to planning evaluation programmes and improving their ability to measure programme effects.

Basic Considerations

Several considerations underlie the decision-making process about HIV/AIDS programme evaluation. The selection of an appropriate evaluation concept for an AIDS prevention programme is crucial because it determines the guiding philosophy behind the actual evaluation process. A number of theorists and evaluation practitioners have proposed various conceptual approaches to evaluation. These approaches differ in their conception as to what evaluation is, what the relationship with the primary client and other stakeholders should be, who should be making the relevant value judgements regarding the programme, and the criteria for judging the evaluation process itself.

The conceptual approach debate was, and is for the most part, a debate about the best ways to measure and interpret change. It has highlighted a series of methodological dimensions among which there are variations in emphasis. These dimensions focus attention on some of the options available for making decisions about methods. Today, for example, there is consensus that both quantitative and qualitative data are valued and recognized as legitimate for programme evaluation. In fact, these methods are by no means incompatible and should be used in combination.

Deciding what and how much data to gather in an evaluation involves difficult methodological decisions and trade-offs between the quality and utility of information. An evaluation approach that uses multiple data collection methods, both quantitative and qualitative, is more likely to address diverse evaluation needs than is a more limited approach. At the same time, research priorities must be sensitive to competing needs for resources in an environment in which the HIV/AIDS epidemic is growing rapidly and evaluation is sometimes considered a luxury. It is a major task of the evaluator to match research methods to the reality of particular evaluation questions and to the available resources.

There is also a need for evaluation researchers to play an active role, not merely a consultative one, in making design decisions for programme assessments. Although a programme evaluator should be a neutral scientific observer, he or she can also mediate between different stakeholder groups, can enable others through a participatory evaluation approach, and can advocate for the dissemination of evaluation results within the larger arena of decisionmaking. Planning evaluation and data collection activities in a participatory fashion is essential for achieving the delicate balance between practical needs and methodological desirability. Key stakeholders should be included in the planning process and every effort should be made for effective use of limited resources. Ensuring active support and participation of key stakeholders who have an interest in the results obtained by various data collection systems is particularly important for programmes funded by external donors that use host country institutions for data collection activities. Data produced by these efforts will have a better chance to be timely and of acceptable quality. Whenever possible, participants, including implementing institutions, host-country collaborators and local representatives of donor agencies, should attempt to reach consensus regarding data needs.

EVALUATION FRAMEWORK FOR COUNTRY PROGRAMMES

HIV/AIDS prevention and care programmes need to be evaluated at different phases of the programme cycle. All stages of evaluation have to be considered together to provide an overall picture of the programme because no single data collection approach can supply all the information necessary to improve programme performance or affect policy change.

Multiple complementary evaluation approaches and multiple methodologies (qualitative and quantitative) have to be applied to address different evaluation needs.

Formative Evaluation

Formative evaluation should be conducted during the planning (or replanning) stage of a prevention and care programme to identify and resolve intervention and evaluation issues before the programme is widely implemented. This is the time when flexibility is greatest and programme sponsors are freer to make decisions about how to proceed.

Formative evaluation explores the need for interventions, provides the information necessary to define realistic goals and objectives for the programme interventions, and helps programme planners make tentative decisions about effective, feasible intervention strategies and how to carry them out. Formative evaluation can also be used as an exploratory tool as the project is being carried out to provide feedback to project managers to help them adjust programme objectives to changing situations. Formative evaluation research can identify unacceptable or ineffective intervention approaches, designs and concepts.

Because of the urgency of the HIV/AIDS problem, many prevention programmes have rushed to carry out interventions without preparing first by conducting thoughtful formative evaluation. The lack of this type of evaluation is particularly felt in community-based interventions designed to reduce sexual transmission of HIV. In many cases, interventions have been based on ideas developed outside of the context of the lives of the people to whom the interventions have been delivered. The literature on behavioural change interventions is full of examples of ideas that made perfect sense in the abstract but failed completely in the "real world", mainly because the ideas were unacceptable to the target audience or were not stated in ways that were relevant to the lives of those people. A fuller understanding of the issues might well have led planners to redesign the intervention to make it more appealing to the selected audience. Fortunately, this situation is changing because formative evaluation is now being applied more frequently in designing prevention programmes.

Formative evaluations use a mix of research methods that can rapidly provide relevant information to programme designers. These methods include:

- Reviews of existing information
- Focus group discussions
- Individual in-depth interviews
- Participant observations
- Short quantitative surveys with structured questionnaires.

The most frequently cited methodological criticism of formative evaluation is its lack of external validity or generalizability. Because the results of the evaluation derive from small-scale rapid assessment procedures and/or pilot studies, one cannot generalize from them to a larger population. Despite this limitation, formative evaluation research can usually identify unacceptable or ineffective intervention approaches, designs and concepts. However, even with adequate formative evaluation at the programme planning stage, there is no guarantee that a prevention programme will be effective when finally implemented; it may not be implemented adequately enough to be effective.

Process Evaluation

Once activities are underway, there is a need to examine whether they are being carried out correctly, on time, and within budget. Process evaluation addresses such basic questions as.

> "To what extent are planned intervention activities actually realized?" and "What services are provided, to whom, when, how often, for how long, and in what context?" Both input (the basic resources required in terms of manpower, money, material and time) and output (the immediate service improvement expressed as distributed commodities, trained staff, and service units delivered) are key elements of process evaluation. These questions are often answered in quantitative terms. Qualitative evidence of how and why a prevention programme works or fails to work is equally important in answering process evaluation questions. Process evaluation requires getting close to data, becoming intimately acquainted with the details of the programme, and observing not only

anticipated effects but also unanticipated consequences. An understanding of the processes through which intervention activities achieve effects can help to explain the outcome of the intervention. Process evaluation, however, does not demonstrate whether interventions are effective.

Process evaluation can also play an important role in improving or modifying interventions by providing the information necessary to adjust delivery strategies or programme objectives in a changing epidemic. Process-oriented evaluation is carried out throughout the course of the programme implementation and should use different methodological approaches to assess service delivery, ranging from reviews of service records and regular reporting systems, key informant interviews, exit interviews of service users, direct observations by 'mystery clients' (for example, in sexually transmitted infection [STI] and voluntary counselling and testing [VCT] services) to quantitative population-based surveys to assess programme coverage and barriers to service use. Different qualitative and quantitative study designs that are complementary to one another provide together the most comprehensive information.

Effectiveness Evaluation

Assessing outcome and Impact Evaluating the effectiveness of AIDS prevention programmes will almost always require quantitative measurements. These measurements will assess the extent to which the objectives of the programme were achieved. Effectiveness evaluation is used to answer the questions, "What outcomes were observed?" "What do the outcomes mean?" and "Does the programme make a difference?"

Taking into account the various implementation stages of HIV/AIDS prevention programmes and the fact that, over time, new age cohorts become sexually active, it is advisable to stratify effectiveness evaluation by short-term and intermediate programme effects (programme outcome) and long-term programme effects (programme impact). Changes in HIV/AIDS-related attitudes, the reduction of risk behaviours and adoption of protective behaviours, and changes in STI rates are considered to be the most appropriate short-term or intermediate (also called proximate) outcome measures for interventions designed to reduce sexual transmission of HIV. Long-term effects include impact on HIV/AIDS trends, sustainability issues, and improved societal response.

Outcome and impact evaluation is intimately connected with process evaluation. Process information can help the evaluator to understand how and why interventions have achieved their effects and, perhaps, what is actually making the difference. Examining outcome/impact indicators without assessing the process of programme implementation could lead to erroneous conclusions regarding the effectiveness of the intervention.

Programme goals and objectives have to be carefully defined to allow the selection of appropriate outcome and impact measures to assess the effectiveness of an AIDS prevention programme. Effectiveness evaluation is generally based on indicators that provide quantitative value from which the outcome and impact of interventions can be measured. Because multiple interventions working synergistically together are most effective in producing behaviour change, surveys should not be typically designed to capture the effects of one single intervention. Rather, they should be designed to measure behavioural trends in population groups who are exposed to combined interventions. The evaluation of one intervention is usually conducted through rigorous and expensive controlled trials.

Cost-effectiveness Analysis

Cost-effectiveness analysis also measures programme effectiveness, but expands the analysis by adding a measure of programme cost per unit of effect (for example, per number of HIV infections averted). By comparing the costs and consequences of various interventions, cost analyses and cost effectiveness estimates can assist in priority setting, resource allocation decisions, and programme design.

The Attribution Dilemma

Are observed changes a result of prevention interventions?

The ultimate goal of any HIV prevention programme is to reduce the number of new infections. Programme evaluation is intrinsically complex, however, due to the temporal evolution of epidemics and our poor understanding of how different behaviours and epidemiologic factors influence epidemic patterns as they move from an epidemic phase to an endemic state. Several factors unrelated to intervention effects can contribute to the observed stabilization or decreases in the prevalence or incidence of HIV in a given setting. They include:

- Mortality, especially in mature epidemics;
- Saturation effects in populations at high risk;
- Behavioural change in response to the experience of HIV/AIDS among friends and relatives;
- Differential migration patterns related to the epidemic; and
- Sampling bias and/or errors in data collection and analysis.

Determining whether observed changes in HIV incidence and prevalence are a reflection of the natural history of the epidemic or due to intervention effects is a critical evaluation issue. This is particularly true when evaluating behaviour changes in the face of growing numbers of people with AIDS-related illnesses because there is evidence that secular trends toward risk reduction will occur. For example, having a friend or relative with HIV/AIDS may influence adolescents to delay the onset of sexual relations or motivate those with non-regular sex partners to use condoms. Human sexual behaviour is influenced and shaped by many factors and exposure to an HIV prevention programme is only one of them.

The question of whether behaviour changes can be attributed to prevention programmes, especially in countries with advanced HIV epidemics, has created some friction between stakeholders and programme implementers at the field level. Their different perspectives on this issue also reflect fundamental differences regarding the criteria for judging the process of programme evaluation itself. From a public health perspective, it may not matter whether the observed changes are due to a particular intervention. What is most important is that sexual practices have become safer and HIV infection should subsequently decrease.

From the cost-effectiveness or policy perspective, however, it is important to determine what caused the observed changes in sexual behaviour. If the changes would have occurred without a particular intervention that was designed to contribute to the observed changes, the costs of the intervention could be considered as resources better spent on something more useful. Prevention programmes are under growing pressure to estimate which approaches work best for specific target populations in different epidemiologic settings with a given level of inputs in order to allocate resources in a cost-effective manner. Effectiveness evaluation, therefore, is critical because it can answer a basic question, "Does the programme make a difference?"

A vexing task of assessing programme effectiveness is to disentangle the attributable affects of a prevention programme from the gross outcome and impact observed. Such estimates can be made with varying degrees of plausibility, but not with certainty. A general principle applies here: The more rigorous the research design, the more convincing the resulting estimate. A hierarchy of evidence based on the study design can be established that reflects the degree of certainty in concluding that a given proportion of the observed changes in behaviour is attributable to the intervention programme and is not the result of other factors.

Non-experimental observational methods with no control groups have been routinely used in behavioural outcome evaluations. It is important to recognize, however, that a before-and-after evaluation design with no comparison groups may be useful for assessing a prevention programme's proficiency in delivering services, but it is not a very convincing design to measure programme effectiveness. The inference of cause and effect from such a design is problematic because competing explanations for across-time behavioural changes cannot be ruled out.

In some situations, the evaluation could assess "exposure" to an intervention programme or a specific element, and determine the extent of the association of that exposure with the desired outcome. This method, however, can be limited in its utility by factors such as lack of association of services or products with the intervention and inaccurate reporting by respondents of their participation in the intervention.

The interpretation of programme evaluation data should always be approached with caution. In most situations, the programme and evaluation process as a whole is not a rigorously controlled experimental trial. The ability of an evaluation to precisely determine the true extent of a programme's effectiveness is often limited by time, resources, and the lack of a rigorous design. Many factors can confuse or confound the results measured, and biases can be introduced by a range of factors inherent to the problem of HIV/AIDS, the available measurement options, and those conducting the evaluation. One of the most difficult questions to answer in any evaluation is that of attributing any measured effect to the programme being evaluated. Defining the web of interacting and overlapping influences is extremely difficult, and is one of the reasons why so many programmes have difficulty attributing results to their actions. At some point, we need to stop worrying about attribution in such settings and focus on monitoring the changes as they occur.

The Role of Triangulation

Triangulation can be achieved through using multiple data sources, different researchers, multiple perspectives to interpret a single set of data, or multiple methods applied to a single programme, problem, or issue. In the absence of rigorous controlled trials, data triangulation procedures must be applied to substantiate a link between interventions and observed behaviour changes. For example, process evaluation data on condom sales, the intensity of peer education, or the quality and coverage of media campaigns can be combined with an analysis of behavioural outcome data to provide an understanding of the process through which an intervention has achieved its effects. Results from behavioural surveys should be analyzed together with findings from qualitative evaluation research that is carried out in sub-samples of surveyed target populations. Such research can include focus group discussions, key informant interviews, and rapid ethnographic studies. This type of analysis will allow a more appropriate interpretation of observed outcome data because they are the likely results of the aggregate effects of multiple interventions as well as environmental and personal factors.

Many of the areas that need to be measured to evaluate HIV/AIDS programmes are sensitive and very personal in nature, such as sexual behaviours or personal attitudes toward persons with HIV/AIDS. Validity and reliability are critical issues for sexual behaviour research because the behaviours cannot be directly observed. Self-reports of sexual behaviours in the absence of additional evidence are often considered invalid and unreliable by stakeholders for whom such data are sensitive and run against firmly held cultural norms.

One of the best methods for promoting reliability and validity, therefore, is to triangulate behavioural data with all other available and relevant biological, behavioural, and process data to explain more comprehensively the context in which risk behaviours take place.

Given the abundance of AIDS-related research conducted in many countries, secondary data are a source of material for triangulation. Multiple-method triangulation is probably the most common triangulation technique. Rapid ethnographic research, combining semistructured information gathering with mapping, participant observation, and in-depth interviews, is another possibility. Focus group discussions have been widely used, as have individual in-depth interviews or key informant interviews, to obtain stakeholders' (or other key individuals') opinions about target groups' behaviour.

Finally, it is important to realize that behaviour change interventions have to be in place for sufficient amounts of time and on a large enough scale to have an impact on personal behaviour, social norms in communities, and ultimately on the epidemic. The example of Thailand shows that a focused intervention strategy implemented on a national scale can result in substantial declines in HIV incidence and prevalence in targeted populations. It is also an example of applied triangulation of data: STI/HIV trends were systematically collected by sentinel surveillance systems, and behavioural surveillance data provided the necessary supplementary information to interpret the observed epidemiological trends. There is now growing consensus that country programmes need to monitor risk behaviour trends together with trends in HIV infection.

Choice of Indicators

One of the critical steps in designing and carrying out an evaluation of an HIV/AIDS programme, or any programme for that matter, is selecting appropriate indicators. This can be a fairly straightforward process if the objectives of the programme have been clearly stated and presented in terms that define quantity, quality, and time frame of a particular aspect of the programme. Even with well-defined objectives, however, the choice of indicators for the evaluation of many programmes requires careful thought and consideration of both theoretical and practical elements.

The following questions can be helpful in selecting indicators:

- Is the focus of the objective a parameter that can be measured accurately and reliably?
- Are there alternative measures that need to be considered?

- What resources (human and financial) does the indicator require?
- Are there areas for congruency, either in the content of the indicator or the means of gathering the data?
- Are there any additional measures that would help in interpreting the results of the primary objective?

Selecting indicators and setting targets is usually done during the process of programme planning and replanning, preferably in a participatory way with the implementing agency and key stakeholders. Setting targets and benchmarks should also include information from similar types of interventions, so that the targets set are realistic from the perspective of the target population, resource allocation, and intervention type.

While the level of attainment to be measured by the indicator is not actually part of the indicator itself, it is a critical factor. The magnitude of the level to be measured affects the size of the sample of the population needed to estimate that level accurately. It may also help evaluators select additional or supplemental indicators that might assist in later interpretations of the results.

Ideally, indicators should be:

- *Valid*: They should measure the condition or event they are intended to measure.
- *Reliable*: They should produce the same results when used more than once to measure the same condition or event.
- *Specific*: They should measure only the condition or event they are intended to measure.
- *Sensitive*: They should reflect changes in the state of the condition or event under observation.
- *Operational*: It should be possible to measure or quantify them with developed and tested definitions and reference standards.
- *Affordable*: The costs of measuring the indicators also should be reasonable.
- *Feasible*: It should be possible to carry out the proposed data collection.

Validity is inherent in the actual content of the indicator and also depends on its potential for being measured. Reliability is inherent in the methodology used to measure the indicator and in the person using the methodology. Many familiar outcome indicators in HIV/AIDS prevention, such as measures of condom use, provide challenges to the evaluator with respect to validity and reliability.

Interpreting outcome indicators for behavioural interventions that promote safer sex is further complicated by the fact that risk behaviours are measured in relative terms. For example, percentage figures of condom use measure the proportion of sexual exposures that are considered to be safe. These may or may not reflect the absolute number of sex acts that place individuals at risk for exposure to sexual transmission. Ten per cent condom use in 10 HIV-associated sexual episodes is still safer than 75 per cent condom use in 100 HIV-associated sex episodes (9 versus 25 unprotected HIV-associated sex acts, respectively). Therefore, in this example it also would be important to determine the frequency of condom use in absolute terms in a given risk situation. Behavioural surveys have begun to address this dilemma by collecting additional data on "always or consistent" condom use in the context of sexual episodes with non-regular partners.

The advantage of relating indicators to specific evaluation levels is that it also helps to identify opportunities for triangulating data. For example, survey data on condom use can be compared with information on condom distribution and availability in a defined intervention area. Or, available data on incident STIs, such as gonorrhea, in the surveyed population could be correlated with the condom data.

In collaboration with national and international partners, the United Nations AIDS Programme and the World Health Organization (UNAIDS/WHO) have developed a standard set of indicators for country programmes that will refine and expand the prevention indicators (PI) developed by WHO's former Global Programme on AIDS (GPA). Moreover, because HIV/AIDS/STI prevention and care programmes are affected by many factors, including political commitment, available resources, and the socio-cultural and economic context, a new approach is currently being developed to capture the overall effort of national HIV/AIDS programmes. The AIDS Programme Effort Index (API) is a composite score comprised the main components of an effective national response.

The potential advantage of this instrument is that it may yield useful information on the above issues even in the absence of more rigorous monitoring and evaluation systems. Using the key informant assessment approach, it also allows an assessment of areas that are difficult to capture with more objectively measurable indicators (e.g., political support and commitment). However, major concerns have been expressed with regard to the subjectivity and reliability of the API approach. The score depends entirely on the choice of informants, and the informants are likely to change from year to year. Questions have also been raised about the utility of a single composite score in which improvements in some areas may be masked by deterioration in other areas.

Differentiating Evaluation Efforts

Because of the various constraints on time, available funds, and trained staff, programme managers and evaluation planners must balance what is ideal or preferred against what is feasible, useful, relevant, and essential when choosing how to evaluate a particular intervention or programme. A useful approach for differentiating evaluation efforts is to define them in three different dimensions: the individual project dimension, the country programme dimension, and the international dimension. Using this multi-dimensional approach (individual, country and international project) to set priorities for the degree of rigour needed to evaluate programmes and projects may alleviate some of the tension that arises when universal, standardized evaluation practices conflict with the objectives of individual projects.

One can think of the individual project dimension as an area of service delivery that, in most cases, does not require a rigorous research design to judge its proficiency, unless it is piloting a new intervention or responding to an unanswered research question, such as would occur with a demonstration project. Individual projects carrying out standard intervention strategies that have already been shown to be effective in other similar settings should their evaluation activities on formative evaluation (when needed for project planning), process evaluation, and capacity building assessment. The monitoring and evaluation "pipeline" illustrates that there is usually a reduced number of projects that actually warrant the evaluation of the effectiveness of their implemented prevention activities.

Within the dimension of a country programme, several categories of evaluation should be emphasized—intervention outcomes, socioeconomic impact, and changes in societal norms. The guiding principle here is that in a situation in which multiple donors are conducting multiple interventions with overlapping target groups, certain types of evaluation are not appropriate for the scope of an individual project, but rather, should be coordinated and conducted by country or regional programmes. Use of such an evaluation approach, especially in the area of behavioural surveys, not only saves money, but also makes sense in environments where the effects of individual projects from different donors cannot be sorted out anyway.

Country programme evaluation includes (but is not limited to) the analysis of behavioural trends in different population groups in conjunction with an analysis of HIV/STI surveillance data; the evaluation of social marketing activities related to condoms, drugs, and services; STI case management; scoring the overall effort of the national programme (for example, through the AIDS Programme Effort Index); socioeconomic impact assessments; and epidemiological modelling of the country's epidemic. Countries will have different programmes of evaluation activities, reflecting their different information needs, which are determined by the stage of their epidemic, as well as their political and social environment, existing capacity for research, and available financial resources.

Evaluation efforts on the international dimension may address still existing uncertainties about which set of prevention interventions works best, in which setting, for whom, and under what circumstances (emphasis on cost-effectiveness analysis). This type of evaluation, however, requires large-scale community-based controlled trials that are certainly beyond the scope of individual projects or even national programmes.

Given the difficulties and high costs associated with directly measuring the impact of HIV prevention programmes through large-scale incidence studies, more emphasis has now been placed on developing other methods of assessing impacts, for example through modelling.

HIV/AIDS prevention and care programme evaluation is applied socio-epidemiological research whose main purpose is to identify and solve practical problems and guide programme managers and planners in improving the design and implementation of prevention and care activities. This perspective not only determines the role of programme evaluation but also how an evaluation should be conducted, including the choice of indicators and levels of efforts in a given setting.

By applying different methods from several disciplines to many types of problems, programme evaluation is a comprehensive research approach committed to meeting the needs of stakeholder groups as well as the requirements of the scientific community.

Although programme evaluation is context specific, a comprehensive framework as outlined in this chapter is helpful in defining the questions that are to be answered by the different types of evaluation during the programme cycle. We advocate for a utilization-focused evaluation approach that emphasizes the interests of stakeholders as the primary intended information users. To achieve the delicate balance between practical needs and methodological desirability, it is therefore essential that programme evaluations are planned in a participatory fashion with key stakeholders.

Decision-making is a political process and programme evaluators can play a major role in this process when evaluation efforts are expected to provide information of policymaking significance and relevance. Although evaluation researchers should be neutral scientific observers, there is also a need for them to assume a more active role and, if necessary, mediate between stakeholders with different and sometimes conflicting interests, perspectives, and information needs.

Given the limited resources in most developing countries, assessing the effectiveness of HIV prevention programmes will often depart from scientifically ideal designs. In the absence of more rigorous evaluation designs, we urge programme managers and evaluators to apply triangulation procedures using multiple complementary methods as well as different data sources. Such a triangulated analysis will provide information comprehensive enough to allow a plausible and valid interpretation of observed outcome data, such as changes in risk behaviours, because they are the likely results of the aggregate effects of multiple interventions as well as environmental and personal factors.

5

Medical Tourism in India: A Global Comparison

India is hoping to expand its tourist industry—to include visitors with heart conditions and cataracts. Indeed, medical tourism, where foreigners travel abroad in search of low cost, world-class medical treatment, is gaining popularity in countries like India. The field has such lucrative potential that Indian Finance Minister Jaswant Singh called for India to become a "global health destination". And, with prices at a fraction of those in the US or Britain, the concept will likely have broad consumer appeal—if people can overcome their prejudices about healthcare in developing countries. Though the quality of healthcare for the poor in countries like India is undeniably low, private facilities offer advanced technology and procedures on par with hospitals in developed nations. One Indian hospital director maintains, "In a corporate hospital, once the door is closed you could be in a hospital in America."

India is promoting the "high-tech healing" of its private healthcare sector as a tourist attraction. The government hopes to encourage a budding trade in medical tourism, selling foreigners the idea of travelling to India for low-cost but world-class medical treatment.

Naresh Trehan, executive director of Escorts Heart Institute and Research Centre, a leading private healthcare provider, says India has established world-class expertise in practices such as cardiac care, cosmetic surgery, joint replacements and dentistry.

Merging medical expertise and tourism became government policy when Finance Minister Jaswant Singh, in this year's budget, called for India to become a "global health destination".

If foreigners respond, a new medical tourism industry could be generating revenues of Rs. 100 bn ($2.1 bn, ∈1.9 bn, £1.3 bn) by

2012, according to a report by McKinsey Consultants and the Confederation of Indian Industry, a business group.

There is no doubt that the Indian medical industry's main appeal is low-cost treatment. Most estimates claim treatment costs in India start at around a tenth of the price of comparable treatment in America or Britain.

For example, in April 2003, Madras Medical Mission, a Chennai-based hospital, successfully conducted a complex heart operation on an 87-year-old American patient at a reported cost of $8,000 (∈7,000, £4,850) including the cost of his airfare and a month's stay in hospital. The patient claimed that a less complex operation in America had earlier cost him $40,000.

Other procedures such as diagnostic services offer significant cost savings.

Take the rising popularity of "preventive health screening". At one private clinic in London a thorough men's health check-up that includes blood tests, electro cardiogram tests, chest X-rays, lung tests and abdominal ultrasound costs £345 ($574, ∈500). By comparison, a comparable check-up at a clinic operated by Delhi-based healthcare company Max Healthcare costs $84.

Yet cost savings may not be enough to foster a trade in medical tourism. Unfairly or not, most foreigners would not think of India as a land of good health.

The sight of the country's overcrowded public hospitals, open sewers and garbage-littered streets would unsettle most visitors' confidence about public sanitation standards in India.

Private healthcare providers argue that foreigners can be sheltered from such nastiness, and that the quality of India's corporate hospitals are world-class. "In a corporate hospital, once the door is closed you could be in a hospital in America," says P.V.R.K. Prasad, director-general of the Dr Marri Channa Reddy Human Resource Development Institute.

Vishal Bali, vice-president of Wockhardt Hospitals, points out as proof of quality that the US private health insurers Blue Cross and Blue Shield insure patients treated at his group's hospitals.

The British health insurer Bupa also insures the costs of treatment at Wockhardt Hospitals.

Mr Bali adds that Wockhardt is in talks with Britain's National Health Service about outsourcing the treatment of British patients to India.

According to Hari Prasad, vice-president of Apollo Hospitals in Hyderabad, foreigners should have confidence in India's medical system because many Britons and Americans are accustomed to being treated by expatriate Indian doctors.

In any case, most private healthcare providers hold modest ambitions about which foreign patients would come to India seeking treatment.

For instance, of the 5,200 hospital beds run by the Apollo hospital group, about 100 beds are usually occupied by foreign patients, mostly from the Middle East, Africa and countries of south Asia.

Indeed, demand for medical tourism is most likely to come from among the 20 m, strong Indian diaspora, says Deep Kalra, chief executive officer of travel agency makemytrip.com.

Mr Kalra says wealthy first-and second-generation expatriate Indians are aware of the rise of India's high quality, low-cost hospitals.

He estimates there is a potential market of some 12 m expatriate Indians who would combine regular visits to India and save time and money by undergoing non-emergency procedures such as eye operations, dental work, cosmetic surgery and knee surgery. Mr. Kalra's agency plans to launch a medical tourism package later this year.

Still, some remain sceptical about medical tourism's potential. Sumanjit Chaudhry, an executive at India's Max Healthcare group, says: "I imagine if someone is sick and ill they won't want to have a holiday. You'll hardly see a guy who comes here for heart surgery leaping off and going to the beach."

MEDICAL TOURISM AND INDIA'S SUITABILITY

Indian corporate hospitals excel in cardiology and cardiothoracic surgery, joint replacement, orthopedic surgery, gastroenterology, ophthalmology, transplants and urology to name a few. The various specialities covered are Neurology, Neurosurgery, Oncology, Ophthalmology, Rheumatology, Endocrinology, ENT, Pediatrics, Pediatric Surgery, Pediatric Neurology, Urology, Nephrology, Dermatology, Dentistry, Plastic Surgery, Gynecology, Pulmonology, Psychiatry, General Medicine and General Surgery.

The various facilities in India include full body pathology, comprehensive physical and gynecological examinations, dental checkup, eye checkup, diet consultation, audiometry, spirometry, stress and lifestyle management, pap smear, digital chest X-ray, 12 lead ECG, 2D echo colour doppler, gold standard DXA bone densitometry, body fat analysis, coronary risk markers, cancer risk markers, carotid colour doppler, spiral CT scan and high strength MRI. Each test is carried out by professional M.D. physicians, and is comprehensive yet pain-free.

There is also a gamut of services ranging from General Radiography, Ultra Sonography, Mammography to high end services like Magnetic Resonance Imaging, Digital Subtraction Angiography along with intervention procedures, Nuclear Imaging. The diagnostic facilities offered in India are comprehensive to include Laboratory services, Imaging, Cardiology, Neurology and Pulmonology. The Laboratory services include biochemistry, hematology, microbiology, serology, histopathology, transfusion medicine and RIA.

All medical investigations are conducted on the latest, technologically advanced diagnostic equipment. Stringent quality assurance exercises ensure reliable and high quality test results.

As Indian corporate hospitals are on par, if not better than the best hospitals in Thailand, Singapore, etc. there is scope for improvement, and the country may become a preferred medical destination. In addition to the increasingly top class medical care, a big draw for foreign patients is also the very minimal or hardly any waitlist as is common in European or American hospitals. In fact, priority treatment is provided today in Indian hospitals.

The Apollo Group, Escorts Hospitals in New Delhi and Jaslok Hospitals in Mumbai are to name a few which are established names even abroad. A list of corporate hospitals such as Global Hospitals, CARE and Dr L.V. Prasad Eye Hospitals in Hyderabad, The Hindujas and NM Excellence in Mumbai, also have built capabilities and are handling a steadily increasing flow of foreign patients. India has much more expertise than say Thailand or Malaysia. The infrastructure in some of India's hospitals is also very good. What is more significant is that the costs are much less, almost one-third of those in other Asian countries.

Medical Tourism India (a.k.a. Health Tourism India) is a developing concept whereby people from world over visit India for their medical and relaxation needs. Most common treatments are heart surgery, knee transplant, cosmetic surgery and dental care. The reason India is a favourable destination is because of its infrastructure and technology in which is in par with those in USA, UK and Europe. India has some of the best hospitals and treatment centres in the world with the best facilities. Since it is also one of the most favourable tourist destinations in the world. Medication combines with tourism has come into effect, from which the concept of Medical Tourism is derived.

India is promoting the "high-tech healing" of its private healthcare sector as a tourist attraction.

The government hopes to encourage a budding trade in medical tourism, selling foreigners the idea of travelling to India for low-cost but world-class medical treatment.

Naresh Trehan, executive director of Escorts Heart Institute and Research Centre, a leading private healthcare provider, says India has established world-class expertise in practices such as cardiac care, cosmetic surgery, joint replacements and dentistry. Merging medical expertize and tourism became government policy when Finance Minister Jaswant Singh, in the year's budget, called for India to become a "global health destination".

For example, in April 2006 Madras Medical Mission, a Chennai-based hospital, successfully conducted a complex heart operation on an 87-year-old American patient at a reported cost of $8,000 (∈7,000, £4,850) including the cost of his airfare and a month's stay in hospital. The patient claimed that a less complex operation in America had earlier cost him $40,000.

Medical Tourism Packages in India for Orthopedic Surgery

A number of orthopedic procedures are available such as hip and knee replacement, the Illzarov technique, limb lengthening, Birmingham Hip resurfacing technique (which scores over conventional hip replacements and is still unavailable even in the US) etc.

Many hospitals specialize in latest techniques and treatments such as minimal invasive surgery, cartilage and bone transplantation, spine surgery and limb sparing surgery. All kinds of musculoskeletal problems ranging from Arthiritis to sports injuries, to complex broken bones, bone tumours and childhood conditions like scoliosis are treated most effectively.

A wide range of spinal surgeries including fixation, stabilization and fusion are regularly undertaken.

Bone Marrow Transplant

Major hospitals in India have oncology units comprising surgical oncology, medical and radiation therapy as well as the crucial bone marrow transplantation (BMT). The BMT unit with high pressure hipa filters has helped achieve a very high success rate in the various types of transplantation.

Cord Blood Transplant and Mismatched Allogeneic Stem Cell Transplant have been performed successfully, a feat that is remarkable and significant, considering the fact that the treatment costs one-tenth of what it does in the west. Special surgeons are available for individual organs. Plastic surgeons of repute provide treatment for head and neck cancer, breast cancer and other malignancies. Facilities offered include tele therapy which includes simulation work stations to ensure high precision and safety during treatment at the 18 MV linear accelerator or telecobalt machines, brachy therapy and 3-D planning systems. In orthopedics, the Ilizarov technique is practised for the treatment of limb deformities, limb shortening and disfiguration.

Joint Replacement Surgery

Shoulder/hip replacement and bilateral knee replacement surgery using the most advanced keyhole or endosopic surgery and anthroscopy is done at several hospitals in India including the Apollo Hospital, Sir Ganga Ram Hospital and Holy Family Hospital in Delhi, Bombay Hospital, Leelavati and Hinduja Hospital in Mumbai and the Madras Institute of Orthoepedics and Trauma Sciences. Some hospitals like Apollo in Delhi have Operation Theatres with Laminar Air Flow System which compares with the best in the USA and the UK. A knee joint replacement costs about 3000 pounds in India wheras in the UK, a similar surgery using the same implants and medical consumables costs around 10,000 pounds.

In sum, among the Asian countries, India has become a major medical tourism destination, as it offers not only cheap but also sophisticated healthcare services, Health Minister Anbumani Ramadoss said. "We are getting people in thousands from various parts of the world with most of them coming for bypass surgeries, dental and orthopedic treatment, and even for plastic surgeries", Ramadoss told IANS. The Indian Government would soon identify a number of multi-speciality hospitals and expert doctors to cater to the increasing flow of overseas patients.

"The task of identifying hospitals and specialist doctors would be entrusted to a new body called the Accreditation Foundation of India," the minister said.

"The foundation would be of immense help to foreign patients to get treatment as per their needs," he added.

The decision to set up the foundation was taken after India witnessed a rush of patients from the US, Britain, Africa, and the Middle East countries seeking advanced healthcare facilities.

"Medical treatment in India is comparatively very cheap and fast, besides the country today having some of the best doctors in the world and also advanced technologies available," Ramadoss maintained.

"The cost of a bypass surgery in India would be just about one-sixth of the expenses if the same was done in the UK or other countries," he added.

The minister was here to launch the National Rural Health Mission for the region.

"Bypass surgeries apart, hip and knee replacements are fields where we are getting lot of European patients," Ramadoss said.

There are, however no official estimates to the number of foreign patients visiting India. The cheap healthcare facilities apart, people from abroad, especially the US and Britain, are flocking to hospitals in India as there is virtually no waiting time involved.

"For instance, a person in the UK needing a dental check-up needs to remain in the queue for 14 months, eight months for a bypass surgery, and about 75 days for an MRI," Ramadoss said.

"But here in India one can get the best of treatment as and when it happens without any waiting time. Healthcare is a priority sector for us," he asserted. The boom in overseas patients has prompted scores of Indian doctors working abroad to return home.

"Doctors are so well paid here that many of them have since returned from the US and other places. They are getting even more than what they were earning in places like Australia, New Zealand, the UK or even the US," the minister said.

To cash in on the boom, the Indian Government has decided to further encourage the concept of medical tourism.

"We have seen many people coming to India for treatment and then travelling to places of interests soon after their medical checkups," Ramadoss said. "The country is bound to benefit as it is expected to generate lot of direct and indirect employment opportunities. The government would facilitate and help both tourists and the hospitals to make medical tourism a huge success," he added.

World-class Facility

With India firmly establishing itself as a medical tourism destination, top hospitals here are offering facilities hitherto found in only upmarket hotels—travel desks, multi-cuisine menus, translators and the like. "An international travel desk is one of the prime requirements of a hospital servicing foreign patients", said Karan Thakur of the Indraprastha Apollo Hospital here. With the Indian medical tourism industry expanding at the rate of 20 to 30 per cent every year, super-speciality hospitals here are increasingly becoming more sensitive to the needs and requirements of foreigners who come here to take advantage of the cost-effective medical facilities on offer.

Thus top hospitals like Apollo and Sir Ganga Ram here are providing travel facilities akin to the best offered by the hotel industry.

Patients and their families are not just assured of a pleasant and comfortable experience throughout their stay, the hospitals arrange for everything they need from the time they arrive in India till they board their flight home.

From airport pickups and drops to making available language translators, hospitals even arrange accommodation for patients' families.

"We arrange for translators as many of the patients or their families have difficulty in communicating in English," said Mohammad Akmal, Apollo's assistant manager for international marketing.

Some hospitals also take care of the visa and forex requirements of foreign tourists. "We have been helping our foreign patients by providing them money exchange facility," said S.K. Sama, chairman of the Sir Ganga Ram Hospital.

Multi-cuisine facilities are available in almost all big hospitals. "The facilities we provide here are no less than a five-star hotel. It's the requirement of the age and we have to keep pace with it", Sama added. "Some hospitals are even running their own air ambulance services", said Sohail Kadri, an agent with Akbar Travels in Gujarat that caters to tourists coming to super-speciality hospitals located in Ahmedabad. "This also gives hospitals the ability to evacuate injured foreign tourists from adventure sports and trekking sites and transport them to a hospital", Sama added.

NEED FOR MEDICAL TOURISM AND INDIA'S RESPONSE

Medical tourism can be broadly defined as provision of 'cost effective' private medical care in collaboration with the tourism industry for patients needing surgical and other forms of specialized treatment. This process is being facilitated by the corporate sector involved in medical care as well as the tourism industry—both private and public.

Medical or health tourism has become a common form of vacationing, and covers a broad spectrum of medical services. It mixes leisure, fun and relaxation together with wellness and healthcare.

The idea of the health holiday is to offer you an opportunity to get away from your daily routine and come into a different relaxing surrounding. Here you can enjoy being close to the beach and the mountains. At the same time you are able to receive an orientation that will help you improve your life in terms of your health and general well-being. It is like rejuvenation and clean up process on all levels—physical, mental and emotional.

Many people from the developed world come to India for the rejuvenation promised by yoga and Ayurvedic massage, but few consider it a destination for hip replacement or brain surgery. However, a nice blend of top-class medical expertize at attractive prices is helping a growing number of Indian corporate hospitals lure foreign patients, including from developed nations such as the UK and the US.

As more and more patients from Europe, the US and other affluent nations with high medicare costs look for effective options, India is pitted against Thailand, Singapore and some other Asian countries, which have good hospitals, salubrious climate and tourist destinations. While Thailand and Singapore with their advanced medical facilities and built-in medical tourism options have been drawing foreign patients of the order of a couple of lakhs per annum, the rapidly expanding Indian corporate hospital sector has been able to get a few thousands for treatment.

But, things are going to change drastically in favour of India, especially in view of the high quality expertise of medical professionals, backed by the fast improving equipment and nursing facilities, and above all, the cost-effectiveness of the package.

As Indian corporate hospitals are on par, if not better than the best hospitals in Thailand, Singapore, etc. there is scope for improvement, and the country may become a preferred medical destination. In addition to the increasingly top class medical care, a big draw for foreign patients is also the very minimal or hardly any waitlist as is common in European or American hospitals. In fact, priority treatment is provided today in Indian hospitals.

The Apollo Group, Escorts Hospitals in New Delhi and Jaslok Hospitals in Mumbai are to name a few which are established names even abroad. A list of corporate hospitals such as Global Hospitals, CARE and Dr L.V. Prasad Eye Hospitals in Hyderabad, The Hindujas and NM Excellence in Mumbai, also have built capabilities and are handling a steadily increasing flow of foreign patients. India has much more expertise than say Thailand or Malaysia. The infrastructure in some of India's hospitals is also very good. What is more significant is that the costs are much less, almost one-third of those in other Asian countries.

Facts and Figures

India offers world-class healthcare that costs substantially less than those in developed countries, using the same technology delivered by competent specialists attaining similar success rates.

If a liver transplant costs in the range of Rs. 60-70 lakh in Europe and double that in the US, a few Indian hospitals, such as Global in Hyderabad, have the wherewithal to do it in around Rs. 15-20 lakh. Similarly, if a heart surgery in the US costs about Rs. 20 lakh, the Chennai-headquartered Apollo Hospitals Group does it in roughly Rs. 2 lakh.

Table 5.1: Procedure charges in India and US (US $)

Procedure	*Cost (US$)*	
	United States	*India*
Bone Marrow Transplant	2,50,000	69,000
Liver Transplant	3,00,000	69,000
Heart Surgery	30,000	8,000
Orthopedic Surgery	20,000	6,000
Cataract Surgery	2,000	1,250

Table 5.2: A brief comparison of the cost of few of the dental treatment procedures between USA and India

Dental procedure	*Cost in US ($)*		*Cost in India ($)*
	General Dentist	*Top End Dentist*	*Top End Dentist*
Smile Designing	—	8,000	1,000
Metal Free Bridge	—	5,500	500
Dental Implants	—	3,500	800
Porcelain Metal Bridge	1,800	3,000	300
Porcelain Metal Crown	600	1,000	80
Tooth Impactions	500	2,000	100
Root Canal Treatment	600	1,000	100
Tooth Whitening	350	800	110
Tooth Colored Composite Fillings	200	500	25
Tooth Cleaning	100	300	75

In India, the Apollo group alone has so far treated 95,000 international patients, many of whom are of Indian origin. Apollo has been a forerunner in medical tourism in India and attracts patients from South-East Asia, Africa, and the Middle East. The group has tied up with hospitals in Mauritius, Tanzania, Bangladesh and Yemen besides running a hospital in Sri Lanka, and managing a hospital in Dubai.

Another corporate group running a chain of hospitals, Escorts, claims it has doubled its number of overseas patients—from 675 in 2000 to nearly 1,200 in 2006. Recently, the Ruby Hospital in Kolkata signed a contract with the British insurance company, BUPA. The management hopes to get British patients from the queue in the National Health Services soon.

Apollo Hospitals Group

Located at Delhi, Chennai, Hyderabad and Madurai

The Apollo Hospitals Group is today recognized as the "Architect of Healthcare" in India. Its history of accomplishments, with its unique ability of resource management and able deployment of technology and knowledge to the service of mankind, justifies its recognition in India and abroad. Their mission is "to bring healthcare of international standards within the reach of every individual. We are committed to the achievement and maintenance of excellence in education, research and healthcare for the benefit of humanity."

Apollo's capabilities have received international acclaim resulting in the replication of its Indian models at international locations. Apollo group is also in talks with private healthcare groups and government authorities in Nigeria, South Africa, Tanzania, Mauritius, Yemen, Muscat, Bahrain, Vietnam, Malaysia, Thailand and other neighbouring countries to establish its presence.

World Class Clinical Efficiencies

- Among the few providers of quaternary care for complicated medical conditions, Apollo saves millions of lives everyday.
- Touched the lives of over 10 million patients till date.
- Over 4,00,000 preventive health checks done.
- Has the largest and the most sophisticated sleep laboratories in the world.
- Has pioneered orthopedic procedures like total hip and knee replacements, the Illizarov procedure, and the Birmingham Hip Resurfacing technique.
- Has performed over 750,000 major surgeries and over 10,00,000 minor surgical procedures till date.
- Has performed over 49,000 cardiac surgeries at a 98.5 per cent success rate.
- Has performed over 2,00,000 angiograms, 16,200 angioplasties (PTCA) and 3,500 mitral balloon valvuoplasties.
- First heart transplant patient is alive, 7 years after the operation.
- Has performed over 9,400 renal transplants.
- 130 bone marrow transplants performed at high success rates.
- Over 30 liver transplants done (Live and cadaver).

- Has over 4,000 specialists and super specialists, 3,000 medical officers spanning 53 clinical departments in patient care.

International Affiliations

- Apollo Hospitals is recognized as a training centre by the National Board of Examination in India for postgraduate training in 16 medical departments.
- The Department of Radiology at Apollo is recognized by the Royal College of Radiologists, United Kingdom for training for fellowship examinations like FRCR.
- Recognized as a centre for conducting research work leading to Ph.D. of the Anna University, Chennai, in medical physics and digital signal processing.
- Apollo Hospitals is recognized by the Royal College of Physicians and Surgeons in Edinburgh for training postgraduates in radiology, surgery and trauma care.
- Apollo Hospitals is the only international training organization for the American Heart Association Technical support from Texas Heart Institute and Minneapolis Heart Institute for Cardiology and Cardio Thoracic surgery.
- Apollo Hospitals has exchange programmes with the hospitals in the US and Europe.
- Apollo Hospitals have an association with Mayo Clinic and Cleveland Heart Institute, USA.
- Apollo Hospitals is also associated with Johns Hopkins University.

Escorts Heart Institute and Research Centre

Located at Delhi and Faridabad (Haryana)

Escorts is steadily consolidating its presence in healthcare, which is likely to emerge as the largest service sector industry. Currently, Escorts is operating three large hospitals in New Delhi, Faridabad and Amritsar. Together with 11 heart command centres and associate hospitals, Escorts is managing nearly 900 beds.

Escorts excellence in providing healthcare services has received due recognition. Escorts Heart Institute and Research Centre (EHIRC), New Delhi, has been ranked as the best cardiac hospital in India by an Outlook-Cfore survey and has been given the highest grade by CRISIL—an acknowledgement of the quality of delivered patient care.

EHIRC is a leader in the fields of cardiac surgery, interventional cardiology and cardiac diagnostics. The Institute has introduced innovative techniques of minimally invasive and robotic surgery. The Institute's latest addition of state-of-the-art Cardiac Scan Centre providing a combined power of CV-MRI and Smart Score CT Scanner to diagnose coronary artery disease at its very early stage. This facility is the first of its kind outside America. State-of-the-art infrastructure and equipment has made this set-up technically the largest and the best dedicated cardiac hospital in the world. The 332-bed Institute has nine operating rooms and carries out nearly 15,000 procedures every year.

Dr. Vivek Saggar's Dental Care and Cure Centre

Located at Ludhiana (Punjab)

Dental Care and Cure Centre is, centrally located in Ludhiana, easily approachable from any part of Punjab by rail or road. It takes not more than two hours from any part of Punjab to reach this place. Theirs is a six-chair operatory with an in-house dental lab, the Dental Caps, Crowns and Beyond Dental Lab, which has been designed on the European standards. The office has been designed to provide an environment of comfort that combines exceptional skill levels, a respectful approach to treatment, clinical and technical excellence with an individualized care approach by providing the most advanced, optimal dental care to the best of our ability.

Theirs is a full service cosmetic and general dental office specializing in creating beautiful smiles. The in-house facility of Dental Caps, Crowns and Beyond... Dental Lab gives them the unmatched time advantage plus international quality control. For NRI's and foreigners they provide special care in the form of appointments at a short notice and the work is completed within the span of 3-5 days keeping in mind your tight schedule.

Standard Procedures

- Oral prophylaxis (gum cleaning and polishing)
- Sub gingival root planing
- Invisible composite fillings

- Simple tooth extractions
- Root canal therapy.

Advanced Technology

- Smile designing
- Crown and bridge work
- Tooth whitening
- Dental implants (single tooth or entire set of teeth)
- Oral and maxillofacial surgery (third molar extractions, apicoectomy surgeries, management of mandible fractures)
- Geriatric patient (partial and complete dentures, implant supported dentures, complete extractions under local anesthesia)
- Diagnostic and preventive (cancer screening, occlusal splints, tooth desensitization)
- Care of the child patient (fluoride treatment, milk teeth as well as permanent teeth restorations, preventive orthodontics, fixed orthodontics, habit breaking appliances, sedation dentistry (licensed anesthesiologist)).

The Lab

Dental Caps, Crowns and Beyond Dental Lab was established in with the goal of supporting Dental Care and Cure Centre and providing dentists of north India with restorations of superior quality and value. The lab has been set up as per European standards. They specialize in crown and bridge metal ceramic and metal free ceramic restorations. Their highly skilled technicians with state-of-the-art techniques, materials, and equipment guarantee exceptional quality restorations with correct fit and shading. Quality is the cornerstone of their work. They were the first lab in north India to start metal free ceramic work.

NM Excellence

Located at Mumbai

NM Excellence was formed from one man's vision to provide a healthier future for the citizens of Mumbai. Established in 2001 by M.D. Radiologist Dr. Nilesh Shah, this modern and sophisticated preventive health checkup centre aims to revolutionize the way healthcare is perceived and practised in India. Backed by over two decades of diagnostic experience under the banner of NM Medical, NM Excellence employs the latest, top-of-the-line imagining modalities, operated by qualified and professional doctors, with a friendly and efficient staff to make a client's experience as memorable as possible. Having viewed the vast range of diseases that can be prevented if detected early enough through its diagnostic experience, NM Excellence philosophises that a preventive health checkup in today's age is an absolute must. NM Excellence is one of Mumbai's foremost preventive healthcare centres boasting of top-of-the-line diagnostic equipment, highly qualified doctors, a well-trained service staff, and a professional yet warm environment that makes one feel at home immediately.

Health Packages

Their diagnostic experience has guided them in forming their health packages for different age and professional categories of people. They believe their health plans are comprehensive enough in covering the entire spectrum of life-threatening ailments you face in today's fast-paced, constantly stressful world. The health plans range from those for busy executives, to senior citizens, from housewives to working women, from kids to pre-employment clients. The health plans are most affordably priced, mostly discounted to the tune of forty per cent.

Health Plan for NRI's and Foreigners

The plan price starts from US$ 225+ and includes the following:

- *Pathology tests*: Complete haemogram, test for diabetes, test for liver disease, test for kidney disease, test for heart disease.
- *Diagnostic tests*: Digital chest X-ray, ECG, Sonography, Stress test, 2D Echo, Spirometry, Dexa bone densitometry, Body fat analysis, Mammography, Transvaginal sonography.
- *Consultations*: Physical examination by MD physician, Dental checkup, Eye checkup, Diet consultation, Gynecological checkup, Pap-smear.

Highlights of the package are

- International quality of equipment
- Highly qualified doctors
- Life and stress presentation
- View reports on Net
- Reports on CD
- Health gift certificates.

PD Hinduja National Hospital and Medical Research Centre

Located at Mumbai

An ultramodern hospital on the busiest artery in Central Mumbai, PD Hinduja National Hospital and Medical Research Centre was established by the Hinduja Foundation in collaboration with Massachusetts General Hospital (MGH), Boston. The fulfillment of Founder Parmanand Deepchand Hinduja's dream, the 351-bed hospital offers comprehensive services covering the gamut from diagnosis and investigation to therapy, surgery and postoperative care. As a tertiary care hospital, the services offered are comprehensive covering investigation and diagnosis to therapy, surgery and postoperative care.

The inpatient services are complemented with a day centre, out-patient facilities and an exclusive centre for health check for executives. Hinduja Hospital was the first multi-disciplinary tertiary care hospital to have been awarded the prestigious ISO 9002 Certification from KEMA of Netherlands for quality management system.

The Hinduja Foundation's quest for upgradation of healthcare facilities in India has prompted it to join hands with the 32,000 member American Association of Physicians of Indian origin (AAPI), with the objective of bringing to India well-qualified and experienced doctors from USA to upgrade the expertise of HNH doctors, provide quality medical care and continuing medical education; to ensure co-operation in research and pursue joint projects in the fields of Coronary artery disease, Osteoporosis and Asthma; and to provide consultancy, technology and treatment support to AAPI dispensaries in India on case to case basis.

Cutting Edge Technology in Diagnostics

Hinduja Hospital has a fully automated Laboratory Medicine Department. The laboratory offers over 500 different types of tests some of, which are exclusive. It also offers an emergency/Stat menu of tests with a very short turn around time.

The department participates in International Quality Control programme conducted by the College of American Pathologists, WHO and National Quality Control Programme where it has achieved and maintained a high ranking consistently for a number of years. Imaging forms a key part of the diagnostic facility at the hospital.

Technology Upgrades

The hospital keeps upgrading its technology by acquiring new state-of-the-art diagnostic and therapeutic equipment. Hinduja Hospital was the first in India to acquire the Gamma Knife-gold standard in Radio Surgery, a non-invasive neurosurgical tool. The hospital was also the first to acquire the Holmium Laser in the country thus replacing the surgeon's scalpel. The oncology services are wholistic and complete with installation of the Linear Accelerator with Multileaf Collimator (MLC) and Micro MLC. The hospital is the first centre in India to have installed the sophisticated state-of-the-art GE-LCA Digital Subtraction Angiography System. In keeping with the quest for continuous improvement in quality and technological advancement, the hospital has recently commissioned the Bone Mineral Densitometer (DEXA), an addition to the Imaging department.

L.V. Prasad Eye Institute

Located at Hyderabad

In October 1987, L.V. Prasad Eye Institute began the work of realizing its mission to achieve excellence, equity and efficiency in eye care. In addition to treating patients dealing with a wide range of vision problems, LVPEI began to conduct research into eye diseases and vision-threatening conditions, train eye care workers, product development and rehabilitate those with incurable visual disability. The focus, right from the start, has been on providing eye-care services to underprivileged populations in the developing world.

Set up as a not-for-profit trust, LVPEI has now come a long way in its journey towards realizing these goals. However, our changing world continues to throw up new challenges and new threats to health, and LVPEI too continues to search for ways in which these challenges can be overcome, in the field of eye health. In partnership with international health organizations such as the World Health Organization and the International Agency for the Prevention of Blindness, LVPEI designs and implements innovative eye health programmes that reach people in the most remote rural areas. While the range of our research and training activities is international, our focus is on bringing this quality of care to the poorest segments of India and the developing world. Our successes include the establishment of rural eye health centres that provide high-quality eye care at the lowest possible cost, or at no cost to those to whom such care would otherwise be inaccessible. In fact it is the same model that operates successfully in our nodal centre in Hyderabad, Andhra Pradesh. At the L.V. Prasad Eye Hospital, nearly 50 per cent of our patients are treated free of cost.

The Eye Hospital forms the nucleus of the Institute's activities. Designed along the lines of the finest eye hospitals in the world. Patients with a wide range of eye disorders are treated which is staffed by a world-class team of dedicated doctors representing all ophthalmic sub-specialities and a highly competent support staff. The Hospital's comprehensive facilities also include the in-house expertise of physicians, microbiologists, pathologists and biochemists trained to apply their knowledge and skills to eye care.

MEDICAL TOURISM IN INDIA: A GLOBAL COMPARISON

That medical tourism is widely prevalent is yesterday's news. Today's news is that many US insurers and hospitals have taken note of the fact that India is fast emerging as a most wanted destination for elective surgeries. To stem the tide as it were, they are embarking on aggressive marketing strategies to make sure that the average American gets his surgeries done in-house.

It is reported that 1.5 lakh medical tourists went to India last year. This number is expected to surge by 15 per cent this year and by 2012 it could net $2.3 billion annually for India. Richard Merli, managing editor, Health Care Insider, KPMG notes that consumers in the low to middle income brackets may be dismissed by American hospitals since they lack insurance, "But industry observers say that the exotic locales and prospect of a vacation is attracting many wealthy patients to have elective surgeries done abroad." But he adds that if a procedure were to fail, Americans have no alternative except to keep quiet and cannot seek legal redress as they can back home. "All the protection afforded by the US healthcare system—board-certified physicians, the FDA and a legal system that supports patient rights—are void as soon as one steps out of the country," said Saul Helman, Pharmaceuticals Practice, MD, KPMG.

But Anne Marie Moncure, MD, Indraprastha Apollo Hospitals in Delhi disagrees and says that the same techniques and care are used in India as in the US, "Every year, 98,000 patients die in US hospitals due to medical negligence and three to four times that number is left permanently disabled," she points out. Indian hospitals feel that if they are getting the same care at a lesser cost, then patients will naturally look at the greener grass, something that American hospitals are noting with concern.

Cost Comparison: India vs United Kingdom (UK)

Significant cost differences exist between U.K. and India when it comes to medical treatment. Accompanied with the cost are waiting times which exist in U.K. for patients which range from 3 months to over months.

India is not only cheaper but the waiting time is almost nil. This is due to the outburst of the private sector which comprises hospitals and clinics with the latest technology and best practitioners.

Table 5.3: Cost comparison analysis

Nature of Treatment	*Approximate Cost in India ($) **	*Cost in other Major Healthcare Destination ($) **	*Approximate Waiting Periods in USA/ UK (in months)*
Open Heart Surgery	4,500	> 18,000	9 - 11
Cranio-facial Surgery and skull base	4,300	> 13,000	6 - 8
Neuro-surgery with Hypothermia	6,500	> 21,000	12 - 14
Complex spine surgery with implants	4,300	> 13,000	9 - 11
Simple Spine Surgery	2,100	> 6,500	9 - 11
Simple Brain Tumor			
—Biopsy	1,000	> 4,300	6 - 8
—Surgery	4,300	> 10,000	
Parkinsons	2,100		
—Lesion	17,000	> 6,500	9 - 11
—DBS		> 26,000	
Hip Replacement	4,300	> 13,000	9 - 11

* These costs are an average and may not be the actual cost to be incurred.

UK Patient Avoided the NHS List and Flew to India for a Heart Bypass. Is Health Tourism the future? (Article from the Guardian's dated February 1, 2005)

Three months ago George Marshall fretted about the choice offered by his doctor in Britain. Diagnosed with coronary heart disease, the violin repairer from Bradford was told he could either wait upto six months for a heart bypass operation on the National Health Service or pay £19,000 to go under the scalpel immediately.

In the end, Mr. Marshall chose to outsource his operation to India. Last month he flew 5,000 miles to the southern Indian city of Bangalore where surgeons at the Wockhardt Hospital and Heart Institute took a piece of vein from his arm to repair the thinning arteries of his heart. The cost was £4,800, including the flight.

"Everyone's been really great here. I have been in the NHS and gone private in Britain in the past, but I can say that the care and facilities in India are easily comparable," says Mr. Marshall, sitting in hospital-blue pyjamas. "I'd have no problem coming again."

The 73-year-old found the hospital in Bangalore after a few hours surfing the internet. Mr. Marshall decided to come after an email conversation with Wockhardt's vice-president and a chat with other "medical tourists" from Britain who had undergone surgery in the hospital.

"Once I knew others had come I thought, why not? In Europe hospitals in Germany and Belgium would do the operation for less than doctors in Britain. But Europe was still more expensive than here. And the staff speak English in India."

With patients such as Mr. Marshall willing to travel across the globe to get treatment sooner or more cheaply than they could at home, Indian hospital groups see a huge market for their services.

Cost Comparison: India vs United States of America (USA)

Significant cost differences exist between U.K. and India when it comes to medical treatment.

India is not only cheaper but the waiting time is almost nil. This is due to the outburst of the private sector which comprises of hospitals and clinics with the latest technology and best practitioners.

Table 5.4: Procedure charges in India and US (US $)

Procedure	*Cost (US $)*	
	United States	*India*
Bone Marrow Transplant	2,50,000	69,000
Lover Transplant	3,00,000	69,000
Heart Surgery	30,000	8,000
Orthopedic Surgery	20,000	6,000
Cataract Surgery	2,000	1,250

Here's a brief comparison of the cost of few of the Dental Treatment procedures between USA and India:

Table 5.5: Comparison of dental treatment procedures between USA and India

Dental Procedure	*Cost in USA ($)**		*Cost in India ($)**
	General Dentist	*Top End Dentist*	*Top End Dentist*
Smile Designing	—	8,000	1,000
Metal Free Bridge	—	5,500	500
Dental Implants	—	3,500	800
Porcelain Metal Bridge	1,800	3,000	300
Porcelain Metal Crown	600	1,000	80
Tooth Impactions	500	2,000	100
Root Canal Treatment	600	1,000	100
Tooth Whitening	350	800	110
Tooth Colored Composite Fillings	200	500	25
Tooth Cleaning	100	300	75

* These costs are an average and may not be the actual cost to be incurred.

Americans Flock to India for Treatment (Article from Hindustan Times, 16 February, 2005)

Robert Walter Beeney was unable to walk due to a stiff hip when he landed in India on January 24. Twenty days later, he not only recovered after a rare hip replacement surgery at Apollo Hospital here but also visited the famous Taj Mahal in Agra after that.

The 64-year-old real estate consultant from San Francisco underwent successful surface replacement surgery using the anatomic surface replacement (ASR) hip system on January 27, reportedly becoming the first US national to come to India for the treatment.

Another patient from Florida will be landing in Chennai for a similar procedure at the Apollo Hospital there later this week.

A team of doctors, led by orthopedic surgeon Vijay Bose, carried out the procedure for Beeney.

Jayaramchander Pingle, a member of the medical team, told a news conference on Tuesday that while in the conventional hip replacement surgery, the total hip was replaced, in the new system, the patient's original head and neck of femur were preserved and only their surface is replaced with metal on metal articulation.

With the use of very advanced metallurgy in this device, the wear and tear is reduced to a fraction in the artifical joint as opposed to the conventional total hip replacement.

Another advantage of the latest procedure is that in the envent of any problem that may occur in the long term, the conventional total hip replacement can be done at a later stage.

Beeney, who came to know about the procedure in India through the Internet, said that since this was not yet cleared by the US Food and Drug Administration, he decided to come to India.

"This is despite the fact that the device that is fixed in the hip is made in the US," he said.

He also had other options like going to Britain or Belgium for treatment. "But I preferred India as the treatment costs there are huge," he said.

The treatment in India cost him $6,600 (Rs. 300,000) while the same as a part of clinical trial in US would have cost $24,000. Even in Britain, where this procedure was first developed a few years ago, it would have cost 12,000 pounds.

COST COMPARISON—INDIA VS. UNITED ARAB EMIRATES (UAE)

Significant cost differences exist between UAE and India when it comes to medical treatment.

India is not only cheaper but the waiting time is almost nil. This is due to the outburst of the private sector which comprises hospitals and clinics with the latest technology and best practitioners.

Why have routine (and not so routine) medical and dental services performed in the US when you can have them done cheaper elsewhere and get a free vacation out of it to boot?

Medical Tourism in India is a developing concept whereby people from world over visit India for their medical and relaxation needs. Most common treatments are heart surgery, knee transplant, cosmetic surgery and dental care. The reason India is a favourable destination is because of its infrastructure and technology in which is in par with those in USA, UK and Europe. India has some of the best hospitals and treatment centers in the world with the best facilities.

Table 5.6: Dental services

Dental Procedure	*Cost in USA ($)*		*Cost in India ($)*
	General Dentist	*Top End Dentist*	*Top End Dentist*
Smile Designing	—	8,000	1,000*
Metal Free Bridge	—	5,500	500*
Dental Implants	—	3,500	800*
Porcelain Metal Bridge	1,800	3,000	300*
Porcelain Metal Crown	600	1,000	80*
Tooth Impactions	500	2,000	100*
Root canal Treatment	600	1,000	100*
Tooth Whitening	350	800	110*
Tooth Colored Composite Fillings	200	500	25*
Tooth Cleaning	100	300	75*

Heart Surgery

A heart care surgery which costs in the region of USD 30,000 in USA can cost as low as USD 8,000 in India.

Cardiac care has become a speciality in India with institutions like the Escorts Heart Institute and Research Centre, All India Institute of Medical Sciences and Apollo Hospital becoming names to reckon with. They combine the latest innovations in medical electronics with unmatched expertise in leading cardiologists and cardothoracic surgeons. These centres have the distinction of providing comprehensive cardiac care spanning from basic facilities in preventive cardiology to the most sophisticated curative technology. The technology is contemporary and world class and the volumes handled match global benchmarks. They also specialize in offering surgery to high risk patients with the introduction of innovative techniques like minimally invasive and robotic surgery.

Renowned Indian hospitals like Apollo and Escorts Heart Institute are equipped to handle all phases of heart diseases from the elementary to the latest clinical procedures like interventional cardiac catherisation and surgical cardiac transplants. Their success rate at an average of 98.50 per cent is at par with leading cardiac centres around the world.

Leading heart centres like The Escorts Heart Institute have Cardiac Care Units with sophisticated equipment and investigative facilities like Echocardiography with coloured Doppler, Nuclear Scanning and Coronary Angiography. The Jayadeva Institute of Cardiology in Bangalore, the Cardiology Hospital in Kanpur, the Heart Hospital in Calicut and the Sree Sudhindra Medical Mission Hospital in Cochin are some hospitals in India devoted exclusively to cardiac treatment.

6

Healthcare in India and Related Tourism Activities

HEALTHCARE IN INDIA: AN INTRODUCTION

Confederation of Indian Industries (CII) estimates that around 150,000 patients came to India for treatment in 2003-04. They are mostly from the SAARC, Middle East and Africa. There has been a growing trend of patients coming from the UK and the US.

CII is playing a major role in taking this initiative forward. It released a guide to select cities and corresponding hospitals on November 17, 2004. Besides, it is working on formulating Price Bands corresponding to various specialized areas of services.

One of the major initiatives is providing accreditation to hospitals. The Government of India, along with CII, is working on Accreditation of Hospitals. CII is also working on developing the Minimum Quality Standards for all hospitals and the first draft is ready. This will give comfort to patients seeking treatment in India.

The Government has also been supportive. Ministry of Health and Family Welfare as well as Ministry of Tourism have formed Task Forces to take this initiative forward.

India's healthcare sector has made impressive strides in recent years. From a US $ 20.6 billion industry in 2001 it is expected to touch US $ 46.4 billion by 2012. This includes the Pharma market, Government spending and Private spending. India's healthcare industry is expected to grow by around 15 per cent a year for the next six years.

So, why is there a revolution in healthcare in India?

First, there are some Economic Factors which make India such an exciting market. Since healthcare is dependent on the people served, India's huge population of a billion people, represents a big opportunity. The middle income group in this vast base, is also a large 300 million.

Today, people are spending more on healthcare. A middle-level manager with a family of four, spends between US $ 170 and US $ 255 a year on healthcare—compared to just US $ 43 in the late 1980s. Most users of healthcare have been paying from their own pocket and preferring private services to government ones.

Major corporations like the Apollo Group, Fortis, Max, Wockhardt and Escorts Group have made significant investments in setting up state-of-the-art private hospitals in cities like Mumbai, New Delhi, Chennai and Hyderabad. Using the latest technical equipment and the services of highly skilled medical personnel these hospitals are in a position to provide a variety of general as well as specialists services. These services are available at extremely competitive prices, encouraging patients not only from developing countries but even from a number of developed ones to come to India for specialized treatment.

In the next ten years, Tertiary Care in India will be predominantly Private Healthcare and extensive Public and Private partnerships. The Secondary Care would be Private and Public Healthcare and selective public and private partnerships. The Primary Care would be predominantly public, especially in the rural areas.

Opportunities Exists in the Areas

Service Providers (Hospitals)	*Curative & Preventive in Primary, Secondary and Tertiary Care Rehabilitative - Geriatric & Others*
Manpower Training	Doctors Managers Nurses Technicians
Infrastructure	Medical Equipments Service Equipments
Insurance	Hospitalization
Materials	Medicines Disposables

Role of the Government

The Indian Constitution charges the states with "the raising of the level of nutrition and the standard of living of its people and the improvement of public health." However, many critics of India's National Health Policy, endorsed by Parliament in 1983, point out that the policy lacks specific measures to achieve broad stated goals. Particular problems include the failure to integrate health services with wider economic and social development, the lack of nutritional support and sanitation, and the poor participatory involvement at the local level.

Central Government efforts at influencing public health have focused on the five-year plans, on coordinated planning with the states, and on sponsoring major health programmes. Government expenditures are jointly shared by the central and state governments. Goals and strategies are set through central-state government consultations of the Central Council of Health and Family Welfare. Central government efforts are administered by the Ministry of Health and Family Welfare, which provides both administrative and technical services and manages medical education. States provide public services and health education.

The 1983 National Health Policy is committed to providing health services to all by 2000. In 1983 healthcare expenditures varied greatly among the states and union territories, from Rs. 13 per capita in Bihar to Rs. 60 per capita in Himachal Pradesh, and Indian per capita expenditure was low when compared with other Asian countries outside of South Asia. Although government healthcare spending progressively grew throughout the 1980s, such spending as a percentage of the gross national product (GDP) remained fairly constant. In the meantime, healthcare spending as a share of total government spending decreased. During the same period, private-sector spending on healthcare was about 1.5 times as much as government spending.

Expenditures

In the mid-1990s, health spending amounted to 6 per cent of GDP, one of the highest levels among developing nations. The established per capita spending is around Rs. 320 per year with the major input from private households (75%). State governments contribute 15.2 per cent, the central government 5.2 per cent, third-party insurance and employers 3.3 per cent, and municipal government and foreign donors about 1.3, according to a 1995 World Bank study. Of these proportions, 58.7 per cent goes toward primary healthcare (curative, preventive and promotive) and 38.8 per cent is spent on secondary and tertiary inpatient care. The rest goes for nonservice costs.

The fifth and sixth five-year plans (FY 1974-78 and FY 1980-84, respectively) included programmes to assist delivery of preventive medicine and improve the health status of the rural population. Supplemental nutrition programmes and increasing the supply of safe drinking water were high priorities. The sixth plan aimed at training more community health workers and increasing efforts to control communicable diseases. There were also efforts to improve regional imbalances in the distribution of healthcare resources.

The Seventh Five-Year Plan (FY 1985-89) budgeted Rs. 33.9 billion for health, an amount roughly double the outlay of the sixth plan. Health spending as a portion of total plan outlays, however, had declined over the years since the first plan in 1951, from a high of 3.3 per cent of the total plan spending in FY 1951-55 to 1.9 per cent of the total for the seventh plan. Mid-way through the Eighth Five-Year Plan (FY 1992-96), however, health and family welfare was budgeted at Rs. 20 billion, or 4.3 per cent of the total plan spending for FY 1994, with an additional Rs. 3.6 billion in the nonplan budget.

Primary Services

Healthcare facilities and personnel increased substantially between the early 1950s and early 1980s, but because of fast population growth, the number of licensed medical practitioners per 10,000 individuals had fallen by the late 1980s to three per 10,000 from the 1981 level of four per 10,000. In 1991 there were approximately ten hospital beds per 10,000 individuals.

Primary health centres are the cornerstone of the rural healthcare system. By 1991, India had about 22,400 primary health centres, 11,200 hospitals, and 27,400 dispensaries. These facilities are part of a tiered healthcare system that funnels more difficult cases into urban hospitals while attempting to provide routine medical care to the vast majority in the countryside. Primary health centres and subcentres rely on trained paramedics to meet most of their needs. The main problems affecting the success of primary health centres are the predominance of clinical and curative concerns over the intended emphasis on preventive work and the reluctance of staff to work in rural areas. In addition, the integration of health services with family planning programmes often causes the local population to perceive the primary health centres as hostile to their traditional preference for large families. Therefore, primary health centres often play an adversarial role in local efforts to implement national health policies.

According to data provided in 1989 by the Ministry of Health and Family Welfare, the total number of civilian hospitals for all states and union territories combined was 10,157. In 1991 there was a total of 811,000 hospital and healthcare facilities beds. The geographical distribution of hospitals varied according to local socioeconomic conditions. In India's most populous state, Uttar Pradesh, with a 1991 population of more than 139 million, there were 735 hospitals as of 1990. In Kerala, with a 1991 population of 29 million occupying an area only one-seventh the size of Uttar Pradesh, there were 2,053 hospitals. In light of the central government's goal of healthcare for all by 2000, the uneven distribution of hospitals needs to be reexamined. Private studies of India's total number of hospitals in the early 1990s were more conservative than official Indian data, estimating that in 1992 there were 7,300 hospitals. Of this total, nearly 4,000 were owned and managed by central, state, or local governments. Another 2,000, owned and managed by charitable trusts, received partial support from the government, and the remaining 1,300 hospitals, many of which were relatively small facilities, were owned and managed by the private sector. The use of state-of-the-art medical equipment, often imported from Western countries, was primarily limited to urban centres in the early 1990s. A network of regional cancer diagnostic and treatment facilities was being established in the early 1990s in major hospitals that were part of government medical colleges. By 1992 twenty-two such centres were in operation. Most of the 1,300 private hospitals lacked sophisticated medical facilities, although in 1992 approximately 12 per cent possessed state-of-the-art equipment for diagnosis and treatment of all major diseases, including cancer. The fast pace of development of the private medical sector and the burgeoning middle class in the 1990s have led to the emergence of the new concept in India of establishing hospitals and healthcare facilities on a for-profit basis.

By the late 1980s, there were approximately 128 medical colleges—roughly three times more than in 1950. These medical colleges in 1987 accepted a combined annual class of 14,166 students. Data for 1987 show that there were 320,000 registered medical practitioners and 219,300 registered nurses. Various studies have shown that in both urban and rural areas people preferred to pay and seek the more sophisticated services provided by private physicians rather than use free treatment at public health centres.

Healthcare in India

Indigenous or traditional medical practitioners continue to practice throughout the country. The two main forms of traditional medicine practised are the ayurvedic (meaning science of life) system, which deals with causes, symptoms, diagnoses, and treatment based on all aspects of well-being (mental, physical and spiritual), and the unani (so-called Galenic medicine) herbal medical practice. A *vaidya* is a practitioner of the ayurvedic tradition, and a *hakim* (Arabic for a Muslim physician) is a practitioner of the unani tradition. These professions are frequently hereditary. A variety of institutions offer training in indigenous medical practice. Only in the late 1970s did official health policy refer to any form of integration between Western-oriented medical personnel and indigenous medical practitioners. In the early 1990s, there were ninety-eight ayurvedic colleges and seventeen unani colleges operating in both the governmental and nongovernmental sectors.

Primary Services

Healthcare facilities and personnel increased substantially between the early 1950s and early 1980s, but because of fast population growth, the number of licensed medical practitioners per 10,000 individuals had fallen by the late 1980s to three per 10,000 from the 1981 level of four per 10,000. In 1991 there were approximately ten hospital beds per 10,000 individuals.

Primary health centers are the cornerstone of the rural healthcare system. By 1991, India had about 22,400 primary health centres, 11,200 hospitals, and 27,400 dispensaries. These facilities are part of a tiered healthcare system that funnels more difficult cases into urban hospitals while attempting to provide routine medical care to the vast majority in the countryside. Primary health centres and subcentres rely on trained paramedics to meet most of their needs. The main problems affecting the success of primary health centres are the predominance of clinical and curative concerns over the intended emphasis on preventive work and the reluctance of staff to work in rural areas. In addition, the integration of health services with family planning programmes often causes the local population to perceive the primary health centres as hostile to their traditional preference for large families. Therefore, primary health centres often play an adversarial role in local efforts to implement national health policies.

According to data provided in 1989 by the Ministry of Health and Family Welfare, the total number of civilian hospitals for all states and union territories combined was 10,157. In 1991 there was a total of 811,000 hospital and healthcare facilities beds. The geographical distribution of hospitals varied according to local socioeconomic conditions. In India's most populous state, Uttar Pradesh, with a 1991 population of more than 139 million, there were 735 hospitals as of 1990. In Kerala, with a 1991 population of 29 million occupying an area only one-seventh the size of Uttar Pradesh, there were 2,053 hospitals. In light of the central government's goal of healthcare for all by 2000, the uneven distribution of hospitals needs to be reexamined. Private studies of India's total number of hospitals in the early 1990s were more conservative than official Indian data, estimating that in 1992 there were 7,300 hospitals. Of this total, nearly 4,000 were owned and managed by central, state, or local governments. Another 2,000, owned and managed by charitable trusts, received partial support from the government, and the remaining 1,300 hospitals, many of which were relatively small facilities, were owned and managed by the private sector. The use of state-of-the-art medical equipment, often imported from Western countries, was primarily limited to urban centres in the early 1990s. A network of regional cancer diagnostic and treatment facilities was being established in the early 1990s in major hospitals that were part of government medical colleges. By 1992 twenty-two such centres were in operation. Most of the 1,300 private hospitals lacked sophisticated medical facilities, although in 1992 approximately 12 per cent possessed state-of-the-art equipment for diagnosis and treatment of all major diseases, including cancer. The fast pace of development of the private medical sector and the burgeoning middle class in the 1990s have led to the emergence of the new concept in India of establishing hospitals and healthcare facilities on a for-profit basis.

By the late 1980s, there were approximately 128 medical colleges—roughly three times more than in 1950. These medical colleges in 1987 accepted a combined annual class of 14,166 students. Data for 1987 show that there were 320,000 registered medical practitioners and 219,300 registered nurses. Various studies have shown that in both urban and rural areas people preferred to pay and seek the more sophisticated services provided by private physicians rather than use free treatment at public healthcentres.

CRITICAL ANALYSIS OF HEALTHCARE SYSTEM IN INDIA

Mr. Deshpande was in the Military Engineering Service for over two decades before he opted for VRS last year to start a business. A communication centre near the Bandra Kurla Centre ran well for a year, but was washed out in the July floods.

They say bad news rarely comes in isolation. He was diagnosed with cancer of the colon a few weeks ago. He took the news of his illness with a stoic calm. This helped his family as they could now concentrate on the treatment. The family had an advantage — Mrs. Deshpande was a senior nurse at a government hospital and, as per service rules, her husband could get subsidized treatment at another government hospital. After two days of standing in long queues, they decided the trouble was not worth it, after all.

"First I had to wait in a line to get the admission form/case paper. Then it was another long wait to see the doctor. I was then asked do a series of investigations, for each of which I had to wait in a line, just to make the payment."

"All this just set me up for yet another appointment with the doctor — which would happen only the next day. The fortitude I had built up to face the deadly disease dissipated by end of that one day," said Mr. Deshpande. The Deshpandes were forced to take a decision that they previously had not considered. They decided to go for a costlier but, 'easier on the patient' private facility. The fortnightly chemotherapy treatment that is likely to last months has begun. They know it is going to be a costly process that will erode their savings.

The compromise the Deshpandes made has come by way of a decision to put off their daughter's marriage by a couple of years.

While this instance is a reflection of the ills of the public healthcare system in the country, it is not as if everything is hunky dory in the private hospitals.

If it is slow treatment that is dogging public healthcare, it is 'over-treatment' that is the bane of some of the leading hospitals in the city, according Dr K. Sanjay, a consulting orthopedic surgeon.

"Everyone knows that private sector healthcare is a big business. Like in retailing or consumer durables, it all boils down to how you are able to market your wares".

"The onus is on doctors to convince the patients to go in for, say, a joint replacement or a spine surgery. The patient may be able to get on a while longer without it, but the question is whether he can afford it. Once it is clarified that the patient has sufficient medical cover or other means of making payment, it is time to talk business," says Dr Sanjay.

According to him, if a doctor who works in a 'five star' or 'seven star' hospital is to hold on to his star billing, he needs to bring in surgeries on a regular basis.

And this becomes possible, says the doctor candidly, only by way of frantic networking at the grassroots level.

"The smart surgeon nowadays has his web cast far and wide. He connects at many levels in his search for potential clients but none are as effective as that with the friendly neighbourhood family physician. Just as in any other business deals, here too, some gratis is paid to those who throw business your way," Dr Sanjay explains.

Thus, the Deshpandes anguished over the slow treatment, and were quick to switch to the private hospitals. But it may be time for many of us who insist on speedy treatment to make sure we actually don't over-treat ourselves.

Positioned somewhere between these two extremes — the snail-paced public healthcare system and the rat race that characterizes at least some of the private hospitals—is the kind of healthcare the country could do with.

These are the days of public-private joint initiatives in many sectors and perhaps such a venture in healthcare could deliver the goods.

HEALTHCARE TOURISM IN INDIA

India's healthcare services industry is poised to become a major driver of economic growth as first world patients, driven out of their own systems by high costs and crowded conditions, look for cheaper places for medical care. For India, new terms such as health tourism, healthcare outsourcing and medical back office support are suddenly gaining currency.

Already, with healthcare costs having spiralled to prohibitive levels across much of the developed world, the British government, for instance, is contemplating flying its ailing to India to clear up long waiting periods for treatment and surgery in the UK's overcrowded hospitals. India's hospital care and education facilities are rapidly improving after having been freed from the yoke of 50 years of a command economy. Hospitals in Kolkata have long queues of patients from Bangladesh, waiting for appointments with Indian medical specialists. The opening of bus service between India and Lahore is expected to bring Pakistani patients as well.

The statistics are impressive. According to India's Ministry of External Affairs, the US$17 billion Indian healthcare industry comprises roughly 4 per cent of the country's GDP. Hospital services, healthcare equipment, managed care and pharmaceuticals are poised to grow by 13 per cent annually for the next six years. According to the Insurance Regulatory and Development Authority (IRDA), India's healthcare industry could grow exponentially, as have software and pharmaceuticals over the past decade. The government believes that only 10 per cent of the market potential has been tapped. With global revenues an estimated $2.8 trillion, healthcare is the world's largest industry.

The industry's growth is being fueled by the rising purchasing power of the Indian middle class, which is willing to pay more for quality healthcare. Indeed, healthcare is becoming steadily more available as the private sector becomes more involved in the industry and hospital management. With the kind of interest in Indian services that is being shown by other countries, industry analysts believe growth could outstrip current calculations.

Privatization is the key to the sector's resurgence. A Central Bureau of Health Intelligence study indicates that middle and high-income groups have more confidence in healthcare products and services offered by private hospitals than in government-owned agencies. On average, private service is 60 per cent more expensive than government-owned service.

Although private healthcare is a more expensive alternative for domestic residents, it is cheaper for the British government to fly patients over and back after treatment than it is to treat them at home. In fact, the cost-benefit advantage is phenomenal. Open heart surgery costs run $34,000 to $70,000 in the UK. In the US, routine open heart surgery runs as high as $150,000, with complicated problems considerably more. In India, open heart surgery could cost $3,000 to $10,000 in the best of hospitals. Cost differentials therefore could be anywhere from 200 per cent to 800 per cent to off the chart. Analysts believe effective marketing could divert patients from African and West Asian countries who are going to the US or UK for treatment to India.

Another niche area that could be exploited is procedures that are generally not insurance-covered in advanced countries, like cosmetic and plastic surgeries and other high-end lifestyle treatments such as breast implants.

While quality remains an issue, it seems to be improving in India, with private hospitals increasingly able to import high-tech medical equipment, a situation that should improve further with the Indian Government's announcement that import duties on medical equipment are to be reduced as well. In addition, for decades, doctors and other professionals have been fleeing India for more developed countries where they could practice medicine or other professions profitably. The US Immigration and Naturalization Service says a startling 48 per cent of "H1-B" category workers admitted to the United States—those with advanced degrees, exceptional abilities or professionals with bachelor's degrees or equivalent and skilled workers—are from India. As healthcare salaries and medical facilities improve in India, that brain drain should start to reverse, as it has in the information technology industry.

A report published by Dr. Vinay Kothari, the managing director of Hospihealth, a hospital and healthcare planner and management consultancy, states that a decade ago India was roughly 50 years behind the US. However, the report says, over the last 10 to 15 years this gap has begun to close fast, with high-tech super-speciality hospitals coming up all over the country. Most Indian private hospitals are trying to improve quality by employing quality manpower, better salary structure, training and arranging for continuing education for their doctors.

It is therefore increasingly likely that Indian healthcare will be close to global standards in the coming years. According to the

Frost and Sullivan Indian Healthcare Industry Forecast 1996-2006, the industry's growth very much depends on India's continuing macroeconomic liberalization, including further tax cuts, a broader tax base and reduced interest rates for borrowers. The forecast says that the introduction of product patents in India is expected to boost the industry by encouraging multinationals to launch specialized life-saving drugs.

India's natural advantages of lower production costs and its skilled work force are expected to attract multinationals to set up research and development and production centres. The export of bulk drugs and formulations is set to increase at a compounded annual growth rate of 20 per cent and 10 per cent respectively between 2002 and 2006. Over-the-counter drugs are likely to drive the market for formulations during this period.

KARNATAKA: A CASE STUDY IN HEALTHCARE TOURISM

After biting deep into the IT pie, Karnataka says it is set to do another Bangalore on the world, this time with healthcare tourism.

Bangalore and Mysore, together with their super-speciality hospitals and a range of good hotels—even a few ISO certified government hospitals—are being pitched at global tourists and businesspeople.

Still flush from the limelight it got from hosting little Noor Fatima, Pakistani heart patient, Karnataka is now looking at snaring at least 20 per cent of the 3.2 lakh total international inflow as healthcare tourists, according to Mr. Mahendra Jain, State Tourism Commissioner.

In a first-of-its kind concerted action from a State Government, it will showcase its top-class corporate and government hospitals and star hotels as the new business opportunity offering the best mix of cost-effective medical treatment and tourist proposition.

The State Government, along with CII, the hospitality and hospital sector is also hosting a two-day 'Quality summit—health tourism' here on November 25 and 26, 2004 as part of CII's Annual Quality Summit.

"We want to position Karnataka as an ideal health tourism destination with its best hospitals and tourism spots," Mr. Jain said.

If Kerala tops in ayurveda treatments, Bangalore, with its unusual offer of a mix of traditional systems like ayurveda and yoga and modern medical expertise, was uniquely poised to capture the health tourism market that currently thrives in Singapore, Malaysia and Thailand. It has the highest number of approved health systems and alternative therapies. The department has done limited promotion campaigns in the country and in the Gulf, Pakistan and the UK to highlight what it can offer.

Mr. Vishal Bali, summit Chairman and VP, Wockhardt Hospitals, said Indian medical care also came at a tenth of the cost of similar services in the West and about a seventh of the South-East Asian pricing, at equally good or better quality. Indian services would be pitched at the numerous international business visitors and make them stay on longer.

Mr. Bali said a CII-McKinsey study done last year showed the domestic healthcare industry as one of the largest service sector employers providing over four million jobs. Healthcare tourism had grown 30 per cent over last year and can add revenues of $2 billion in eight years.

Driven by health insurance cover, healthcare spending is set to double in 10 years to Rs. 1,56,000 crore, especially in private institutions.

In the bargain, domestic patients too, would gain as hospitals upgrades services to international quality, Mr. Bali said.

"We are witnessing an increasing trend of international tourists enquiring about the healthcare services available in the country," said Mr. Suresh Kumar, summit co-Chairman and VP, ITC Hotels.

Mr. Jain said the State does not have specific number on the current inflow of the health tourist, estimated at 8,000 a year. Each of the dozen hospitals that are in the loop could be treating up to 500 foreigners a year. The department is putting up a database on such travellers while on the health front the State Government is sprucing up its district hospitals as part of the game plan.

RAJASTHAN: A CASE STUDY IN MEDICAL TOURISM

Rajasthan is to unveil an ambitious roadmap to boost medical education and medical tourism but there's a catch—investors will have to cough up at least Rs. 50 million (a million dollars) to take advantage of the scheme. Education Minister Ghanshyam Tiwari will unveil the "Policy to Promote Private Investment in Health Care Facilities 2006" at the Rajasthan Association of North America (RANA) conference in New York July 1-4.

Tiwari told IANS that special emphasis would be laid on promoting and developing the concept of medical tourism, as also the level of medical education in the state.

For this, land would be provided at special prices to all new private medical institutions, including medical and dental colleges, diagnosis centres, blood banks, and nursing and paramedical training institutes.

The policy will also boost other medical streams like ayurveda, homoeopathy and naturopathy. A "land bank" will be created to give land to medical institutions that are promoting and practising alternative medical therapies.

To benefit from the policy, nursing and paramedical institutions will have to make an investment of at least Rs. 50 million.

Similarly, nursing homes and 15-bed hospitals planning a facility within 50 km from regional headquarters or 20 km from district headquarters or in a village or town with a population of less than 50,000 will have to invest at least Rs. 5 million.

Investors will also have to abide by environment protection rules for hospital waste disposal and follow the rules and regulations set by the committee of standards.

The policy also provides for better medical facilities for those living below the poverty line (BPL).

Medical establishments will have to reserve 10 per cent of their beds for BPL families and provide services and medicines at discounted prices.

7

Promoting Medical Tourism in India: Holiday and Hospital Packages Approach

INTRODUCTION

Medical tourism focuses on treatment of acute illness, elective surgeries such as cardiology and cancer, among others. From October 2007, the Government planned to start overseas marketing of India as a medical tourism destination. Senior Government officials say that the formalities for marketing medical facilities to a global audience have already started and they hope to complete the process of price-banding of hospitals in various cities by the third quarter of the year. The Government of India is of the opinion that by marketing India as a global medical tourism destination, it could capitalize on the low-cost, high-quality medical care available in the country.

Statistics show that the medical tourism industry in India is worth \$333 million (Rs. 1,450 crore) while a study by CII-McKinsey estimates that the country could earn Rs. 5,000-10,000 crore by 2012. Probably realizing the potential, major corporates such as the Tatas, Fortis, Max, Wockhardt, Piramal, and the Escorts group have made significant investments in setting up modern hospitals in major cities. Many have also designed special packages for patients, including airport pickups, visa assistance and board and lodging, healthcare industry officials said.

Among the factors that make India an attractive proposition for medical treatment is cost efficiency. The estimated cost for a heart surgery in the US is \$30,000, however the same could be performed in India for about \$6,000. Similarly, a bone marrow transplant could cost about $2,50,000 in the US while it could be done here for about $26,000.

Foreigners have already started trickling into India for medical treatment thus officials are hopeful that this will become a flood once the various initiatives being taken by the Government take off. The Government has also introduced various policy measures such as the National Health Policy recognizes the treatment of international patients as an export, which allows private hospitals treating such patients to enjoy benefits such as lower import duties, increase in the rate of depreciation (from 25 per cent to 40 per cent) for life-saving medical equipment, and several other tax sops in order to encourage medical tourism in India.

Holiday Destinations in India

In a country as diverse and complex as India, it is not surprising to find that people here reflect the rich glories of the past, the culture, traditions and values relative to geographic locations and the numerous distinctive manners, habits and food that will always remain truly Indian.

Beaches in India

Thousands of sun-deprived tourists visit India because it incredibly has the most diverse varieties of beaches anywhere in the world. Placid backwaters and lagoons, bays and rough lava-rocked seas, marine estuaries with fish, crashing surf, powdery golden sand or palm fringed shores—Incredible India has them all.

The West Coast with the Arabian Sea and the East Coast with the Bay of Bengal offer many a verdant vistas to the traveller. The coasts of India have their own seafood cuisine, relaxing spas, diving and water sports and great places to stay for a balmy holiday.

Hill Stations and Retreats

India offers several hill stations with excellent tourist attractions and facilities.

Royal Retreats

Having had a glorious past ranging from old civilizations to the more recent kingdoms, India offers royal retreats which are nowhere to be seen elsewhere. Staying at beautiful palaces with lush green fields, huge borders etc., make some of these retreats a memory of a lifetime.

Some of the holiday destinations covered by us are:

- Agra
- Rajasthan
- Kerala
- Goa
- Delhi
- Mumbai (Bombay)
- Karnataka

India Holiday Packages

Golden Triangle Tour

Destination Covered: Delhi—Agra—Jaipur—Delhi.
Duration: 7 Days—6 Nights

Rajasthan Cultural Tour

Destination Covered: Delhi—Varanasi—Agra—Fatehpur Sikri and more cities.
Duration: 24 Days—23 Nights

Wildlife Tour

Destination Covered: Delhi—Sariska—Jaipur—Ranthambore—Bharatpur—Agra and more cities.
Duration: 22 Days—23 Nights

Kerala Backwater Tour

Destination Covered: Cochin—Periyar—Kumarakom—Houseboat—Marari—Cochin.
Duration: 8 Days—7 Nights

Taj Mahal and Tiger Tour

Destination Covered: Delhi—Agra—Bandhavgarh—Delhi.
Duration: 10 Days—9 Nights

Palace on Wheels Tour

Destination Covered: Delhi—Jaipur—Jaisalmer—Jodhpur—Sawai Madhopur and more cities.
Duration: 8 Days—7 Nights

Heritage Trip to Rajasthan

Destination Covered: Delhi—Jaipur—Mukundgarh—Bikaner—Jaisalmer and more cities.
Duration: 21 Days—20 Nights

Golden Triangle Trip

Destination Covered: Delhi—Agra—Jaipur—Delhi.
Duration: 7 Days—6 Nights

Day 01: Arrive Delhi

Meeting and Assistance at the airport and transfer to hotel for overnight stay.

Day 02: Delhi

Morning after breakfast enjoy combined city tour of Old and New Delhi visiting Red Fort, Jama Masjid, Rajghat, India Gate, President House etc. Entrances to Monuments are not included (only guide with driver). Overnight at hotel.

Day 03: Delhi—Agra

After breakfast drive to Agra and transfer to your hotel. Afternoon visit Taj Mahal-The Eternal symbol of India and Agra, built in white marble. Taj Mahal was built by Mughal Emperor Shahjahan for his Empress Mumtaz Mahal. 20,000 workmen worked for 22 years to complete it. Overnight stay at hotel.

Day 04: Agra—Fatehpur Sikri—Jaipur

Morning breakfast at the hotel and drive to Jaipur. En route visiting Fatehpur Sikri—named as The Abondoned City. Built by great Mughal Emperor Akbar, as his capital but after few years abondoned due to scarcity of water. The whole city is built of Red Sand Stone.

Day 05: Jaipur

Breakfast at the hotel and drive to Jaipur. Jaipur is the Gateway to Rajasthan. Also known as Pink City, as all buildings have a pink tint to them. It is an unselfconsciously medieval city, with stately palaces, colourful bazaars (markets) and a fort brooding over the city. Graceful women in swirling skirts and veils of red, yellow, orange and magenta, laden with silver jewellery, straight tall men in Turbans and luching carts drawn by camels, do nothing to dispel the illusion. Morning excursion to Amber Fort, enjoy elephant ride over there. Afternoon city tour of Jaipur visit City Palace museum, Observatory and Palace of Winds. Overnight stay at hotel.

Day 06: Jaipur—Delhi

Morning breakfast at the hotel and drive back to Delhi. On arrival checkin at hotel for overnight stay.

Day 07: Delhi Depart

Breakfast at the hotel and checkout at 12.00 hrs.

Rajasthan Cultural Tour

Destination Covered: Delhi—Varanasi—Agra—Fatehpur Sikri—Bharatpur—Jaipur—Pushkar—Udaipur—Ranakpur—Jodhpur—Jaisalmer—Bikaner—Mukundgarh—Delhi.
Duration: 24 Days—23 Nights

Day 01: Arrive Delhi

Meeting and Assistance at the airport and transfer to hotel for overnight stay.

Day 02: Delhi

Morning after breakfast enjoy combined city tour of Old and New Delhi visiting Red Fort, Jama Masjid, Rajghat, India Gate, President House etc. Entrances to Monuments are not included (only car with Guide). Overnight at hotel.

Day 03: Delhi—Varanasi

Day free. Later transfer to railway station to board train for Varanasi. Overnight on board train.

Day 04: Varanasi

Arrive Varanasi and transfer to Hotel. Afternoon visit Sarnath, the buried Buddhist city, where Lord Buddha gave his first sermon. Visit the ruins, the stupa, the Buddhist temple and the museum.

Day 05: Varanasi

Early morning boat excursion on the holy river Ganges to see the bathing ghats and cremetion site. Watching people bathing and worshipping at the ghats is one of the most extraordinary experiences of a visit to India. Later visit the Bharat Mata Temple, Durga Temple, Tulsi Manas Mandir, Banaras Hindu University which has an art gallery.

Day 06: Varanasi—Agra

Day free. Evening transfer to railway station to board train for Agra. Overnight on board train.

Day 07: Agra

Arrive Agra and transfer to your hotel. Afternoon visit Taj Mahal—The Eternal symbol of India and Agra, built in white marble. Taj Mahal was built by Mughal Emperor Shahjahan for his Empress Mumtaz Mahal. 20,000 workmen worked for 22 years to complete it. Overnight stay at hotel.

Day 08: Agra—Fatehpur Sikri—Bharatpur

Morning breakfast at the hotel and drive to Bharatpur. En route visiting Fatehpur Sikri—named as The Abondoned City. Built by great Mughal Emperor Akbar, as his capital but after few years abondoned due to scarcity of water. The whole city is built of Red Sand Stone. Bharatpur is a famous Bird Sanctuary mainly known for the migrated bird from Siberia. Explore the park by bicycle or rickshaw. On arrival transfer to hotel Chandra Mahal Haveli (Heritage) for overnight stay.

Day 09: Bharatpur—Jaipur

Breakfast at the hotel and drive to Jaipur. Jaipur is the Gateway to Rajasthan. Also known as Pink City, as all buildings have a pink tint to them. It is an unselfconsciously medieval city, with stately palaces, colourful bazaars (markets) and a fort brooding over the city. Graceful women in swirling skirts and viels of red, yellow, orange and magenta, laden with silver jewellery, straight tall men in turbans and luching carts drawn by camels, do nothing to dispel the illusion. On arrival transfer to hotel Maharani Palace. Overnight stay at hotel.

Day 10: Jaipur

Morning breakfast at the hotel. Full day free to enjoy. You may visit Amer Fort (on Elephant back), City Palace museum, Observatory and Palace of Winds. Overnight stay at hotel.

Day 11: Jaipur—Pushkar

Morning after breakfast drive to Pushkar. Pushkar is a small village famous for its cultural charm. Here you can interact with local people and take a know-how of their living etc. Overnight stay at hotel Pushkar Palace (heritage hotel).

Day 12: Pushkar—Udaipur

Breakfast at the hotel and drive to Udaipur. Udaipur is referred as a Lake city, situated in the valley of Aravalis and on the banks of the Shimmering Lake Pichola. On arrival transfer to hotel for overnight stay.

Day 13: Udaipur

Morning breakfast at the hotel and proceed for half day city tour, visit City Palace Musuem, Jagdish Temple. Also you can go for Boating on Lake Pichola. Overnight stay at hotel.

Day 14: Udaipur—Ranakpur—Jodhpur

Morning after breakfast drive to Jodhpur, located on the edge of Thar Deserts. The city is known for its Striking Forts, Stately Palaces and gracious buildings. On arrival transfer to hotel. En route visit Ranakpur—famous for 500 years old Jain temples with intricate carvings. Overnight stay at hotel.

Day 15: Jodhpur

Morning breakfast at the hotel. Morning visit Mehrangarh Fort...most impressive fort in whole Rajasthan and Jaswant Thada Museum. Rest of the day free to enjoy on your own. Overnight stay at hotel.

Day 16: Jodhpur—Jaisalmer

Breakfast at the hotel and drive to Jaisalmer. An exotic little desert town that was once on the caravan route into Central Asia. Jaisalmer is a golden city, of the entire town, its fort, is magnificent mansions and markets are all built out of the rich, golden sandstone typical of the area. Overnight stay at hotel.

Day 17: Jaisalmer

Morning breakfast at the hotel and visit Gadisar Lake, Jaisalmer Fort and Old Mansions. You can also visit Sam Sand Dunes. Overnight stay at hotel.

Day 18: Jaisalmer

Breakfast at the hotel. Full day free for independent activities. Overnight stay at hotel.

Day 19: Jaisalmer—Bikaner

Breakfast at the hotel and drive to Bikaner. Bikaner is referred as the Gateway to the Great Indian Deserts. On arrival checkin at hotel. Bikaner was a major trading port between Africa, West Asia and Far east. Visit Fort and Lallgarh Palace. Overnight stay at hotel.

Day 20: Bikaner—Mukundgarh

Morning breakfast at the hotel and drive to Mukundgarh. Mukundgarh is situated in the Shekawati region of Rajasthan, which is famous for its painted mansions (Havelis). You can view the Real Indian Culture and Art around this place. Afternoon visit of various old painted mansions. Overnight stay at Mukundgarh Fort. (Heritage hotel...Old Palace converted into hotel).

Day 21: Mukundgarh—Delhi

Morning breakfast at the hotel and drive to Delhi. On arrival direct transfer to airport to board flight back home.

Uday Tour: A Case Study of Global Medicare Tie upto Tap Medical Tourism Mart

Healthcare consultancy firm Global Medicare and Uday Tour and Travel have entered into an agreement to promote Indian medical facilities overseas with a view to tap the growing medical tourism industry.

As per the MoU, Global Medicare would provide technical know-how and professional inputs, while Uday Tours would undertake promotional activities overseas and make all travel arrangements of clients, Uday Tour said in a release.

The companies would target clients in the US, UK, South Africa, Middle East and Australia.

The treatment would be offered in areas such as cardiac surgery, orthopaedics, oncology and plastic surgery. Further, Uday Tour also planned to offer Ayurvedic treatment and Yoga in Kerala for post-operative recovery, it said.

What is the Procedure?

We would need to follow the following steps:

Step 1: You need to send us your query alongwith specific details.
Step 2: We identify a suitable doctor and hospitals based on your query.
Step 3: Doctors get back to you with their suggestions and how to proceed further.
Step 4: We finalize on which treatment to follow and how to go about it.
Step 5: We give you the options such as where to stay pre-hospitalization and post-hospitalization.
Step 6: You finalize details and make advance payment.
Step 7: Arrival in India.
Step 8: We arrange airport pick-up and hotel check-in. We also arrange translator if required.
Step 9: We arrange your meetings with the requisite doctors.

Step 10: We proceed further with the treatment as discussed in Step 4.

Step 11: We proceed for your short holiday break if required.

Step 12: Hotel check-out, you return to your country.

Agra Hospitals: A Case Study of Modernize to Promote Medical Tourism

In what should be welcome news for tens of thousands of visitors to this city, private hospitals and nursing homes are modernizing and entering into tie-ups with well-known groups, hoping to benefit from the growing trend in medical tourism.

Half a dozen super speciality hospitals have come up in a year, in addition to scores of smaller general hospitals catering to locals and those from Rajasthan, Madhya Pradesh and other parts of Uttar Pradesh.

Said Ravi Pachauri, who is director of the joint venture between Noida-based Fortis hospital and Ravi Hospital, here: "Agra is definitely moving in the direction of a well developed medical tourism centre. With the new international airport coming up soon, and competent city doctors working abroad, this process will start soon enough.

"Medical facilities in Agra have expanded immensely. Earlier we referred our patients to hospitals in Delhi, now with the latest gadgetry and facilities available locally, patients take advantage and save both money and time."

Apollo Hospitals has also entered into partnership with Pankaj Mahendru's medical outfit. The new venture is called Apollo Pankaj.

Said Apollo Pankaj director Pankaj Mahendru: "Earlier during the British and Mughal empires also, Agra was the main centre of health services. Now embassies and corporate houses are referring patients to hospitals here which have a fairly competent base of manpower and facilities."

An American company Mefcom Agro Ind has acquired stakes in Kamayani Patients Care India, a multi-speciality hospital, providing speciality cancer treatment.

UK Boy Flying to India for Private Healthcare: A Case Study

A British mother has chosen to pay to fly her son to India for a private healthcare operation rather than wait for more than a year to get the treatment through the National Health Service (NHS).

Fourteen-year-old Elliot Knot injured his back in an ice skating accident on New Year's Eve, and now suffers from spondylolisthesis, where a vertebra moves out of position and presses on a nerve.

His mother was told by Southampton General Hospital that he would have to wait 17 weeks to see a consultant, and would then be placed on a nine-month waiting list.

Concerned about the pain her son is in, and the psychological effects his immobility may have over the course of a year, she has opted to send him to Delhi to have the specialist operation through affordable private healthcare.

AYURVEDIC THERAPIES: ONE OF THE WAYS FOR CASHING IN ON MEDICAL TOURISM

Medical tourism is a growing business in Asia. Foreigners often come to this side of the content to get therapies and treatment, which would be extremely expensive in their own countries.

More and more Globetrotters are making a beeline for the state of Kerala in India during the monsoons. Why you may ask? Well it is believed strongly that the best time to undergo natural Ayurveda healing therapy is in the rainy months of June, July and August. A statement made by Mr. M. Narayanan, head of the premier Poovar Island Resort, said, compared to the previous year monsoon tourism had gone up by 20 per cent in India.

"Ayurveda seems to have clicked much more than expected. We have occupancy of 60 per cent now. This year we got quite a few tourists from Australia. Our regular clientele is from Europe, mainly Germany," said Mr. Narayanan.

The packages can cost anything between about 60 euros and 180 euros a day. However, two-week packages carry discounts compared to daily packages. And hence the most popular packages are those spanning one week, two weeks and three weeks.

Many entrepreneurs are cashing on this new growing trend offering massages with different types of herbal oils and powders. Much preferred is the treatment for ailments of the nose, mouth and throat called "sirovasthi", in which lukewarm herbal oils are poured into a cap fitted on the head.

Most of the major Ayurveda resorts have also formulated special ayurveda kitchens to enhance the effect of the oil treatment. Clients while gcing through the Ayruvedic experience are put on a strict vegetarian diet regime, which helps to detoxify their body and add a glow to their skins. In fact, several resorts have been known to throwing in cooking classes to help clients maintain their new look and lifestyle change, which they can take back with them.

Many of the Ayurvedic therapies are quite effective, however one cannot expect a hundred per cent cure. Still, some of the high demanding therapies are for arthritis patients, treatment to arrest the ageıng process, high blood cholesterol, diabetes, body slimming, stress management and beauty treatments. Although good wholestic Aryvedic treatments can come at a high cost many health conscious individuals are opting for the Ayurvedic experience.

History of Ayurveda

The true history of Ayurveda starts from the time of the Holy books, Vedas. The ancient mythology presents that the knowledge of Ayurveda was delivered directly by the lord Brahma who is considered as the creator of the world. There are four Vedas called Rigveda, Yajurveda, Samaveda and Atharvaveda. These Vedas were written during the time 3-5 thousand years before. All these Vedas especially Atharvaveda contains the medical knowledge based on the principle of Ayurveda

India offers world-class healthcare that costs substantially less than those in developed countries, using the same technology delivered by competent specialists attaining similar success rates.

Following are some hospitals that are highly known for their respective specialities:

- AIIMS
- Apollo Hospital
- B.M.Birla Heart Research Centre
- Christian Medical College
- Tata Memorial Hospital
- Apollo Cancer Hospital
- Indraprastha Medical Corporation

- Institute of Cardiovascular Diseases

India Hospital Packages

Our Affiliate Hospitals

- AIIMS, New Delhi
- Apollo Hospital
- B.M.Birla Heart Research Centre
- Christian Medical College, Vellore
- Tata Memorial Hospital
- Apollo Cancer Hospital, Chennai
- Indraprastha Medical Corporation
- Institute of Cardiovascular Diseases
- Escorts Heart Institute and Research Centre
- PD Hinduja National Hospital and Medical Research Centre

All India Institute of Medical Science, Delhi

AIIMS' contribution in the fields of medical education, research and specialized treatment is widely acknowledged. The main object of the institute is to demonstrate high-standard of medical education, training of personnel and to conduct experiments and research in various disciplines of medical sciences.

Escorts Heart Institute and Research Centre

Located at Delhi and Faridabad

Escorts is steadily consolidating its presence in healthcare, which is likely to emerge as the largest service sector industry. Currently, Escorts is operating three large hospitals in New Delhi, Faridabad and Amritsar. Together with 11 heart command centres and associate hospitals, Escorts is managing nearly 900 beds.

Escorts excellence in providing healthcare services has received due recognition. Escorts Heart Institute and Research Centre (EHIRC), New Delhi, has been ranked as the best cardiac hospital in India by an Outlook-Cfore survey and has been given the highest grade by CRISIL—an acknowledgement of the quality of delivered patient care.

EHIRC is a leader in the fields of cardiac surgery, interventional cardiology and cardiac diagnostics. The Institute has introduced innovative techniques of minimally invasive and robotic surgery. The Institute's latest addition of state-of-the-art Cardiac Scan Centre providing a combined power of CV-MRI and Smart Score CT Scanner to diagnose coronary artery disease at its very early stage. This facility is the first of its kind outside America. State-of-the-art infrastructure and equipment has made this set-up technically the largest and the best dedicated cardiac hospital in the world. The 332-bed Institute has nine operating rooms and carries out nearly 15,000 procedures every year.

PD Hinduja National Hospital and Medical Reserch Centre

Located at Mumbai

An ultramodern hospital on the busiest artery in Central Mumbai, PD Hinduja National Hospital and Medical Research Centre was established by the Hinduja Foundation in collaboration with Massachusetts General Hospital (MGH), Boston. The fulfillment of Founder Parmanand Deepchand Hinduja's dream, the 351-bed hospital offers comprehensive services covering the gamut from diagnosis and investigation to therapy, surgery and post-operative care. As a tertiary care hospital, the services offered are comprehensive covering investigation and diagnosis to therapy, surgery and post-operative care.

The inpatient services are complemented with a day centre, out-patient facilities and an exclusive centres for health check for executives. Hinduja Hospital was the first multi-disciplinary tertiary care hospital to have been awarded the prestigious ISO 9002 Certification from KEMA of Netherlands for Quality Management System.

The Hinduja Foundation's quest for up gradation of healthcare facilities in India has prompted it to join hands with the 32,000 member American Association of Physicians of Indian origin (AAPI), with the objective of bringing to India well-qualified and experienced doctors from USA to upgrade the expertise of HNH doctors, provide quality medical care and continuing medical education; to ensure co-operation in research and pursue joint projects in the fields of: Coronary artery disease, Osteoporosis and

Asthma; and to provide consultancy, technology and treatment support to AAPI dispensaries in India on case to case basis.

Cutting Edge Technology in Diagnostics

Hinduja Hospital has a fully automated Laboratory Medicine Department. The Laboratory offers over 500 different types of tests some of, which are exclusive. It also offers an emergency/Stat menu of tests with a very short turn around time.

The department participates in International Quality Control programme conducted by the College of American Pathologists, WHO and National Quality Control Programme where it has achieved and maintained a high ranking consistently for a number of years. Imaging forms a key part of the diagnostic facility at the hospital.

Technology Upgrades

The hospital keeps upgrading its technology by acquiring new state-of-the-art diagnostic and therapeutic equipment. Hinduja Hospital was the first in India to acquire the Gamma Knife-gold standard in Radio surgery, a non-invasive neurosurgical tool. The hospital was also the first to acquire the Holmium Laser in the country thus replacing the surgeon's scalpel. The Oncology Services are wholistic and complete with installation of the Linear Accelerator with Multileaf Collimator (MLC) and Micro MLC. The hospital is the first centre in India to have installed the sophisticated state of the art GE-LCA Digital Subtraction Angiography System. In keeping with the quest for continuous improvement in quality and technological advancement, the hospital has recently commissioned the Bone Mineral Densitometer (DEXA), an addition to the Imaging department.

MEDICAL TOURISM PACKAGES IN INDIA FOR HEALTH CHECK-UPS

Many common and life-threatening conditions can be treated successfully if detected early. Many leading hospitals in India have health check-up programmes that screen every part of the body meticulously and professionally. A proper health check-up scans your bio-history, interprets signals and provides the opportunity for the proverbial "stitch in time." A heart check-up constituting echocardiography, consultation by a senior cardiologist, blood test, general test and haemogram can go a long way in ensuring a healthy heart. The test can be done at any of the leading cardiac hospitals or private clinics.

A comprehensive health check-up contains the following tests:

- Doctors consultation and full medical examination
- Blood tests
- Complete Haemogram (hb, TLC, DLR, ESR, Haemotocrit, Peripheral Smear)
- Blood group (ABO, RH)
- Blood Sugar
- Blood Urea
- Serum Uric Acid
- Serum Creatinine
- Serum Cholesterol
- Lipid Profile
- Urine and Faeces Examimation
- X-Ray Chest PA
- ECG
- Exercise Stress Test (TMT)
- Stress Screening by Psychologist
- Eye Examination
- Gynaecologist Consultation and Pap Smear Test
- Post Check-up Consultation
- Optional Test

Some additional tests may be advised by your doctor which may include:

- Pulmonary Function Tests
- Ultrasound Screening for the Abdomen
- ENT Examination
- Screening for Liver Disease
- Screening for Thyroid Disease
- Hepatitis-B Screening to Assess Immunity and for Detection of Carriers.
- A test for AIDS can also be requested
- Screening for Kidney Disease

- Serum Cholesterol
- Lipid Profile
- Urine and Faeces Examination
- X-Ray Chest PA
- ECG
- Exercise Stress Test (TMT)
- Stress Screening by Psychologist
- Eye Examination
- Gynaecologist Consultation and Pap Smear Test
- Post Check-up Consultation
- Optional Test

These tests can be done at any leading hospital, private and public. Many pioneering hospitals have comprehensive health check-up packages at rates that can cost between 2,000 and 2,500.

Child Health

Adolescent Health Care

- Age 10-18 years
- Complete physical and mental health check-up
- Check-up including Dentist, Skin, Endocrinologist, ENT. Gynaecologist, Orthopaedic, Eye Specialist etc.

Antenatal Care (Pre-Delivery)

- Diagnosis and treatment of disease in antenatal period
- Treatment of congenital abnormalities

All Childhood Related Acute and Chronic Illnesses

- Jaundice in the newborn
- Biliary atresia
- Growth failure
- Chronic diarrhea
- Celiac disease
- Abdominal pain
- Recurrent vomiting
- Blood in the stools with or without diarrhea
- Constipation
- Anorexia/ Poor Appetite
- Jaundice

- Chronic lever disease
- Pancreatitis

Paediatric Surgery

- Common operations
- Only one-day stay in hernia, hydrocele, undescended testis
- Counselling
- Your fatty child
- Speech therapy
- Behavioural therapy
- Immunisation programme

Ear, Nose and Throat Care

Complete ENT Care

Cochlear Implant

- For severely deaf children and adults

Sinus Endoscopy

- Nasal and sinus endoscopy diseases in the pituitary, naso-pharynx and orbit for endoscopic procedures.

Paediatric Otorhinolaryngology

- Early detection of deafness management of subglottic and tracheal stenosis.

Diagnostic Facilities

- Complete audiometric set-up
- Electronystagmography testing
- Brain Stem Evoked Response Audiometry (BSERA) and Oto-Aciostic Emission (OAE)
- Facial nerve monitoring
- Speech therapy facilities
- Acoustic Immitance Studies including Tympanogram, Stapedial reflex, Reflex decay, Eustachain tube function test (ETF! & ETF2).
- Special Tests of Hearing:

- — SISI
- — Tine Decay Threshold
- — STAT
- — DLI
- — DLF
- — ABLB
- — MLB
- — MLD
- — MCL
- — UCL Loudness Scaling.

Minimal Access Surgeries in ENT (Endoscopic)

- Ear surgery for chronic and acute diseases

Surgeries

- Reconstructive middle ear surgery.
- Surgery of the facial nerve.
- Congenital ear anomalies.
- Microlaryngeal surgery.
- Surgery for snoring and sleep apnoea.
- Thyroplasty.
- Septoplasty and septorhinoplasty.
- Functional endoscopic sinus surgery.
- Head and neck cancer surgeries.
- Revision ear surgeries.
- Laser surgeries for several head and neck lesions.
- Phonosurgery.

Gastroenterology

Gastroenterology and Hepatology

- Upper GI Endoscopy Colorectal Neoplasia
- Colonoscopy
- ERCP (Endoscopic Retrograde Cholangio Pancreatography)
- Sclerotherapy and band ligation of varices
- Oesophageal dilations
- Balloon treatment for Achalasia cardia
- Prosthesis placement

- Extraction of stone from CBD
- Stenting of CBD and pancreatic ducts
- Percutaneous endoscopic gastrostomy
- Colorectal Neoplasia
- Liver Transplant Clinic.

Surgical Gastroenterology and Minimally Invasive Surgery

- Surgery for benign and malignant conditions of : Oesophagus, Stomach, Intestines, livers and pancreas.

Minimally Invasive Surgeries

- Cholecystectomy, Appendectomy, Splenectomy, Intestinal Resections, Surgery for Hiatus Hernia.
  - Benign and malignant diseases of the food pipe (oesophagus).
  - Diseases of stomach including tests for H. Pylori for peptic ulcer.
  - Diseases of small bowel including Malabsorption Syndrome.
  - Benign and Malignant disorders of the biliary tract.
  - Acute and chronic Pancreatic diseases.
  - Diseases of large bowel.
  - Liver Diseases including tests for Viral Profile in Hepatitis and Alcohol related problems.

Liver Diseases

- Medical
- Pediatric

Surgical

- Control of Variecal Bleeding
- Oesophageal Protheses for Malignancy
- ERCP
- Endoscopic removal of Bile Duct Stones
- Stent Placement in Bile Duct and Pancreatic Duct
- Early Detection of Gastric and Colonic Malignancies
- Polypectomies

Nephrology

Clinical Nephrology

- Angiographic, genetic and HLA studies
- Immunofluorescence and immuno-histochemistry

Dialysis

Vascular Access for Haemodialysis
Continuous Renal Replacement Therapy

- SCUF (Slow Continuous Ultrafiltration)
- CVVH (Continuous Veno-Venous Hemofiltration)
- CVVHD (Continuous Veno-Venous Hemodialysis)
- CVVHDF (Continuous Veno-Venous Hemodiafiltration)
- Plasmapheresis

Plasmapheresis and Plasma Exchange

- CAPD (Continuous Ambulatory Peritoneal Dialysis)

Renal Transplantation (As per Rules of Government of India)

Neuro Surgery

The Gamma Knife

- Parkinsons
- Trigeminal neuralgia
- Arterioveous malformation
- Essential tumours
- Benign tumours
- Malignant tumours
- Epilepsy

Brain Tumour Surgery

All type of brain tumours are removed microscopically. Examples of brain tumours operated are meningiomas, pituitary tumours, craniopharyngioma, glioma, hemangioblastoma ependymoma, acoustic tumours, trigeminal neuromas, base of skull tumours, skull tumours, orbital tumours, intraventricular tumours etc.

Vascular Surgery

Clipping of all type of aneurysms of both anterior and posterior circulation, small to giant aneurysms, surgery of arterio-venous malformations, carotid endarterectomy, arterial bypass surgery.

Spinal Surgery

- Spinal tumours viz. bony, extradural tumours, intradural tumours, intramedullary tumour, spinal fixation.
- Microsurgery for cervical and lumbar disc surgery.
- Endoscopic lumbar disc surgery.

Paediatric Neurosurgery

- All type of congenital, neoplastic, traumatic, vascular problems. Hydrocephalus, craniostenosis, spinal dysraphism, Chiari malformations.
- All type of paediatric brain tumours like craniopharyngioma, gliomas, ependymoma, medulloblastoma, etc.

Endoscopic Brain Surgery

- Endoscopic transnasal surgery for pituitary tumours.
- Endoscopic third ventriculostomy for hydrocephalus.
- Intraventricular tumours—colloid cyst, cysticercus.

Endoscopic Disc Surgery

- Lumbar disc surgery (Band-Aid surgery).

Stereotactic and Functional Neurosurgery

- Stereotaxy.
- Deep brain stimulation.
- Pallidotomy and thalamotomy.
- Epilepsy surgery—vagal nerve stimulation.

Peripheral Nerve Surgery

- Surgery of brachial plexus and other peripheral nerves.
- All type of traumatic, neoplastic, entrapment disorders of nerves.

- Carpal tunnel syndrome.

Interventional Neuroradiology

Coiling of aneurysms, embolization of intracranial and spinal AVMs, AV fistulas, embolization of tumours, stenting of intra or extracranial vessels e.g. carotid angioplasty, cerebral and spinal angiography.

Pain and Spasticity Surgery

- Radiofrequency ablation for trigeminal neuralgia
- Facet joint ablation
- Microvascular decompression for trigeminal neuralgia and glossopharyngeal neuralgia
- Intrathecal baclofen pump implantation for spasticity.

Interventional Neuroradiology

- Head and Spine Injuries
- Strokes
- Aneurysm
- AV malformations
- Congenital Disorders like Hydrocephalus
- Spinal Dysraphisms
- Spinal Tumours
- Disc Disorders
- Treatment of Trigeminal Neuralgias
- Parkinson's Disease
- Aneurysm Coiling
- Carotid Stenting
- Angioplasty
- Neuroendoscopic System
- Stereotactic system, operating microscopes, ultrasonic aspirator etc.

Oncology

Medical Oncology

- Chemotherapy of solid tumours

- Chemotherapy of haematological malignancies
- Immunotherapy and targeted therapy of solid tumour and haematological malignancies including Interleukin, herceptin, Avastin and Mabthera
- Diagnostic tests
- Day care chemotherapy
- Chemoport insertion
- Bone marrow and stem cell transplantation

Radiation Oncology

- Intensity Modulated Radiation Therapy (IMRT)
- 3D Conformal Radiation Therapy (3D-CRT)
- Linear Accelerator (LINAC)
- Cobalt Unit
- Brachytherapy
- Simulator

Pediatric Hematology and Oncology

Surgical Oncology

Brain Tumour Surgery

All type of brain tumours are removed microscopically. Examples of brain tumours operated are meningiomas, pituitary tumours, craniopharyngioma, glioma, hemangioblastomaependymoma, acoustic tumours, trigeminal neuromas, base of skull tumours, skull tumours, orbital tumours, intraventricular tumours etc.

Reconstruction Post Cancer Surgery

- Head and neck reconstruction after cancer surgery
- Breast and nipple reconstruction after cancer surgery
- Skull base cancer surgery and reconstruction

Ophthalmology

Cataract

- Microincision sutureless cataract surgery
- "Cold Phaco" — Less Tissue Damage

Glaucoma

- Retinal Nerve Fibre Layer Analysis with GDxVCC and Optical Coherence Tomography (OCT)
- Selective Laser Trabeculoplasty (SLT)

LASIK

- Epi LASIK (for thinner corneas and higher spectacle powers)

Retinal Disorder

- Advanced Vitreo-Retinal Surgery (for Macular holes, severe Diabetic Retinopathy, Complex Retinal Disorders).

Detachments and Eye Injuries

- Photodynamic Therapy (PDT)—for Aging Macular Degeneration
- Advanced Diagnostic Modalities
- OCT and Ocular Electrophysiology
  - Low Vision Aids
  - Macular Degeneration
  - Orbit and Oculoplasty
  - Corneal Disorders
  - Contact Lens
  - Diabetic Retinopathy
  - Strabismus
  - Uveitis
  - Strabismus
  - Neuro Ophthalmology
  - Ocular Electrophysiology

Psychiatry

- Consult Psychiatrist for any psychiatric illness
- Depression
- Anxiety
- Obsessive Compulsions

- Unusual Stresses
- Psychosomatic Problems
- Sleep Problems
- Drug Addiction
- Alcoholism
- Sexual Disorders
- Marital Problems
- Counselling for positive mental health

Clinical Neurophysiologic Services (Electrodiagnosis)

- Electromyography (NCV/EMG)
- Evoked Potentials (EP)
- Electroencephalography (EEG)
- Sleep studies (polysomnography)

Medical Tourism Packages Available for India

Several medical packages are available to suit your needs. The medical package suitable for a patient depends on past treatment and current condition, based on which the most appropriate treatment will be made available.

Some of the medical packages available are for:

- Dental Care
- Eye Care
- Heart Care
- Heart Surgery
- Health Check Up
- Cosmetic Treatment
- Orthopaedic Surgery

Medical Tourism in India for Dental Care

There are several Dental Care packages available. However, these will be based on the requirements of the person and his holiday needs.

Small cost comparison of dental treatment procedures between USA and India is given below. There is a huge difference between the pricing (about 7/8 times when we speak of Top-end dentists).

Dental procedure	Cost in USA ($)		Cost in India ($)
	General Dentist	Top End Dentist	Top End Dentist
Smile designing	—	8,000	1,000*
Metal Free Bridge	—	5,500	500*
Dental Implants	—	3,500	800*
Porcelain Metal Bridge	1,800	3,000	300*
Porcelain Metal Crown	600	1,000	80*
Tooth Impactions	500	2,000	100*
Root Canal Treatment	600	1,000	100*
Tooth Whitening	350	800	110*
Tooth Colored Composite fillings	200	500	25*
Tooth Cleaning	100	300	75*

* *These figures do not suggest the actual cost. Actual cost of treatment varies Raro from case to case.*

Some of the facilities offered by the dental clinics are:

- Dental Scanning—Intra mouth
- Surgical Intervention under general anaesthesia
- Whitening of teeth
- Ceramic caps without gold under microscopic control
- Prosthesis on the implant
- Vertical and horizontal bone grafting
- Gum grafting
- Palatal orthodontics
- Fluoride treatment for children
- Maxillary surgery
- Over denture
- Combined prostheses with milling

Medical Tourism in India for Eye Care

The cost difference for most eye care procedures varies as high as 8-10 times from that of USA and UK. Some of the treatments available are:

- Eye Lasik Refractive Packages
- Lasik Eye Surgery
- Eye Care Treatment
- Lasik Treatment
- Refractive Surgery in India

- Laser Refractive Surgery
- Refractive Eye Correction Package
- Natural Eye Care Treatment
- Vision and Eye Care
- Eye Refractive Care Packages

Medical Tourism Packages in India for Heart Care

India offers world-class healthcare that costs substantially less than those in developed countries, using the same technology delivered by competent specialists attaining similar success rates. Hospitals in India use some of the best know-how and technology and the procedures include cardiothoracic, neurology, gastrointestinal, orthopaedic, renal, obstetric, ENT, ophthalmology, dental, plastic, cosmetic and tumour surgeries.

A heart care surgery which costs in the region of USD 30,000 in USA can cost as low as USD 8,000 in India. This clearly states the price difference that exists in India when compared to the west.

Conditions operated on include:

- Valvular diseases
- Arrhythmias
- Coronary artery disease
- Hypercholesterolemia
- Family history of coronary disease
- Heart disease symptoms

Some of the procedures available are:

- Directional coronary atherectomy
- Rotablation
- Coronary artery stenting
- Intravascular ultrasound
- Balloon valvuloplasty
- Non-surgical closure of holes in the heart such as ASD, VSD and PDA.

Medical Tourism Packages in India for Heart Surgery

A heart care surgery which costs in the region of USD 30,000 in

USA can cost as low as USD 8,000 in India. This clearly states the price difference that exists in India when compared to the west.

Cardiac care has become a speciality in India with institutions like the Escorts Heart Institute and Research Centre, All India Institute of Medical Sciences and Apollo Hospital becoming names to reckon with. They combine the latest innovations in medical electronics with unmatched expertise in leading cardiologists and cardo-thoracic surgeons. These centres have the distinction of providing comprehensive cardiac care spanning from basic facilities in preventive cardiology to the most sophisticated curative technology. The technology is contemporary and world class and the volumes handled match global benchmarks. They also specialise in offering surgery to high risk patients with the introduction of innovative techniques like minimally invasive and robotic surgery.

Renowned Indian hospitals like Apollo and Escorts Heart Institute are equipped to handle all phases of heart diseases from the elementary to the latest clinical procedures like interventional cardiac catherisation and surgical cardiac transplants. Their success rate at an average of 98.50 per cent is at par with leading cardiac centres around the world.

Leading heart centers like The Escorts Heart Institute have Cardiac Care Units with sophisticated equipment and investigative facilities like Echocardiography with coloured Doppler, Nuclear Scanning and Coronary Angiography. The Jayadeva Institute of Cardiology in Bangalore, the Cardiology Hospital in Kanpur, the Heart Hospital in Calicut and the Sree Sudhindra Medical Mission Hospital in Cochin are some hospitals in India devoted exclusively to cardiac treatment.

Surgical treatment packages are offered in following areas:

- Cardiac Surgery and Cardiology
- Open Heart Surgery
- Angiographies
- Angioplasties
- Paediatric Cardiac Surgery
- Paediatric Intervention
- Cardiology Robotic Surgery

Some other procedures available are:

- Directional coronary atherectomy
- Rotablation
- Coronary artery stenting
- Intravascular ultrasound
- Balloon valvuloplasty
- Non-surgical closure of holes in the heart such as ASD, VSD and PDA.

Medical Tourism Packages for Cosmetic Surgery

A new dimension of the medical field taking off in India is cosmetic surgery which utilizes some of the latest techniques in corrective procedures. Some disfigurations corrected include hair restoration (hair implants, hair flaps and scalp reductions), rhinoplasties (reshaping or recontouring of the nose), stalling of the aging process (face life, cosmetic eyelid surgery, brow lift, sub-metal lipectomy for double chin), demabrasions (sanding of the face,) otoplasty for protruding ears, chin and cheek enlargement, lip reductions, various types of breast surgery and reconstruction and liposuction.

Non-invasive surgical procedures like streotactic radiosurgery and radiotherapy for brain tumours are practised successfully.

Medical Tourism Packages in India for Orthopedic Surgery

A number of orthopedic procedures are available such as hip and knee replacement, the Illizarov technique, limb lengthening, Birmingham Hip resurfacing technique (which scores over conventional hip replacements and is still unavailable even in the US) etc.

Many hospitals specialize in latest techniques and treatments such as minimal invasive surgery, cartilage and bone transplantation, spine surgery and limb sparing surgery. All kinds of musculoskeletal problems ranging from Arthiritis to sports injuries, to complex broken bones, bone tumours and childhood conditions like scoliosis are treated most effectively.

A wide range of spinal surgeries including fixation, stabilization and fusion are regularly undertaken.

Bone Marrow Transplant

Major hospitals in India have oncology units comprising surgical oncology, medical and radiation therapy as well as the crucial Bone Marrow Transplantation (BMT). The BMT unit with high pressure hipa filters has helped achieve a very high success rate in the various types of transplantation.

Cord Blood Transplant and Mismatched Allogeneic Stem Cell Transplant have been performed successfully, a feat that is remarkable and significant, considering the fact that the treatment costs one-tenth of what it does in the west. Special surgeons are available for individual organs. Plastic surgeons of repute provide treatment for head and neck cancer, breast cancer and other malignancies. Facilities offered include tele-therapy which includes simulation work stations to ensure high precision and safety during treatment at the 18 MV linear accelerator or telecobalt machines, brachy therapy and 3-D planning systems. In orthopedics, the Illizarov technique is practised for the treatment of limb deformities, limb shortening and disfiguration.

Joint Replacement Surgery

Shoulder/hip replacement and bilateral knee replacement surgery using the most advanced keyhole or endosopic surgery and anthroscopy is done at several hospitals in India including the Apollo Hospital, Sir Ganga Ram Hospital and Holy Family Hospital in Delhi, Bombay Hospital, Leelavati and Hinduja Hospital in Mumbai and the Madras Institute of Orthopedics and Trauma Sciences. Some hospitals like Apollo in Delhi have Operation Theatres with Laminar Air Flow System which compares with the best in the USA and the UK. A knee joint replacement costs about 3000 pounds in India whereas in the UK, a similar surgery using the same implants and medical consumables costs around 10,000 pounds.

Doctors Attitude and Costs Plays a Vital Role in Boosting Medical Tourism in India

A leading Indian cosmetic surgeon, Narendra Pandya, says he foresees a dramatic rise in medical tourism to India because of not just the low costs involved but a more humane approach towards patients.

"What we are seeing now (in medical tourism) is just the beginning. At the Apollo Victor Hospital in Goa, where I do surgery, over 90 per cent of the patients are British expatriates," Pandya told IANS in an interview.

While the lower costs in India were a major factor in attracting medical tourists, Pandya said there was also a difference in the approach to patients.

"In the US the patient is only a number. In the East, we are more involved with them as humans. It makes a difference."

Pandya said Indian physicians and surgeons treated a large number of patients, giving them a definite advantage over their American counterparts.

"An American surgeon for example will not be performing more than 15 cleft lip operations in an entire year. My resident-in-training in Mumbai performs more than 500 cleft operations in a year. Where is the comparison?"

"The on-the-job medical training in India is infinitely better. People in the US cannot grasp the quantum of work we do. We also have only 24 hours," he pointed out.

He said he was increasingly seeing more patients from the West flocking to India for treatment, such as dentistry, cosmetic surgery, joint replacements and eye surgery, given the low costs and the world class facilities available.

"A nose job costs $8,000 in the US while it cost $1,500 in India. If you trust me in Chicago for $8,000 dollars, how am I, as a physician, inferior in India?" he asked.

In fact, on this visit, Pandya had scheduled consultations with prospective patients in Boston, followed by similar consultations in London.

The desire for cosmetic surgery, said the surgeon, was "commensurate with affluence". "If you do not have enough to eat, you do not worry about your nose," said the skilled surgeon.

But he added that cosmetic surgery had won wide acceptance among both women and men in India.

Although the favourite cosmetic surgeon to Bollywood stars, Pandya said he normally did not have the time to attend Bollywood concerts or watch movies.

But on his visit, he squeezed in time to attend the Rockstars concert, on a special invitation from the participating stars.

"I have a professional association with almost 90 per cent of Bollywood stars," the doctor said diplomatically.

Pandya, who holds a diploma from the American Board of Plastic Surgery, had trained under Sumner Koch at Northwestern University in Chicago and was an assistant director at the Cook County Hospital Burns unit in the late 1960s.

Despite a successful career in the US, Pandya and his wife (a gynecologist) decided to go back to India in 1971 where he began his career treating burns and leprosy-affected patients.

Later, he shifted to rhinoplasty (nose jobs) and then began sculpting faces, and was branded India's 'father of plastic surgery'.

8

Medical Tourism: Conclusion and Recommendation

Medical tourism can be broadly defined as provision of 'cost effective' private medical care in collaboration with the tourism industry for patients needing surgical and other forms of specialized treatment. This process is being facilitated by the corporate sector involved in medical care as well as the tourism industry—both private and public.

Medical or Health tourism has become a common form of vacationing, and covers a broad spectrum of medical services. It mixes leisure, fun and relaxation together with wellness and healthcare.

The idea of the health holiday is to offer you an opportunity to get away from your daily routine and come into a different relaxing surrounding. Here you can enjoy being close to the beach and the mountains. At the same time you are able to receive an orientation that will help you improve your life in terms of your health and general well-being. It is like rejuvenation and clean up process on all levels—physical, mental and emotional.

Many people from the developed world come to India for the rejuvenation promised by yoga and Ayurvedic massage, but few consider it a destination for hip replacement or brain surgery. However, a nice blend of top-class medical expertize at attractive prices is helping a growing number of Indian corporate hospitals lure foreign patients, including from developed nations such as the UK and the US.

As more and more patients from Europe, the US and other affluent nations with high medicare costs look for effective options, India is pitted against Thailand, Singapore and some other Asian countries, which have good hospitals, salubrious climate and tourist destinations. While Thailand and Singapore with their advanced medical facilities and built-in medical tourism options have been drawing foreign patients of the order of a couple of lakhs per annum, the rapidly expanding Indian corporate hospital sector has been able to get a few thousands for treatment.

But, things are going to change drastically in favour of India, especially in view of the high quality expertise of medical professionals, backed by the fast improving equipment and nursing facilities, and above all, the cost-effectiveness of the package.

Promoting Medical Tourism in India

Medical tourism focuses on treatment of acute illness, elective surgeries such as cardiology and cancer, among others. From October this year, the Government plans to start overseas marketing of India as a medical tourism destination. Senior Government officials say that the formalities for marketing medical facilities to a global audience have already started and they hope to complete the process of price-banding of hospitals in various cities by the third quarter of this year. The Government of India is of the opinion that by marketing India as a global medical tourism destination, it could capitalise on the low-cost, high-quality medical care available in the country.

Statistics show that the medical tourism industry in India is worth $333 million (Rs. 1,450 crore) while a study by CII-McKinsey estimates that the country could earn Rs. 5,000-10,000 crore by 2012. Probably realising the potential, major corporates such as the Tatas, Fortis, Max, Wockhardt, Piramal, and the Escorts group have made significant investments in setting up modern hospitals in major cities. Many have also designed special packages for patients, including airport pick-ups, visa assistance and board and lodging, healthcare industry officials said.

Among the factors that make India an attractive proposition for medical treatment is cost efficiency. The estimated cost for a heart surgery in the US is $ 30,000, however, the same could be performed India for about $ 6,000. Similarly, a bone marrow transplant could cost about $ 2,50,000 in the US while it could be done here for about $ 26,000.

India is hoping to expand its tourist industry – to include visitors with heart conditions and cataracts. Indeed, medical tourism, where foreigners travel abroad in search of low cost, world-class medical treatment, is gaining popularity in countries like India. The field has such lucrative potential that Indian Finance Minister Jaswant Singh called for India to become a "global health destination." And, with prices at a fraction of those in the US or Britain, the concept will likely have broad consumer appeal – if people can overcome their prejudices about healthcare in developing countries. Though the quality of healthcare for the poor in countries like India is undeniably low, private facilities offer advanced technology and procedures on par with hospitals in developed nations. One Indian hospital director maintains, "In a corporate hospital, once the door is closed you could be in a hospital in America." – YaleGlobal ....

For someone about to undergo surgery to remove gallstones, David Potter, a 63-year-old Briton, is remarkably chipper. Pushing a walking-frame he hardly seems to need, he testifies to the success of an earlier operation, to replace a hip. Both are standard surgical procedures....

Health and medical tourism is perceived as one of the fastest growing segments in marketing 'Destination India' today. While this area has so far been relatively unexplored, we now find that not only the ministry of tourism, Government of India, but also the various state tourism boards and even the private sector consisting of travel agents, tour operators, hotel companies and other accommodation providers are all eying health and medical tourism as a segment with tremendous potential for future growth.

With an increasing number of foreign patients flocking to India for treatment, the country could earn Rs. 100 billion (US$ 2.3 billion) through 'Medical Tourism' by 2012, a study has indicated.

According to the study conducted by the Confederation of Indian Industry and McKinsey consultants, last year some 150,000 foreigners visited India for treatment, with the number rising by 15 per cent a year.

With a large pool of highly trained doctors and low treatment cost, healthcare aims to replicate the Indian software sector's success. Built on acres of land the new sleek medical centres of excellence offer developed world treatment at developing world prices, a report in 'The Guardian' said.

India could earn more than $1 billion annually and create 40 million new jobs by sub-contracting work from the British National Health Service, the head of India's largest chain of private hospitals told rediff.com.

Houston-trained Dr. Prathap C. Reddy, chairman, Apollo Hospitals, also said he was waiting for a reply to his proposal to carry out operations at a fraction of what they would cost in the United Kingdom.

Details of the multi-million dollar package are also carried in this week's edition of India Abroad.

They include surgery for hip and knee replacements and coronary bypass that would slash waiting times dramatically, reducing the queues of British patients waiting to see their doctors.

"We have well-equipped, state-of-the-art hospitals and we can offer the same level of care as anywhere else in the world," Dr. Reddy said.

"There is no reason why we should not become the healthcare destination of the world."

A Worldwide Market

What's called medical tourism—patients going to a different country for either urgent or elective medical procedures—is fast becoming a worldwide, multibillion-dollar industry.

The reasons patients travel for treatment vary. Many medical tourists from the United States are seeking treatment at a quarter or sometimes even a 10th of the cost at home. From Canada, it is often people who are frustrated by long waiting times. From Great Britain, the patient can't wait for treatment by the National Health Service but also can't afford to see a physician in private practice. For others, becoming a medical tourist is a chance to combine a tropical vacation with elective or plastic surgery.

And more patients are coming from poorer countries such as Bangladesh where treatment may not be available.

Medical tourism is actually thousands of years old. In ancient Greece, pilgrims and patients came from all over the Mediterranean to the sanctuary of the healing god, Asklepios, at Epidaurus. In Roman Britain, patients took the waters at a shrine at bath, a practice that continued for 2,000 years. From the 18th century wealthy

Europeans travelled to Spas from Germany to the Nile. In the 21st century, relatively low-cost jet travel has taken the industry beyond the wealthy and desperate.

Countries that actively promote medical tourism include Cuba, Costa Rica, Hungary, India, Israel, Jordan, Lithuania, Malaysia and Thailand, Belgium, Poland and Singapore are now entering the field. South Africa specializes in medical safaris—visit the country for a safari, with a stopover for plastic surgery, a nose job and a chance to see lions and elephants.

India

India is considered the leading country promoting medical tourism and now it is moving into a new area of "medical outsourcing," where subcontractors provide services to the overburdened medical care systems in western countries.

India's National Health Policy declares that treatment of foreign patients is legally an "export" and deemed "eligible for all fiscal incentives extended to export earnings." Government and private sector studies in India estimate that medical tourism could bring between $1 billion and $2 billion US into the country by 2012. The reports estimate that medical tourism to India is growing by 30 per cent a year.

India's top-rated education system is not only churning out computer programmers and engineers, but an estimated 20,000 to 30,000 doctors and nurses each year.

With an increasing number of foreign patients flocking to India for treatment, India could earn Rs.100 billion through 'Medical Tourism' by 2012, a study has indicated.

According to the study conducted by the Confederation of Indian Industry and McKinsey consultants, some 150,000 foreigners visited India for treatment, with the number rising by 15 per cent a year.

With a large pool of highly trained doctors and low treatment cost, healthcare aims to replicate the Indian software sector's success. Built on acres of land the new sleek medical centres of excellence offer developed world treatment at developing world prices, a report in 'The Guardian' said today.

A number of private hospitals also offer packages designed to attract wealthy foreign patients, with airport-to-hospital bed car service, in-room internet access and private chefs. Another trend is to combine surgery in India with a yoga holiday or trip to the world famous Taj Mahal.

The report said it is not just cost but competency that is India's selling point. Naresh Trehan, who worked as a heart surgeon in Manhattan but returned to start Escorts hospital group in India, was quoted as saying that his hospital in Delhi completed 4,200 heart operations.

Many people from the developed world come to India for the rejuvenation promised by yoga and ayurvedic massage, but few consider it a destination for hip replacements or brain surgery.

Yet that's exactly what the government in the Indian state of Maharashtra hopes will happen soon.

Together with the state's business sector and private health-care providers it recently launched the Medical Tourism Council (MTC) of Maharashtra.

Its aim: To make India a prime destination for medical tourists.

At its Swish offices in central Bombay, also known as Mumbai, members of the council explain the concept.

Bombay, they argue, has private hospitals on a par with the best in the world.

Many of the surgeons at hospitals such as the Hinduja are leaders in their field, working with the best equipment available.

But they can provide their expertize at a fraction of the price that comparable surgery would cost in Europe or the United States.

A nice blend of top-class medical expertize at attractive prices is helping a growing number of Indian corporate hospitals lure foreign patients, including from developed nations such as the UK and the US.

If a liver transplant costs in the range of Rs. 60 lakh-70 lakh in Europe and double that in the US, a few Indian hospitals, such as Global in Hyderabad, have the wherewithal to do it in around Rs. 15 lakh-20 lakh. Similarly, if a heart surgery in the US costs about Rs. 20 lakh, the Chennai-headquartered Apollo Hospitals Group does it in roughly Rs. 2 lakh.

As more and more patients from Europe, the US and other affluent nations with high medicare costs look for effective options, India is pitted against Thailand, Singapore and some other Asian countries, which have good hospitals, salubrious climate and tourist destinations.

While Thailand and Singapore with their advanced medical facilities and built-in medical tourism options have been drawing foreign patients of the order of a couple of lakhs per annum, the rapidly expanding Indian corporate hospital sector has been able to get a few thousands for treatment.

But, things are going to change drastically in favour of India, especially in view of the high quality expertize of medical professionals, backed by the fast improving equipment and nursing facilities, and above all, the cost-effectiveness of the package, said some of the hospitals Business Line spoke to.

Medical tourism is likely to be the next major foreign exchange earner for India as an increasing number of patients, unwilling to accept long queues in Europe or high costs in the US, are travelling to the country to undergo surgery, according to a media report.

Medical tourism is on the rise with more people from the United States, Europe and the Middle East seeking Indian hospitals as a cheap and safe alternative, says an article in an upcoming issue of Bloomberg Markets magazine.

The article says Indian doctors are setting up what could be a medical renaissance in their country and the next great boom for the Indian economy.

Many Indian hospitals are coming together to improve the quality of healthcare, boost first impressions and aiming for $2.3 billion in annual revenue by 2012, it says.

Instead of paying $2,00,000 for a mitral valve surgery in the US, a patient could travel to India and receive the same treatment for $6,700.

Similarly, rather than paying 15,000 pounds Sterling for hip resurfacing in the UK, a patient can get the same procedure for 5,000 pounds in India, including surgery, airfare and hotel stay, the magazine says.

Would you do it? Has a cheaper workforce enabled India to compete in a field many thought could never flourish in that country? These are the questions many people throughout the world have been asking themselves, and increasingly the answer is yes, Bloomberg Markets says.

Medical insurance is seen as the fastest growing segment in the Indian economy, says Supriya Saxena.

A recent outcome of the privatization of health services in India has been the growth of medical tourism to the extent that this sector is perceived as a fast-growing segment of the economy. India is a recent entrant into this industry and is expected to become a $2-billion business by 2012.

The driving force behind medical tourism is its cost effectiveness and the possibility of attracting substantial tourism revenue. Medical care, packaged with traditional therapies like yoga, meditation, ayurveda, allopathy, and other traditional systems of medicines, attract high-end tourists especially from European countries and the Middle East.

Kerala has pioneered health and medical tourism in India. But low cost treatment is the ultimate factor weighing in favour of India. Medical care costs only one-fifth of the costs in the West. So if a particular surgery costs $30,000 in the West, it would cost only $6,000 in India.

India has gained acceptance in areas of medical care such as organ transplant, knee replacement, open-heart surgery and others because of the efforts of the corporate sector in the medical as well as tourism industry. The state-of-the-art equipment and well-qualified practitioners at these hospitals is what attract patients from other countries.

It is estimated that foreigners account for about 12 per cent of all patients in top hospitals of Mumbai, like Lilavati, Jaslok, Breach Candy, Bombay Hospital, Hinduja Hospital, Apollo and Wockhardt.

Bariatric Surgery Solution to Obesity: A Model Way to Boost Medical Tourism

Bariatric surgery is the surgery done for obesity. This type of surgery is in high demand as in the US as 30 per cent of its population is estimated to be overweight. Bariatric surgery in India could bring patients from US and Europe to the country.

A private hospital in Kolkata launched a world class Bariatric surgery clinic here to treat people suffering from severe obesity, a disease that is fast attaining epidemic proportions in India.

The star-studded launch of the clinic at Apollo Gleneagles Hospitals here saw at least 25 people queuing up for surgery to get rid of excessive body weight and in turn associated diseases like high blood pressure, diabetes and cardiac ailments.

The new facility, first of its kind in eastern India after sporadic attempts elsewhere in the country, is also eyeing patients from the west, where the cost of treatment is 15 per cent more and the waiting time enormous.

"The facility, being backed by a support group for obese people, is a comprehensive unit, which will benefit not only domestic patients but also thousands of patients in the Americas and Europe, who are showing interest in flying down to get operated," says advanced laparoscopic and Bariatric surgeon Dr B Ramana, who heads the clinic.

Quoting the WHO, he says 17 per cent of men and 15 per cent women in India were confirmed to be obese and the numbers were growing by leaps with changing lifestyles and eating habits.

"Globally, over 1.7 billion people are affected by the disease. In the US, over 300,000 people die of obesity while in Europe around 250,000 people are killed by the scourge," he says.

Though a systematic survey of obesity mortality has not been conducted in the country, Ramana says the numbers could be high in the next five years.

For Indians, the risk of obesity is more as the population traditionally exhibits low muscle mass, high fat content and a pot belly syndrome.

This propensity to deposit fat around the abdomen makes Indians more prone to diabetes and heart diseases, Dr. Ramana says. "Ninety per cent of adult diabetics in India are obese and Bariatric surgery offers them hope for a better living. In India, the cases of obesity are trebling every year, much faster than the western world," he says.

The surgery, wherein the stomach is stapled and stitched to a part of the small intestine, has gained popularity throughout the world as it reduces the body weight of patients by 80 per cent.

Through procedures called laparoscopic gastric bypass and sleeve gastrectomy, where the digestive system is short-circuited to decrease absorption of fats, Bariatric surgery reduces the intake capacity of the stomach.

"This makes for lesser food intake and subsequent reduction of weight. The patient, however, is kept on essential vitamins and nutritional supplements for normal functioning of body systems," Ramana says.

Bariatric Surgery Clinic to Boost Medical Tourism

In a development that could bring patients from US and Europe to the country, a private hospital today launched a world class bariatric surgery clinic here to treat people suffering from severe obesity, a disease that is fast attaining epidemic proportions in India. The star-studded launch of the clinic at Apollo Gleneagles Hospitals here saw at least 25 people queuing up for surgery to get rid of excessive body weight and in turn associated diseases like high blood pressure, diabetes and cardiac ailments.

Tourism industry never had it so good! After witnessing successive setbacks on various counts like SARS or adverse travel advisories issued by the US and a number of countries, the tourism sector is witnessing a boom both in domestic as well as inflows of foreign tourists.

With robust economic growth and ongoing peace talks between India and Pakistan, the foreign tourist arrivals almost touched the three million marks during the year, which saw emergence of a healthy trend in the domestic sector as well.

"India is the natural destination for the world today", an upbeat tourism minister Renuka.

During the year, the country saw a record number of 29,83,453 foreign tourist arrivals in the country till November this year, registering a growth of 24 per cent over the previous year and the government proposed several new initiatives to strengthen the "incredible India" overseas.

Brimming with new ideas, Chowdhury says several initiatives have been launched in the sphere of medical tourism in partnership with the private sector to make India emerge as a major global hub.

A joint task force comprising tourism and health ministries along with Confederation of Indian Industry (CII) has been set up to tap this market which has a huge potential, she says.

The government is also contemplating offering a package to foreign tourists, keen on medical tourism, by dovetailing allopathic with alternative medicines.

Efforts to modernize Delhi and Mumbai airports as also upgrade facilities at 22 non-metro airports in the next two years and upgrade infrastructure facilities at Buddhist circuit in six states is expected to attract more tourists.

With a view to increasing India's share in the growing business of Meetings, Incentives, Conferences and Events (MICE) segment, it has been decided to support the setting up of large convention centres with exhibition facilities in Delhi, Mumbai and Bangalore and small convention facilities in Goa and Jaipur.

Laying emphasis on quality of tourism rather than the number of tourists visiting the country, Chowdhury says the visa on arrival, a long pending proposal, was only a facilitator and not a crucial factor to attract foreign tourists.

"My ministry has asked the home ministry to look into the issue. When Sri Lanka with its school of terrorism gives visa on arrival, why not India? At the same time, there is no visa on arrival in China but it witnesses a booming tourist inflow. Visa on arrival is not a crucial issue but only a facilitator," she says.

Strongly pitching for bringing tourism in the concurrent list of the Constitution, Chowdhury says the issue is being examined in consultation with the state governments in order to give a new impetus to the development of this sector.

The ministry is contemplating launching a strong campaign "athithi devo bhava" (guest is like God) in order to boost domestic tourism which has a multiplier effect on the employment potential with the growth of various facets of tourism like travel components and infrastructure development.

The infrastructure upgradation of Buddhist circuit in six states has been started in a big way to attract more tourists.

The ministry has identified 31 tourism hotspots in various states to develop as rural tourism hubs so as to help rural poor to get employment through various tourism related projects.

During the year, the ministry has evolved a concept of "night bazaars" as an attempt to provide a unique shopping experience as well as to preserve and nourish the traditional art and cultural forms of the country. The Hauz Khas area in New Delhi has been selected for the first night bazaar project.

In a bid to beef up security arrangements for foreign tourists, the government has asked the state governments to deploy tourist police at all important tourist destinations to check crimes against tourists.

In a novel arrangement, the Tourism Ministry also plans to train taxi drivers operating at the airports and urged the airport authority of India to tie up with state governments for operation of radio taxis to airports in order to ensure the safety of passengers.

Glossary of Terms

Abduction

A form of logical inference, commonly applied in the process of medical diagnosis. Given an observation, abduction generates all known causes.

Ablative Surgery

Surgical procedure performed at peripheral or central neural structures to relieve pain by permanent disruption of nerve pathways.

Access

An individual's ability to obtain appropriate healthcare services. Barriers to access can be financial (insufficient monetary resources), geographic (distance to providers), organizational (lack of available providers) and sociological (e.g., discrimination, language barriers). Efforts to improve access often focus on providing or improving health coverage.

Accessibility

The degree to which the healthcare system inhibits or facilitates the ability of an individual to gain entry and to receive services. Accessibility involves geographic, architectural, transportation, social, time, and economic consideration. It may be measured either by utilization, non-utilization or the relative strength and absence of barriers to utilization.

Accreditation

A process whereby a programme of study or an institution is recognized by an external body as meeting certain predetermined standards. For facilities, accreditation standards are usually defined in terms of physical plant, governing body, administration, and medical and other staff. Accreditation is often carried out by organizations created for the purpose of assuring the public of the quality of the accredited institution or programme. State or Federal governments can recognize accreditation in lieu of, or as the basis for licensure or other mandatory approvals. Public or private payment programmes often require accreditation as a condition of payment for covered services. Accreditation may either be permanent or may be given for a specified period of time.

Acupuncture

The piercing of specific sites of the body surface with needles to produce pain relief.

Acute Care

Medical treatment given to individuals whose illnesses or health problems are short-term (usually under 30 days) or episodic. Acute care facilities are those hospitals that mainly serve persons with short-term health problems.

Addiction (Psychological Dependence)

Pattern of compulsive drug use characterized by a continued craving for a drug and the need to use the drug for effects other than pain relief.

Adequacy of Prenatal Care

See Kessner Index.

Adjuvant Analgesic Drug

A drug that has independent or additive analgesic properties. Adjuvant are used to provide analgesia for specific types of pain, e.g. naturopathic pain, to augment the efficacy of other agents such as uploads.

Administrative Services Only

A service requiring a third party to deliver administrative services to an employer group and requiring the employer to be at risk for the cost of healthcare services provided. This is a common arrangement when an employer sponsors a self-funded healthcare programme.

Aeromedical Evacuation

The movement of patients, under medical supervision, to and between medical treatment facilities by air transportation.

Affiliation

An agreement, usually formal, between two or more otherwise independent entities or individuals which defines how they will relate to each other. Affiliation agreements between hospitals may specify procedures for referring or transferring patients from one facility to another, joint faculty, and/or medical staff appointments, teaching relationships, sharing of records or services, or provision of consultation between programmes.

AFI

Acute febrile illness.

Age-Adjusted Death Rate

(Direct method) A summary of age-specific death rates, applied to a standard population to calculate what rate would be expected if the selected population had the same distribution as the standard population. The total of expected deaths divided by the total of the standard population and multiplied by 100,000 yields the age-adjusted death rate per 100,000.

Agent

Computer software constructed to operate with a degree of autonomy from its user, e.g. an agent may search the Internet for information based upon loose specifications provided by its user.

Age-Specific Rate

The number of events to individuals in a specific age group per 100,000 individuals in the population in the same age group.

Air Force Security Assistance Training (AFSAT) Squadron

The U.S. Air Force agency responsible for the management of the Air Force international training programme.

Algorithm

A set of instructions to programmatically carry out some task. In clinical practice algorithms usually, bút not always, involve some form of numerical calculation.

Alien

Any person not a citizen or national of the United States.

Allied Health Professional (AHP)

AHPs are individuals trained to support, complement, or supplement the professional functions of physicians, dentists, and other health professionals in the delivery of healthcare to patients. They include physician assistants, dental hygienists, medical technicians, nurse midwives, nurse practitioners, physical therapists, psychologists, and nurse anesthetists.

Allodynia

Pain produced by a stimulant that is not normally painful, such as after nerve injury.

Alma-Ata Conference

Alma-Ata International Conference on Primary Healthcare, held 6-12 September 1978, in Alma-Ata, USSR. The first such international conference, it was sponsored by the World Health Organization and UNICEF and attended by delegates from 134 countries. It presented the manifesto to attain global health for the 21st century by providing basic healthcare aimed at the urban and rural poor of the developing world.

Alphabet

The set of symbols that defines a particular language. *See*: Language.

Alternative Delivery Systems

A catch-all phrase used to cover all forms of healthcare delivery except traditional fee-for-service, private practice. The term includes HMOs, PPOs, IPAs, and other systems of providing healthcare.

Alternative Splicing Product

Variation in the way pre-mRNA is spliced together. Introns are typically spliced (removed) from pre-mRNA and the remaining exons are pieced together to form a contiguous transcript of mRNA (*see* Exon). However, the same set of introns may not always be spliced out, and the resultant mRNA may have a different combination of introns and exons. These alternative versions of the mRNA result in different downstream proteins being formed (alternative splicing products). Alternative splicing products are one reason why the number of gene products is much larger than the number of genes.

Ambulatory Care

All types of health services that are provided on an outpatient basis, in contrast to services provided in the home or to persons who are inpatients. While many inpatients may be ambulatory, the term ambulatory care usual implies that the patient must travel to a location to receive services that do not require an overnight stay.

Ambulatory Payment Classification (APC)

This is the method used by CMS to implement prospective payment for ambulatory procedures. APC clusters many different ambulatory procedures into groups for purposes of payment.

Ambulatory Setting

A type of institutional organized health setting in which health services are provided on an outpatient basis. Ambulatory care settings may be either mobile (when the facility is capable of being moved to different locations) or fixed (when the person seeking care must travel to a fixed service site).

Ambulatory Surgery Centres

Surgical facilities that provide outpatient (same day) surgery, including single and multi-speciality centres, and independent, corporate or hospital owned centres. Procedures performed in ambulatory surgical centres include ophthalmology, gynecology, gastroenterology, ear nose throat (ENT), orthopedics, general, reconstructive and cosmetic and podiatry.

AMMP

Adult Morbidity and Mortality Project. A joint project of the Tanzania Ministry of Health and the University of Newcastle Upon Tyne, funded by the Department for International Development, United Kingdom.

Analgesia

A deadening or absence of pain without loss of consciousness.

Analgesic

A medication that reduces or eliminates pain.

Ancillary Service

Diagnostic and therapeutic services generally provided by hospitals and consisting of specific departments such as X-ray and laboratory.

Anxiolysis

Sedation or hypnosis used to reduce anxiety, agitation, or tension.

Anxiolytic

Medication used to reduce anxiety, agitation, or tension.

Any Willing Provider

Laws that require managed care plans to contract with all health care providers that meet their terms and conditions.

Application

Synonym for a computer programme that carries out a specific type of task. Word-processors or spreadsheets are common applications available on personal computers.

Appropriateness

Appropriate healthcare is when the expected health benefits exceeds the expected negative consequences by a wide enough margin to justify treatment.

Arden Syntax

A language created to encode actions within a clinical protocol into a set of situation-action rules, for computer interpretation, and also to facilitate exchange between different institutions.

ARPA Net

Advanced Research Projects Network. A computer network developed by the United States Department of Defence in the late 1960s, and the forerunner of today's Internet.

Artificial Intelligence (AI)

Any artefact, whether embodied solely in computer software, or a physical structure like a robot, that exhibits behaviours associated with human intelligence. Also the study of the science and methods for constructing such artefacts.

Artificial Intelligence in Medicine

The application of artificial intelligence methods to solve problems in medicine e.g. developing expert systems to assist with diagnosis, or therapy planning.

Assessment

A surveillance process for identifying public health threats and trends.

Assurance

The pledge that necessary services, including personal health services for the protection of public health in the community will be available and accessible to all persons.

Asynchronous Communication

A mode of communication between two parties, when the exchange does not require both to be active participant in the conversation at the same time e.g. sending a letter.

ATM

Asynchronous Transfer Mode. A packet-based communication protocol that provides the high bandwidth transmission rates required for multimedia communication.

Average Length of Stay

The average stay, in days, of inpatients in a given time period. This can be calculated by dividing the number of patient days by either the number of admissions or the number of discharges and death.

Average Wholesale Price (AWP)

Average Wholesale Price of brand-name pharmaceuticals, as stated by the manufacturer, is used as a basis for determining discounts and rebates.

Bandwidth

Amount of data that can be transmitted across a communication channel over a given period of time.

Base Pair

The chemical structure that forms the units of DNA and RNA and that encode genetic information. The bases that make up the base pairs are adenine (A), guanine (G), thymine (T), cytosine (C), and uracil (U) (*see* DNA).

Bayes' Theorem

Theorem used to calculate the relative probability of an event given the probabilities of associated events. Used to calculate the probability of a disease given the frequencies of symptoms and signs within the disease and within the normal population.

BCG

Bacillus of Calmette-Guérin vaccine, administered by injection to protect against tuberculosis.

Behavioural Risk Factors

Actions or habits (e.g., smoking, use of seat belts, exercise) that contribute to a person's health.

Behavioural Technique

A coping strategy in which patients are taught to monitor and evaluate their own behaviour and to modify their reactions to pain.

Benchmark

A term meaning a measurement taken at the outset of a series of measurements of the same variable, sometimes meaning the best or most desirable value of the variable.

Beneficiary

Persons eligible for benefits under the MHS.

Biofeedback

A process in which a person learns to reliably influence physiologic responses of two kinds: those that are not ordinarily under voluntary control and those that ordinarily are easily regulated but for which regulation has broken down because of trauma or disease.

Bioinformatics

The collection, organization, and analysis of large amounts of biological data, using computers and databases. Historically, bioinformatics concerned itself with the analysis of the sequences of genes and their products (proteins), but the field has since expanded to the management, processing, analysis, and visualization of large quantities of data from genomics, proteomics, drug screening, and medicinal chemistry. Bioinformatics also includes the integration and "mining" of the ever-expanding databases of information from these disciplines.

Biphosphonates

A class of medication that decreases the turnover of bone.

Birth Weight

The first weight of a fetus or infant at time of delivery. This weight is usually measured during the first hour of life, before postnatal weight loss occurs.

B-ISDN

Broadband ISDN. A set of communication system standards for ATM systems.

Bit

One binary digit, in base 2. The basic unit for electronically stored or transmitted data.

Bits-Per Second

A measure of data transmission rate.

Bluetooth

Wireless communication system designed to allow many personal devices such as computers, mobile phones and digital cameras to communicate with each other over a short-range.

Boolean Logic

A system of logic devised by Georges Boole that defined the meaning of linguistic notions like *and, or* and *not* to produce 'laws of thought' which had a clear syntax and semantics.

Breakthrough Pain

Intermittent exacerbations of pain that can occur spontaneously or in relation to specific activity despite ongoing analgesic therapy.

Broadband Network

General term for a computer network capable of high-bandwidth transmission rated.

Browser

A programme used to view data e.g. examining the contents of a database or knowledge base, or viewing documents on the World Wide Web.

Burden of Disease

A general term used in public health and epidemiological literature to identify the cumulative effect of a broad range of harmful disease consequences on a community, including the health, social, and economic costs to the individual and to society. Since the broad range of information is not consistently available for many of the conditions described in this report, measures of mortality were used in making comparative assessments of disease burden, allowing a contrast the variety of conditions using a common unit of measure.

Burden of Disease Profile

An annual document used in planning and priority setting that graphically presents population health information from a sentinel Demographic Surveillance System in easily understood computer-generated charts and tables. It presents results not in terms of individual diseases, but in terms of aggregated intervention-addressable shares of the burden of disease.

Byte

Eight bits. Bytes are usually counted in kilobytes (1024 bytes), megabytes and gigabytes.

Capitation

A method of payment for health services in which an individual or institutional provider is paid a fixed amount for each person insured, regardless of actual use or expense. Capitation is the characteristic payment method for certain health maintenance organizations.

Care Management Protocols (CMPs)

Care Management Protocols specify utilization and treatment standards for various diagnoses.

Care Pathway

It describes the expected course of the patient's management and what actions need to be taken at every stage.

Carrier

A ship, aircraft, train, road vehicle, or other means of transport, including military.

Carve Out

An arrangement whereby an employer eliminates coverage for a specific category of services (e.g., vision care, mental health/ psychological services, or prescription drugs) and contracts with a separate set of providers for those services according to a predetermined fee schedule or capitation arrangement. May also refer to a method of coordinating dual coverage for an individual.

Case Mix

A measure of the types of cases being treated by a particular health-care provider that is intended to reflect the patients' different needs for resources. Case mix is generally established by estimating the relative frequency of various types of patients seen by the provider during a given time period, and may be measured by factors such as diagnosis, severity of illness, utilization of services and provider characteristics.

Case-Based Reasoning

An approach to computer reasoning that uses knowledge from a library of similar cases, rather than by accessing a knowledge base containing more generalized knowledge, such as a set of rules.

Causal Reasoning

A form of reasoning based on following from cause to effect, in contrast to other methods in which the connection is weaker, such as probabilistic association.

Cause of Death

The underlying cause of death determined to be the primary condition leading to death, based on the international rules and sequential procedure set forth for manual classification of the underlying causes of death by the National Centre for Health Statistics and the World Health Organization (International Classification of disease, Ninth Revision).

CERN

Conseil Européan pour la Recherche Nucléaire. The European Particle Physics Laboratory. It was here that the initial set of standards were developed to create the World Wide Web.

Certificate of Need

A certificate issued by a governmental body to an individual or organization proposing to construct, modify, or close a health facility, acquire major new medical equipment, modify a health facility, or offer a new or different health service or discontinue a service. Such issuance recognizes that a facility or service, when available, will meet the needs of those for whom it is intended. CON is intended to control expansion of facilities and services by preventing excessive or duplicative development of facilities and services.

Certification

Certification is a voluntary system of standards that practitioners can choose to meet to demonstrate accomplishment or ability in their profession. Certification standards are generally set by non-governmental agencies or associations.

Channel

The connection between two parties that transports their messages, such as a telephone or e-mail.

Channel Capacity

Amount of data that can be transmitted per unit time along a communication channel. Synonym: Bandwidth.

Child Survival Revolution

An initiative launched by James Grant, Executive Director of UNICEF, in its December 1982 *State of the World's Children* report. The initiative later included child development. Through this initiative, UNICEF proposed to vanquish common infections of early childhood using simple, low-cost technologies: growth monitoring, oral rehydration therapy for diarrhea, breastfeeding, and immunization against the 6 vaccine-preventable childhood killers: tuberculosis, diphtheria, whooping cough, tetanus, polio, and measles.

Chromosome

One of the physically separate segments that together forms the genome, or total genetic material, of a cell. Chromosomes are long strands of genetic material, or DNA, that have been packaged and compressed by wrapping around proteins. The number and size of chromosomes varies from species to species. In humans, there are 23 pairs of chromosomes (a pair has one chromosome from each parent). One pair forms the sex chromosomes because they contain genes that determine sex. The chromosome carrying the male determining genes is designated Y and the corresponding female one is the X chromosome. The remaining pairs are called autosomes. Chromosome 1 is the largest and chromosome 22 the smallest. Each chromosome has two "arms" designated p and q.

Chronic Care

Treatment and care given to individuals whose health problems are long term and continuing. Rehabilitation facilities, nursing homes, and mental hospitals may be considered chronic care facilities.

Chronic Disease

A disease with one or more of the following characteristics: permanence, leaves residual disability, caused by non-reversible pathological alternation, requires special training of the patient for rehabilitation, or may require a long period of supervision, observation, or care.

Chronic Illness

Diseases which have one or more of the following characteristics: they are permanent, leave residual disability, are caused by nonreversible pathological alteration, require special training of the patient for rehabilitation, or may be expected to require a long period of supervision, observation, or care.

CIDA

Canadian International Development Agency.

Circuit-Switched Network

A communication network that connects parties by establishing a dedicated circuit between them.

Civilian Health and Medical Programme of the Uniformed Services (CHAMPUS)

Programme administered by the Department of Defense that cost-shares for care delivered by civilian healthcare providers.

Client

A computer connected to a network that does not store all the data or software it uses, but retrieves it across the network from another computer that acts as a server.

Client-Server Architecture

A computer network architecture that places commonly used resources on centrally accessible server computers, which can be retrieved as they are needed across the network by client computers on the network.

Closed-Loop Control

Completely automated system control method in which no part of the control system need be given over to humans.

CMS

Centres for Medicare and Medicaid Services.

Coast Guard International Training Office

Commandant Coast Guard (G-CI) office responsible for the management of the Coast Guard International training programe.

COBRA

Consolidated Omnibus Budget Reconciliation Act of 1986.

Code

In medical terminological systems, the unique numerical identifier associated with a medical concept, which may be associated with a variety of terms, all with the same meaning.

Cognitive Reappraisal

A coping strategy in which patients are taught to monitor and evaluate negative thoughts and replace them with more positive thoughts and images.

Cognitive Science

A multi-disciplinary field studying human cognitive processes, including their relationship to technologically embodied models of cognition.

Collective Bargaining

Collective bargaining refers to bargaining by union members, which is authorized by the NLRA, or non-unionized physicians' attempts to obtain the right to bargain collectively.

Communicable Diseases

Illnesses due to infectious agents or their toxic products, which may be transmitted from a reservoir to a susceptible host, either directly or indirectly.

Communicable Period

Period or periods during which the etiologic agent may be transferred directly or indirectly from the body of the infected person or animal to the body of another.

Communication Protocol

The rules governing how a conversation may proceed between well-behaved agents.

Community Voice Tool

An approach known as participatory action research that can assist in bringing the demands of the community into the district planning process.

Complementary DNA (cDNA)

DNA that is synthesized from a messenger RNA template; the single-stranded form is often used as a probe in physical mapping or for detecting RNA. Since cDNA is constructed from messenger RNA (after introns have been spliced out), it does not contain introns.

Computerized Physician Order Entry (CPOE)

Computerized physician order entry (CPOE) is an electronic prescribing system. With CPOE, physicians enter orders into a computer rather than on paper. Orders are integrated with patient information, including laboratory and prescription data. The order is then automatically checked for potential errors or problems.

Computerized Protocol

Clinical guideline or protocol stored on a computer system, so that it may be easily accessed or manipulated to support the delivery of care.

Conditional Probability

The probability that one event is true, given that another event is true.

Confidence Interval (CI)

An interval (range of values) within which the population parameter (the "true" value) is expected to lie with a given degree of certainty (e.g., 95%).

Connectionism

The study of the theory and application of neural networks.

Conscious Sedation

"Light sedation" during which the patient retains airway reflexes and responses to verbal stimuli.

Contamination

The presence of undesirable substances or material which may contain infectious agents or their toxic products.

Continuous Variable

1. Any characteristic that can be measured on a continuous scale (e.g., blood pressure, height, pain intensity score).
2. Correlation association or interdependence between two variables (characteristics).

Continuum of Care

A comprehensive set of services ranging from preventive and ambulatory services to acute care to long-term and rehabilitative services. By providing continuity of care, the continuum focuses on prevention and early intervention for those who have been identified as high risk and provides easy transition from service to service as needs change.

Control System

A system that utilizes measurement of its output and feedback to influence future behaviour based upon a measurement of past performance.

Coronary Artery Bypass Graft (CABG)

Surgical therapy of ischemic coronary artery disease, achieved by grafting a section of saphenous vein, internal mammary artery, or other substitute between the aorta and the obstructed coronary artery distal to the obstructive lesion.

Cost

The total level of economic investment required for the provision of health services. This level of investment includes all financial expenditures, especially expenditures for capital and operating requirements. Charges, the price of a service or amount billed to an individual or third party, may or may not be equal to service costs.

Cost Containment

A wide variety of strategies or methods whose primary goal is to control the rising cost of healthcare, thus making healthcare more affordable. These strategies and methods may include, but are not limited to government regulation, managed care programmes, payment policies, global budgets, rate setting, consumer education, and utilization management.

Cost Sharing

Provisions in a health insurance plan that require the insured to pay some portion of the covered medical expenses. Typical forms of cost sharing include coinsurance, co-payments, and deductibles.

Cost Shifting

The practice of increasing revenues from one type of payer (e.g., privately insured patients) in order to cover the costs of uncompensated care or other shortfalls in reimbursements from other payers.

Cost-Effectiveness

The cost to avert the loss of a Disability Adjusted Life Year.

Counter Stimulation

Application of moderate to intense sensory stimulation, such as cold, heat, rubbing, pressure, or electrical current, so as to decrease perception of pain at the same or a distant site.

CPR

Computer-based Patient Record. *See*: Electronic Medical Record.

Critical Loss Analysis

A two-step analysis is used to perform a critical loss analysis. The first step identifies, for any given price increase, the amount of sales that can be lost before the price increase becomes unprofitable. The second step considers whether or not the actual level of sales lost due to the price increase will exceed this amount.

Crude Rate

The number per 100,000 population. This rate should not be used for making comparisons between different populations when the age, race and sex distributions of the populations are different.

Cryotherapy

The therapeutic use of cold to reduce discomfort; limit progression of tissue edema; or break a cycle of muscle spasm.

CSCW

Computer supported co-operative work. The study of computer systems developed to support groups of individuals work together.

Cybernetics

A name coined by Norbert Weiner in the 1950s to describe the study of feedback control systems and their application. Such systems were seen to exhibit properties associated with human intelligence and robotics, and so was an early contributory to the theory of artificial intelligence.

Cyberspace

Popular term now associated with the Internet, which describes the notional information 'space' that is created across computer networks.

DALY

Disability Adjusted Life Years. The DALY extends the concept of potential years of life lost due to premature death to include years of "healthy" life lost by virtue of being in states of ill-health. DALYs for a disease or risk factor are calculated as the annual sum of the years of life lost due to premature mortality in the population and the "years lived with disability" for incident cases of the health condition.

DANIDA

Danish International Development Agency.

Database

A structured repository for data, consisting of a collection of data and their associated data model, and usually stored on a computer system. The existence of a regular and formal indexing structure permits rapid retrieval of individual elements of the database.

Deafferentation Pain

Pain due to loss of sensory input into the central nervous system, as occurs with avulsion of the brachial plexus or other types of lesions of peripheral nerves.

Decision Support System

General term for any computer application that enhances a human's ability to make decisions.

Decision Tree

A method of representing knowledge which structures the elements of a decision into a tree-like fashion. Chance nodes in a decision tree represent alternative possibilities, and decision nodes represent alternative choices. The leaf nodes of the tree represent outcomes, which may be assigned a numerical utility.

Declaration of Alma-Ata

A manifesto issued at the close of the September 1978 Alma-Ata Conference on Primary Health Care, which stated that "This conference strongly reaffirms that health is a state of complete physical, mental and social well-being and not merely the absence of disease or infirmity... A major social target of governments, international organizations and the whole world community in the coming decades should be the attainment by all people of the world by the year 2000 of a level of health that will permit them to lead socially and economically productive lives."

DECT

Digital European Cordless Telephony standard, which defines the architecture for wireless voice and data communication systems restricted to campus-size areas, rather than wide-area systems that would be publicly available.

Deduction

A method of logical inference. Given a cause, deduction infers all logical effects that might arise as a consequence.

Defense Enrolment Eligibility Reporting System (DEERS)

An operational programme to determine eligibility for medical benefits.

Defense Security Cooperation Agency (DSCA)

Formerly the Defense Security Assistance Agency (DSAA), the DoD agency responsible for the management of Security Assistance and other international programmes.

Defense Institute of Security Assistance Management (DISAM)

The DoD school responsible for Security Assistance education and training.

Deferred Non-Emergency Care

Medical, surgical, or dental care that, in the opinion of a medical authority, could be performed at another time or place and without risk of patient's life, limb, health or well-being.

Demand

The amount of a given service sought by consumers in response to their perceived need for that service. Demand is influenced by availability of services by accessibility of the service and by ability to pay for the service.

Dental Care

Oral healthcare.

Dental Certification

A statement signed by a competent dentist that certifies the individual meets the dental requirements for the course of instruction and that major dental work will not be required prior to or during their participation in training.

Dental Emergency

When dental treatment is required for the relief of painful or acute conditions.

Deoxyribonucleic Acid (DNA)

The chemical that forms the basis of the genetic material in virtually all living organisms. Structurally, DNA is composed of two strands that intertwine to form a spring-like structure called the double helix. Attached to each backbone are chemical structures called bases (or nucleotides), which protrude away from the backbone toward the centre of the helix, and which come in four types: adenine, cytosine, guanine and thymine (designated A, C, G and

T). In DNA, cytosine only forms optimal hydrogen bonding with guanine and adenine only with thymine. These interactions across the many nucleotides in each strand hold the two strands together.

Detention

The temporary holding of a person, ship, aircraft, or other carrier, animal, or thing in such placed and for such period of time as may be determined.

DHMT

District Health Management Team. A key component of Tanzania's health sector reforms was the establishment of DHMTs in each of the country's 123 districts. Comprised members with complementary skills and multiple areas of expertise, DMHTs are responsible for health planning, managing and monitoring. (Now called Council Health Management Teams in Tanzania.)

Diagnostic Related Groups

A patient classification scheme that categorizes patients who are medically related with respect to diagnoses and treatment, and are statistically similar in their length of stay. The classification system is generally used to set uniform rates for the payment of hospital care. The DRG system was adopted by the medicare programme in 1983 to create incentives for hospitals to provide more cost-effective care.

Dichotomous Variable

Observations that occur in one of two possible states, often labelled 0 and 1. Commonly occurring examples include "dead/alive" and "improved/not improved".

Direct Medical Services

Services delivered by a health professional to a patient in an office, clinic, or emergency room. Basic services include what most consider ordinary medical care, inpatient and outpatient medical services, allied health services, drugs, laboratory testing, X-ray services, dental care, and pharmaceutical products and services.

Disability

Any temporary or long-term condition (physical and/or mental) that results from an acute or chronic condition that may prevent the performance of regular duties.

Disease Burden

See Burden of Disease.

Disinfection

The killing of infectious agents or inactivation of their toxic products outside the body by direct exposure to chemical or physical agents.

Disinfestation

Any chemical or physical process serving to destroy or remove undesired small animal forms, particularly arthropods or rodents, present upon the person, the clothing or the environment of an individual, or upon animals and carriers.

Disproportionate Share

A programme that provides additional financial aid to hospitals having excessive numbers of indigent patients.

Distraction

The cognitive strategy of focusing attention on stimuli other than pain or negative emotions that accompany pain.

Distributed Computing

Term for computer systems in which data and programmes are distributed across different computers on a network and shared.

District Cost Information System

A custom database managed at the district level and used to store information from the Health Management Information System (HMIS), including the sex, age group, in/outpatient status, repeat patient status, and diagnosis, as well as the drugs, surgical procedures, and laboratory tests prescribed. Its primary purpose is to identify technical efficiency in the delivery of essential clinical and public health interventions.

District Health Accounts Tool

Also known as the District Health Expenditures Mapping Tool: A customized Microsoft Excel application designed to help CHMTs analyze their budgets and expenditures by providing a one page analytical summary and several graphical "pictures" of key aspects of their annual plan.

District Health Service Mapping Tool

A simplified "point and click" geographic information software application (GIS) designed by WHO. Called Health Mapper, it is used to facilitate entry of HMIS data into a district level database and its graphical display on local maps of the district.

DOTS

Directly Observed Treatment Short Course.

DSS

Demographic Surveillance System. A method of continuously monitoring a geographically defined population to provide timely data on all births, deaths, causes of deaths and migrations.

DTMF

Dial Tone Multi-Frequency. The tones generated by punching in numbers on a telephone key-pad.

Durable Medical Equipment (DME)

Devices which are very resistant to wear and may be used over a long period of time. DME includes items such as wheelchairs, hospital beds, artificial limbs, etc.

Dysesthesia

An unpleasant abnormal sensation, whether spontaneous or evoked.

Early and Periodic Screening Diagnosis and Treatment Programme

A programme mandated by law as part of the Medicaid programme. The law (section 1905(a) (4)(B) of the Social Security Act) requires that all States have in effect a programme for eligible children under age 21 to ascertain their physical or mental defects, and to provide such healthcare treatments, and other measures to correct or ameliorate defects and chronic conditions discovered.

EDI

Electronic Data Interchange. General term describing the need for healthcare applications to be able to exchange data, requiring the adoption of agreed common standards for the form and content of the messages passing between applications.

EDP

Essential Drugs Programme.

Effect Size

Refers to the size (or the distance from null value indicating no treatment effect) of the summary measure (or point estimate) of the treatment effect and the values included in the corresponding 95 per cent confidence interval.

EHIP

Essential Health Interventions Project, precursor of TEHIP.

Elective Healthcare

Healthcare not medically necessary to provide relief from pain and suffering, or a potential health problem.

Electronic Mail

See E-mail.

Electronic Medical Record

A general term describing computer-based patient record systems. It is sometimes extended to include other functions like order entry for medications and tests, amongst other common functions.

Electrophoresis

The use of electrical fields to separate charged biomolecules such as DNA, RNA and proteins. DNA and RNA carry a net negative charge because of the numerous phosphate groups in their structure. In the process of gel electrophoresis, these biomolecules are put into wells of a solid matrix typically made of an inert substance such as agarose. When this gel is placed into a bath and an electrical charge applied across the gel, the biomolecules migrate and separate according to size in proportion to the amount of charge they carry. The biomolecules can be stained for viewing and isolated and purified from the gels for further analysis. Electrophoresis can be used to isolate pure biomolecules from a mixture or to analyze biomolecules (such as for DNA sequencing).

Eligible Partnership for Peace (PFP) Members

A military member of a PFP nation, who has a SOFA on file at the U.S. Department of State, is on active duty and who, in connection with official duties, is stationed in or passing through the United States.

E-mail

Electronic mail. Messaging system available on computer networks, providing users with personal mail-boxes from which electronic messages can be sent and received.

Emergency Medical Services

The services provided to accident victims and patients suffering from severe acute illness and psychiatric emergencies. Services include the detection and reporting of medical emergencies, initial care, transportation and care for patients in route to healthcare facilities, medical treatment for the acutely ill and severely injured within emergency departments, and the provision of linkages to continued care or rehabilitation services.

Employee Retirement Income Security Act

A federal law enacted in 1974 that set minimum standards of information disclosure and fiduciary responsibilities in the establishment, operation and administration of employee benefit plans, including group, life pensions and health plans. Employers who operate their own insurance plans for employees, or "self-insure" under ERISA, are exempt from state insurance regulation.

EMR

See: Electronic Medical Record.

EMTALA

Emergency Medical Treatment and Active Labour Act of 1986.

End-Stage Renal Disease (ESRD)

An irreversible and usually progressive reduction in renal function in which both kidneys have been damaged by a variety of diseases to the extent that they are unable to adequately remove the metabolic products from the blood and regulate the body's electrolyte composition and acid-base balance. Chronic kidney failure requires hemodialysis or kidney transplantation.

Environmental Health

Characteristics of health that result from the aggregate impact of both natural and man-made surroundings, including health effects of air pollution, water pollution, noise pollution, solid waste disposal, and housing; occupational disease and injuries; and those diseases related to unsanitary surroundings.

Enzyme

A protein that catalyzes chemical reactions in a living cell. Enzymes are protein molecules whose function it is to speed the making and breaking of chemical bonds required for essential physiochemical reactions.

EPI

Expanded Programme on Immunization.

Epidemiology

A branch of medical service that deals with the incidence, distribution, and control of disease in a population, or the sum of the factors controlling the presence or absence of a disease.

Epidural

Situated within the spinal canal, on or outside the duramater (tough membrane surrounding the spinal cord); synonyms are "extradural" and "peridural".

Epistemology

The philosophical study of knowledge.

EPR

Electronic patient record. *See*: Electronic medical record.

Equianalgesic

Having equal pain-killing effect; morphine sulfate, 10 mg intramuscularly is widely used for opioid analgesic comparisons.

ERISA

Employee Retirement Income Security Act.

Evidence-Based Medicine

A movement advocating the practice of medicine according to clinical guidelines, developed to reflect best-practice as captured from a meta-analysis of the clinical literature. Conscientious, explicit, and judicious use of current best evidence in making decisions about the care of individual patients.

Exclusive Provider Organization

An organization that provides coverage only for contracted providers.

Exon

The protein-coding DNA sequences of a gene.

Expected Value

For a decision option, its expected value is the sum of the utilities of each different possible outcome of that option, each weighted by their own probability.

Expert System

A computer programme that contains expert knowledge about a particular problem, often in the form of a set of if—then rules that is able to solve problems at a level equivalent or greater than human experts.

External Validity

Degree to which the results of a study can be applied to situations other than those under consideration of the study, such as for routine clinical practice.

Family Member

A spouse, child or parents authorized on the Invitational Travel Order which meet the dependency criteria that applies to U.S. military family members.

FAQ

Frequently Asked Questions. Common term for information lists available on the Internet, which has been compiled to newcomers to a particular subject, answering common questions that would otherwise often be asked by submitting e-mail requests to a Newsgroup.

Feedback

Taking some or all of the output of a system and adding it to a system's own input.

Fee-for-Service

A method of payment in which each service provided to the patients is associated with a corresponding fee to be paid to the provider. It is the method of billing used by the majority of U.S. physicians.

Fetal Death

Death prior to the complete expulsion or extraction from the mother of a product of conception, which has passed through at least the 20th week of gestation. The fetus shows no signs of life such as heartbeat, pulsation of the umbilical cord, or movement of voluntary muscles.

Finite State Machine

A knowledge representation that makes different states in a process explicit, and connects them with links that specify some transition condition that specifies how one traverses from one state to another.

Firewall

A security barrier erected between a public computer network like the Internet and a local private computer network.

First-Principles, Reasoning From

Use of a model of the mechanisms that control a system to predict or simulate the likely outcome if some of the inputs or internal structure of the system is altered.

Fixed or Random Effects Model

Statistical methods used to produce weighted summary estimates of an effect of interventions across many studies. The fixed effects model assumes that all studies are studying the same true effect and that variability is due to random error only. The random effects model assumes that the true effect differs among studies and therefore must be represented by a distribution of values instead of a single value.

Foreign Military Sales (FMS)

That portion of the U.S. Security Assistance authorized by the Arms Export Control Act (AECA), as amended, and conducted on the basis of formal contracts or agreements between the United States Government and an authorized recipient government or international organization. FMS includes government-to-government sales of defense articles or defense services, from DoD stocks or through new procurements under DoD-managed contracts, regardless of the source of financing.

Formative Assessment

Evaluation of the performance of an information system against user needs.

Formulary

A list of approved drugs for treating various diseases and conditions.

Freestanding

An independent facility without financial or administrative attachment or support from another facility.

FTP

File Transfer Protocol. A computer protocol that allows electronic files to be sent and received in a uniform fashion across a computer network.

Functional Genomics

The use of genetic technology to determine the function of newly discovered genes by determining their role in one or more model organisms. Functional genomics uses as its starting point the isolated gene whose function is to be determined, and then selects a model organism in which a homolog of that gene exists. This model organism can be as simple as a yeast cell or as complex as a nematode worm, fruit fly, or even a mouse.

Fuzzy Logic

An artificial intelligence method for representing and reasoning with imprecisely specified knowledge, for example defining loose boundaries to distinguish 'low' from 'high' values.

G-8

Group of 8 an informal group of 8 countries—Canada, France, Germany, Italy, Japan, Russia, the United Kingdom, and the United States. Each year, G-8 leaders and representatives from the European Union meet to discuss broad economic and foreign policies.

Gatekeeper

A healthcare professional, who coordinates, manages, and authorizes all healthcare services provided to a covered beneficiary.

May be a nurse, a social worker, a physician's assistant, or a physician (e.g., internist, family/general practitioner, pediatrician, and in some cases, OB/GYN). Gatekeepers are frequently used by managed care plans to control costs by limiting unnecessary utilization of services.

Gene

The basic unit of heredity; the sequence of DNA that encodes all the information to make a protein. A gene may be activated or "switched on" to make protein (referred to as gene expression) by these proteins that control when, where, and how much protein is expressed from the gene. In the human genome, there are an estimated 30,000 genes (although recent studies suggest a larger number).

Gene Product

The biochemical material, either RNA or protein, resulting from expression of a gene. The amount of gene product is used to measure how active a gene is; abnormal amounts can be correlated with disease-causing alleles. As gene products include all the alternative splicing products, there are estimated to be at least 100,000 distinct such products.

Gene Therapy

The technology that uses genetic material for therapeutic purposes. This genetic material can be in the form of a gene, representative of a gene or cDNA, RNA, or even a small fragment of a gene. The introduced genetic material can be therapeutic in several ways. It can make a protein that is defective or missing in the patient's cells (as would be the case in a genetic disorder), or that will correct or modify a particular cellular function, or that elicits an immune response.

Gestational Age

The number of completed weeks elapsed between the first day of the last normal menstrual period and the date of delivery.

Global Fund to Fight AIDS, Tuberculosis and Malaria

A fund established in January 2002 to dramatically increase

resources to fight three of the world's most devastating diseases, and to direct those resources to areas of greatest need. An outgrowth of work undertaken by the G-8 group of countries, leaders of African states, and UN Secretary General Kofi Annan, it is a partnership between governments, civil society, the private sector, and affected communities.

Grammar

The set of rules that together specify the allowed ways an alphabet can be put together to form strings of symbols in a given language.

Group

A group collects together a number of different codes associated with medical events that are considered to be sufficiently similar for some purpose e.g. the determination of an appropriate reimbursement for approximately similar clinical procedures or diseases.

Group Model Health Maintenance Organization

A healthcare model involving contracts with physicians organized as a partnership, professional corporation, or other association. The health plan compensates the medical group for contracted services at a negotiated rate, and that group is responsible for compensating its physicians and contracting with hospitals for care of their patients.

Group Practice

The provision of medical services by three or more physicians formally organized to provide medical care, consultation, diagnosis, and/or treatment through the joint use of equipment and personnel, and with income from the medical practice distributed in accordance with methods previously determined by members of the group. Group practices have a single-speciality or multi-speciality focus.

Group Practice without Walls

Typically a network of physicians who have formed a single legal entity, but maintain their individual practices. The assets of individual practices may be acquired by the larger entity, but some autonomy is retained at each site. The central management provides administrative support. *See* Integrated Delivery System.

Group Purchasing Organization (GPO)

A shared service which combines the purchasing power of individual organizations or facilities in order to obtain lower prices for equipment and supplies.

Groupware

A computer application that assists communication and shared working amongst groups of individuals with access to a common computer network, but who may be geographically or temporarily separated.

GSM

The Global System of Mobility. A widely adopted international standard for the architecture and operation of digital cellular telephony systems that can carry voice and data circuits, as well as short packet-data messages.

GUI

Graphical User Interface. That part of a computer application seen and interacted with by its user. Specifically, that part of the interface that is based upon visual structures like icons, which act as metaphors for the different functions supported by the application e.g. deleting a file is enacted by dragging a visual symbol representing the file onto a trash can icon.

Guideline

An agreed set of steps to be taken in the management of a clinical condition.

Hardware

For a computer system, all its physical components, as distinguished from the programmes and data that are manipulated by the computer.

Health

A state of physical, mental, and social well-being and productive functioning, not merely the absence of disease or infirmity.

Health Alliances or Regional Health Alliances

Purchasing pools responsible for negotiating health insurance arrangements for employers and/or employees. Alliances would use their leverage to negotiate contracts that would ensure care is delivered in economical and equitable ways. (Also referred to as health insurance purchasing cooperatives or health plan purchasing cooperatives).

Health Care Financing Administration

An agency of the U.S. Department of Health and Human Services responsible for administrating the Medicare programme and overseeing the administration of state Medicaid programmes.

Health Delivery System

A coordinated complex of resources, including manpower, facilities, equipment, etc. that provides healthcare to the populace of a given area.

Health Education

A continuing process of informing people how to achieve and maintain good health; of motivating them to do so; and of promoting environmental and lifestyle changes to facilitate their objective.

Health Maintenance Organization

An entity that provides, offers, or arranges for coverage of designated health services needed by plan members for a fixed, prepaid premium. There are four basic models of HMOs: group models, individual practice association, network model, and staff model. Under the Federal HMO Act, an entity must have three characteristics to call itself an HMO: (1) an organized system for providing healthcare or otherwise assuring healthcare delivery in a geographic area; (2) an agreed upon set of basic and supplemental health maintenance and treatment services; and (3) a voluntarily enrolled group of people.

Health Mapper

See District Health Service Mapping Tool.

Health Plan

A health maintenance organization, preferred provider organization, insured plan, self-funded plan, or other entity that covers healthcare services.

Health Plan Employer Data and Information Set

A core set of comparable performance measures of managed care plans on quality, access, patient satisfaction, membership, utilization, finance, and descriptive information on health plan management and activities.

Health Plan Employer Data and Information Set (HEDIS)

A set of standardized performance measures designed to ensure that purchasers and consumers have reliable information with which to compare the performance of Managed Care Organizations (MCOs).

Health Professional Shortage Area

An area or group that the U.S. Department of Health and Human Services designates as having an inadequate supply of healthcare providers. It can be an urban or rural geographical area, a population group for which access barriers can be demonstrated that prevent members from using local providers, or medium- and maximum-security correctional institutions, and public or non-profit private residential facilities.

Health Status

The level of illness or wellness of a population at a particular time.

Health Systems

All services, functions and resources in a geographic area whose primary purpose is to affect the state of health of the population.

Healthcare Provider

Physicians, Dentists, Nurses and medical ancillary personnel who provide healthcare.

Hepatitis B

A viral disease that affects the liver.

Heterogeneity

Diversity, such as may exist between studies. In that context, heterogeneity may be due to identifiable factors or statistical factors or both, especially the component that cannot be explained by random error. If there is significant heterogeneity, this suggests that the trials are not estimating a single common treatment effect.

Heuristic

A rule of thumb that describes how things are commonly understood, without resorting to deeper or more formal knowledge.

HIPAA

Health Insurance Portability and Accountability Act of 1996.

HIS

Hospital information system. Typically used to describe hospital computer systems with functions like patient admission and discharge, order entry for laboratory tests or medications and billing functions.

Hispanic Ethnicity

Refers to people whose origins are from Spain, the Spanish-speaking countries of Central America, South America and the

Caribbean, or persons of Hispanic origin identifying themselves as Spanish, Spanish-American, Hispanic, Hispano, Latino and so on. In Connecticut, the birth, death and fetal death certificates have a separate line item for the individual's Hispanic status to attempt to distinguish Hispanic ethnicity from race. Individuals identifying themselves as "Hispanic" can be of any race.

HIV/AIDS

Human Immunodeficiency Virus/Acquired Immune Deficiency Syndrome.

HL7 (Health Level 7)

An international standard for electronic data exchange in healthcare, which defines the format and content of messages that pass between medical applications.

HMIS

Health Management Information System. A system to collect routine data from hospitals and community health facilities.

Home Health Care

A broad spectrum of services (physical health, psycho-social and environmental support) provided to persons living at home for the purpose of promoting, maintaining, or restoring health; or minimizing the effects of illness and disability. Services are delivered by a variety of professional and non-professional personnel, generally through a provider agency which may be voluntary (non-profit) or proprietary (for profit); or through the efforts of an assessment and coordinating programme or group.

Home PagSe

A document on the World Wide Web that acts as a front page or point of welcome to a collection of documents that may introduce an individual, organization, or point of interest.

Homeostasis

The use of feedback systems to keep a desired state. Often used to describe physiological steady-states.

Hospice

A multi-disciplinary service programme for the dying person and his/her family which provides the supports needed to keep the dying person comfortable and free from pain until the time of death.

HTML

Hypertext Mark-up Language. The description language used to create hypertext documents that can be viewed on the World Wide Web.

HTTP

Hypertext Transfer Protocol. Communication protocol used on the Internet for the transfer of HTML documents.

Human Immunodeficiency Virus (HIV)

A viral disease that affects the immune system.

Human-Computer Interaction

The study of the psychology and design principles associated with the way humans interact with computer systems.

Human-Computer Interface

The 'view' presented by a programme to its user. Often literally a visual window that allows a programme to be operated, an interface could just as easily be based on the recognition and synthesis of speech, or any other medium with which a human is able to sense or manipulate.

Hybridisation

The interaction of complementary nucleic acid strands. Since DNA is a double-stranded structure held together by complementary interactions (in which C always binds to G and A to T), complementary strands favourably renewal or "hybridize" to each other when separated.

Hyperalgesia

Exaggeration (to an abnormal degree) of the intensity of a normally painful stimulus.

Hyperlink

A connection between hypertext documents that allows a reader to trace concepts appearing in one document to related occurrence in other documents.

Hyperpathia

A painful syndrome characterized by increased reaction to a stimulus, especially a repetitive stimulus, as well as an increased threshold.

Hypertext

A method of presenting documents electronically that allows them to be read in a richly interconnected way. Rather than following a single document from beginning to end, sections of each document are connected to related occurrences in other documents via hyperlinks, permitting 'non-linear' reading following concepts of interest to the reader.

Hypnosis

A state of heightened awareness and focused concentration that can be used to manipulate the perception of pain.

Iatrogenic

Induced by a medical treatment or other procedure, e.g., surgery.

ICD-9

The International Classification of Diseases, 9th edition. Published by World Health Organization.

IDRC

International Development Research Centre, Canada.

IEC

Information, education and communication.

Ill Person

A person who has a temperature of 100°F (or 38°C) or greater, accompanied by a rash, glandular swelling, or jaundice, or which has persisted for more than 48 hours; or has diarrhea.

Imagery

A cognitive-behavioural strategy that uses mental images as an aid to relaxation.

IMAI

Integrated Management of Adolescent and Adult Illness. A health care strategy that focuses on the main clinical conditions that account for most adolescent and adult deaths and disability across the world, and integrates the prevention of illness and care of the adolescent and adult in a single healthcare package. This includes pneumonia, malaria, sexually transmitted infections, key women's health issues, mental health disorders, and the detection and care of priority chronic conditions that can be prevented or treated with cost-effective measures, such as epilepsy, tuberculosis and HIV.

IMC

Integrated Management Cascade. A hierarchical communications and supervisory structure that allows delegation of responsibilities from the DHMT level down to the lower levels of the district health system.

IMCI

Integrated Management of Childhood Illnesses. A health strategy developed by WHO and UNICEF that targets children under 5 and addresses 5 leading causes of death — malaria, pneumonia, diarrhea measles and malnutrition.

Immigration and Nationality Act (INA), as Amended

The law that governs entry to the United States by aliens. Also referred to as 8 USC-Aliens and Nationality.

Immunization

An inclusive term denoting the process of inducing or providing immunity artificially by administering vaccines, toxoids, or antibody-containing preparation.

Incidence

The number of new cases of a specific disease occurring during a certain period of time.

Incident Pain

See "movement-related pain".

Indemnity Plans Protection

Against loss an indemnity policy pays money to an insured in the event of hospitalization or illness, or a predetermined amount for the medical or surgical procedures incurred.

Independent Practice Associations (IPAs)

IPAs are networks of independent physicians that contract with MCOs and employers. IPAs may be organized as sole proprietorships, partnerships, or professional corporations.

INDEPTH Network

An international network of field sites with continuous demographic evaluation of populations and their health. This umbrella organization embraces 40 field sites in Africa, South-East Asia and Oceania. Their focus includes data analysis and capacity strengthening, technical support to field sites, comparative assessments of mortality, and equity with and emphasis on applications to policy and practice.

Indicator

A measurable factor which reflects or is highly correlated with either a health problem or outcome (e.g., infant mortality or disability days) or particular characteristics of health systems service delivery (e.g., cost per patient day, per cent of area residents with a regular control course of care, or time or distance from primary care). A proxy indicator can be used to bring to light social or environmental conditions, values, interests and concerns.

Individual Practice Association Model HMO

A healthcare model that contracts with an entity, which in turn contracts with physicians, to provide healthcare services in return for a negotiated fee. Physicians continue in their existing individual or group practices and are compensated on a per capita, fee schedule, or fee-for-service basis.

Infant Death

Death occurring to an individual of less than one year (365 days) of age, comprising the sum of neonatal death and post neonatal death.

Infant Mortality Rate

The number of deaths reported among infants under one year of age in a calendar year per 1,000 live births reported in the same year and place.

Inpatient

A person who must stay overnight in a health facility (usually a hospital) for medical treatment.

Inpatient Medical Care

Care provided to individuals admitted to a hospital.

Inpatient Prospective Payment System (IPPS)

Medicare's payment system for inpatient hospitals and facilities. The specific amount that is paid is based on the DRG for the hospital admission.

Integrated Delivery

The ability to provide comprehensive healthcare services through a coordinated, person-centered continuum designed to improve the health of people in a specified community within economic limits.

Integrated Delivery System

A group of healthcare service units that typically includes hospitals, physicians (for example, medical groups and independent practice associations), and other non-hospital providers) for example, ambulatory surgery centres, home health providers, skilled nursing facilities). These units are coordinated in their efforts to service one or more target markets. The integration may take a variety of forms, including joint venture, merger, or contract.

Integrated Service Networks

Any plan that incorporates a network of providers that can provide the full continuum of necessary medical and social service needs for enrollees, and accepts financial risk for that care.

Intentional Injury

Injuries and deaths that are self-inflicted or perpetrated by another person. Intentional injuries can be caused by homicide, suicide, assault, domestic violence and intentional use of firearms.

Internal Validity

Degree to which the inferences drawn from a study are warranted when account is taken of its design, conduct and reporting (e.g., blinding, randomization and dropouts).

International Military Education and Training (IMET) Programme

That component of the U.S. Security Assistance Programme that provides training to selected foreign military and defence associated civilian personnel on a grant basis. Training is provided at U.S. military facilities and with U.S. Armed Forces in the U.S. and overseas, and through the use of Mobile and Education

Training Teams. Contract technicians, contractors (including instructors at civilian institutions), may also provide training. The IMET Programme is authorized by the Foreign Assistance Act of 1961 (FAA), as amended.

International Military Student (IMS)

A national of a foreign government, with military or civilian status, who is receiving education or training or is touring U.S. government activities under sponsorship of the Security Assistance Training Programme (SATP).

International Military Student Office (IMSO)

The U.S. military office that is designated to coordinate and monitor the local SATP and provides required administrative support for IMS in training at that activity. Also responsible for the conduct of the DoD Informational Programme.

International Narcotics Law (INL)

Training provided to paramilitary in support of International Narcotics and Law Enforcement, Department of State.

International Voyage

A voyage involving entry into a country other than the country in which that person begins his/her voyage.

Intervention-Addressable Shares of Burden of Disease

A method of expressing burden of disease data in terms of the aggregated percentage of disease burden addressed by available, cost-effective interventions (for example, IMCI would address the combined burden of disease in children under 5 years of age caused by malaria, pneumonia, diarrhea, malnutrition and measles).

Intrathecal

The space enclosed by the arachnoids meanings and containing cerebrospinal fluid and the spinal cord.

Invitational Travel Order (ITO)

A written authorization (either the DD Form 2285 or computer generated letter format) for IMS to travel to, from and between U.S. activities for the purpose of training.

Isolation

The separation of a person or group of persons from other persons, except the health staff on duty, in such a manner as to prevent the spread of infection.

ITNs

Insecticide-treated mosquito nettings.

Kessner Index (Modified)

The Kessner Index is a composite indicator of the adequacy of prenatal care a mother receives during her pregnancy. Prenatal care is categorized as adequate, intermediate, or inadequate based on three items from the birth certificate: timing of the first prenatal visit; total number of prenatal visits; and length of gestation.

Lancinating

Characterized by piercing or stabbing sensations.

Licensure

A form of business licensure in which an applicant is granted a license or permit to conduct or engage in the provision of health services within a specific type of institution or setting. Inpatient, outpatient, and non-patient health facilities are licensed by State regulatory agencies with statutory authority to license, certify, inspect, or otherwise approve or disapprove the operation of specific types of health facilities.

Linkages

A set of relationships between two or more providers for purposes of providing continuous care, avoiding duplication of services, assuring appropriate placement, expanding the range of services available, or assuring the most economical use of available resources.

Live Birth

The complete expulsion or extraction from the mother of a product of conception, regardless of the duration of pregnancy; after such separation, shows signs of life (e.g., heartbeat, pulsation of the umbilical cord, or movement of voluntary muscles).

Local Health Department

A governmental public health agency, which is in whole or in part responsible to a sub-state governmental entity or entities (e.g., a city, county, borough, township). A local health department employs one or more full-time professional public health employees (e.g., public health nurse, sanitarian), delivers public health services (e.g., immunization, food inspection), serves a definable geographic area, and has identifiable expenditures and/or budgets in the political subdivision(s) it serves.

Local Health District

A local governmental entity consisting of two or more towns that is responsible for the public health of its constituent towns.

Local Nerve Block

Infiltration of a local anesthetic around a peripheral nerve so as to produce anesthesia in the area supplied by the nerve.

Local Public Health Authority

The agency charged with responsibility for meeting the health needs of the community. Usually this is the Board of Health, a city/county/regional authority, and its administrative arm, the local health department.

Long Term Care

A continuum of broad-ranged maintenance and health services delivered to the chronically ill, disabled and others. Services may be provided on an inpatient, outpatient, or at-home basis.

Low Birth Weight

A birth weight of less than 2,500 grams (approximately 5 lbs., 8 oz.).

Managed Care

A system of healthcare delivery that influences utilization and cost of services and measures performance. The goal is a system that delivers value by giving people access to quality, cost-effective healthcare.

Managed Care Organizations (MCOs)

MCOs integrate, to varying degrees, the financing and delivery of healthcare services.

Managed Health Care Plan

One or more products which integrate financing and management with the delivery of healthcare services to an enrolled population; employ or contract with an organized provider network which delivers services and which (as a network or individual provider) either shares financial risk or has some incentive to delivery quality, cost-effective services; and use an information system capable of monitoring and evaluating patterns of covered persons' use of medical services and the cost of those services.

Management Service Organization

A legal entity that provides practice management, administrative and support services to individual physicians or group practices. It may be a direct subsidiary of a hospital or may be owned by investors.

Marine Corps Combat Development Command (MCCDC)

The Marine Corps office responsible for the management of the Marine Corps international training programme.

Maternal and Child Care

Services for the prevention, diagnosis and treatment of diseases and conditions which are specific to mothers and children or for which mothers and children are considered particularly vulnerable populations with special needs.

Maximum Allowable Cost (MAC)

Maximum Allowable Cost or Charge. The maximum that a vendor may charge for something. This term is often used in pharmaceutical contracting.

MDGs

United Nations Millennium Development Goals. A set of 8 goals adopted in September 2000 that bind countries to do more and join forces in the fight against poverty, illiteracy, hunger, lack of education, gender inequality, child and maternal mortality, disease and environmental degradation. The goals set targets to be achieved by 2015.

Medicaid (Title XIX)

A Federally aided, State-operated and administered programme that provides medical benefits for certain indigent or low-income persons in need of health and medical care. The programme, authorized by Title XIX of the Social Security Act, is basically for the poor. It does not cover all of the poor, however, but only persons who meet specified eligibility criteria. Subject to broad Federal guidelines, states determine the benefits covered, programme eligibility, rates of payment for providers, and methods of administering the programme.

Medicaid HEDIS

A set of health plan performance measures specially targeted to meet the needs of programmes that serve Medicaid beneficiaries with particular focus on women and children.

Medicaid Waivers

A waiver of current federal Medicaid law obtained from the HCFA that exempts states from a number of federal Medicaid statutes and regulations that would otherwise hinder their efforts to create Medicaid managed care programmes. The two most common types of waivers obtained for this purpose are:

(1) 1115 waiver 1115 waivers allow states to use federal funds in ways that are not otherwise permitted under federal law to implement and test innovations in their Medicaid programmes. These programmes, often known as demonstrations, usually include the creation of capitated managed care programmes that alter eligibility requirements and benefit packages.

(2) 1915 (b) waiver 1915 (b) waivers exempt states from the freedom-of-choice requirements that allow Medicaid beneficiaries the same liberty to select among providers as the privately insured. By waiving this requirement, states are able to mandate the enrolment of certain Medicaid recipients into a managed care programme. They also allow states to waive requirements of uniform statewide operation (statewide effectiveness) and identical benefits for different types of beneficiaries (comparability).

Medical Care/Healthcare

Inpatient, outpatient, dental and related professional services.

Medical Certification

A statement signed by a competent physician that certifies the individual has received a thorough physical examination, has received prescribed immunizations, and is free of communicable disease.

Medical Eligibility

Eligible to receive medical care from a Department of Defence medical treatment facility based on approved programme, international treaty or agreement.

Medical Treatment Facility (MTF)

A facility established for the purpose of furnishing medical and/or dental care. The term applies to civilian or military hospitals and clinics.

Medically Indigent

Individuals with little or no health insurance and who are without sufficient resources to pay for essential healthcare.

Medically Underserved Area

An urban or rural geographic area designated by the federal Department of Health, Education and Welfare as having a shortage of personal health services, or a population group designated by the Secretary as having a shortage of such services.

Medicare

A federally funded nationwide hospital and medical-care insurance programme for the elderly (over age 64) and some people with disabilities.

Medicare + Choice (M+C)

Also known as Medicare Part C. The Balanced Budget Act of 1997 (BBA) established the Medicare + Choice programme. Under this programme, an eligible individual may elect to receive Medicare benefits through enrolment in a Medicare + Choice plan, which generally takes the form of a MCO.

Medicare Advantage (MA)

As of 2003, the new name for Medicare + Choice (M+C).

Medicare Payment Advisory Commission (MedPAC)

The Commission was created by the BBA through a merger of the Prospective Payment Assessment Commission and the Physician Payment Review Commission. MedPAC reviews payment policies under Medicare Parts A and B and the effects of Medicare Part C. MedPAC also evaluates the effect of prospective payment policies and their impact on healthcare delivery in the US.

Medigap

1. Private insurance policies that supplement Medicare coverage.
2. A supplemental health insurance policy sold by private insurance companies that is designed to pay for healthcare costs and services

that are not paid for by Medicare and any private health insurance benefits.

Mental Health

The capacity of an individual to form harmonious relations with his/her social and physical environment and to achieve a balanced satisfaction of his/her own drives.

Meta-Analysis

Synthesis and quantitative summary of the results from several studies identified in a systematic review.

Metropolitan Statistical Areas (MSAs)

Standard metropolitan statistical areas are defined by the U.S. Census so that institutions and individuals gathering statistics on urban areas can use a common definition.

Military Health System (MHS)

The DoD organization that provides health/dental care.

Military Services/Armed Forces

The U.S. Army, U.S. Air Force, U.S. Navy, U.S. Marine Corps and U.S. Coast Guard.

Mixed Opioid Agonist-Antagonist: A compound that has an affinity for two or more types of opioid receptors and blocks opioid effects on one receptor type while producing opioid effects on a second receptor type.

MMA

Medicare Prescription Drug, Improvement and Modernization Act of 2003.

MoH

Ministry of Health.

Morbidity

The extent of illness, injury, or disability in a defined population, expressed in general or specific rates of incidence or prevalence. Sometimes used to refer to any episode of disease.

Mortality Rate

The mortality rate (death rate) expresses the number of deaths in a unit of population within a prescribed time and may be expressed as crude death rates (e.g., total deaths in relation to total population during a year) or as rates specified for disease and, sometimes, for age, sex, or other attributes (e.g., number of deaths from cancer in white males in relation to the white male population during a year).

Most Favoured Nation (MFN)

A "Most Favoured Nation" (MFN) clause is a contractual agreement between a supplier and a customer that requires the supplier to sell to the customer on pricing terms at least as favourable as the pricing terms on which that supplier sells to other customers. These clauses are sometimes found in the contracts health insurers enter into with providers.

Movement-Related Pain

A type of breakthrough pain related to specific activity, such as eating, defecation, socializing, or walking. Also referred to as incident pain.

Mucositis

Inflammation of a mucous membrane. Oral mucositis is a common complication of chemotherapy and radiation therapy.

Music Therapy

A form of distraction that uses music as an aid to relaxation.

Myofascial Pain

A group of painful muscle disorders characterized by the presence of hypersensitive points, called trigger points, within one or more muscles and/or the investing connective tissue together with a syndrome of pain, muscle spasm, tenderness, stiffness, limitation of motion, weakness, and occasionally autonomic dysfunction.

National Health Care

A system of health insurance administered by the government that insures all citizens. The government serves as the single insurer (single-payer) and sets all fees for hospitals, physicians and other health providers.

Naval Education and Training Security Assistance Field Activity (NETSAFA)

The U.S. Navy agency responsible for the management of the Navy international training programme.

Neonatal Death

Death occurring to an infant less than 28 days of age.

Network

A defined group of providers, typically linked through contractual arrangements, which provide either specific benefits or a full range of acute and long-term care services.

Network Model HMO

An HMO type that contracts with more than one physician group, and may contract with single-and multi-speciality groups. The physician works out of his/her own office. The physician may share in utilization savings, but does not necessarily provide care exclusively for HMO members.

Neuraxial

Within the spinal canal. Term used to indicate administration of drugs to the intrathecal or epidural space.

Neurolytic Block

The injection of a chemical agent to cause destruction and consequent prolonged interruption of peripheral somatic or sympathetic nerves, or in some cases, the neuraxis.

Neuropathic Pain

Pain that results from a disturbance of function or a pathologic process in a nerve; in one nerve, mononeuropathy; in several nerves, mononeuropathy multiplex; if diffuse, polyneuropathy.

NGO

Non-governmental organization.

Nociception

The neural process by which tissue injury or nerve dysfunction is detected, transmitted through the nervous system, and in conscious individuals perceived in pain.

Nociceptive Pain

Pain produced by activation of nociceptors as a result of heat, mechanical pressure, or the release of chemical mediators of inflammation or as a result of tissue injury.

Non-Community Water System

A public water system which serves at least twenty-five (non-residents) persons at least sixty days out of the year and is not a community or a seasonal water system.

Non-NATO

A term used to describe any country that is not a member of NATO or is an eligible PFP country.

Nonsteroidal Anti-Inflammatory Drug (NSAID)

Aspirin-like drug that reduces inflammation (and hence pain) arising from injured tissue.

Non-Transient Non-Community Water System

A public water system that is not a community system and that regularly serves at least twenty-five of the same persons over six months per year.

Normal and Usual Care

Healthcare that is normally and usually available in a DoD MTF to include pharmaceutical products usually stocked in DoD Pharmacies.

North Atlantic Treaty Organization (NATO) Member

A military member of a NATO nation, who is on active duty and who, in connection with official duties, is stationed in or passing through the U.S.

Nursing Homes

A wide range of licensed health facilities, other than hospitals, that provide various levels of maintenance and personal or nursing care to people who are unable to care for themselves and who may have health problems which range from minimal to very serious. The term includes free-standing institutions, or identifiable components of other health facilities that provide nursing care and related services, personal care and residential care.

Observer Training (OBT)

Special training conducted to permit IMSs to observer U.S. DoD techniques and procedures.

Opiate Receptor

Opiate-binding sites found throughout primary afferents and the neuraxis.

Opioid

Any synthetic narcotic that has morphine-like activities. Also denotes non-morphine-like molecules such as naturally occurring peptides (e.g., enkephalins), that exert morphine-like effects by interacting with opioid receptors.

Opioid Agonist

Any morphine-like compound that produces bodily effects, including pain relief, sedation, constipation and respiratory depression.

Opioid Partial Agonist

A compound that has an affinity for and stimulates physiologic activity at the same cell receptors as opioid agonists but that even at maximal doses produces only a partial (i.e., sub maximal) bodily response.

Organized Delivery Systems

Networks of providers and payers that provide care and compete with other systems for enrollees in regions. Systems include hospitals, primary care physicians, speciality care physicians, and other providers and sites that offer a full range or preventive and treatment services. Also refers to accountable health plans, coordinated care networks, community care networks, integrated health systems, and integrated service networks.

Outpatient

A patient who receives ambulatory care at a hospital or other facility without being admitted to the facility. Usually, it does not mean people receiving services from a physician's office or other programme that does not provide inpatient care.

Outpatient Medical Care

Care provided to individuals that visit an MTF and return home the same day.

Outpatient Prospective Payment System (OPPS)

Medicare's system for payment to outpatient departments of hospitals and other outpatient facilities. The specific amount that is paid is determined by the relevant APC.

Pain

An unpleasant sensory and emotional experience associated with actual or potential tissue damage or described in terms of such damage.

Pain Intensity Difference (PID)

Outcome measure in analgesic trials. The difference between pain intensity at a given time and at baseline (start time of an observation period).

Pain Relief

Reduction in pain intensity.

Palliative Therapy

A procedure such as chemotherapy, radiation therapy, or surgery that is performed to relieve or ease pain.

Pancoast Tumor

Tumor originating from the superior sulcus of the lung that invades all or a portion of the brachial plexus.

PAR

Participatory action research.

Patient Flow Data

Patient flow data identifies the zip code of each patient discharged from a hospital.

Patient-Controlled Analgesia (PCA)

Self-administration of analgesics by a patient instructed in doing so; usually refers to self-dosing with intravenous opioid (e.g., morphine) administered by means of a programmable pump.

Pharmacy Benefit Manager (PBM)

A company under contract with managed care organizations, self-insured companies and government programmes to manage pharmacy network management, drug utilization review, outcomes management and disease management.

Physical Dependence

Adaptation of the body to the presence of a drug, such as an opioid or benzodiatepine, such that sudden drug discontinuation or exposure to an antagonist will precipitate an abstinence syndrome.

Physical Modalities

Therapeutic interventions that use physical methods, such as heat, cold, massage, or exercise, to relieve pain.

Physician-Hospital Organization

A legal entity formed and owned by one or more hospitals and physician groups in order to obtain payer contracts and to further mutual interests. Physicians maintain ownership of their practices while agreeing to accept managed care patients under the terms of the agreement. The PHO serves as a negotiating, contracting and marketing unit. (*See* integrated delivery system).

Plausibility Design

A rigorous method of summative evaluation of health interventions or programmes, as delivered in real-life health systems, that assesses the programme's utilization, coverage, or impact. The objective is to provide plausible inferences to decision-makers and policymakers. The approach may use historical, internal or external control groups and places a heavy emphasis on contextual factors. It answers the question: Did the programme have an effect above and beyond what may have been caused by other external factors?

Point of Service (POS)

A health insurance plan in which members do not have to choose how to receive services until they need them. The most common use of the term applies to a plan that enrols each member in both an HMO (or HMO-like) system and an indemnity plan. These plans provide different benefits, depending on whether the member chooses to use plan providers or go outside the plan for services.

Point-of-Service Plan

A health plan allowing the covered person to choose to receive a service from a participating or non-participating provider, with different benefit levels associated with the use of participating providers. Point-of-service can be provided in several ways: (1) an HMO may allow members to obtain limited services from non-participating providers; (2) an HMO may provide non-participating benefits through a supplemental major medical policy; (3) a PPO may be used to provide both participating and non-participating levels of coverage and access; or (4) various combinations of the above may be used.

Policy Development

The process of selecting the most appropriate response to public health threats and trends.

Population Based Services

Preventive interventions and personal health services, developed and available for the entire population rather than for individuals in a one-on-one situation. Disease prevention, health promotion, and statewide outreach are major components. Common among these services are immunization campaigns, injury prevention, lead poisoning prevention and screening programmes, outreach and public education, newborn metabolic screening, and counselling for a family whose infant has died from Sudden Infant Death Syndrome.

Population Health

The health, well-being and functioning of a clearly defined population. "The health outcomes of a group of individuals, including the distribution of such outcomes within the groups" (Kindig and Stoddart 2003).

Postneonatal Death

Death occurring to an infant aged 28 days to 364 days.

Pre-Existing Medical/Dental Condition

A medical or dental condition that existed prior to sponsorship of the SATP. Examples are hearing losses, dental caries, poor eyesight, congenital defects, wounds, etc.

Preferred Provider Organization (PPO)

A programme in which contracts are established with providers of medical care. Providers under such contracts are referred to as preferred providers. Usually, the benefit contract provides significantly better benefits (fewer co-payments) for services received from preferred providers, thus encouraging covered persons to use these providers. Covered persons are generally allowed benefits for non-participating providers' services, usually on an indemnity basis with significant co-payments. A PPO arrangement can be insured or self-funded. Providers may be, but are not necessarily, paid on a discounted fee-for-service basis.

Premature

A live birth or fetal death that occurs before the completion of the 37th week of gestation.

Prenatal

Existing or taking place prior to birth.

Prepayment

Usually refers to any payment to a provider for anticipated services (such as an expectant mother paying in advance for maternity care). Sometimes prepayment is distinguished from insurance as referring to payment to organizations which, unlike an insurance company, take responsibility for arranging for and providing needed services as well as paying for them (such as health maintenance organizations, prepaid group practices and medical foundations).

Prevalence

The number of cases of a disease, infected persons, or persons with some other attribute present during a particular interval of time. Prevalence is often expressed as a rate.

Preventive Care

Comprehensive care emphasizing patients' behaviours that encourage health promotion and disease prevention, early detection, and early treatment of conditions, generally including routine physical examinations, immunization, and well-person care.

Preventive Health Services

Refers to the extensive array of procedures and services provided to the individual by medical providers and other practitioners which are designed to prevent disease or arrest its development. Services such as immunization, screening tests, chemoprophylaxis and contraception are included.

Primary Care

Basic or general healthcare focused on the point at which a patient ideally first seeks assistance from the medical care system. Primary care is considered comprehensive when the primary provider enters into a sustained partnership with the patient to take responsibility for the overall coordination for the care of the patient's health problems; biological, behavioural, or social. Physicians have traditionally provided the care, but, increasingly, it is provided by other personnel such as nurse practitioners or physician assistants.

Primary Care Case Management

A Medicaid managed care arrangement in which the State Medicaid agency contracts directly with primary care providers to act as "gatekeeper", approving and monitoring all covered services for the patient. For this case management service, the primary care providers are paid a per patient per month case management fee (usually between three and five dollars). In addition, the providers are reimbursed by the state on a fee-for-service basis for all services provided.

Primary Care Physicians

Internists or general/family practitioners who treat a variety of medical problems across all patient age groups and who frequently serve as the patient's first point of contact with the healthcare system. In some cases, obstetricians, gynecologists and pediatricians are considered primary care physicians.

Professional Authority

The Chief of the medical service, medical clinic or dental clinic located in the medical centre, hospital or dental clinic.

Progressive Muscle Relaxation

A cognitive-behavioural strategy in which muscles are alternately tensed and relaxed in a systematic fashion.

Prosthetic Devices

Artificial limbs, hearing aids, orthopedic footwear and spectacles.

Provider

Sponsored Organization within the Medicare programme, HCFA allows hospitals and doctors to group together to form this entity for the Medicare programme. Similar to HMOs except the entity is run by medical providers.

Pseudo-Addiction

Pattern of drug-seeking behaviour of pain patients receiving inadequate pain medication; can be mistaken for addiction.

Psychological Dependence

See Addiction.

Psychosocial Intervention

A therapeutic intervention that uses cognitive, cognitive-behavioural, behavioural, and supportive interventions to relieve pain. These include patient education, interventions aimed at aiding relaxation, psychotherapy, and structured or peer support.

Public Health

One of the efforts organized by society to protect, promote and restore the people's health. The combination of sciences, skills, and beliefs directed to the maintenance and improvement of the health of all the people through collective or social actions. A social institution, a discipline, and a practice with the goal to reduce the amount of disease, premature death, and disease-produced discomfort and disability in the population.

Quality Improvement Organization (QIO)

Organizations that contract with CMS to review care provided to Medicare beneficiaries.

Quality of Care

A measure of the degree to which delivered healthcare services meet established professional standards and judgements of value by the consumer. Quality may also be seen as the degree to which actions taken or not taken maximize the probability of beneficial health outcomes and minimize risk and other untoward outcome, given the existing state of medical science and art. Quality is frequently described as having three dimensions: quality of input resources (certification, and/or training of providers); quality of the process of services delivery (the use of appropriate procedures for a given condition), and quality of outcome of service use (actual improvement in condition or reduction of harmful effects).

Race

A population of individuals who identify themselves from a common history, nationality, or geographical place. When responses in the "race" line item on vital records are associated with the definition of Hispanic origin, they are re-coded to "white race", as described in the National Centre for Health Statistics instruction manuals for coding vital records. Individuals identifying themselves as either "white", "black", or "other" race can be of any ethnic group.

Random Effects Model

See "Fixed effects model".

Real-Time Automated Personnel Identification System (RAPIDS)

An operational programme in support of resources/benefits management, critical defence missions, and the Uniformed Services Identification (ID) Card programme.

Reciprocal Healthcare Agreement

International agreement pursuant to Title 10, USC, Chapter 151, Section 2549 which authorizes care in military treatment facilities at no cost based on comparable care and comparable numbers. Services and categories of persons covered vary.

Rehabilitation

The combined and coordinated use of medical, social, educational and vocational measures used for training or re-training individuals disabled by disease or injury to the highest possible level of functional ability.

Relative Risk

One of several ways to quantitatively describe the strength of association between a suspected cause and its presumed effect. The relative risk is a ratio of two risks — the risk of the outcome in those exposed to the suspected cause compared with the risk of the outcome in those not exposed.

Relaxation

A state of relative freedom from both anxiety and skeletal muscle tension.

Residence

The usual place of abode of the person to whom the vital event occurred. For births and fetal deaths, residence is defined as the mother's usual place of residence.

Resource-Based Relative Value Scale (RBRVS)

The RBRVS determines the rate at which Medicare reimburses physicians on an FFS basis. The RBRVS is calculated based on the cost of physician labour, practice overheads, materials and liability insurance. The resulting figures are adjusted for geographical differences and are updated annually.

Risk ratio

See Relative risk.

Risk Sharing

The distribution of financial risk among parties furnishing a service. For example, if a hospital and a group of physicians from a corporation provide healthcare at a fixed price, a risk-sharing arrangement would entail both the hospital and the physician group being held liable if expenses exceed revenues.

Roll Back Malaria Partnership

A global initiative—made up of more than 90 partners—whose goal is to halve the burden of malaria by 2010. The partnership was launched in 1998 by the World Health Organization, UNICEF, UNDP and the World Bank to provide a coordinated international approach to fighting malaria.

SAPs

Structural Adjustment Programmes created in the late 1970s, SAPs are aimed at changing the structure of a developing country's economy to correct underlying problems that lead to economic declines. Initiated by the World Bank, structural adjustment programmes aim to increase developing countries' ability to service their international debt and have generally increased privatization of government functions and increased support for export production of agriculture commodities.

Security Assistance (SA)

A group of programmes authorized by the Foreign Assistance Act of 1961, as amended, and the Arms Export Control Act, as amended, or other related statutes, by which the United States provides defence articles, military training and other defence related services, by grant, credit, cash sale, lease, or loan, in furtherance of national policies and objectives.

Security Assistance Organization/Office (SAO)

The generic term SAO encompassing all DoD elements, regardless of actual title, located in a foreign country with assigned responsibilities for carrying out security assistance management functions.

Security Assistance Training Field Activity (SATFA)

The U.S. Army agency responsible for the management of the Army international training programme.

Security Assistance Training Programme (SATP)

Education and training provided under the auspices of Security Assistance.

Self-Statement

Involves instructing patients to substitute positive thoughts such as "I can withstand this experience" for such negative ones as "I can't stand this" or "How much longer will this go on?"

Sensitivity Analysis

Any test of the stability of the conclusions of an evaluation over a range of probability estimates, value judgements, and assumptions.

Single Speciality Hospital (SSH)

Specialized hospitals that provide treatment relating to a single speciality (e.g., cardiac or orthopedic services). Many of the physicians who refer patients to an SSH have an ownership interest in the facility.

SMI

Safe Motherhood Initiative.

Somatic Pain

Pain that arises from the surface of the body (e.g., skin).

SPID

Sum of pain intensity differences following administration of a different analgesic to two or more groups of patients, or a single patient studied at different times.

State Action Doctrine

First articulated in Parker v. Brown, the state action doctrine shields certain anticompetitive conduct from federal antitrust scrutiny.

State Board of Medical Examiners

State Boards of Medical Examiners are typically responsible for licensure and promulgate regulations governing physicians and AHPs.

State Children's Health Insurance Programme (SCHIP)

Also referred to as Children's Health Insurance Programme (CHIP). A programme created by the federal government to encourage states to provide insurance coverage for children. SCHIP is funded through a combination of federal and state funds, and administered by the states in conformity with federal requirements.

Status of Forces Agreement (SOFA)

An agreement between states the parties to international treaties on the status of their forces.

STD

Sexually transmitted disease.

Suffering

A state of severe distress associated with events that threaten the wholeness of the person.

Supplemental Care-Non-CHAMPUS

MTF operating and maintenance funds that the MTF uses to obtain civilian healthcare for active duty members and non-CHAMPUS beneficiaries when the care is not available in the MTF. The patient must remain under the clinic supervision of a member of the MTF staff.

Surveillance

The systematic collection, analysis, interpretation, and

dissemination of health data to assist in the planning, implementation and evaluation of public health interventions and programmes.

Surveillance

The temporary supervision of a person who may have or has been exposed to a communicable disease.

SWAp

Sector-wide approach a SWAp is a process in which funding for the sector—from both government and donor partner—is conducted in partnership as a means to increase donor-government collaboration, consolidate local management of resources, and undertake the policy and systems reform necessary to achieve a greater impact on health issues.

Systematic Review

The process of systematically locating, appraising and synthesizing evidence from scientific studies in order to obtain a reliable answer to a specific question posed a priori.

Technology

Mechanical devices, pharmaceuticals and techniques used in medical and surgical diagnostic and therapeutic procedures. These devices and techniques are often related to innovations in treatment methods and advances in patient care.

Teenage Mother

A woman under 20 years of age on the date of delivery.

TEHIP

Tanzania Essential Health Interventions Project.

Telemedicine

Telemedicine involves the use of electronic communication and information technologies to provide or support clinical care at a distance.

Third-Party Administrator (TPA)

A firm that performs administrative functions (e.g., claims processing, membership) for a self-funded plan or a start-up MCO.

Third-Party Payer

Any organization, public or private, that pays or insures health or medical expenses on behalf of beneficiaries or recipients. An individual pays a premium for such coverage in all private and in some public programmes; the payer organization then pays bills on the individual's behalf. Such payments are called third-party payments and are distinguished by the separation among the individual receiving the service (the first party), the individual or institution providing it (the second party), and the organization paying for it (the third party).

Tolerance

A common physiologic result of chronic use of drugs such as opiods or benzodiazepines; connotes the requirement for doses progressively higher across time to maintain the same analgesic effect.

Transient Non-Community Water System

A non-community water system that does not meet the definition of a non-transient non-community water system.

Treatment

A procedure or medical service which medical personnel expect to lead to or assist in the patient's recovery.

TRICARE

The DoD health care programmes which combines medical care from both military and civilian sources.

Trimester of Pregnancy

One-third of the total gestation period of a full-term pregnancy, or 13 weeks per trimester. The "third trimester" classification comprises pregnancies of 27 or more weeks gestation. The weekly count begins on the first day of last menstrual period.

TZS

Tanzanian shilling (in 2004, 1 USD = 1 094 TZS).

U.S. Port

Any seaport, airport, or border crossing point under the control of the United States.

UNAIDS

Joint United Nations Programme on HIV/AIDS.

Underinsured

People with public or private insurance policies that do not cover all necessary medical services, resulting in out-of-pocket expenses.

Underlying Cause of Death

The disease or injury that initiated the sequence of events leading directly to death, or the circumstances of the accident or violence that produced the fatal injury.

UNESCO

United Nations Educational, Scientific and Cultural Organization.

UNICEF

United Nations Children's Fund.

Unintentional Injury

Injuries and deaths that are considered accidental. Unintentional injuries can be a result of residential fires, falls, motor-vehicle-related and drownings.

United States

The states, the District of Columbia, Guam, The Commonwealth of Puerto Rico, the Northern Mariana Islands, the Virgin Islands, American Samoa and the Trust Territory of the Pacific Islands.

United States Public Health Service (PHS)

The organizational part of the United States Department of Health and Human Services that is responsible for public health and related policies.

Universal Access/Coverage

The provision of a standard minimum level of healthcare benefits to all individuals residing in an area (may be a region, state, or the U.S. as a whole).

Utilization

Patterns or rates of use of a single service or type of service (e.g., hospital care, physician visits, prescription drugs). Use is also expressed in rates per unit of population at risk for a given period.

Utilization Review

A cost-control mechanism used by some insurers and employers that evaluate healthcare on the basis of appropriateness, necessity and quality.

Utilization Review

An organized procedure carried out through committees to review admissions, duration of stay, professional services furnished, and to evaluate the medical necessity of those services and promote their most efficient use.

Variable

Some characteristics that differs from subject to subject or from time to time.

Vector

An animal (including insects) or thing which conveys or is capable of conveying infectious agents from a person or animal to another person or animal.

Verbal Autopsy

A method of assigning the cause of death based on an interview with next of kin or other caregivers.

Very Low Birth Weight

A birth weight of less than 1,500 grams (approximately 3 lbs., 5 oz.).

Village Health Account

An account established by villages to fund health-related activities and to which villagers contribute through local taxes on their products.

Visceral Pain

Pain that arises from injury of or psychophysiology involving internal organs (viscera) or their innervation.

Visual Analog Scale (VAS)

Typically a 10-centimeter horizontal line on which the left side represents no pain and the right side represents the worst imaginable pain. Variants according to orientation (i.e., vertical), size and design (e.g., cross-hatched) are common.

WDR93

World Development Report 1993: Investing in Health, published by the World Bank.

WHO Analgesic Ladder (or Staircase)

A method for management of cancer pain that focuses on selecting analgesics on the basis of pain intensity. There are three steps, from mild pain—suggesting use of a nonopioid analgesics and the possibility of an adjuvant analgesic—to severe pain, suggesting an opioid with the possibility of nonopioid and adjuvant analgesics.

World Health Organization (WHO)

An agency of the United Nations whose objective is the attainment by all peoples of the highest possible level of health.

Years of Potential Life Lost

A measure of the relative impact of various diseases and lethal forces on society. It highlights the loss to society as a result of youthful or early deaths. The figure for potential years of life lost due to a particular cause is the sum, over all persons dying from that cause, of the years that these persons would have lived had they experienced normal life expectation.

YLLs

Years of life lost. A measure of time lost due to premature death.

ZTC

Zonal Training Centre (also known as Zonal Continuing Education Centre). A number of institutions set up and run by the Ministry of Health distributed across the country to provide continuing health education to the various levels of health managers and health personnel.

Bibliography

Agency for Health Care Administration. A Blueprint for Health Security, Interim Florida Health Plan, 1992.

Ailing, P.M. speaks out: Urges all not to Spread Rumours About his Health *Kantipur Report*, July 7, 2006, Retrieved September 12, 2006.

Alpha Center, *Glossary of Terms Commonly Used in Health Care*, Washington, D.C., 1996.

Archer, B.H. (1995). The Impact of International Tourism on the Economy of Bermuda. *Journal of Travel Research*, 34(2), 27-30.

Archer, B.H. & Fletcher, J.E. (1990). Tourism. *Its Economic Significance*. In M. Quest (ed.), Horwath Book of Tourism (pp. 10-25). London: The MacMillan Press.

Boerma, T., Schwartländer, B., Mertens, T., A Proximate Determinants Framework for Monitoring and Evaluation of HIV/AIDS/STD Programs. From: Towards Improved Monitoring and Evaluation of HIV Prevention, AIDS Care and STD Control Programs. A Joint UNAIDS, WHO, USAID/MEASURE Evaluation Workshop, Nairobi (Kenya); November 17-20, 1998.

Britton, S.G. (1982). "The Political Economy of Tourism in the Third World", *Annals of Tourism Research*, 9(3): 331-358.

Cater, E. (1993). *Ecotourism in the Third World: Problems for Sustainable Tourism Development*. Tourism Management, 14,85-90.

Carrera, Percivil M. http://content.healthaffairs.org/cgi/content/full/25/5/1453.

CBC News Indepth. Parts 1 and 2. June 18, 2004 www.cbc.ca/news/background/healthcare/medicaltourism.html.

Certron, Martin 2006. www.udel.edu/PR/UDaily/2005/mar/tourism072505.html.

Clement, The Hon.Tony. Federal Minister of Health *www.hc-sc.gc.ca/ahc-asc/minist/health sante/speeches-discours/2006_04_13_e.html.*

Connecticut Department of Public Health. MCH Block Grant, Title V Application, Hartford, CT, 1997.

Cook, T.D., Campbell, D.T., editors. *Quasi-experimentation: Design and analysis issues for field settings.* Chicago: Rand McNally; 1979, pp. 95-146.

Coyle, S., Boruch, R., Turner, C., editors. *Evaluating AIDS prevention programs.* Washington (DC): National Academy Press; 1991, pp. 50-82.

Edgell, D.L. (1999). *Tourism Policy*: The Next Millennium. Advances in Tourism Applications Series, Sagamore Publishing.

Elgood, C., *A Medical History of Persia* (Cambridge Univ. Press), p. 173.

Erbes, R. (1973). International Tourism and the Economy of Developing Countries. Paris: Organization for Economic Cooperation and Development.

Harrison, L.C., and Husbands, W. (1996). *Practicing Responsible Tourism: International Case Studies in Tourism. Planning, Policy and Development.* John Wiley & Sons, Inc.

Heinz, E. Muller-Dietz. *Historia Hospitalism* (1975).

India Fosters Growing 'Medical Tourism' Sector by Ray Marcelo, The Financial Times, 2 July, 2003 retrieved September 29, 2006.

Incision Care. *American Academy of Family Physicians*, July, 2005, retrieved September 18, 2006.

Indian Medical Care Goes Global, Aljazeera. Net, June 18, 2006 accessed at November 11, 2006.

Just what the hospital ordered: Global accreditations by Zeenat Nazir, Indian Express, September 18, 2006 retrieved September 29, 2006.

Institute of Medicine. The Future of Public Health, 1988.

Kongstvedt, Peter R., MD, The Managed Health Care Handbook, Second Edition, 1993.

Last, JM (Ed). A Dictionary of Epidemiology, 2nd ed., New York: Oxford University Press, 1988.

Loomis, J.B. and Walsh, R.G. (1996). *Recreation Economic Decisions: Comparing Benefits and Costs* (2nd Edition) Venture Publishing, Inc. State College Pennsylvania.

Lundberg, D.E., Stavenga, M.H. and Krishnamoorthy, M. (1995). *Tourism Economics*, New York: Longman Scientific and Technical.

Mathieson. A., & Wall, G. (1982). *Toursm: Economic, physical and social impacts.* New York: Longman scientific and Technical.

Medical conference makes Asia debut http://www.breakingtravelnews.com/article/20061212190313304.

Medical tourism growing worldwide by Becca Hutchinson, *UDaily*, July 25, 2005, retrieved September 5, 2006.

Medical Tourism: Hidden dimensions by Rabindra Seth, *Express Hospitality*, June, 2006, retrieved September 12, 2006.

Medical Tourism: Need surgery, will travel *CBC News Online*, June 18, 2004, retrieved September 5, 2006.

Mertens, T.E., Caraël M. *Evaluation of HIV/STD Prevention, Care and Support: An Update on WHO's Approaches.* AIDS Educ Prev 1997; 9(2), pp. 133-145.

Mill, R.C. and Morrison, A.M. (1999). *The Tourism System: An Introductory Text* (3rd Edition) Kendall/Hunt Publishing Company, Dubuque, lowa.

Patton, M.Q., editor. *Qualitative Evaluation and Research Methods.* 2nd edition. Newbury Park (CA): Sage Publications; 1990, pp. 11-12.

Patton, M.Q., editor. *Utilization-focused Evaluation*, 2nd edition. Beverly Hills (CA): Sage Publications; 1986, pp. 177-217.

Pleumarom, A. (1999). "Tourism, Globalization and Sustainable Development" in Third World Network Dossier for CSD 7, Third World Network, Malaysia.

Prof. Arjuna Aluvihare. "Rohal Kramaya Lovata Dhayadha Kale Sri Lankikayo", *Vidhusara Science Magazine*, November, 1993.

Roderick, E. McGrew. *Encyclopedia of Medical History* (Macmillan 1985), pp.134-35.

Roderick, E. McGrew. *Encyclopedia of Medical History* (Macmillan 1985), p.135.

Roderick, E. McGrew. *Encyclopedia of Medical History* (Macmillan 1985), pp. 135-36.

Roderick, E. McGrew. *Encyclopedia of Medical History* (Macmillan 1985), p.139.

Rossi, P.H., Freeman, H.E., editors. *Evaluation: A Systematic Approach*, 5th edition, Newbury Park (CA)· Sage Publications; 1993, pp. 215-259.

State of Connecticut. One Hundred and Forty-eighth Registration Report, 1995, July, 1997.

Susser, M. "Some principles in Study Design for Preventing HIV

Transmission: Rigor or Reality." *Am J Public Health 1996;* 86(12):1713-16.

Thompson, J.C., Program evaluation within a health promotion framework. *Can J Public Health* 1992;83 (Suppl 1) : S67-S71.

UNAIDS/00.17E. National AIDS programmes: A guide to monitoring and evaluation. Geneva: Joint United Nations Programme on HIV/AIDS (UNAIDS); 2000.

U.S. Department of Health and Human Services. Agency for Health Care Policy and Research, Assessing Roles, Responsibilities and Activities in a Managed Care Environment, Washington D.C.

United Health Care Corporation. The Managed Care Resource, 1994.

Vacation, Adventure And Surgery? *CBS News: 60 Minutes,* September 4, 2005, retrieved September 12, 2006.

Wikipedia Encyclopedia *http://en.wikipedia.org/wiki/Medical_tourism.*

WHO/GPA/TCO/SEF/94.1. Evaluation of a National AIDS Programme: A Methods Package, Geneva: World Health Organization; 1994.

Waiver Application Development Council discussions, July 30, 1997.

Index